# ASSESSMENT OF CHILDREN
## WISC-III AND WPPSI-R SUPPLEMENT

# ASSESSMENT OF CHILDREN
## WISC-III AND WPPSI-R SUPPLEMENT

Jerome M. Sattler
*San Diego State University*

Jerome M. Sattler, Publisher, Inc.
San Diego

Editorial Services: Sally Lifland and Janice Ostock,
    Lifland et al., Bookmakers
Interior Design: Sally Lifland and Jerome M. Sattler
Interior Design Consultant: Kathi Townes
Cover Designer: Jerome M. Sattler and E. Gail Magin
Proofreaders: Gladys Moore and Jerome M. Sattler
Cover Printer: Maple Vail Book Manufacturing Group
Printer and Binder: Maple Vail Book Manufacturing Group

*This text was set in Times Roman and Gill Sans and printed on
50# Hi-Brite Vellum paper.*

Cover: Black and white reproduction of Tridem-K by Vasarely, ©
S.P.A.D.E.M., Paris/V.A.G.A., New York, 1986.

**Library of Congress Cataloging-in-Publication Data**

Sattler, Jerome M.
    Assessment of children : WISC-III and WPPSI-R supplement / Jerome
M. Sattler.
        p.   cm.
    Includes bibliographical references and indexes.
    ISBN 0-9618209-3-4
    1. Wechsler Intelligence Scale for Children.   2. Wechsler
Preschool and Primary Scale of Intelligence.   I. Title.
    BF432.5.W42S28   1992
    155.4'1393 – dc20                                        92-90725
                                                                      CIP

16   15   14   13   12   11   10   9   8   7   6   5   4   3   2   1      99   98   97   96   95   94   93   92
Printed in the United States of America

# _ CONTENTS _____

# LIST OF TABLES

# _LIST OF FIGURES

# _LIST OF EXHIBITS

# _PREFACE

*Assessment of Children: WISC-III and WPPSI-R Supplement* contains the seven WISC-III and WISC-R appendixes added to the main 1988 text. The supplement *must* be used in conjunction with the main text, *Assessment of Children, Third Edition*, to have the full complement of tables and guidelines needed to interpret the WISC-III and WPPSI-R.

The supplement follows the format of the main text. However, changes have been made to make the text more readable and comprehensive. In addition, Appendixes I, J, and K include a "Thinking Through the Issues" section, designed to stimulate further thought about several issues raised in these appendixes.

Appendix G on the WPPSI-R parallels Chapter 9 on the WPPSI. Appendixes I and J on the WISC-III parallel Chapters 6 and 7 on the WISC-R. Appendix K, on interpreting the WISC-III and report writing, parallels parts of Chapter 8 and extends the content of Chapter 23.

References added after the main text was published in 1988 are placed at the end of Appendix I, J, or K or in Appendix G proper. All other references cited in the supplement and in the main text appear in the Reference section in the main text.

The seven appendixes in the supplement are also incorporated in the latest version of the main text, entitled *Assessment of Children, Revised and Updated Third Edition*, a 1992 publication (ISBN 0-9618209-2-6).

Both the WISC-III and the WPPSI-R are refinements of a clinical tool that first appeared in the 1930s. David Wechsler's work is being carried on by the staff of The Psychological Corporation. And, although David Wechsler died in 1981, he is still listed as the author of the revised versions of his tests.

The material in the supplement was written to help readers become master clinicians in administering and interpreting the WISC-III and WPPSI-R. Your comments about this work will be most appreciated.

# _ACKNOWLEDGMENTS_____

I have been fortunate in obtaining wise counsel from many individuals about the seven new WPPSI-R and WISC-III appendixes. The following individuals read two or more of the appendixes:

Dr. Leslie Atkinson, Surrey Place Centre
Ms. Angela Ballantyne, San Diego State University
Dr. Jeannine Feldman, San Diego State University
Dr. James Gyurke, The Psychological Corporation
Dr. Larry Hilgert, Valdosta State College
Dr. William A. Hillix, San Diego State University
Ms. Tina S. Oprendeck, San Diego State University
Dr. Aurilio Prifitera, The Psychological Corporation
Ms. Bonnie J. Sattler, Kaiser Permanente
Dr. Arthur B. Silverstein, University of California, Los Angeles
Ms. Naomi Singer, San Diego State University
Dr. John R. Slate, Arkansas State University
Dr. Lawrence Weiss, The Psychological Corporation
Dr. Irla Lee Zimmerman, Private Practice in Los Angeles

Thank you, Leslie, Angela, Jeannine, James, Larry, Al, Stephie, Aurilio, Bonnie, Art, Naomi, John, Lawrence, and Irla for your valuable suggestions and for your efforts to make the text more readable, thorough, comprehensive, and scholarly. Readers will appreciate your fine contributions.

The staff and faculty of the Department of Applied Psychology at University College Cork, Cork, Ireland assisted me in the preparation of the WPPSI-R appendixes. Thank you all for your help.

I also wish to acknowledge the help of other individuals who contributed to the work incorporated in the WISC-III appendixes:

Michael Irwin, from the Test Office at San Diego State University, was of great assistance in writing the computer programs necessary to generate most of the tables in Appendix L. Thank you, Mike, for your excellent work and generosity.

Professors Fred Hornbeck and Jeff Bryson, from the Psychology Department at San Diego State University, assisted me in conducting and interpreting the factor analyses. Thank you, Fred and Jeff, for your assistance.

Rachel Litonja-Witt and James Edwards, from the Media Technology Center at San Diego State University, were extremely helpful in enabling me to master some of the intricacies of WordPerfect. Thank you, Rachel and Jim. It is always comforting to know that your guidance is available when I get into trouble with the computer, and I do get into trouble.

Valerie Brew and Beverly Dexter, students in the psychology master's program at San Diego State University, were helpful in proofreading the WISC-III appendixes. Thank you, Valerie and Beverly, for taking the time from your busy schedule to proofread the galleys.

My student assistants, Jennifer Mayes and Deborah Walker, have been wonderful to work with. They typed various sections of the manuscript, helped in proofreading, and rechecked many of the table entries. Thank you, Jennifer and Deborah, for your excellent work.

Coleen Beaudoin, the office manager at Jerome M. Sattler, Publisher, has been helpful in coordinating many of the details involved in the production of the text. Thank you, Coleen, for your efficiency and interest in the project.

I also wish to thank the staff at Harrison Typesetting for doing an excellent job in converting my WordPerfect files to camera-ready copy.

Roy Wallace, representing Maple Vail Book Manufacturing, has again been excellent to work with. Thank you, Roy, for your help and assistance. Also convey my thanks to the production staff at Maple Vail for printing a high-quality text.

And finally, I wish to thank Sally Lifland and Janice Ostock, from Lifland et al., Bookmakers, for doing a superlative job in editing the manuscript. Sally Lifland also coordinated the numerous production details, for which she deserves additional thanks.

March 1992

Jerome M. Sattler
San Diego State University
Psychology Department
San Diego, CA 92182

# ASSESSMENT OF CHILDREN
## WISC-III AND WPPSI-R SUPPLEMENT

# APPENDIX G

## WECHSLER PRESCHOOL AND PRIMARY SCALE OF INTELLIGENCE— REVISED (WPPSI-R)

*Thought once awakened does not slumber.*

—Thomas Carlyle

Standardization

Deviation IQs, Scaled Scores, and Test-Age Equivalents

Reliability

Validity

Intercorrelations Between Subtests and Scales

Factor Analysis

IQ Ranges and Subtest Scaled-Score Ranges

Normative Changes on Animal Pegs

Comparison of the WPPSI-R and the WPPSI

Administering the WPPSI-R

WPPSI-R Subtests

Interpreting the WPPSI-R

Assets of the WPPSI-R

Limitations of the WPPSI-R

Psychological Evaluation

Test Your Skill

Summary

This appendix describes the latest version of the Wechsler Preschool and Primary Scale of Intelligence—Revised (WPPSI-R) [D. Wechsler (1989), *Wechsler Preschool and Primary Scale of Intelligence—Revised* (San Antonio: The Psychological Corporation)]. The test is one of the major instruments for assessing the cognitive ability of young children. The content of this appendix is based primarily on the WPPSI-R manual, a factor analysis for each age level of the scale, and research based on the prior edition of the test. The appendix should be read in conjunction with Appendixes J and K on the WISC-III and Chapter 8 on the WISC-R. Because the WISC-R (WISC-III) and the WPPSI-R are so similar, psychometric, clinical, and psychoeducational approaches used on the WISC-R (WISC-III) can also be applied to the WPPSI-R. However, because the WPPSI (and the WPPSI-R) has not been as widely used or researched as the WISC-R (WISC-III), more caution is needed in interpreting test findings and in generating hypotheses about the implications of children's performance on the WPPSI-R.

The WPPSI-R (see Figure G-1) was published 22 years after the original version. The length of time between revisions is somewhat long, but it is comparable to that for the other Wechsler scales. The WPPSI-R is more elaborate than its predecessor. It has a more extensive age range (from 3 years, 0 months to 7 years, 3 months) and one additional subtest (Object Assembly). The new age range is approximately two years wider than that of the original WPPSI—one year downward and one year upward. Unfortunately, the WPPSI-R is not completely distinct from the WISC-III; some items overlap with those on four WISC-III subtests (Picture Completion, Mazes, Vocabulary, and Information). As noted later in the appendix, this overlap is a limitation in the retesting of children. It would have been preferable to have the scale completely distinct from the other Wechsler scales.

The WPPSI-R contains 12 subtests (see Exhibit G-1), 6 in the Performance Scale and 6 in the Verbal Scale. Five of the six subtests in each scale are designated as the standard subtests. They are Object Assembly, Geometric Design, Block Design, Mazes, and Picture Completion in the Performance Scale and Information, Comprehension, Arithmetic, Vocabulary, and Similarities in the Verbal Scale. The optional subtests are Animal Pegs in the Performance Scale and Sentences in the Verbal Scale. Nine of the 12 subtests are similar to those in the WISC-III (Object Assembly, Block Design, Mazes, Picture Completion, Information, Comprehension, Arithmetic, Vocabulary, and

**Figure G-1. Wechsler Preschool and Primary Scale of Intelligence—Revised.** From the *Wechsler Preschool and Primary Scale of Intelligence—Revised*. Copyright © 1989 by The Psychological Corporation. Reproduced by permission. All rights reserved.

**Exhibit G-1**

**WPPSI-R–Like Items**

**Object Assembly** (6 items)

There are two types of tasks: (a) placing pieces into a form board and (b) assembling jigsaw puzzles. An example of an Object Assembly item is shown below.

**Geometric Design** (16 items)

The task for the first seven items is to select the matching design from four choices. The task for the last nine items is to copy a geometric design shown on a printed card. The designs include a circle, square, triangle, and diamond.

**Block Design** (14 designs)

The task is to reproduce designs using three or four blocks.

**Mazes** (11 mazes)

The task is to complete a series of mazes.

**Picture Completion** (28 items)

The task is to identify the essential missing part of the picture.
A picture of a doll without a leg.
A picture of a rabbit without an ear.
A picture of a car without a wheel.

**Animal Pegs**

The task is to place appropriate colored pegs in the corresponding holes on a board. The colored pegs are matched with four different animals. The Animal Pegs task is shown in the photograph of the WPPSI-R (see Figure G-1).

**Information** (27 items)

Point to the picture that shows the one you cut with.
How many legs does a cat have?

In what kind of store do we buy meat?
How many pennies make a dime?

**Comprehension** (15 items)

Why do you need to take a bath?
Why do we have farms?
What makes a sailboat move?

**Arithmetic** (23 items)

A card with squares of different sizes is placed in front of child. Examiner says, "Here are some squares. Which one is the biggest? Point to it."
Bill had one penny and his mother gave him one more. How many pennies does he now have?
Judy had 4 books. She lost 1. How many books does she have left?
Jimmy had 7 bananas and he bought 8 more. How many bananas does he have altogether?

**Vocabulary** (25 items)

Examiner shows child a picture of a dog and says, "What is this?"
What is a boot?
What does "nice" mean?
What does "annoy" mean?

**Similarities** (20 items)

Examiner shows child a picture of objects that go together and says, "Look at these pictures. They're all alike—they all go together. Now look at these pictures. Which one is like these?"
You can read a book and you can also read a _____.
In what way are a quarter and a dollar alike?
In what way are a cow and a pig alike?

**Sentences** (12 items)

The task is to repeat sentences given orally by the examiner.
Birds fly.
Ted eats apples in the morning.
The children like to visit the city every Saturday during the summer.

Similarities), and three are unique to the WPPSI-R (Sentences, Animal Pegs, and Geometric Design). Essentially, the WPPSI-R can be considered a downward extension of the WISC-R (WISC-III), except at 6 to 7¼ years, where the two tests overlap.

## STANDARDIZATION

The WPPSI-R was standardized on 1,700 children, 100 boys and 100 girls in each of eight age groups from 3 to 7 years and one group of 50 boys and 50 girls from 7 years,

0 months to 7 years, 3 months. The 1986 U.S. census data were used to select representative children for the normative sample. White children and nonwhite children were included in the sample, based on the ratios found in the census for four geographical regions in the United States (Northeast, North Central, South, and West).

## DEVIATION IQS, SCALED SCORES, AND TEST-AGE EQUIVALENTS

The WPPSI-R, like the WISC-III and the WAIS-R, employs the Deviation IQ ($M = 100$, $SD = 15$) for the Verbal, Performance, and Full Scale IQs, and scaled scores ($M = 10$, $SD = 3$) for the 12 individual subtests. The IQs are obtained by comparing the examinee's scores with the scores earned by a representative sample of his or her own age group. A raw score is first obtained on each subtest and then converted to a scaled score within the examinee's own age group through use of a table in the WPPSI-R manual (Table 25, pages 170–186). Age groups are divided into 16 three-month intervals from 2-11-16 (years, months, days) to 6-11-15 and 1 four-month interval from 6-11-16 to 7-3-15.

The table in the WPPSI-R manual used to obtain IQs (Table 27, pages 188–189) is based on the 10 standard subtests. The two optional subtests are excluded from the calculation of the IQ unless a subtest is spoiled or not given. When a subtest is excluded on the Performance Scale, Animal Pegs is substituted, and when one is excluded on the Verbal Scale, Sentences is substituted. When an optional subtest is substituted for a standard subtest, little is known about the reliability and validity of the IQs generated by the altered combination of subtests because neither optional subtest was used in the construction of the tables used to generate the IQs.

### Prorating Procedure

When fewer than 10 subtests are administered, IQs can be computed either by prorating or by a special short-form procedure designed to estimate the Performance, Verbal, and Full Scale IQs. Although the WPPSI-R manual provides a table (Table 26, page 187) for prorating the scores when four of the subtests are administered in each scale, it is advisable to compute IQs by using the procedure described later in this chapter whenever fewer than 10 subtests are administered. The special short-form procedure takes into account the intercorrelations between the specific subtests administered for each age of the child; prorating does not take this factor into account.

### Test-Age Equivalents

The WPPSI-R manual provides a table of test-age equivalents (Table 28, page 190) to facilitate interpretation of a child's performance. The test ages were arrived at for each age level by obtaining the raw score corresponding to a scaled score of 10. Because a scaled score of 10 represents the mean, the test-age equivalents of the raw scores shown in Table 28 can be understood as reflecting the average score for each particular age group. The assets and limitations associated with test-age equivalents are discussed on pages 20–21 and pages 75–76 of this text.

## RELIABILITY

The WPPSI-R Performance, Verbal, and Full Scale IQs have excellent reliability in eight of the nine age groups covered by the test. From ages 3 through 6½ years, the reliabilities for each of the three IQs range from .90 to .97; this range is excellent. However, at age 7 years the reliability coefficients for the Performance and Verbal Scale IQs ($r_{xx} = .85$ and .86, respectively) are less satisfactory than that for the Full Scale IQ ($r_{xx} = .90$). The WPPSI-R manual attributes the lower reliability coefficients at the 7-year level to ceiling effects, but provides no research evidence to support this hypothesis. (Ceiling effects exist when a test has too few items at the upper levels to measure reliably the ability of bright children.) Across the nine age groups, the average internal consistency reliabilities are .92 for the Performance Scale IQ, .95 for the Verbal Scale IQ, and .96 for the Full Scale IQ (see Table G-1).

### Subtest Reliabilities

The reliabilities for the subtests are lower than those for the three scales (see Table G-1). The average subtest reliabilities range from a low of .63 for Object Assembly to a high of .86 for Similarities. For the nine age groups, median reliabilities are highest for ages 3, 3½, 4, 4½, and 5 ($Mdn\ r_{xx}$'s range from .830 to .870), followed by age 6 ($Mdn\ r_{xx} = .780$), age 5½ ($Mdn\ r_{xx} = .775$), age 6½ ($Mdn\ r_{xx} = .745$), and age 7 ($Mdn\ r_{xx} = .660$). The lowest subtest reliabilities are found at age 7 (see Table G-2).

### Standard Errors of Measurement

The average standard errors of measurement ($SE_m$) in IQ points are 3.00 for the Full Scale, 4.24 for the Performance Scale, and 3.35 for the Verbal Scale (see Table G-1).

**Table G-1**
**Average Reliability Coefficients and Standard Errors of Measurement for WPPSI-R Subtests and Scales**

| Subtest or scale | Average reliability coefficient | Average standard error of measurement |
|---|---|---|
| Object Assembly | .63 | 1.82 |
| Geometric Design | .79 | 1.37 |
| Block Design | .85 | 1.16 |
| Mazes | .77 | 1.44 |
| Picture Completion | .85 | 1.16 |
| Animal Pegs | .66 | 1.75 |
| Information | .84 | 1.20 |
| Comprehension | .83 | 1.24 |
| Arithmetic | .80 | 1.34 |
| Vocabulary | .84 | 1.20 |
| Similarities | .86 | 1.12 |
| Sentences | .82 | 1.27 |
| Performance IQ | .92 | 4.24 |
| Verbal IQ | .95 | 3.35 |
| Full Scale IQ | .96 | 3.00 |

*Note.* Reliability coefficients for all subtests except Animal Pegs are split-half coefficients corrected by the Spearman-Brown formula. For Animal Pegs the reliability coefficient is a test-retest coefficient.
*Source:* Adapted from Wechsler (1989).

**Table G-2**
**Median Subtest Reliabilities at Nine Age Groups and at the Average of the Nine Age Groups on the WPPSI-R**

| Age | Range | Median |
|---|---|---|
| 3 | .63–.90 | .850 |
| 3½ | .63–.89 | .845 |
| 4 | .66–.89 | .870 |
| 4½ | .56–.93 | .840 |
| 5 | .59–.86 | .830 |
| 5½ | .57–.86 | .775 |
| 6 | .66–.86 | .780 |
| 6½ | .66–.83 | .745 |
| 7 | .54–.86 | .660 |
| Average | .63–.86 | .825 |

Thus, as with all of the Wechsler scales, more confidence can be placed in an IQ based on the Full Scale than in one based on either the Performance or Verbal Scale alone.

The average standard errors of measurement for the subtests in scaled-score points range from 1.16 to 1.82 for the Performance Scale subtests and from 1.12 to 1.34 for the

Verbal Scale subtests. Within the Performance Scale, Block Design and Picture Completion have the smallest $SE_m$ (1.16 for both). Within the Verbal Scale, Similarities, Information, and Vocabulary have the smallest $SE_m$ (1.12, 1.20, and 1.20, respectively).

**Test-Retest Reliablity**

When the WPPSI-R was readministered to 175 children in the standardization group after a period of approximately 3 to 7 weeks ($M = 4$ weeks), average increases of 6.3, 2.8, and 5.1 IQ points (which were all significant at $p < .001$) were found on the Performance, Verbal, and Full Scales, respectively (see Table G-3) (Wechsler, 1989). Respective

**Table G-3**
**Test-Retest WPPSI-R IQs for 175 Children at Two Age Groups—3 Through 4-11 and 5 Through 7¼ Years of Age**

| Scale | First testing | | Second testing | | |
| | Mean IQ | SD | Mean IQ | SD | Change[a] |
|---|---|---|---|---|---|
| Performance IQ | 101.8 | 14.4 | 108.1 | 16.6 | + 6.3 |
| Verbal IQ | 101.4 | 14.7 | 104.2 | 16.3 | + 2.8 |
| Full Scale IQ | 101.7 | 14.4 | 106.8 | 16.6 | + 5.1 |

[a] All mean change scores are significant at $p < .001$.
*Source:* Adapted from Wechsler (1989).

test-retest correlations were .87, .89, and .91 for the Performance, Verbal, and Full Scales. The changes in subtest scaled scores, which were probably related to practice effects, were as follows: Object Assembly, +1.2; Geometric Design, 0; Block Design, +1.3; Mazes, +1.0; Picture Completion, +.9; Animal Pegs, +.7; Information, +.4; Comprehension, +.4; Arithmetic, +.4; Vocabulary, −.2; Similarities, +.9; and Sentences, +.4.

The preceding changes, which ranged from −.2 (Vocabulary) to +1.3 (Block Design), were significant for 10 of the 12 subtests. The two exceptions were Geometric Design, where there was no change, and Vocabulary, where the change was extremely small. Generally, subtests on the Performance Scale showed greater practice effects ($M$ change $= .85$) than did subtests on the Verbal Scale ($M$ change $= .45$). (Differences in test–retest change scores for the three scales and 12 subtests were evaluated by using a *t* test for differences between correlated means.)

## Precision Range

Table H-1 in Appendix H shows the confidence intervals for the 68, 85, 90, 95, and 99 percent levels for the WPPSI-R Performance, Verbal, and Full Scale IQs by age level. The precision ranges (or confidence intervals) on the WPPSI-R are generally similar throughout the nine age groups. For the Full Scale IQ, they range between 6 and 8 points at the 95 percent confidence level. The precision ranges are narrower for the Full and Verbal Scale IQs than for the Performance Scale IQ and narrower at ages 3 to 5 than at ages 5½ to 7. *The child's specific age group should be used to obtain the most accurate confidence interval.* For further discussion of precision ranges and how to report them, see pages 28–29 and 729–730.

## VALIDITY

Although approximately 42 percent of the items on the WPPSI-R are new, much of the research on the validity of the WPPSI probably is pertinent to the WPPSI-R. Studies related to the validity of the WPPSI, reviewed on pages 195–198 of this text, indicate that it has adequate construct, concurrent, and predictive validity for many different types of normal and handicapped children in the age range from 4 to 6½ years.

## Concurrent Validity

Because the WPPSI-R is a newly published test, little is known about how valid it is over its entire age range, except for the few studies reported in the WPPSI-R manual. These studies are summarized in Table G-4 and are discussed below.

1. *WPPSI-R and WPPSI.* Full Scale IQs on the WPPSI-R were found to be about *8 points lower*, on the average, than those on the WPPSI in a sample of 144 children between the ages of 48 and 79 months. Similarly, IQs on the Performance Scale and Verbal Scale were lower on the WPPSI-R than on the WPPSI by about 9 and 5 IQ points, respectively, on the average.

For the 11 subtests in common, correlations ranged from a low of .58 for Mazes to a high of .79 for Sentences (*Mdn r* = .69). Correlations between subtests on the Perfor-

**Table G-4**
**Summary of Concurrent Validity Studies Reported in WPPSI-R Manual**

| Study | N | Age range | Test-retest interval | Scale | Test | | $D^a$ | r |
|-------|---|-----------|---------------------|-------|------|------|------|---|
| 1 | 144 | 48–79 mos. (*M* = unknown) | 3–5 weeks | | WPPSI-R | WPPSI | | |
| | | | | Performance | | | | |
| | | | | *M* | 102.8 | 112.2 | − 9.4 | .82 |
| | | | | *SD* | 15.9 | 15.7 | − | − |
| | | | | Verbal | | | | |
| | | | | *M* | 104.0 | 109.1 | − 5.1 | .85 |
| | | | | *SD* | 15.9 | 16.9 | − | − |
| | | | | Full Scale | | | | |
| | | | | *M* | 103.9 | 111.6 | − 8.3 | .87 |
| | | | | *SD* | 16.2 | 16.3 | − | − |
| 2 | 50 | 72–86 mos. (*M* = 79 mos.) | 3–30 days (*M* = 19 days) | | WPPSI-R | WISC-R | | |
| | | | | Performance | | | | |
| | | | | *M* | 99.8 | 108.7 | − 8.9 | .71 |
| | | | | *SD* | 13.1 | 12.3 | − | − |
| | | | | Verbal | | | | |
| | | | | *M* | 106.9 | 111.6 | − 4.7 | .77 |
| | | | | *SD* | 11.3 | 15.3 | − | − |
| | | | | Full Scale | | | | |
| | | | | *M* | 103.8 | 111.3 | − 7.5 | .85 |
| | | | | *SD* | 11.6 | 11.7 | − | − |

*(Table continues next page)*

**Table G-4 (cont.)**

| Study | N | Age range | Test-retest interval | Scale | Test | | $D^a$ | r |
|---|---|---|---|---|---|---|---|---|
| 3 | 115 | 4-0 to 7-2 yrs. (M = 5-10) | 1–90 days (M = 16.7 days) | Performance | WPPSI-R | Stanford-Binet –4th Ed. | | |
| | | | | M | 104.8 | – | – | .56 |
| | | | | SD | 13.2 | – | – | – |
| | | | | Verbal | | | | |
| | | | | M | 104.1 | – | – | .73 |
| | | | | SD | 15.1 | – | – | – |
| | | | | Full Scale | | | | |
| | | | | M | 105.3 | 107.2[b] | – 1.9 | .74 |
| | | | | SD | 14.0 | 12.8 | – | – |
| 4 | 93 | 4–6 yrs. (M = 62.5 mos.) | 7–21 days (M = 14 days) | Performance | WPPSI-R | McCarthy Scales | | |
| | | | | M | 101.2 | – | – | – |
| | | | | SD | 14.4 | – | – | .66 |
| | | | | Verbal | | | | |
| | | | | M | 103.3 | – | – | .77 |
| | | | | SD | 12.9 | – | – | – |
| | | | | Full Scale | | | | |
| | | | | M | 102.4 | 104.8[c] | – 2.4 | .81 |
| | | | | SD | 13.5 | 14.3 | – | – |
| 5 | 59 | 37–76 mos. (M = 61 mos.) | 5–14 days (M = 9.5 days) | Performance | WPPSI-R | K-ABC | | |
| | | | | M | 100.4 | – | – | .41 |
| | | | | SD | 13.5 | – | – | – |
| | | | | Verbal | | | | |
| | | | | M | 94.4 | – | – | .42 |
| | | | | SD | 12.5 | – | – | – |
| | | | | Full Scale | | | | |
| | | | | M | 96.8 | 103.1[d] | – 6.3 | .49 |
| | | | | SD | 12.6 | 13.1 | – | – |

[a]Difference.
[b]Using Composite Score.
[c]Using General Cognitive Index.
[d]Using Mental Processing Composite.

mance Scale were slightly lower (range of .58 to .74, *Mdn r* = .64) than those on the Verbal Scale (range of .59 to .79, *Mdn r* = .69). These somewhat low correlations suggest that the subtests in common on the WPPSI-R and the WPPSI do not share a close degree of correspondence. It is not clear why the correlations between the subtests on the two tests were not higher.

2. *WPPSI-R and WISC-R*. In another sample of 50 children, ages 72 to 86 months, the WPPSI-R yielded *lower* Full Scale IQs than the WISC-R by about *8 points*, on the average. Performance Scale IQs on the WPPSI-R were lower by about 9 points and Verbal Scale IQs were lower by about 5 points, on the average, than the respective WISC-R IQs.

3. *WPPSI-R and Stanford-Binet Intelligence Scale—4th Edition*. In a sample of 115 children between 4-0 and 7-2 years, IQs were found to be *similar* on the WPPSI-R and Stanford-Binet Intelligence Scale—4th Edition. The mean

Full Scale IQ on the WPPSI-R was about 2 points lower than the mean Composite Score on the Stanford-Binet—4th Edition.

4. *WPPSI-R and McCarthy Scales of Children's Abilities.* The WPPSI-R yielded scores that were *similar* to those on the McCarthy Scales of Children's Abilities in a sample of 93 children, ages 4 to 6 years. The mean WPPSI-R Full Scale IQ was about 2 points lower than the mean General Cognitive Index on the McCarthy Scales.

5. *WPPSI-R and K-ABC.* The WPPSI-R yielded lower IQs than did the K-ABC in a sample of 59 children ages 37 to 76 months. The mean WPPSI-R Full Scale IQ was about *6 points lower* than the mean K-ABC Mental Composite.

### Construct Validity

The principal components analysis cited later in this appendix, as well as the factor analyses cited in the WPPSI-R manual, indicates that the test measures adequately two factors that correspond to the Verbal and Performance Scales of the test. In addition, the test provides a fair measure of general intelligence. Thus, there is support for the construct validity of the WPPSI-R.

### Comment on the Validity of the WPPSI-R

The validity studies in the WPPSI-R manual suggest that the WPPSI-R has adequate concurrent and construct validity. This conclusion, however, may not pertain to all ages covered by the test, particularly ages 36 to 48 months, which are new to the revision. Because only one of the studies cited in the WPPSI-R manual sampled this age period, much additional research is needed to investigate the validity of the WPPSI-R at the earliest age levels of the test. It also would be helpful to have additional studies for children who are 7 years old, because this age group is new to the test, and for children between 4 and 6½ years as well.

The WPPSI-R and the WISC-R should not be considered parallel forms. The study cited above suggests that children tested first with the WPPSI-R and then with the WISC-R will probably show an increase of about 8 IQ points, on the average. (This generalization may not hold for handicapped or exceptional children, particularly for those at the lower or upper levels of the IQ distribution.) This increase in WISC-R scores may have *nothing* to do with any intervening events resulting in changes in the child or in the child's environment and *likely is associated with the two different sets of norms.* Almost 15 years separate the standardization of the two instruments, and

any differences in scores may be *solely* a function of the different standardization samples. It is also possible that the WPPSI-R is a more difficult test than the WISC-R. Changes greater than 8 points may reflect genuine changes in performance, however.

Similarly, children first tested with the WISC-R (say at the age of 6 years) and then retested with the WPPSI-R (say at the age of 7 years) may show a *decrease* in scores of up to 8 points, on the average. Again, this decrease should be understood solely as a function of the different instruments, and not attributed to decrements in the intellectual ability of the children. Decreases beyond 8 points may suggest decrements in performance, however.

The other concurrent validity studies cited in the WPPSI-R manual suggest that the WPPSI-R yields IQs that are similar to those of the Stanford-Binet Intelligence Scale—4th Edition and McCarthy Scales of Children's Abilities for children in the normal range of functioning. The comparability of the WPPSI-R and Stanford-Binet—4th Edition and WPPSI-R and McCarthy Scales needs further study in samples of exceptional children. The WPPSI-R yielded IQs that were not comparable to those on the K-ABC. Scores on the K-ABC were generally about 6 points higher than those on the WPPSI-R. Again, the relationship between the two tests needs to be studied in samples of exceptional children and additional samples of normal children.

## INTERCORRELATIONS BETWEEN SUBTESTS AND SCALES

Intercorrelations between subtests and scales permit us to observe the degree of relationship between various parts of the WPPSI-R. Average intercorrelations between the 12 subtests range from a low of .25 (Object Assembly and Sentences) to a high of .66 (Information and Comprehension). The median intercorrelation is .41. The six *highest* subtest average intercorrelations are between Information and Comprehension (.66), Information and Vocabulary (.60), Comprehension and Vocabulary (.60), Information and Arithmetic (.59), Information and Similarities (.57), and Information and Sentences (.55). The seven *lowest* subtest average intercorrelations (seven are listed instead of six because of ties) are between Mazes and Sentences (.24), Object Assembly and Sentences (.25), Geometric Design and Vocabulary (.26), Object Assembly and Comprehension (.26), Mazes and Comprehension (.26), Mazes and Vocabulary (.26), and Animal Pegs and Vocabulary (.26). The Verbal subtests have higher intercorrelations than the Performance subtests. The lowest correlations are found between the subtests of the two different scales.

## FACTOR ANALYSIS

A principal components analysis with varimax rotation was performed on the standardization data. (See pages 31–34 of this text for a brief explanation of factor analysis.) Two principal factors were found at all age levels, with the exception of age 7, where a three-factor solution was also appropriate. (In the three-factor solution Mazes and Animal Pegs were the only subtests that had loadings above .40 on the third factor.) The two-factor solution best ex-

plains the WPPSI-R throughout all of its age levels. The Verbal factor (or Verbal Comprehension) is best represented at all ages by the six subtests in the Verbal Scale: Comprehension, Information, Vocabulary, Sentences, Similarities, and Arithmetic. The Performance factor (or Perceptual Organization) is best represented at most ages by five of the six subtests in the Performance Scale: Block Design, Geometric Design, Object Assembly, Mazes, and Animal Pegs (see Table G-5).

Picture Completion does not consistently load on the Performance factor at all ages. It has higher loadings on the Verbal than Performance factor at age 3 and loads well on both the Verbal and Performance factors at ages 3½, 4, 4½, 6½, and 7. It clearly loads on the Performance factor *only* at ages 5, 5½, and 6. For all ages combined, Picture

**Table G-5**
**Factor Loadings of WPPSI-R Subtests for Nine Age Groups and the Average Following Varimax Rotation**

| Subtest | Age group | | | | | | | | | |
|---|---|---|---|---|---|---|---|---|---|---|
| | 3 | 3½ | 4 | 4½ | 5 | 5½ | 6 | 6½ | 7 | Av. |
| **Factor A — Verbal** | | | | | | | | | | |
| Object Assembly | 21 | 15 | 08 | 12 | 23 | 13 | 06 | 30 | 02 | 14 |
| Geometric Design | 38 | 29 | 22 | 19 | −03 | 17 | 20 | 16 | 09 | 18 |
| Block Design | 12 | 22 | 34 | 26 | 45 | 23 | 18 | 39 | 15 | 26 |
| Mazes | 25 | 15 | 26 | 23 | 13 | −04 | 24 | 06 | 13 | 15 |
| Picture Completion | 63 | 55 | 49 | 53 | 32 | 22 | 22 | 41 | 41 | 41 |
| Animal Pegs | 18 | 19 | 30 | 28 | 41 | 26 | 15 | 24 | 24 | 24 |
| Information | 83 | 79 | 81 | 77 | 80 | 73 | 78 | 79 | 70 | 78 |
| Comprehension | 80 | 87 | 85 | 84 | 80 | 77 | 79 | 75 | 75 | 81 |
| Arithmetic | 59 | 69 | 70 | 63 | 62 | 52 | 64 | 65 | 66 | 62 |
| Vocabulary | 79 | 79 | 77 | 83 | 81 | 79 | 78 | 82 | 70 | 79 |
| Similarities | 73 | 72 | 78 | 74 | 72 | 75 | 68 | 71 | 65 | 72 |
| Sentences | 72 | 77 | 71 | 76 | 73 | 75 | 76 | 61 | 73 | 74 |
| **Factor B — Performance** | | | | | | | | | | |
| Object Assembly | 70 | 68 | 75 | 76 | 64 | 66 | 76 | 68 | 77 | 72 |
| Geometric Design | 69 | 75 | 75 | 77 | 80 | 67 | 65 | 72 | 55 | 72 |
| Block Design | 69 | 77 | 74 | 76 | 65 | 80 | 78 | 72 | 78 | 75 |
| Mazes | 69 | 69 | 63 | 63 | 79 | 73 | 69 | 75 | 50 | 69 |
| Picture Completion | 37 | 53 | 55 | 56 | 65 | 62 | 66 | 55 | 44 | 57 |
| Animal Pegs | 52 | 58 | 64 | 65 | 38 | 50 | 48 | 31 | 36 | 52 |
| Information | 32 | 33 | 34 | 37 | 25 | 22 | 28 | 26 | 30 | 31 |
| Comprehension | 21 | 20 | 19 | 21 | 07 | 10 | 04 | 13 | 08 | 16 |
| Arithmetic | 43 | 39 | 38 | 44 | 50 | 54 | 40 | 36 | 30 | 44 |
| Vocabulary | 13 | 13 | 18 | 16 | 08 | 17 | 21 | 18 | 26 | 17 |
| Similarities | 25 | 30 | 24 | 28 | 29 | 20 | 30 | 25 | −05 | 26 |
| Sentences | 22 | 13 | 27 | 19 | 22 | 13 | 13 | 29 | 16 | 19 |

*Note.* Av. = Average. Decimal points omitted. Factors based on principal components analysis.

Completion has a substantial loading on *both* the Verbal and Performance factors, but somewhat higher loadings on the Performance factor. At 3 years, a purer measure of the Performance factor can be obtained by using only Object Assembly, Geometric Design, Block Design, and Mazes (and also adding Animal Pegs if desired).

## WPPSI-R Subtests as Measures of *g*

The extent to which the WPPSI-R subtests measure general intelligence or *g* can be determined by examining the loadings on the first unrotated factor in the principal component analysis. Overall, the WPPSI-R is a fair measure of *g*, with 45 percent of its variance attributed to *g*. Higher *g* loadings are found at ages 3 to 5 (average loadings range from 45 to 50 percent) than at ages 5 to 7 (average loadings range from 34 to 44 percent), with age 7 having the *lowest* *g* loadings (average loading is 34 percent).

With respect to the measurement of *g*, the WPPSI-R subtests form two clusters: (a) Information, Arithmetic, Comprehension, Similarities, and Vocabulary are *good measures of g*, and (b) Picture Completion, Block Design, Sentences, Geometric Design, Object Assembly, Mazes, and Animal Pegs are *fair measures of g* (see Table G-6). The subtests in the Verbal Scale have higher *g* loadings than those in the Performance Scale. In the Verbal Scale, Information has the *highest* loading, whereas in the Performance Scale, Picture Completion and Block Design have the *highest* loadings. Any of the five standard Verbal subtests may serve as a good measure of *g*. Although none of the Performance subtests are good measures of *g*, Block Design and Picture Completion, with 47 percent of their variance attributed to *g*, could be used if nonverbal measures of *g* are needed.

At each age level, the Verbal subtests have, on the average, consistently higher *g* loadings than do the Performance subtests. The consistency of this finding is striking. There are only two age levels at which any Verbal subtest contributes less than 40 percent to the measurement of *g*: at age 6, Comprehension (38 percent), and at age 7, Similarities (26 percent). Block Design is a fair-to-good measure of *g* at each of the nine age levels. Picture Completion is a fair-to-good measure of *g* at every age level of the test.

## WPPSI-R Subtest Specificity

Subtest specificity refers to the proportion of a subtest's variance that is both reliable (that is, not due to errors of measurement) and distinctive to the subtest (see pages 32–34 of this text for further information about subtest specificity). Although the individual subtests on the WPPSI-R overlap in their measurement properties (that is, the majority of reliable variance for most subtests is common factor variance), most possess sufficient specificity at some age levels to justify interpretation of specific subtest functions (see Table G-7).

Throughout the entire age range covered by the WPPSI-R, Picture Completion is the only subtest that has *ample*

**Table G-6**
**WPPSI-R Subtests as Measures of *g***

| | Good measure of g | | | Fair measure of g | |
|---|---|---|---|---|---|
| Subtest | Average loading of g | Proportion of variance attributed to g (%) | Subtest | Average loading of g | Proportion of variance attributed to g (%) |
| Information | .79 | 63 | Picture Completion | .69 | 47 |
| Arithmetic | .76 | 57 | Block Design | .68 | 47 |
| Comprehension | .72 | 52 | Sentences | .68 | 46 |
| Similarities | .72 | 51 | Geometric Design | .61 | 37 |
| Vocabulary | .71 | 51 | Object Assembly | .57 | 33 |
| | | | Mazes | .56 | 32 |
| | | | Animal Pegs | .52 | 27 |

*Note.* Following were the criteria used to classify subtests as good, fair, or poor measures of *g*: *good*—variance attributed to *g* was approximately 50 percent or higher; *fair*—variance attributed to *g* was between 26 percent and 49 percent; *poor*—variance attributed to *g* was between 0 percent and 25 percent. The proportion of variance attributed to *g* was based on a five-place decimal number.

**Table G-7**
**Amount of Specificity in WPPSI-R Subtests**

| WPPSI-R subtest | Ages with ample specificity | Ages with adequate specificity | Ages with inadequate specificity |
|---|---|---|---|
| Object Assembly | – | – | 3–7, Av. |
| Geometric Design | 6,7 | 3–3½, 4½, Av. | 4, 5–5½, 6½ |
| Block Design | 3 | 3½–5, 6, 7, Av. | 5½, 6½ |
| Mazes | 3–4½, 6, 7, Av. | – | 5–5½, 6½ |
| Picture Completion | 3–7, Av. | – | – |
| Animal Pegs | 3, 5, 6–7, Av. | – | 3½–4½, 5½ |
| Information | – | 3½, 4½ | 3, 4, 5–7, Av. |
| Comprehension | – | 3, 5–5½ | 3½–4½, 6–7, Av. |
| Arithmetic | 3, 5½, 6½ | 3½, 4½, 6, Av. | 4, 5, 7 |
| Vocabulary | 4 | 3, 5–5½, Av. | 3½, 4½, 6–7 |
| Similarities | 3–3½, 4½–6, Av. | 4 | 6½–7 |
| Sentences | 3–4 | 4½–5, Av. | 5½–7 |

*Note.* Av. = average of the nine age groups. Kaufman's (1975a) rule of thumb was used to classify the amount of specificity in each subtest. Subtests with *ample specificity* have specific variance that (a) reflects 25 percent or more of the subtest's total variance *and* (b) exceeds the subtest's error variance. Subtests with *adequate specificity* have specific variance that (a) reflects between 15 to 24 percent of the subtest's total variance *and* (b) exceeds the subtest's error variance. Subtests with *inadequate specificity* have specific variance that is either (a) less than 15 percent of the subtest's total variance *or* (b) equal to or less than the subtest's error variance.

*specificity* and Object Assembly is the only subtest that has *inadequate specificity.* Each of the 10 other subtests shows a unique pattern of specificity — that is, the ages at which each one has ample, adequate, or inadequate specificity differ. More subtests have inadequate specificity at ages 4, 5½, 6½, and 7 than at the other ages, however.

Subtests with inadequate specificity should not be interpreted as measuring specific functions, and cautious interpretation is required for those subtests falling within the adequate specificity category. Subtests with inadequate specifity, however, still can be interpreted as measuring *g* (see Table G-6) and the appropriate principal factor (Verbal or Performance) (see Table G-5).

#### Factor Analysis of the WPPSI-R Compared to the WISC-R

The factor structure of the WPPSI-R is generally similar to that of the WISC-R, particularly in regard to the Verbal (or Verbal Comprehension) factor and Performance (or Perceptual Organization) factor. The primary difference between WPPSI-R and WISC-R factor structures is that a Freedom from Distractibility factor emerges on the WISC-R but not on the WPPSI-R. Conceivably, sustained directed attention, partly measured by the Freedom from Distractibility factor, is a part of every subtest at younger age levels and emerges as a separate factor only at some-

what older age levels. Alternatively, it may be that the Freedom from Distractibility factor does not emerge on the WPPSI-R because the test does not include either Digit Span or Coding; these two subtests, along with Arithmetic, generally defined Freedom from Distractibility on the WISC-R.

## IQ RANGES AND SUBTEST SCALED-SCORE RANGES

Information about the range of IQs available at each age level of the test will help you (a) to determine whether the WPPSI-R is an appropriate instrument for evaluating children at the extreme ranges of intelligence and (b) to monitor children's performance over time. Knowing about the available range of subtest scaled scores at each age level of the test will help in profile analysis. This section of the chapter discusses the range of IQs and subtest scaled scores in the WPPSI-R and provides guidelines for evaluating IQs and subtest scaled scores that are at the extremes of the range.

### IQ Ranges

*The range of Full Scale IQs from 41 to 160, as shown in Table 26 of the WPPSI-R manual, cannot be obtained at every age level of the test*. When the rule of thumb recommended in the WPPSI-R manual for computing IQs is followed—that IQs be computed only when the child has a minimum of three raw scores of 1 on the Performance Scale and three raw scores of 1 on the Verbal Scale—it is not until 5¾ years that a Full Scale IQ of 41 can be obtained (six raw scores of 1 and four raw scores of 0). The lowest Full Scale IQ possible at 3 years, for example, is 65, which is barely below two standard deviations from the mean (see Table G-8). (The lower limits of the ranges shown in Table

### Table G-8
### Performance, Verbal, and Full Scale IQ Ranges by Three-Month Age Intervals on the WPPSI-R

| Age[a] | Performance Scale | Verbal Scale | Full Scale |
|---|---|---|---|
| 3 | 66–160 | 71–160 | 65–160 |
| 3¼ | 62–160 | 67–160 | 61–160 |
| 3½ | 60–160 | 66–160 | 59–160 |
| 3¾ | 56–160 | 63–160 | 56–160 |
| 4 | 52–160 | 58–160 | 51–160 |
| 4¼ | 49–160 | 54–160 | 47–160 |
| 4½ | 48–160 | 54–160 | 46–160 |
| 4¾ | 47–160 | 53–160 | 45–160 |
| 5 | 47–160 | 48–160 | 43–160 |
| 5¼ | 45–160 | 48–160 | 42–160 |
| 5½ | 45–160 | 47–160 | 42–160 |
| 5¾ | 45–160 | 46–160 | 41–160 |
| 6 | 45–160 | 46–160 | 41–160 |
| 6¼ | 45–160 | 46–160 | 41–160 |
| 6½ | 45–156 | 46–157 | 41–160 |
| 6¾ | 45–156 | 46–152 | 41–160 |
| 7 | 45–156 | 46–152 | 41–160 |

*Note.* Age 7 represents a four-month interval. Ranges were obtained by using data from Table 25, "Scaled Score Equivalents of Raw Scores," and Table 27, "IQ Equivalents of Sums of Scaled Scores," in the WPPSI-R manual. Ranges based on the 10 standard subtests using the suggested criterion in the WPPSI-R manual that examinees must have three raw scores of at least 1 on the Performance Scale and three raw scores of at least 1 on the Verbal Scale in order for an IQ to be computed. The lower limits of the IQ range represent the lowest IQs that can be obtained. Other combinations of successes and failures will produce slightly higher IQs at the lower limits of the range.
[a] In years.

G-8 may vary depending on the combination of subtests for which raw-score points are earned.) The lowest possible Performance Scale IQ at 3 years is 66 and the lowest possible Verbal Scale IQ is 71 (three scores of 1 point and two scores of 0 points on each scale). Because the lower limit of IQs provided by the WPPSI-R is not consistent throughout the scale, monitoring changes in the performance of children functioning more than two standard deviations below the mean of the test will be difficult.

**IQs at the lower limits.** The following example illustrates the IQs given to a 3-year-old child who has raw scores of 1 on the Object Assembly, Geometric Design, Block Design, Information, Arithmetic, and Vocabulary subtests and raw scores of 0 on each of the four remaining subtests. Six 1-point raw scores will yield a Performance Scale IQ of 66 (22 scaled-score points), a Verbal Scale IQ of 71 (26 scaled-score points), and a Full Scale IQ of 65 (48 scaled-score points). This example demonstrates that the WPPSI-R may not provide precise IQs for children who are functioning two or more standard deviations below the mean of the test. Research is needed to determine the validity of the WPPSI-R for mild and moderately mentally retarded children. If a child fails all or most of the items on the WPPSI-R, it is advisable to administer a test that may provide a more accurate estimate of the child's ability.

Another example illustrates how the restricted range of IQs at the earliest year levels of the test may seriously affect the interpretation of a child's performance. A 3-year-old boy obtains a Full Scale IQ of 65, and when retested at 5¼ years, he obtains a Full Scale IQ of 41. The 24-point drop between the first and second examinations may be purely an artifact of the IQs available at each age level of the test. As previously noted, at the earliest year levels of the test, the floor is much higher than at the later year levels—that is, the lowest IQs cannot be obtained at the early ages. *Thus, in the case of low-functioning children, when the results of two (or more) examinations given two (or more) years apart are compared, there is simply no way of knowing whether there was a serious decrement in the children's performance.* In the preceding example (and in similar cases), it would be best to assume that no decrement in mental ability occurred during the interval between the two examinations.

**IQs at the upper limits.** In contrast to the restricted and variable range of IQs at the lower limits of the WPPSI-R, the upper limit of the WPPSI-R IQ range—a Full Scale IQ of 160—can be obtained at every age level of the test. On the one hand, the uniform ceiling is a definite advantage in follow-up evaluations of children who are functioning three or four standard deviations above the mean. On the other hand, the uniform ceiling also represents a low ceiling level for extremely bright 3-year-olds who answer every item correctly. For example, if every item of the test were answered correctly by both a 3-year-old and a 7-year-old, both children would obtain the exact same IQ of 160. It is quite likely that the 3-year-old is brighter than the 7-year-old, but this is not reflected in his or her score.

The failure of the WPPSI-R to differentiate between the brightest of the 3-year-olds and the brightest of the 7-year-olds happens in part because at the 3-year level (and at adjacent ages) several raw scores at the upper limits of each subtest are awarded the *exact* same scaled score of 19. For example, raw scores from 21 to 47 on the Vocabulary subtest are given a scaled score of 19, as are raw scores from 24 to 42 on the Block Design subtest. The failure of the WPPSI-R to differentiate among young children who are functioning more than four standard deviations above the mean is not a major criticism of the scale, however. None of the leading measures of cognitive ability have a range of IQs greater than that of the WPPSI-R.

Although the ceiling level on the Full Scale is uniform throughout the WPPSI-R, the ceiling level on the Performance and Verbal Scales is somewhat less uniform (see Table G-8). The highest Performance IQ available at ages 6½ through 7 is 156, whereas the highest Verbal IQ available at age 6½ is 157 and at ages 6¾ and 7 is 152. These somewhat restricted ranges at the upper ages should not cause too much of a problem in interpreting IQs on the Performance and Verbal Scales.

## Subtest Scaled-Score Ranges

The major problem with the scaled-score ranges occurs at the first year level of the test, where points are awarded to children who fail every item. For example, children who fail every item on Geometric Design, Mazes, Picture Completion, Information, Comprehension, Similarities, or Sentences are given 5 or 6 scaled-score points (see Table G-9). At 3 years, Object Assembly is the only subtest on which a scaled score of 1 can be obtained. This problem is related to the limited floor discussed previously. For example, 3-year-old children receive up to 43 scaled-score points even when they fail every item on the 10 standard subtests; the corresponding IQ is 62. It is also noteworthy that at none of the 17 separate age groups listed in Table 25, "Scaled Score Equivalents of Raw Scores," of the WPPSI-R manual (pages 170–186) is it possible to obtain the entire range of scaled-score points from 1 to 19 on all subtests.

The WPPSI-R manual, as noted before, advises that IQs not be computed (as was done in the previous example) unless children obtain at least one success on three Verbal and on three Performance subtests. Research is needed, however, to determine the validity of this recommendation.

**Table G-9**
**Subtest Scaled-Score Ranges by Three-Month Age Intervals on the WPPSI-R**

|          |      |      |      |      |      | Subtest |      |      |      |      |      |      |
| -------- | ---- | ---- | ---- | ---- | ---- | ------- | ---- | ---- | ---- | ---- | ---- | ---- |
| Age[a]   | OA   | GD   | BD   | MA   | PC   | AP      | I    | C    | A    | V    | S    | Se   |
| 3        | 1–19 | 5–19 | 4–19 | 5–19 | 5–19 | 2–19    | 5–19 | 6–19 | 3–19 | 3–19 | 6–19 | 5–19 |
| 3¼       | 1–19 | 4–19 | 4–19 | 4–19 | 4–19 | 1–19    | 4–19 | 6–19 | 3–19 | 2–19 | 5–19 | 4–19 |
| 3½       | 1–19 | 4–19 | 4–19 | 3–19 | 4–19 | 1–19    | 4–19 | 5–19 | 3–19 | 2–19 | 5–19 | 3–19 |
| 3¾       | 1–19 | 3–19 | 3–19 | 2–19 | 3–19 | 1–19    | 3–19 | 5–19 | 2–19 | 2–19 | 4–19 | 3–19 |
| 4        | 1–19 | 2–19 | 3–19 | 1–19 | 2–19 | 1–19    | 2–19 | 4–19 | 1–19 | 2–19 | 3–19 | 3–19 |
| 4¼       | 1–19 | 1–19 | 3–19 | 1–19 | 1–19 | 1–19    | 2–19 | 3–19 | 1–19 | 1–19 | 3–19 | 2–19 |
| 4½       | 1–19 | 1–19 | 3–19 | 1–19 | 1–19 | 1–19    | 2–19 | 3–19 | 1–19 | 1–19 | 3–19 | 2–19 |
| 4¾       | 1–19 | 1–18 | 2–19 | 1–19 | 1–19 | 1–19    | 1–19 | 3–19 | 1–19 | 1–19 | 2–19 | 2–19 |
| 5        | 1–19 | 1–18 | 1–19 | 1–19 | 1–19 | 1–19    | 1–19 | 2–19 | 1–19 | 1–19 | 2–19 | 1–19 |
| 5¼       | 1–19 | 1–17 | 1–19 | 1–19 | 1–19 | 1–19    | 1–19 | 2–19 | 1–19 | 1–19 | 2–19 | 1–19 |
| 5½       | 1–18 | 1 17 | 1–19 | 1–19 | 1–19 | 1–19    | 1–19 | 2–18 | 1–19 | 1–19 | 1–19 | 1–19 |
| 5¾       | 1–18 | 1–17 | 1–19 | 1–19 | 1–19 | 1–19    | 1–19 | 1–18 | 1–19 | 1–19 | 1–19 | 1–19 |
| 6        | 1–17 | 1–17 | 1–19 | 1–19 | 1–19 | 1–19    | 1–19 | 1–18 | 1–19 | 1–19 | 1–19 | 1–19 |
| 6¼       | 1–17 | 1–17 | 1–19 | 1–19 | 1–19 | 1–19    | 1–19 | 1–18 | 1–18 | 1–19 | 1–18 | 1–19 |
| 6½       | 1–16 | 1–16 | 1–18 | 1–18 | 1–19 | 1–19    | 1–18 | 1–17 | 1–17 | 1–19 | 1–18 | 1–19 |
| 6¾       | 1–16 | 1–16 | 1–18 | 1–18 | 1–18 | 1–19    | 1–17 | 1–17 | 1–16 | 1–19 | 1–17 | 1–19 |
| 7        | 1–16 | 1–16 | 1–18 | 1–18 | 1–18 | 1–19    | 1–17 | 1–17 | 1–16 | 1–19 | 1–17 | 1–17 |

*Note.* Abbreviations: OA = Object Assembly, GD = Geometric Design, BD = Block Design, MA = Mazes, PC = Picture Completion, AP = Animal Pegs, I = Information, C = Comprehension, A = Arithmetic, V = Vocabulary, S = Similarities, Se = Sentences. Age 7 represents a four-month interval. Ranges based on Table 25, "Scaled Score Equivalents of Raw Scores," in WPPSI-R manual.
[a] In years.

It should be considered as tentative because the WPPSI-R manual fails to indicate the basis for it. We don't know, for example, whether IQs derived from four (or five) raw scores of 1 are reliable and valid. In addition, we need to know more about the reliability and validity of IQs obtained using the rule of thumb given in the WPPSI-R manual.

A minor problem occurs at the upper limits of the last two years of the test. At age 7, for example, it is possible to obtain 19 scaled-score points on only two of the subtests— Animal Pegs and Vocabulary. In addition, at age 7, there is a low ceiling (scaled score of 16) on three subtests: Object Assembly, Geometric Design, and Arithmetic. Finally, on some subtests the ceiling level of 19 scaled-score points is reached midway through the age range (for example, at age 4½ for Geometric Design and at age 5¼ for Object Assembly and Comprehension), after which the ceiling level goes down.

The failure to have a uniform scaled-score range throughout all age levels of the test means that profile analysis cannot be performed in a routine manner, particularly at the lower and upper limits of the scaled-score range. *Therefore, in interpreting children's profiles, you must take into account the range of scaled scores available for that child's specific age.*

## NORMATIVE CHANGES ON ANIMAL PEGS

Because Animal Pegs is the only subtest that has exactly the same number of items, scoring procedure, and time limits in the WPPSI and in the WPPSI-R, it is of interest to see how the norms have changed over the 22-year period between the publication of the original and revised versions of the test. At ages 4 through 6½, where the two forms overlap, children, in most cases, must earn more raw-score points on the WPPSI-R than on the WPPSI to obtain the same scaled score. The changes range from −1 to 17 raw-score points (*Mdn* change = 4 raw-score points).

### Changes Related to Age and Ability Level

The normative changes on the Animal Pegs subtest tend to be related to both age and ability level. *The groups usually most affected by the changes are (a) children between 4 and 4½ years with above-average ability (for example, with scaled scores above 10) and (b) children between 4¾ and 6½ years with below-average ability (for example, with scaled scores below 10). These groups, in most cases,*

need to be more proficient (in either speed, accuracy, or some combination of the two) to maintain the same relative position on the WPPSI-R that they had on the WPPSI. In contrast, 4-year-olds with below-average ability and 5- to 6½-year-olds with above-average ability have not changed appreciably (see Table G-10). Overall, changes are greatest at age 4 (*Mdn* change = 7 raw-score points) and smallest at age 6½ (*Mdn* change = 1 raw-score point) (see Table G-11).

**Table G-10**
**Median Additional Raw-Score Points Needed on WPPSI-R Animal Pegs to Obtain Same Scaled Score as on WPPSI at Younger and Upper Ages for Low and High Scaled-Score Ranges**

| Scaled-score range | Ages | | |
|---|---|---|---|
| | 4–4½ | 4¾–5¾ | 6–6½ |
| 1–9 | 1 | 8 | 6 |
| 11–19 | 8 | 3 | 1 |

**Table G-11**
**Additional Points Needed on WPPSI-R Animal Pegs to Obtain Same Scaled Score as on WPPSI at Ages 4, 5¼, and 6½ Years**

| Scaled score | Age | | | |
|---|---|---|---|---|
| | 4 | 5¼ | 6½ | Mdn[a] |
| 1 | 0 | 0 | 0 | 0 |
| 4 | 1 | 7 | 17 | 7 |
| 7 | 2 | 13 | 1 | 9 |
| 10 | 7 | 7 | 1 | 7 |
| 13 | 11 | 3 | 0 | 3 |
| 16 | 9 | 3 | 0 | 3 |
| 19 | 13 | 5 | 2 | 5 |
| Mdn[b] | 7 | 4 | 1 | 4 |

*Note.* Based on Table 25 in the WPPSI-R manual and Table 21 in the WPPSI manual. The raw scores shown in the table are at the lower limits of the range of raw scores for each scaled score. Animal Pegs is called Animal House on the WPPSI.
[a]Over 11 age intervals from 4 through 6½ years.
[b]Over the range of scaled scores from 1 through 19.

These trends are examined in more detail in Table G-11, which shows the additional raw-score points needed for seven representative scaled scores at ages 4, 5¼, and 6½ years. A 4-year-old child needs, for example, 13 more raw-score points on the WPPSI-R than on the WPPSI to earn a scaled score of 19. Translated into time requirements, this means that to earn the highest scaled score, a 4-year-old with a perfect performance must work 1 minute *faster* on the WPPSI-R than on the WPPSI (30″ on the WPPSI-R and 1′30″ on the WPPSI). Another way to understand the changes on Animal Pegs is to note, for example, that a 4-year-old with a raw score of 52 earns a scaled score of 19 on the WPPSI, but a scaled score of only 15 on the WPPSI-R. For a 6½-year-old child, a raw score of 15 earns a scaled score of 4 on the WPPSI, but a scaled score of only 1 on the WPPSI-R. These are some of the most dramatic normative changes on the Animal Pegs subtest.

### Accounting for Normative Changes on Animal Pegs

It is not easy to account for the normative changes that have taken place on the Animal Pegs subtest. Perhaps during the years between the initial standardization and the revision, young children have had better nutrition or increased exposure to manipulative experiences at preschool or at home. The normative changes also may be due to unknown differences in the WPPSI-R and WPPSI standardization groups.

Examining the changes in relation to both age and ability level suggests that changes have been minimal for younger children with below-average ability. However, during the years between the original test and the revision, school-aged children with below-average ability appear to have become more proficient in the skills measured by the Animal Pegs subtest. On the original norms, the school-age children with above-average ability were already near or at the ceiling level, and therefore few changes could be expected in their performance. Overall, the data indicate that children must be more proficient on the WPPSI-R than on the WPPSI Animal Pegs subtest to maintain their same relative position.

### COMPARISON OF THE WPPSI-R AND WPPSI

Although similar to its predecessor, the WPPSI-R differs from it in some important ways.

1. As previously noted, the age range is greater for the revision. On the WPPSI the age range was from 4 to 6½, whereas on the WPPSI-R it goes from 3 to 7¼ years. To increase the range, 91 new items were added, and the total number of items expanded from 182 to 217.

2. The revision contains a new subtest, Object Assem-

bly, which makes the WPPSI-R more similar to the WISC-R.

3. The Animal House subtest has been renamed Animal Pegs and made an optional subtest, and the retest (Animal House Retest) is not included in the revision.

4. Full-color art is included in some of the pictorial materials in the revision.

5. Scoring guidelines and administrative procedures for some subtests have been modified in the revision.

6. Speed (coupled with correct performance) is awarded additional bonus points on the Block Design subtest in the revision.

7. Reliability coefficients for the Performance, Verbal, and Full Scales differ somewhat in the two tests. On the WPPSI reliability coefficients for the IQs on the three scales were .90 or above at all ages, whereas on the WPPSI-R reliability coefficients for the Performance and Verbal Scale IQs are in the .80s at the 7-year level and in the .90s at other age levels.

8. The WPPSI-R is more of a test of speed than the WPPSI was, because Object Assembly and Block Design have bonus points for speed.

9. At the upper age levels of the test, the WPPSI-R covers a more extensive IQ range than does the WPPSI — 41 to 160 instead of 45 to 155.

Examiners familiar with the WPPSI should study carefully the administrative and scoring procedures on the WPPSI-R. Although many of the procedures are the same for both tests, some modifications have been made and these new procedures must be mastered.

### ADMINISTERING THE WPPSI-R

The general administrative suggestions described for the WISC-III (see pages 1051–1067 of this text) are also appropriate for the WPPSI-R. In addition, the two scales have common problems in administration and scoring. Because many subtest names are the same in both scales, care must be taken not to substitute WISC-III directions for WPPSI-R directions or vice versa. The suggestions shown in Exhibit G-2, which supplement those given in other parts of this appendix, and the checklist shown in Exhibit G-3 should help you learn to administer the WPPSI-R. You can review the checklist before you administer the test, complete it as you review a videotape of your test administration, and have another student complete it as he or she observes you administer the test (in person or on videotape). Your course instructor (or teaching assistant) may also use the checklist. Figure G-2 shows the cover of the WPPSI-R record form.

**Exhibit G-2**

## Administering the WPPSI-R

1. Complete the top of the record form.
2. Using date of testing and date of birth, calculate the chronological age (CA) and put it in the box provided. On the WPPSI-R, CA must be stated in years, months, and days.
3. Administer the subtests in the order presented in the manual, except in rare circumstances. Do not change the wording on any subtest. Read the directions exactly as shown in the manual. Do not ad lib.
4. Start with the appropriate item on each subtest and follow discontinuance criteria. You must know correct scoring criteria *before* you give the test.
5. Write out all responses completely and legibly. Do not use unusual abbreviations. Record time accurately.
6. Question all ambiguous or unscorable responses, writing a (Q) after each questioned response.
7. Be patient when working with children in the WPPSI-R age group. Several breaks may be needed during the testing.
8. On Comprehension, if a child only gives one reason to Question 11, request a second reason.
9. Carefully score each protocol, recheck the scoring, and transfer subtest scores to the front of the record form under Raw Score. If you have failed to question a response when you should have and the response is obviously not a 0 response, give the child the most appropriate score.
10. If a subtest was spoiled, write *spoiled* by the subtest total score and on the front of the record form where the raw and scaled scores appear. If for some reason a subtest was not administered, write *NA* in the margin in the record form next to the subtest name and on the front of the record form.
11. Transform raw scores into scaled scores by using Table 25 on pages 170–186 of the WPPSI-R manual. Be sure to use the page of the table that is appropriate for the child's age and the correct row and column for each transformation.
12. Base the Performance Score on the total of the scaled scores on the five standard Performance Scale subtests. Base the Verbal Score on the total of the scaled scores on the five standard Verbal Scale subtests. Do not use Animal Pegs to compute the Performance Score unless you substitute it for another Performance subtest. Similarly, do not use Sentences to compute the Verbal Score unless you substitute it for another Verbal subtest. Add the Performance Score and the Verbal Score together to get the Full Scale Score.
13. If fewer than five subtests were administered in the Performance section or fewer than five subtests in the Verbal section, use the Tellegen and Briggs short-form procedure described on page 138 of this text to compute the IQ.
14. Obtain the IQs from Table 27 in the WPPSI-R manual. Be sure to use the correct section of the table for each of the three IQs—page 188 for the Performance and Verbal IQs and page 189 for the Full Scale IQ. Record the IQs. Next, recheck all of your work. If the IQ was obtained by use of a short form, write *SF* beside the appropriate IQ.
15. Look up the confidence intervals for the Full Scale IQ, Performance Scale IQ, and Verbal Scale IQ in Table H-1 in Appendix H. Normally, the confidence intervals are not used with the Performance or Verbal IQs unless these were the only IQs reported.
16. Look up the percentile rank and classification for each of the IQs in Tables BC-1 and BC-2 on the inside back cover of this text.
17. If desired, use the material on page 190 (Table 28) of the WPPSI-R manual to obtain test-age equivalents. They can be placed (in parentheses) in the right-hand margin of the cover page of the record form next to the scaled score. For test-age equivalents above those in the table, use the highest test-age equivalent and a plus sign. For test-age equivalents below those in the table, use the lowest test-age equivalent and a minus sign.
18. In summary, be sure to read directions verbatim, pronounce words clearly, query at the appropriate times, start with the appropriate item, discontinue at the proper place, place items properly before the child, use correct timing, and follow the specific guidelines in the manual for administering the test.

*Source:* Adapted and revised from material written by M. L. Lewis for the WPPSI. Courtesy of M. L. Lewis.

**Exhibit G-3**

**Administrative Checklist for the WPPSI-R**

ADMINISTRATIVE CHECKLIST FOR THE WPPSI-R

*Name of examiner:* _____  *Date:* _____

*Name of examinee:* _____  *Name of observer:* _____

(Note. *If an item is not applicable, mark NA next to the item.*)

**Object Assembly**                          *Circle One*

1. Reads directions verbatim                  Yes  No
2. Reads directions clearly                   Yes  No
3. Administers all items                      Yes  No
4. Uses shield correctly                      Yes  No
5. Presents puzzles with pieces arranged
   properly                                   Yes  No
6. Records time accurately                    Yes  No
7. Gives appropriate prompt once only if child
   dawdles on items 1 and 2                   Yes  No
8. Demonstrates correct arrangement if child
   fails item 1                               Yes  No
9. Does not demonstrate correct arrangement
   on items 2 through 6 if child fails these
   items                                      Yes  No
10. Gives no prompts on items 3–6             Yes  No
11. Discontinues at proper place              Yes  No

Comments: _____

_____

**Information**

1. Reads items verbatim                       Yes  No
2. Reads items clearly                        Yes  No
3. Queries at appropriate times               Yes  No
4. Demonstrates the correct answer if child fails
   item 1                                     Yes  No
5. Does not demonstrate correct answer if child
   fails on items 2–27                        Yes  No
6. Discontinues at proper place               Yes  No

Comments: _____

_____

**Geometric Design**

1. Reads directions verbatim                  Yes  No
2. Reads directions clearly                   Yes  No
3. Uses prompts appropriately for items 1–7   Yes  No
4. Gives correct answer to item 1 if child fails
   item                                       Yes  No
5. Does not give correct answer on items 2–16
   if child fails these items                 Yes  No

6. Uses black-lead primary pencils with
   erasers                                    Yes  No
7. Uses sheet of cardboard or other firm,
   smooth surface for items 8–16 if table top is
   not smooth                                 Yes  No
8. Folds sheets correctly on items 8–16       Yes  No
9. Queries appropriately                      Yes  No
10. Discontinues at proper place              Yes  No

Comments: _____

_____

**Comprehension**

1. Reads items verbatim                       Yes  No
2. Reads items clearly                        Yes  No
3. Queries at appropriate times               Yes  No
4. Asks for a second response on item 11 if
   child gives only 1 answer                  Yes  No
5. Gives correct answers to items 1 and 2 if
   child gives a 0- or 1-point response       Yes  No
6. Does not give correct answers to items 3–15
   if child fails or does not give a 2-point
   response                                   Yes  No
7. Discontinues at proper place               Yes  No

Comments: _____

_____

**Block Design**

1. Reads directions verbatim                  Yes  No
2. Reads directions clearly                   Yes  No
3. Starts at appropriate item                 Yes  No
4. Places blocks and cards properly           Yes  No
5. Provides demonstration and an explanation
   when administering items 1–3 and item 6 on
   first trial                                Yes  No
6. Provides demonstration without explanation
   when administering items 4, 5, and 7–14 on
   first trial                                Yes  No
7. Provides demonstration and an explanation
   when administering items 6, 8, and 10–14 on
   second trial                               Yes  No

*(Exhibit continues next page)*

**Exhibit G-3 (cont.)**

*Circle One*

8. Provides demonstration without explanation when administering items 1–5, 7, and 9 on second trial    Yes    No
9. Discontinues at proper place    Yes    No

Comments: _____

_____

**Arithmetic**

1. Reads items verbatim    Yes    No
2. Reads items clearly    Yes    No
3. Starts with appropriate item    Yes    No
4. Uses correct timing    Yes    No
5. On items 1–11 proceeds to next item if child shows no sign of responding after 10 or 15 seconds    Yes    No
6. Asks for clarification when two responses are given    Yes    No
7. Gives credit when child answers correctly by holding up fingers only    Yes    No
8. Gives no credit when child holds up correct number of fingers but gives incorrect verbal response    Yes    No
9. Probes on item 11 if child leaves incorrect number of blocks    Yes    No
10. Probes on item 14 if child says "one"    Yes    No
11. Places items properly    Yes    No
12. Discontinues at proper place    Yes    No

Comments: _____

_____

**Mazes**

1. Reads directions verbatim    Yes    No
2. Reads directions clearly    Yes    No
3. Uses red-lead pencil    Yes    No
4. Gives child black-lead primary pencils without erasers    Yes    No
5. Starts with appropriate item    Yes    No
6. Exposes sheet properly    Yes    No
7. Gives correct demonstration    Yes    No
8. Provides "cautions" correctly    Yes    No
9. Uses correct timing    Yes    No
10. Discontinues at proper place    Yes    No

Comments: _____

_____

**Vocabulary**

1. Reads directions verbatim    Yes    No
2. Reads directions clearly    Yes    No

3. Pronounces words clearly    Yes    No
4. Queries at appropriate times    Yes    No
5. Gives correct answer for item 1 if child misses item    Yes    No
6. Does not give correct answers for items 2–25 if child misses items    Yes    No
7. Discontinues at proper place    Yes    No

Comments: _____

_____

**Picture Completion**

1. Reads directions verbatim    Yes    No
2. Reads directions clearly    Yes    No
3. Reads words clearly    Yes    No
4. Starts with appropriate item    Yes    No
5. Places booklet properly    Yes    No
6. Gives child at least 15 seconds to respond to items 1 and 2    Yes    No
7. Gives child at least 30 seconds to respond to items 2–28    Yes    No
8. Gives child correct answers for items 1–4 if child gives incorrect answers    Yes    No
9. Gives the prompt "Yes, but what is missing?" no more than twice for items 4–28    Yes    No
10. Gives the prompt "A part is missing in the picture. What is it that is missing?" no more than twice for items 4–28    Yes    No
11. Inquires correctly on items 16, 17, 22, and 28 when certain responses are given    Yes    No
12. Discontinues at proper place    Yes    No

Comments: _____

_____

**Similarities**

1. Reads directions verbatim    Yes    No
2. Reads directions clearly    Yes    No
3. Reads items verbatim and clearly    Yes    No
4. Queries at appropriate times    Yes    No
5. Gives child correct answers for items 1, 7, 13, and 14 if child gives incorrect answers    Yes    No
6. Does not give correct answers for items 2–6, 8–12, and 15–20 if child gives incorrect answers    Yes    No
7. Gives an example of a 2-point response if child gives a 1-point response to item 13    Yes    No

*(Exhibit continues next page)*

**Exhibit G-3 (cont.)**

                                                                        *Circle One*

8. Queries at appropriate times                              Yes   No
9. Discontinues at proper place                              Yes   No

Comments: _____

_____

**Animal Pegs**

1. Reads directions verbatim                                 Yes   No
2. Reads directions clearly                                  Yes   No
3. Demonstrates tasks clearly                                Yes   No
4. Uses correct timing                                       Yes   No
5. Gives correct prompt or caution when child
   hesitates after completing first row                      Yes   No
6. Gives correct prompt or caution when child
   loses the sense of the task                               Yes   No
7. Gives correct prompt or caution no more than
   twice when child selects pegs of one color and
   completes that color before starting another              Yes   No
8. Gives correct prompt or caution when child
   removes pegs after finishing one row and starts
   over again                                                Yes   No

Comments: _____

_____

**Sentences**

1. Reads directions verbatim                                 Yes   No
2. Reads directions clearly                                  Yes   No
3. Reads items verbatim                                      Yes   No
4. Reads items clearly                                       Yes   No
5. Starts with correct item                                  Yes   No
6. Gives correct answers if child fails items 1, 2,
   and 6                                                     Yes   No
7. Does not give correct answers to items 3–5 and
   7–12 if child fails any of these items                    Yes   No
8. Discontinues at proper place                              Yes   No

Comments: _____

_____

**Overall Assessment of Test Administration**

*Circle one:*

Excellent   Above Average   Average   Poor   Failing

Overall strengths: _____

Overall weaknesses: _____

Other comments: _____

_____

## Physical Abilities Necessary for the WPPSI-R

The physical abilities children need to take the WPPSI-R are, for the most part, the same as those required for the WISC-III (see Table I-15 on page 1073). Adequate visual-motor skills, in particular, are needed to handle the Performance Scale materials. Alternative ways of adminstering the WPPSI-R items are limited because young children who cannot speak usually will not be able to write their answers, and those who cannot hear usually will not be able to read the questions. The specific suggestions for administering the WISC-III to handicapped children also are useful for the WPPSI-R (see pages 1072–1074). This material should be carefully reviewed before the WPPSI-R is administered to physically handicapped children.

## Testing-of-Limits on the WPPSI-R

The general testing-of-limits suggestions presented in Chapter 5 (see pages 110–112) are also useful with the WPPSI-R.

## WPPSI-R Short Forms

Short forms of the WPPSI-R have the same advantages and disadvantages as those of the WISC-III (see page 1071). *Of crucial importance is that short forms never be used for classification or selection purposes.* A short form may be useful for screening or research studies, however. The information in Table H-6 in Appendix H can aid you in the selection of a short form. This table, based on the average of the total standardization group, shows the best WPPSI-R short forms for combinations of two, three, four, and five subtests. Because the short forms of a given length are, for all practical purposes, mutually interchangeable, clinical or other considerations can be used to select the short form. Estimated WPPSI-R Full Scale IQ equivalents for the 10 best short-form dyads, triads, and tetrads are shown in Tables H-7, H-8, and H-9 in Appendix H, respectively.

An inspection of the coefficients in Table H-6 indicates that the four- and five-subtest combinations yield the highest reliability coefficients (.927 and above) and validity coefficients (.910 and above). Consequently, if time per-

**RECORD FORM**

Name _____     Parent's Name _____

Address _____

School _____     Grade _____

Place of Testing _____     Examiner _____

Age _____     Sex _____     Handedness _____

|  | Year | Month | Day |
|---|---|---|---|
| Date Tested |  |  |  |
| Date of Birth |  |  |  |
| Age |  |  |  |

| Performance Tests | Raw Score | Scaled Score |
|---|---|---|
| Object Assembly |  |  |
| Geometric Design |  |  |
| Block Design |  |  |
| Mazes |  |  |
| Picture Completion |  |  |
| (Animal Pegs) | ( ) | ( ) |

Total Performance Tests [ ]

| Verbal Tests | Raw Score | Scaled Score |
|---|---|---|
| Information |  |  |
| Comprehension |  |  |
| Arithmetic |  |  |
| Vocabulary |  |  |
| Similarities |  |  |
| (Sentences) | ( ) | ( ) |

Total Verbal Tests [ ]

|  | Scaled Score | IQ |
|---|---|---|
| Performance Score |  |  |
| Verbal Score |  |  |
| Full Scale Score |  |  |

**WPPSI-R PROFILE**

Clinicians who wish to draw a profile should first transfer the child's *scaled scores* to the row of boxes below. Then mark an X on the dot corresponding to the scaled score for each test, and draw a line connecting the X's.*

Performance Tests          Verbal Tests

Object Assembly, Geometric Design, Block Design, Mazes, Picture Completion, (Animal Pegs)          Information, Comprehension, Arithmetic, Vocabulary, Similarities, (Sentences)

Scaled Score [ ][ ][ ][ ][ ][ ]          Scaled Score [ ][ ][ ][ ][ ][ ]          Scaled Score

19 . . . . . .   19   . . . . . .   19
18 . . . . . .   18   . . . . . .   18
17 . . . . . .   17   . . . . . .   17
16 . . . . . .   16   . . . . . .   16
15 . . . . . .   15   . . . . . .   15
14 . . . . . .   14   . . . . . .   14
13 . . . . . .   13   . . . . . .   13
12 . . . . . .   12   . . . . . .   12
11 . . . . . .   11   . . . . . .   11
10 . . . . . .   10   . . . . . .   10
9 . . . . . .   9   . . . . . .   9
8 . . . . . .   8   . . . . . .   8
7 . . . . . .   7   . . . . . .   7
6 . . . . . .   6   . . . . . .   6
5 . . . . . .   5   . . . . . .   5
4 . . . . . .   4   . . . . . .   4
3 . . . . . .   3   . . . . . .   3
2 . . . . . .   2   . . . . . .   2
1 . . . . . .   1   . . . . . .   1

*See the Manual for a discussion of the significance of differences between scores on the tests.

Ⓨ THE PSYCHOLOGICAL CORPORATION
HARCOURT BRACE JOVANOVICH, INC.

**Figure G-2.     Cover page of WPPSI-R record form.** From the *Wechsler Preschool and Primary Scale of Intelligence—Revised*. Copyright © 1989 by The Psychological Corporation. Reproduced by permission. All rights reserved.

mits, a four- or five-subtest combination is preferable to a two- or three-subtest combination. In addition, if a purer estimate of verbal and performance abilities is needed, the short form chosen should not include Picture Completion because it does not load primarily on the Performance factor at all ages. If the goal is simply to select a general cognitive screening measure, however, Picture Completion can be used because it is a good measure of cognitive functioning. Because Sentences and Animal Pegs were not used in arriving at the IQ scores shown in the manual, these subtests are not recommended for use in a short form.

Another short-form procedure, initially developed by Yudin (1966) and modified by Silverstein (1968a), can be applied to the WPPSI-R. The procedure uses either every second or every third item in each of the 10 standard subtests (see Table G-12). Once again, Animal Pegs and Sentences are excluded from this short form because they were omitted in establishing the IQ table.

**Table G-12**
**Yudin's Abbreviated Procedure for the WPPSI-R as Modified by Silverstein**

| Subtest | Item used | Multiply score by |
|---|---|---|
| Object Assembly | Odd only | 2 |
| Geometric Design | Odd only | 2 |
| Block Design | Odd only | 2 |
| Mazes | Odd only | 2 |
| Picture Completion | Every 3rd | 3 |
| Information | Every 3rd | 3 |
| Comprehension | Odd only | 2 |
| Arithmetic | Odd only | 2 |
| Vocabulary | Every 3rd | 3 |
| Similarities | Odd only | 2 |

*Note.* Procedure for Object Assembly provided by text author.
*Source:* Adapted from Silverstein (1968a).

**Choosing Between the WPPSI-R and the WISC-R**

The WPPSI-R overlaps with the WISC-R from 6-0-0 to 7-3-15 years. Consequently, a decision must be made about which form to use for these ages. The WPPSI-R manual recommends that the WISC-R be administered to children with average or above-average ability who also have average communication ability, whereas it recommends the WPPSI-R for children who are below average in either of these areas. However, the WPPSI-R manual does not pre-

sent any empirical evidence to support this recommendation. As noted on page 139 of this text, the choice of a test should depend on the validity of the inferences that can be made from it. To this end, research is needed with samples of both normal and exceptional children to investigate which test is more valid at the overlapping ages.

The test with the lowest standard error of measurement also would be preferred. Again, it is difficult to compare the WPPSI-R and the WISC-R at the overlapping ages because standard errors of measurement are not given at ages 6 and 7 for the WISC-R. At age 6½, where standard errors of measurement are available for both tests, they are highly similar for the Performance, Verbal, and Full Scale IQs. Although direct comparisons cannot be made for age 7, the standard errors of measurement provided at ages 6½ and 7½ of the WISC-R and at age 7 of the WPPSI-R suggest that the WISC-R provides lower standard errors of measurement than does the WPPSI-R.

Still another useful criterion is which test provides the more reliable and valid estimate of intelligence at different levels of intelligence. Because neither reliability nor validity coeffients are provided in either manual for different levels of intelligence, it is impossible to evaluate this criterion. However, the WPPSI-R provides a more thorough sampling of ability than does the WISC-R in the overlapping age range, because more WPPSI-R than WISC-R items must be administered in order to obtain the same scaled score. For example, on the WPPSI-R Information subtest 16 raw-score points correspond to a scaled score of 5, whereas on the WISC-R Information subtest 2 raw-score points result in this same scaled score. Similarly, for a scaled score of 10 on the Information subtest, the WPPSI-R requires a raw score of 21 points, whereas the WISC-R requires a raw score of 5 points. Similar relationships exist for the other subtests common to both forms.

Research is needed to determine at what ages the greater sampling of ability on the WPPSI-R results in more reliable and valid scores. As noted previously, the WISC-R may have a lower standard error of measurement than the WPPSI-R at age 7, even though the WPPSI-R provides a greater sampling of ability. (Pages 1071–1072 discuss choosing between the WPPSI-R and WISC-III.)

## WPPSI-R SUBTESTS

This section describes the 12 WPPSI-R subtests. Included is a brief discussion of each subtest, its rationale, factor analytic findings, reliability and correlational highlights, and administrative and interpretive considerations. Reliabilities above .80 are preferred for clinical and psychoeducational tasks, and reliabilities at or above .90 are preferred for decision-making tasks. Subtests with reliabilities between .70 and .79 are *relatively reliable*; between .60 and .69, *marginally reliable*; and below .60, *unreliable*.

## Object Assembly

The Object Assembly subtest requires children to place rectangular pieces in their appropriate recess in a frame (item 1—three pieces) or put jigsaw pieces together to form common objects—a flower (item 2—four pieces in a frame), a car (item 3—three pieces), a teddy bear (item 4—four pieces), a face (item 5—five pieces), and a dog (item 6—four pieces). There is no sample item. On each item, the pieces are laid out in a specified disarranged pattern. All children start with the first item, and the subtest is discontinued after three consecutive failures in which children receive a score of 0. Object Assembly is new to the WPPSI-R.

All items are timed. Items 1 through 4 are given 120 seconds, and items 5 and 6, 150 seconds. A perfect performance is given 3 points for the rectangles, teddy bear, and dog; 2 points for the car; and 5 points for the face. Bonuses of up to 3 points are awarded for speed and accuracy on items 3 through 6. With the bonus points, the face item has a maximum score of 8; the teddy bear and dog, 6; and the car, 5. Points also are given for partially correct solutions, depending on the number of pieces placed correctly.

**Rationale.** The rationale presented for the WISC-III Object Assembly subtest appears to apply to the WPPSI-R Object Assembly subtest (see page 1099). However, there are some subtle differences in the items on the two scales. One is that the first WPPSI-R Object Assembly item is a form-board item and does not require the child to make a meaningful picture; in contrast, there are no form-board items on the WISC-III. A second is that the WISC-III items have more pieces than the WPPSI-R items. And a third is that one WISC-III item has a longer time limit (180 seconds) than any on the WPPSI-R.

**Factor analytic findings.** The Object Assembly subtest overall is a fair measure of $g$ (33 percent of its variance may be attributed to $g$—range of 22 to 44 percent in the nine age groups). The subtest contributes substantially to the Performance factor (*Mdn* loading = .70). Subtest specificity is inadequate at every age level and at the average of the nine age groups.

**Reliability and correlational highlights.** Object Assembly overall has a marginal level of reliability ($r_{xx}$ = .63). Reliability coefficients are *below* .70 at seven of the nine age groups; the two exceptions are at ages 4 and 6, where the reliability coefficients are both equal to .70. The subtest correlates more highly with Block Design ($r$ = .52) than with any other subtest. It has low correlations with the Full Scale ($r$ = .50), Performance Scale ($r$ = .56), and Verbal Scale ($r$ = .37).

**Administrative and interpretive considerations.** The administrative and interpretive considerations presented for the WISC-III Object Assembly subtest (pages 1099–1100) are also relevant for the WPPSI-R Object Assembly subtest. It is especially important to observe the time limits on each item and to record precisely the elapsed time because additional bonus points are awarded for quick execution on the last four items. Profile analysis should take into account that the full range of scaled scores from 1 to 19 is available only at ages 3 to 5¼ years (see Table G-9).

## Geometric Design

The Geometric Design subtest has two parts; in the first children must make visual discriminations, and in the second they copy designs. The subtest contains 16 items. Items 1 through 7 require visual recognition and discrimination, whereas items 8 through 16 require visual-motor coordination. Of the 16 items, 10 are new and 6 are either unchanged or slightly modified from the WPPSI. There is no time limit. Items 1 to 7 are given either 0 or 1 point; items 8 through 16 are given 0, 3, 4, 6, 8, or 12 points.

All children begin the subtest with the first item. Special attention must be given to the discontinuance procedures. There are two distinct discontinuance procedures—one for Part 1 (items 1 through 7) and one for Part 2 (items 8 through 16). Part 1 is discontinued after three consecutive failures. Part 2 is then administered, which begins with item 8 (the first drawing item). Part 2 (and the entire subtest) is discontinued after two consecutive failures. Thus, it is important to remember that Part 2 is always administered, even when Part 1 has been discontinued.

**Rationale.** The first part of the Geometric Design subtest (items 1 through 7) involves perceptual recognition and discrimination ability. The child must match a target figure with one of the four figures below it. Because attention probably is involved, impulsive children who make quick, careless choices may perform poorly, especially if they fail to scan all four choices.

The second part of the subtest (items 8 through 16) involves perceptual and visual-motor ability, visual construction, and eye-hand coordination. Previous experience with paper and pencil may help the child succeed. Adequate reproduction of the designs requires appropriate fine motor development, perceptual discrimination ability, and ability to integrate perceptual and motor processes. The child must shift attention between the stimulus and the reproduction and monitor his or her performance.

It is not known to what extent perceptual recognition and discrimination abilities are forerunners of visual-motor skills. It may be that there are two (or more) distinct processes measured by the two different parts of the Geometric Design subtest; research will be needed to investigate this hypothesis.

Low scores may indicate lags in the developmental process. Even some bright young children may have difficulty obtaining high scores, because the motor ability needed for successful performance (the ability to grasp a pencil appropriately, make contact with paper, and draw appropriate lines) is associated in part with maturational processes that may be independent of the development of cognitive processes.

**Factor analytic findings.** The Geometric Design subtest overall is a fair measure of $g$ (37 percent of its variance may be attributed to $g$ — range of 15 to 53 percent in the nine age groups). The subtest contributes substantially to the Performance factor (*Mdn* loading = .72). Subtest specificity is either ample or adequate at five of the ages and at the average of the nine age groups, and inadequate at ages 4, 5, 5½, and 6½.

**Reliability and correlational highlights.** Geometric Design overall is a relatively reliable subtest ($r_{xx}$ = .79). Reliability coefficients are *above* .70 at eight of the nine age groups; the one exception is at age 7, where the reliability coefficent is .68. It correlates more highly with Block Design ($r$ = .49) than with any other subtest. It has low correlations with the Full Scale ($r$ = .54), Performance Scale ($r$ = .58), and Verbal Scale ($r$ = .41).

**Administrative and interpretive considerations.** The WPPSI-R manual presents detailed guidelines for scoring designs 8 through 16, which will require careful study. Although previous research indicated that the WPPSI Geometric Design subtest was difficult to score (e.g., Morsbach, McGoldrick, & Younger, 1978; Sattler, 1976), research described in the WPPSI-R manual suggests that the new scoring rules have improved the scoring accuracy of

examiners. Additional research will be needed to determine whether the revised scoring criteria have improved scorer reliability with other samples of examiners.

The special copyrighted blank paper obtained from the test publisher for the administration of the Geometric Design subtest is not necessary. You need only cut a sheet of paper in half, writing on each sheet the number of the design and "top" and "bottom" relative to the child's frame of reference. Give the child a *new* half sheet of paper for each drawing so that there is no possible distraction from any other drawing made on the paper.

Profile analysis should take into account that the full range of scaled scores from 1 to 19 is available only at ages 4¼ to 4½ years (see Table G-9).

### Block Design

The Block Design subtest requires children to reproduce designs using flat, two-colored blocks. The subtest contains 14 items, 8 of which are new to the WPPSI-R and 6 of which are unchanged or slightly modified. The child is shown a model constructed by the examiner for the first seven items and designs for the last seven items. Children younger than 6 years of age begin with item 1, whereas children 6 years of age and older begin with item 6. The subtest is discontinued after three consecutive failures. An item is considered failed only when *both* trials are failed.

All of the items are timed. The first six items are given a maximum of 30 seconds; the seventh, 45 seconds; and the eighth through fourteenth, 75 seconds. Items 8 to 14 receive time-bonus credits. On the first seven items, 2 points are given for successful performance on the first trial, 1 point for successful performance on the second trial, and 0 points when both trials are failed. On the last seven items, scores range from 0 (failure) to 4 points, with 3 or 4 points awarded for speed (for example, 4 points are awarded on item 8 if it is completed in 15 seconds or less).

**Rationale.** The rationale described for the WISC-III Block Design subtest appears to apply to the WPPSI-R Block Design subtest (see page 1097).

**Factor analytic findings.** The Block Design subtest overall is a fair measure of $g$ (47 percent of its variance may be attributed to $g$ — range of 26 to 58 percent in the nine age groups). The subtest contributes substantially to the Performance factor (*Mdn* loading = .76). Subtest specificity is adequate or ample at most ages and at the average of the nine age groups, with the exception of ages 5½ and 6½, where it is inadequate.

**Reliability and correlational highlights.** Block Design overall is a reliable subtest ($r_{xx}$ = .85). Reliability coefficients are *above* .70 at every age group. It correlates more highly with Picture Completion ($r$ = .46), Arithmetic ($r$ = .46), and Mazes ($r$ = .45) than with any of the other subtests. It correlates moderately with the Full Scale ($r$ = .62) and the Performance Scale ($r$ = .64) and to a lesser degree with the Verbal Scale ($r$ = .48).

**Administrative and interpretive considerations.** The administrative and interpretive considerations described for the WISC-III Block Design subtest generally apply to the WPPSI-R Block Design subtest (see page 1098). Profile analysis should take into account that the full range of scaled scores from 1 to 19 is available only at ages 5 to 6¼ years (see Table G-9).

## Mazes

The Mazes subtest requires children to solve paper-and-pencil mazes that differ in level of complexity. The subtest consists of 11 mazes, 8 of which are unchanged or modified from the WPPSI and 3 of which are new. Seven of the mazes are very similar to those on the WISC-III. Mazes 1 through 4 are horizontal mazes, and mazes 5 through 11 are box mazes. Mazes is a standard subtest in the WPPSI-R, whereas in the WISC-III it is an optional one. Children below the age of 5 years start with maze 1A; those 5 years of age and older start with maze 3A. The subtest is timed and discontinued after two consecutive failures. On the first four items, an item is considered as failed when *both* trials are failed.

**Rationale.** The rationale described for the WISC-III Mazes subtest appears to apply to the WPPSI-R Mazes subtest (see page 1102).

**Factor analytic findings.** The Mazes subtest overall is a fair measure of *g* (32 percent of its variance may be attributed to *g*—range of 16 to 41 percent in the nine age groups). The subtest contributes substantially to the Performance factor (*Mdn* loading = .69). Subtest specificity is ample at most ages and at the average of the nine age groups, except at ages 5, 5½, and 6½, where it is inadequate.

**Reliability and correlational highlights.** Mazes overall is a relatively reliable subtest ($r_{xx}$ = .77). Reliability coefficients are above .70 at eight of the nine age groups; the one exception is at age 7, where the reliability coefficient is

.65. It correlates more highly with Block Design ($r$ = .45) and Geometric Design ($r$ = .43) than with any of the other subtests. It has low correlations with the Full Scale ($r$ = .50), Performance Scale ($r$ = .54), and Verbal Scale ($r$ = .38).

**Administrative and interpretive considerations.** Although the administrative and interpretive considerations described for the WISC-III Mazes subtest generally apply to the WPPSI-R Mazes subtest (see pages 1102–1103), the administrative procedures differ in timing, scoring, and other details. For example, on the WPPSI-R each of the first seven mazes is allowed a maximum of 45 seconds; maze 8, 60 seconds; maze 9, 75 seconds; and mazes 10 and 11, 135 seconds. These time limits differ from those on the WISC-III. Therefore, you must be sure to use the procedures appropriate for the test being administered. Allow children to finish each maze (especially if they want to or are about to complete it), regardless of the errors made, because interruptions may generate anxiety and confusion and leave them with a sense of failure.

Scoring the Mazes subtest requires considerable judgment. You must become familiar with special terms, such as "blind alley," "clear crossing of a wall," "overshoot," "false exit," and "false start," which designate specific features of the mazes or of the child's performance. Likewise, you must be careful to point out these features of the subtest to the child in the sample item.

Study the child's failures carefully. Note whether there is a pattern to the child's failures, or whether there are signs of tremor or other visual-motor difficulties. When the entire test is finished, you might want to return to the Mazes subtest to inquire into the child's performance on any mazes of interest. For example, you can ask "Why did you go that way?"

A careful evaluation of the failures that occur on the Mazes subtest may prove to be useful. Two examples are shown in Figure G-3. In example 1, the girl failed to complete the maze, but made no errors as far as her performance went. In example 2, the boy entered a blind alley, thereby making an error. In the first case one wonders why the girl stopped short before reaching the goal. Perhaps her perseverance is limited, perhaps she takes things for granted and hopes that others will understand her, or perhaps she is easily distracted. In contrast, the second performance may be that of an impulsive boy who works well until he is about to complete a task and then is unable to do so correctly. These analyses are, of course, only tentative, subject to modification after study of the child's performance on the entire subtest and other subtests

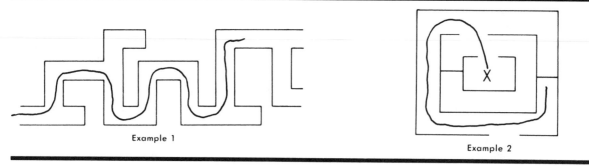

on the test, as well as of other sources of data.

Profile analysis should take into account that the full range of scaled scores from 1 to 19 is available only at ages 4 to 6¼ years (see Table G-9).

### Picture Completion

The Picture Completion subtest requires children to identify the single most important missing element in 28 drawings of common objects, such as a doll, car, and jacket. The subtest contains 12 new items, but 5 of the 28 items are also found on the WISC-III. The child's task is to discover and name or point to the essential missing portion of the incompletely drawn picture. Although there is no exact time limit for each item, items 1 and 2 are allowed a minimum of 15 seconds, and items 3 through 28, 30 seconds. Children younger than 5 years start with the sample item, and those 5 years and older start with item 3. The subtest is discontinued after five consecutive failures.

**Rationale.**   The rationale described for the WISC-III Picture Completion subtest appears to hold for the WPPSI-R Picture Completion subtest (see page 1092).

**Factor analytic findings.**   The Picture Completion subtest overall is a fair measure of $g$ (47 percent of its variance may be attributed to $g$ – range of 34 to 58 percent in the nine age groups). The subtest has a high loading on the Performance factor (*Mdn* loading = .55) *and* on the Verbal factor (*Mdn* loading = .41). These results suggest that verbal reasoning may help children to detect the missing part of the pictures. Subtest specificity is ample at all ages and at the average of the nine age groups.

**Reliability and correlational highlights.**   Picture Completion overall is a reliable subtest ($r_{xx}$ = .85). Reliability

coefficients are *above* .70 at all of the age groups. It correlates more highly with Information ($r$ = .47), Block Design ($r$ = .46), and Arithmetic ($r$ = .45) than with any of the other subtests. It correlates moderately with the Full Scale ($r$ = .61) and to a lesser degree with the Performance ($r$ = .54) and Verbal ($r$ = .54) Scales.

**Administrative and interpretive considerations.**   The administrative and interpretive considerations discussed for the WISC-III Picture Completion subtest generally apply to the WPPSI-R Picture Completion subtest (see pages 1092–1093). The major exception concerns the time limits. Unlike the WISC-III Picture Completion subtest, which allows a maximum of 20 seconds per card, the WPPSI-R Picture Completion subtest has no *absolute* time limits. For qualitative analysis, however, you might want to record the amount of time taken by children to make each response.

Children may have difficulty in identifying the missing part of some pictures because the way in which they are drawn may be confusing (for example, the face item and the suit jacket item).

Profile analysis should take into account that the full range of scaled scores from 1 to 19 is available only at ages 4¼ to 6½ years (see Table G-9).

### Animal Pegs

The Animal Pegs subtest, a substitute for the WISC-R Coding subtest, requires children to place colored pegs in holes on a board according to a key at the top of the board. In the original WPPSI, the subtest was called Animal House and was one of the five standard subtests on the Performance Scale; in the WPPSI-R, it is called Animal Pegs and is optional. The subtest essentially remains the same as it was on the WPPSI, with only minor changes in artwork. However, on the WPPSI-R there are no norms provided for a retest on Animal Pegs as there were on the WPPSI, where the retest (and norms) was referred to as "Animal House Retest."

Animal Pegs is a liberally timed subtest (maximum time of 5 minutes) in which a premium is placed on speed. A perfect score in 9 seconds or less is credited with 70 raw-score points, whereas one obtained in 5 minutes is credited with 12 raw-score points.

**Rationale.** Animal Pegs requires the child to associate signs with symbols. Memory, attention span, goal awareness, concentration, finger and manual dexterity, and learning ability may all be involved in the child's performance. Research with the WPPSI Animal House subtest indicated that it correlated significantly with a measure of learning ($r = .71$) and a measure of motor skill ($r = -.69$) in a sample of 36 children 5 to 6 years old (Sherman, Chinsky, & Maffeo, 1974). (The negative correlation resulted from the association of *lower* motor skill scores, which reflected faster reaction times, with *higher* Animal House scores.) The combination of learning *and* motor scores led to a better prediction of Animal House scores than did the learning scores by themselves. This research suggests that performance on the Animal House (or Animal Pegs) subtest involves both motor and learning abilities.

**Factor analytic findings.** The Animal Pegs subtest is a fair measure of $g$ (27 percent of its variance may be attributed to $g$—range of 15 to 41 percent in the nine age groups). The subtest has a high loading on the Performance factor (*Mdn* loading = .50). It has ample specificity at five ages and at the average of the nine age groups, and inadequate specificity at four ages (3½, 4, 4½, and 5½).

**Reliability and correlational highlights.** Animal Pegs has a marginal level of test-retest reliability ($r_{xx} = .66$). In addition, little is known about its reliability at each specific age level of the test. The only test-retest reliability coefficient reported in the WPPSI-R manual is based on a combined sample of 175 children who were in two age groups: 36 to 59 months and 60 to 87 months of age. Unfortunately, separate test-retest reliability coefficients were not given for each age group. (All tables requiring the use of reliability coefficients in Appendixes G and H of this text use a reliability coefficient of .66 for Animal Pegs.) Animal Pegs correlates more highly with Block Design ($r = .37$) than it does with any other subtest. It has low

correlations with the Full Scale ($r = .45$), Performance Scale ($r = .43$), and Verbal Scale ($r = .37$).

**Administrative and interpretive considerations.** Note whether the child is right- or left-handed before administering the subtest. This information is helpful not only in guiding the placement of the box of pegs, but also for clinical purposes. Children should be encouraged to use the hand they prefer. As on all timed subtests, do not stop timing once the subtest has begun. If the subtest is spoiled, do not score it. (This is true, of course, for any subtest that is spoiled.) Because Animal Pegs is an optional subtest, it does not have to be administered. And if it is administered as the sixth Performance Scale subtest, it is not used in calculating the IQ. However, if time permits, the subtest should be administered because it provides potentially useful information about important developmental skills.

Profile analysis should take into account that the full range of scaled scores from 1 to 19 is available at nearly all ages of the test—from 3¼ to 7 years (see Table G-9).

## Information

The Information subtest requires children to answer a broad range of questions dealing with factual information. The subtest contains 27 questions, 3 of which are exactly the same as in the WISC-III and one of which is essentially the same. Ten new items have been added to the subtest. Most questions require the child to give a simply stated fact or facts.

All children begin the subtest with the first item. Items 1 through 6 use pictures as stimuli and require either a pointing or verbal response. Items 7 through 27 are given orally and require a verbal response. All items are scored 1 or 0 (pass-fail). The subtest is untimed and discontinued after five consecutive failures.

**Rationale.** The rationale presented for the WISC-III Information subtest appears to apply to the WPPSI-R Information subtest (see pages 1080–1081). The WPPSI-R questions, however, appear to assess that part of the child's knowledge of the environment that is gained from experiences rather than from education, especially formal education.

**Factor analytic findings.** The Information subtest overall is the best measure of $g$ in the test (63 percent of its variance may be attributed to $g$—range of 47 to 74 percent in the nine age groups). The subtest contributes substantially to the Verbal factor (*Mdn* loading = .79). Specificity is adequate at ages 3½ and 4½ and inadequate at the other ages and at the average of the nine age groups.

**Reliability and correlational highlights.** Information overall is a reliable subtest ($r_{xx} = .84$). Reliability coefficients are above .70 at eight of the nine age groups; the one exception is at age 7, where the reliability coefficient is .62. It correlates more highly with Comprehension ($r = .66$) than with any other subtest. It correlates moderately with the Full Scale ($r = .71$) and the Verbal Scale ($r = .75$) and to a lesser degree with the Performance Scale ($r = .52$).

**Administrative and interpretive considerations.** The administrative and interpretive considerations presented for the WISC-III Information subtest are also relevant for the WPPSI-R Information subtest (see pages 1081–1082). Some WPPSI-R items require special scoring considerations. For example, the sample answers to question 12 in the WPPSI-R manual do not mention grooming products that come in plastic bottles, such as shampoo or liquid soap. Because the term "etc." appears in the scoring criteria, it seems logical to assume that credit should be given for responses that mention such substances and any other substances that come in plastic bottles. Likewise, the scoring criteria for question 14 do not include "planet," yet a planet shines in the sky at night. It is recommended that credit be given for "planet," "comet," and other astronomical terms. Finally, the suggested answers for question 13 do not mention that acceptable answers should include the names of any mammals because all mammals produce milk when feeding their newly born offspring. Therefore, credit should be given for any mammal named.

Profile analysis should take into account that the full range of scaled scores from 1 to 19 is available only at ages 4¾ to 6¼ years (see Table G-9).

---

Question: What do you call a baby goat?
Answer: Matilda would be a nice name.

---

## Comprehension

The Comprehension subtest requires children to explain situations, actions, or activities that relate to events with which most young children would be familiar. The subtest contains 15 questions, 10 of which are new. None of the items overlap with those in the WISC-III. Several content areas are covered, including health and hygiene, environmental concerns, interpersonal relations, and societal conventions. Items are scored 2, 1, or 0. All children start with item 1. The subtest is untimed and discontinued after four consecutive failures.

**Rationale.** The rationale presented for the WISC-III Comprehension subtest appears to apply generally to the WPPSI-R Comprehension subtest (see page 1088). Linguistic skill and logical reasoning, however, may play a more important role on the WPPSI-R Comprehension subtest than on the WISC-III Comprehension subtest.

**Factor analytic findings.** The Comprehension subtest overall is a good measure of $g$ (52 percent of its variance may be attributed to $g$—range of 38 to 64 percent in the nine age groups). The subtest contributes substantially to the Verbal factor (*Mdn* loading = .80). Specificity is adequate at ages 3, 5, and 5½, and inadequate at the other ages and at the average of the nine age groups.

**Reliability and correlational highlights.** Comprehension overall is a reliable subtest ($r_{xx} = .83$). Reliability coefficients are above .70 at eight of the nine age groups; the one exception is at age 7, where the reliability coefficient is .59. It correlates more highly with Information ($r = .66$) and Vocabulary ($r = .60$) than with any of the other subtests. It correlates moderately with the Full Scale ($r = .61$) and the Verbal Scale ($r = .70$) and to a lesser degree with the Performance Scale ($r = .41$).

**Administrative and interpretive considerations.** The administrative and interpretive considerations discussed for the WISC-III Comprehension subtest generally apply to the WPPSI-R Comprehension subtest (see pages 1088–1089). Because Comprehension responses are occasionally difficult to score, judgment is needed to arrive at appropriate scores. As in all decisions on the scoring of WPPSI-R (and WISC-III and WAIS-R) responses, the content of the response, not the quality of the verbalization, should be considered.

Profile analysis should take into account that the full range of scaled scores from 1 to 19 is available at *none* of the age levels in the test (see Table G-9).

## Arithmetic

The Arithmetic subtest requires children to demonstrate their understanding of concepts that may be precursors to numerical reasoning and to show their knowledge of numerical concepts. The subtest contains 23 problems, 2 of which are also on the WISC-III. Eight new items have been added to the subtest. For the first 7 items, the stimuli are presented via pictures; for the next 3 items, via blocks; and for the last 13 items, via oral questions. Pointing responses are required on the first 7 items and oral responses on the last 16 items.

The subtest is started with item 1 for children under 6 years and with item 8 for children 6 years of age and older. The first 11 problems have no time limit, but the last 12 items have a 30-second time limit. Each item is scored 1 or 0, and the subtest is discontinued after five consecutive failures.

The problems on the Arithmetic subtest reflect various skills. Problems 1 through 7 entail perceptual judgments involving the concepts of biggest, tallest, longest, more, most, shortest, and same. Problems 8 through 10 require direct counting of concrete quantities. Problems 11 through 23 involve simple addition or subtraction, although simple division or multiplication also can be used. Problems 12 to 23 are arithmetical reasoning problems presented orally by the examiner.

**Rationale.** The rationale described for the WISC-III Arithmetic subtest appears to apply generally to the WPPSI-R Arithmetic subtest (see page 1084). The skills required for the WPPSI-R Arithmetic subtest, however, are likely to be less dependent on formal education than are those required for the WISC-III Arithmetic subtest. The first seven WPPSI-R questions, which require the child to make comparisons and perceptual discriminations, appear to measure nonverbal reasoning ability; these seven problems use quantitative concepts without involving the explicit use of numbers.

**Factor analytic findings.** The Arithmetic subtest overall is a good measure of $g$ (57 percent of its variance may be attributed to $g$—range of 50 to 63 percent in the nine age groups). The subtest has a substantial loading on the Verbal factor ($Mdn$ loading = .64) and a moderate loading on the Performance factor ($Mdn$ loading = .40). Its loading on the Performance factor may be accounted for by the fact that some items employ pictures of sets of objects that must be visually analyzed, after which verbal comparisons may be made. Specificity is either ample or adequate at six age groups and at the average of the nine age groups, and inadequate at ages 4, 5, and 7.

**Reliability and correlational highlights.** Arithmetic overall is a reliable subtest ($r_{xx}$ = .80). Reliability coefficients are above .70 at eight of the nine age groups; the one exception is at age 7, where the reliability coefficient is .66. It correlates more highly with Information ($r$ = .59) than with any other subtest. It correlates moderately with the Full Scale ($r$ = .67) and with the Verbal Scale ($r$ = .63) and to a lesser degree with the Performance Scale ($r$ = .55).

**Administrative and interpretive considerations.** The administrative and interpretive considerations discussed for the WISC-III Arithmetic subtest generally apply to the WPPSI-R Arithmetic subtest (see pages 1084–1085). Scoring is for the most part easy—1 or 0 points. The time taken by the child to solve each problem should be recorded. On problems 12 through 23, correct answers given after the time limit has expired should also be noted, but of course not credited in the formal scoring.

Profile analysis should take into account that the full range of scores from 1 to 19 is available only at ages 4 to 6 years (see Table G-9).

**Vocabulary**

The Vocabulary subtest requires children to identify pictured stimuli on the early items and to define words on the later items. The subtest contains 25 words, 4 of which also appear on the WISC-III. Ten new items have been added to the subtest. On items 1 through 3 the child is asked to give the correct name of a pictured object, whereas on items 4 through 25 the child is asked to explain orally the meaning of each word. The first three items are scored 1 or 0, whereas the remainder of the items are scored 2, 1, or 0, depending on the conceptual level of the response. The subtest is untimed, and discontinued after five consecutive failures starting with item 4.

**Rationale.** The rationale presented for the WISC-III Vocabulary subtest generally applies to the WPPSI-R Vocabulary subtest (see page 1086). Formal education, however, is less likely to be an influence in vocabulary development for preschool children than for older children. Experiences at home and in the community are likely to be the major contributing factor to the vocabulary development of preschool children.

**Factor analytic findings.** The Vocabulary subtest overall is a good measure of $g$ (51 percent of its variance may be attributed to $g$—range of 46 to 56 percent in the nine age groups). The subtest contributes substantially to the Verbal factor ($Mdn$ loading = .79). Specificity is ample or adequate at four ages and at the average of the nine age groups, and inadequate at ages 3½, 4½, 6, 6½, and 7.

**Reliability and correlational highlights.** Vocabulary overall is a reliable subtest ($r_{xx}$ = .84). Reliability coefficients are above .70 at all age groups. It correlates more highly with Information ($r$ = .60) and Comprehension ($r$ = .60) than with any of the other subtests. It correlates moderately with the Full Scale ($r = .61$) and with the Verbal Scale ($r = .68$) and to a lesser degree with the Performance Scale ($r = .42$).

**Administrative and interpretive considerations.** All children start the subtest with the first word. This procedure differs from the one used for the WISC-III, where the starting word depends on the child's age. The general administrative and interpretive guidelines presented for the WISC-III Vocabulary subtest should be followed for the WPPSI-R Vocabulary subtest (see pages 1086–1087). Scoring requires considerable judgment, especially because the WPPSI-R manual provides too few sample responses.

The second Vocabulary item is contaminated by a procedure used on a previous subtest. The second Vocabulary picture is *exactly* the same as one of the pictures used on the second Arithmetic item. On Arithmetic, which is administered *before* Vocabulary, *the examiner tells the name of the picture to the child.* Consequently, success on the second Vocabulary item may be a function of short-term memory rather than of vocabulary ability.

Profile analysis should take into account that the full range of scaled scores from 1 to 19 is available from ages 4¼ to 7 years (see Table G-9).

## Similarities

The WPPSI-R Similarities subtest requires children to answer questions about how objects or concepts are alike and to give verbal analogies. Responses may involve perceptual reasoning (and, perhaps, even verbal reasoning) on the early items, and verbal reasoning or conceptual thinking on the later items. The subtest consists of 20 questions, one of which is found on the WISC-III. Eleven new items have been added to the subtest.

Items 1 through 6 require the child to point to the object that is similar to the target object in the pictured array. Items 7 through 12 require a response to simple analogies presented orally by the examiner. Items 13 through 20 require a conceptual reasoning type of response and are similar to those found in the WISC-III.

Items 1 through 12 are scored 1 or 0 (pass-fail), and items 13 through 20 are scored 2, 1, or 0, depending on the conceptual level of the response. The subtest is untimed and discontinued after three consecutive failures on items 1 through 6 or after five consecutive failures on items 7 through 20. All children begin with item 1.

**Rationale.** The rationale described for the WISC-III Similarities subtest generally applies to the WPPSI-R Sim-

ilarities subtest for the conceptual reasoning items (items 13 through 20, see page 1082). Items 1 through 6, however, appear to measure reasoning based on classification involving perceptual elements. And items 7 through 12 involve primarily simple analogic reasoning, but, as noted below, may be solved by other means as well.

Because over half of the items are either perceptual reasoning or simple analogic thinking items, the subtest may be measuring logical thinking (or even vocabulary ability in some cases), rather than verbal concept formation, especially at the earlier levels of the subtest (that is, below 5 years of age). In fact, on items 7 through 12 children may not even have to attend to the first half of the statement in order to get the item correct. For example, children need only attend to the second half of item 8 (". . . you also ride in a _____") to get the right answer. Thus, it is not known to what extent the simple analogy items are a forerunner of conceptual reasoning and to what extent they reflect vocabulary ability or verbal reasoning skills.

**Factor analytic findings.** The Similarities subtest overall is a good measure of $g$ (51 percent of its variance may be attributed to $g$ — range of 26 to 57 percent in the nine age groups). The subtest contributes substantially to the Verbal factor (*Mdn* loading = .72). Specificity is either ample or adequate at most ages and at the average of the nine age groups, except at ages 6½ and 7, where it is inadequate.

**Reliability and correlational highlights.** Similarities overall is a reliable subtest ($r_{xx} = .86$). Reliability coefficients are above .70 at eight of the nine age groups; the one exception is at age 7, where the reliability coefficient is .54. It correlates more highly with Information ($r = .57$) than with any other subtest. It correlates moderately with the Full Scale ($r = .62$) and with the Verbal Scale ($r = .65$) and to a lesser degree with the Performance Scale ($r = .45$).

**Administrative and interpretive considerations.** The administrative and interpretive considerations discussed for the WISC-III Similarities subtest generally apply to the WPPSI-R Similarities subtest (see pages 1082–1083). Scoring procedures, however, differ. Because responses to the first 12 items are scored 1 or 0, few scoring problems should be encountered on these items. As in the WISC-III, however, the items dealing with similarities (13 through 20) are difficult to score. Scoring guidelines should be studied carefully.

Profile analysis should take into account that the full

range of scaled scores from 1 to 19 is available only at ages 5½ to 6 years (see Table G-9).

## Sentences

The Sentences subtest requires children to repeat verbatim sentences given orally by the examiner. The subtest is an optional subtest and contains 12 sentences, ranging from 2 to 18 words. Three new items have been added to the subtest. When it is administered as a sixth Verbal Scale subtest, the subtest is not used in calculating the IQ. Items receive from 0 to 5 points, depending on the length of the sentence and the number of errors made. Errors in reproducing the sentences include omissions, transpositions, additions, and substitutions of words. Children younger than 5 years of age start with sentence 1; those older than 5 years of age start with sentence 6. The subtest is untimed, and it is discontinued after scores of 0 are obtained on three consecutive items.

**Rationale.**    The Sentences subtest is a memory subtest, measuring immediate recall and attention. Short-term auditory memory is involved, which includes attention, concentration, listening comprehension, and auditory processing. Because success may depend on verbal facility, failure may not necessarily reflect poor memory ability. For children 5 years and older, scores may be related primarily to memory ability, but for children younger than 5 years, scores may reflect verbal knowledge and comprehension, rather than immediate recall ability per se.

**Factor analytic findings.**    The Sentences subtest overall is a fair measure of $g$ (46 percent of its variance may be attributed to $g$ – range of 40 to 52 percent in the nine age groups). The subtest contributes substantially to the Verbal factor ($Mdn$ loading = .72). Specificity is either ample or adequate at five ages and at the average of the nine age groups, and inadequate at ages 5½, 6, 6½, and 7.

**Reliability and correlational highlights.**    Sentences overall is a reliable subtest ($r_{xx}$ = .82). Reliability coefficients are above .70 at all age groups. It correlates more highly with Information ($r$ = .55) than with any other subtest. It correlates moderately with the Full Scale ($r$ = .59) and with the Verbal Scale ($r$ = .65) and to a lesser degree with the Performance Scale ($r$ = .41).

**Administrative and interpretive considerations.** Scoring responses on the Sentences subtest requires careful attention to the different types of errors. The quality of the child's responses should also be evaluated. For exam-

ple, note (a) if any idiosyncratic or peculiar words were added; (b) if errors were made primarily at the beginning, middle, or end of sentences; and (c) if sentences were partially or completely missed. Missing a few words suggests minor inefficiencies, whereas missing all or most of the words may be indicative of more serious memory problems.

Profile analysis should take into account that the full range of scaled scores from 1 to 19 is available only at ages 5 to 6¾ years (see Table G-9).

## INTERPRETING THE WPPSI-R

Most of the material in Chapter 8 (see pages 166–190) on the WISC-R also pertains to the WPPSI-R. The methods of interpretation – such as the successive-level approach, profile analysis, Performance/Verbal Scale comparisons, and subtest comparisons – are essentially the same for both the WISC-R (and WISC-III) and the WPPSI-R.

The information in Table C-24 in Appendix C (pages 836–839) can aid you in interpreting the WPPSI-R subtests, as well as in writing reports. It summarizes the abilities thought to be measured by the 12 WPPSI-R subtests. It deserves careful study. A summary of the interpretive rationales for the Full Scale, Verbal Scale, and Performance Scale of the Wechsler batteries can be found in Table C-42 (pages 856–857). Suggested remediation activities for combinations of Wechsler subtests can be found in Table C-43 (page 858).

The classifications associated with WPPSI-R IQs are shown in Table BC-2 on the inside back cover. Table BC-1 on the inside back cover shows the percentile ranks for the WPPSI-R Full Scale, Performance Scale, and Verbal Scale IQs. Percentile ranks associated with subtest scaled scores are shown in Table C-41 in Appendix C (page 855). The WPPSI Structure of Intellect classifications, many of which pertain to the WPPSI-R, can be obtained from Table C-23 in Appendix C (pages 834–836).

The individual subtests should not be viewed as a means of determining specific cognitive skills with precision. Rather, subtest scores should be used as a means of generating hypotheses about the child's abilities. The most reliable estimates of *specific abilities* are derived from the Performance Scale IQ (performance or perceptual organization abilities) and the Verbal Scale IQ (verbal or verbal comprehension abilities), not from individual subtest scores. In fact, of the 108 separate reliability coefficients for the 12 subtests at the nine age groups of the test, 60 are at .80 or above and of these only 3 are at .90 or above –

Information at ages 3 and 4½ years and Picture Completion at age 4½ years. The remaining 48 reliability coefficients are below .80 and are not sufficiently reliable for decision-making or classification purposes (see Table 9 on page 128 of the WPPSI-R manual).

Because there is a great deal of overlap between the WPPSI-R and the WISC-III, especially for the nine subtest types that they share, much of the information in this text on the WISC-III is pertinent to the WPPSI-R. You are encouraged to read Appendix J (pages 1079–1103), which discusses the WISC-III subtests, before reading the rest of this appendix.

## Profile Analysis

Because profile analysis on the WPPSI-R is similar to that on the WISC-R, the material in Chapter 8 (pages 165–180) describing WISC-R profile analysis should be reviewed before a WPPSI-R profile analysis is undertaken. Although much less is known about profile analysis on the WPPSI-R than on other Wechsler scales, the procedures can still be useful in generating hypotheses about a child's strengths and weaknesses.

The five approaches to profile analysis on the WPPSI-R that follow are essentially the same as those described for the WISC-R (see pages 166–171). One difference, however, is that the tables in Appendix H must be used instead of those in Appendix C. Another difference is that the critical values in the tables are based on the child's specific age group instead of on an average value. A third difference is that factor scores are not included in profile analysis on the WPPSI-R because the Performance and Verbal Scales adequately describe the organization of the test.

1. *Comparing Performance and Verbal Scale IQs.* Table H-2 in Appendix H provides the critical values for comparing the Performance and Verbal IQs for the nine age groups of the WPPSI-R. The critical values for each age, as shown in Table H-2, are as follows (.05/.01 significance level):

- 10/13 at ages 3 through 4½
- 11/14 at age 5
- 12/15 at age 5½
- 11/14 at age 6
- 12/16 at age 6½
- 16/21 at age 7

These values indicate that an average critical value based on the entire group would be misleading. Therefore, the values for the child's specific age group should be used in evaluating differences between the child's Performance and Verbal IQs. (Probabilities associated with various differences between the Performance and Verbal Scale are shown in Table H-4 in Appendix H.)

2. *Comparing each Performance subtest scaled score to the mean Performance scaled score.* Table H-3 in Appendix H provides the critical values for each of the nine age groups of the WPPSI-R. Typical values for 3-year-old children for the five standard Performance subtests, for example, range from 2.65 to 3.96 at the .05 level and from 3.16 to 4.72 at the .01 level.

3. *Comparing each Verbal subtest scaled score to the mean Verbal scaled score.* Table H-3 in Appendix H provides the critical values for each of the nine age groups of the WPPSI-R. Typical values for 3-year-old children on the five standard Verbal subtests, for example, range from 2.30 to 3.10 at the .05 level and from 2.75 to 3.70 at the .01 level. These values are lower than those on the Performance Scale.

4. *Comparing each subtest scaled score to the mean subtest scaled score.* Table H-3 in Appendix H provides the critical values for each of the nine age groups in the WPPSI-R for 10, 11, and 12 subtests. For a 3-year-old, for example, they range from 2.62 to 4.72 at the .05 level and from 3.05 to 5.49 at the .01 level for the 10 standard subtests.

5. *Comparing sets of individual subtest scores.* Table H-2 in Appendix H provides the critical values for comparing sets of subtests for each of the nine age groups of the WPPSI-R. They range from 3 to 6 at the .05 level and from 4 to 7 at the .01 level. The values in Table H-2 are overly liberal (that is, lead to too many significant differences) when more than one comparison is made. They are most accurate when a priori planned comparisons are made, such as Comprehension versus Information or Block Design versus Object Assembly. Additional information for making comparisons between subtests can be found on pages 174–179.

Silverstein (personal communication, February 1990) advises determining the difference between the highest and lowest subtest scores before making multiple comparisons. If this difference is 6 scaled-score points or more, a significant difference at the .05 level is indicated. Differences between subtests that are 6 scaled-score points or greater can then be interpreted. If the difference between the highest and lowest subtest scaled scores is less than 6 scaled-score points, multiple comparisons between individual subtest scores should not be made. (The *Note* to Table H-2 in Appendix H shows the formula used to compute the significant difference. The formula considers the average standard error of measurement for each of the 12 subtests and the studentized range statistic.)

Two other tables will assist you in profile analysis. Table 14 (page 136) in the WPPSI-R manual presents the frequencies with which various differences between a child's score on each subtest and his or her average WPPSI-R Verbal, Performance, or overall score occurred in the standardization sample. This table should be used only for differences that first have been shown to be reliable. (See numbers 2, 3, and 4 in the Profile Analysis section above.)

Table H-5 in Appendix H presents the percentage of children in the standardization group who obtained a given discrepancy between the Verbal and Performance Scales. This table shows, for example, that between 25 and 50 percent of the population in each WPPSI-R age group had a 10-point difference (in either direction) between the two IQs.

## ASSETS OF THE WPPSI-R

The WPPSI-R is a well-standardized test, with good reliability and validity. It has 12 subtests divided into two sections and provides three IQs—Performance, Verbal, and Full Scale. This is helpful in clinical and psychoeducational work. Parts of the test also can be administered to children limited by sensory impairments (for example, the Verbal Scale to blind children and the Performance Scale to deaf children).

1. *Excellent standardization*. The standardization procedures were excellent, sampling four geographical regions, both sexes, white children and nonwhite children, and the entire socioeconomic status range. The standardization group well represents the nation as a whole for the age groups covered by the test.

2. *Excellent overall psychometric properties*. The WPPSI-R has excellent reliability for the three IQs generated by the scale, with the minor exception at 7 years, where the Performance and Verbal IQs have reliabilities below .90. The few studies available suggest that the WPPSI-R has adequate concurrent and construct validity, although more research is needed to evaluate the validity of the test, especially at its first and last year levels.

3. *Useful diagnostic information*. The WPPSI-R provides diagnostic information useful for the assessment of cognitive abilities of preschool and early elementary-school age children who are functioning within two standard deviations from the mean. In addition, the test is useful for mildly mentally retarded children who are between 4 and 7 years of age and for moderately mentally retarded children who are between 5 and 7 years of age. It also furnishes data likely to be helpful in planning special

school programs, perhaps tapping important developmental or maturational factors needed for school success in the lower grades.

4. *Good administrative procedures*. The prescribed procedures for administering the WPPSI-R are excellent. Examiners actively probe responses in order to evaluate the breadth of the child's knowledge and determine whether the child really knows the answers. The emphasis on probing questions and queries is extremely desirable.

5. *Good manual*. The WPPSI-R manual is easy to use; it provides clear directions and tables. The examiner's instructions are printed in a different color to facilitate reading of the directions. Helpful suggestions are provided about abbreviations to use in recording reponses.

6. *High interest level*. Most children should enjoy taking the test; the mixture of performance and verbal items, as well as the varied test materials, should maintain their interest.

## LIMITATIONS OF THE WPPSI-R

Although the WPPSI-R is generally an excellent instrument, some problems exist.

1. *Low reliability of individual subtests*. Reliability coefficients for the individual subtests are lower than .80 at some ages. In these cases, the scores may not be dependable. In addition, during the standardization of the scale, test–retest scores for the Animal Pegs subtest were not obtained at each age level of the test. Because the WPPSI-R manual presents only *one* test-retest reliability coefficient for Animal Pegs, the same reliability coefficient had to be used, both by the test publisher and by the text author, to generate the standard errors of measurement and other statistical information for each age level of the test; the accuracy of these estimates is unknown.

2. *Limited floor*. The WPPSI-R is limited by the absence of an adequate floor—that is, it does not clearly differentiate abilities at the lower end of the scale. IQ equivalents of the scores range from 41 to 160, but the lower limit of this range is reached only at 5¼ years.

3. *Nonuniformity of subtest scores*. Because the range of scaled scores on all subtests is not uniform, there are problems in profile analysis, particularly at the lower and upper limits of the scaled-score range.

4. *Long administration time*. Administration time may be too long for some children, although fatigue should not often be a problem for older children. Little is known about how 3- to 4-year-olds will be able to maintain attention on the test. With younger children or with handi-

capped children, two test sessions may be needed. When this procedure is followed, there is no way of determining whether the break between testing sessions affects a child's scores, because the procedure differs from that used in standardizing the scale. Empirical data would be helpful in clarifying the effect of two test sessions on test scores.

5. *Possible difficulties in scoring responses.* Work with the WPPSI suggests that some subtests will be difficult to score. These subtests include the Geometric Design, Vocabulary, Similarities, and Comprehension subtests. The WPPSI-R manual cites a study in which there was high agreement in the scores given to these subtests (and the Mazes subtest as well) by independent examiners. These results are encouraging, but need to be replicated. Consultation with colleagues is recommended when responses are difficult to score.

6. *Problems for some minority children and for children who do not place a premium on speed.* The long administration time, demands for concentration and attention, and need to clarify answers may make some children uncomfortable, particularly those minority children who are unaccustomed to prolonged or intense periods of problem-solving activity. In addition, the test may penalize children who (a) are from a minority group that does not place a premium on speed (see Chapter 19) or (b) work in a slow, deliberate, and thoughtful manner.

7. *Overlap with the WISC-III.* The WPPSI-R and the WISC-III have at least 23 overlapping items, primarily on the Picture Completion, Mazes, Vocabulary, and Information subtests. This overlap is unfortunate for at least two reasons. First, it means that the WPPSI-R and the WISC-III are not independent parallel forms at the overlapping age levels (6 to 7¼ years). Second, it means that children tested with the WPPSI-R and then with the WISC-III (or vice versa) have an advantage on the second test because of practice effects. On the next revision of either test, the overlapping items should be replaced with completely different items.

## PSYCHOLOGICAL EVALUATION

The psychological evaluation in Exhibit 9-3 (pages 216–217) illustrates the application of the WPPSI to evaluation of a developmentally immature child and should be helpful in understanding the WPPSI-R as well. The report summarizes information obtained from parents and from a kindergarten teacher and cites both qualitative and quantitative information obtained during the evaluation. Profile analysis is used to develop some assessment information,

and recommendations are based on the test results and background information.

## TEST YOUR SKILL

The WISC-R Test-Your-Skill Exercises on pages 187–189 also pertain to the WPPSI-R. If you have not reviewed these exercises recently, you are encouraged to do so now. In addition, three exercises that pertain only to the WPPSI-R follow. In each exercise, there is some inadequacy of description or interpretation. Analyze the mistakes, then check your answers with those shown on page 806 (referred to as "Chapter 9: Test-Your-Skill Exercises for the WPPSI").

1. "Tom's excellent performance on Block Design and Geometric Design suggests that he has good ability in analyzing school situations and has high moral judgment."

2. "The Geometric Design subtest presented problems for her and she fell in the slow learning category."

3. The following interpretation was given to these WPPSI-R Performance Scale scores: Object Assembly, 12; Picture Completion, 15; Mazes, 13; Geometric Design, 14; and Block Design, 12. "While her two lowest scores on the Performance Scale were above average, they may suggest some visual acuity problems."

## SUMMARY

1. The WPPSI-R, designed to be used with children between 3 and 7¼ years of age, follows the basic format of the WISC-R (WISC-III), providing Performance, Verbal, and Full Scales IQs.

2. The WPPSI-R contains 12 subtests: Object Assembly, Geometric Design, Block Design, Mazes, Picture Completion, Animal Pegs, Information, Comprehension, Arithmetic, Vocabulary, Similarities, and Sentences. Three of the subtests—Sentences, Animal Pegs, and Geometric Design—do not appear in the WISC-III. Object Assembly is new to the WPPSI-R; it did not appear in the WPPSI.

3. The standardization sample was representative of the 1986 U.S. population and included 1,700 children living in four geographical regions in the United States.

4. Like the other Wechsler scales, the WPPSI-R employs Deviation IQs ($M = 100$, $SD = 15$) for the Performance, Verbal, and Full Scale IQs. Similarly, scaled scores ($M = 10$, $SD = 3$) are provided for each subtest. When fewer than 10 subtests are administered, this text recommends the use of a special short-form procedure to obtain the IQs.

5. The WPPSI-R has excellent reliability for the three IQs (average reliabilities range from .92 to .96), except at age 7,

where the reliabilities for the Performance and Verbal Scale IQs are below .90. The reliabilities for the subtests are less satisfactory (average reliabilities range from .66 to .86) than those for the three scales. The Performance Scale generally shows greater practice effects than does the Verbal Scale.

6. Because the WPPSI-R is a new revision, little is known about its validity, especially for exceptional children. Studies of the prior version indicate that it should have adequate concurrent and predictive validity.

7. Studies cited in the WPPSI-R manual, using such criteria as the WISC-R, Stanford-Binet Intelligence Scale—4th Edition, McCarthy Scales of Children's Abilities, and K-ABC, suggest that the test has good concurrent validity for normal children.

8. Construct validity is adequate as established by factor analytic studies.

9. Little is known about the validity of the WPPSI-R at ages 3 and 7, the two new age levels of the test.

10. Research cited in the WPPSI-R manual indicates that the WPPSI-R and WISC-R cannot be considered parallel forms, because the WISC-R yields IQs that are, on the average, 8 points *higher* than those of the WPPSI-R.

11. Factor analysis indicates that all of the 12 WPPSI-R subtests are either good or fair measures of *g*. Subtest specificity varies throughout the age levels of the test. A Freedom from Distractibility factor does not emerge on the WPPSI-R.

12. The range of Full Scale IQs from 41 to 160 cannot be obtained until 5¾ years. At 3 years the lowest Full Scale IQ that can be obtained is 65. The lack of a uniform floor at all ages of the WPPSI-R will impede the monitoring of changes in the performance of low-functioning children.

13. The range of subtest scaled scores from 1 to 19 cannot be obtained on any subtest at every age level of the WPPSI-R. Profile analysis, consequently, must take into account the non-uniform scaled-score range, especially at the lower and upper limits of the range.

14. Generally, children must be more proficient on the WPPSI-R Animal Pegs subtest than on the WPPSI to maintain their same relative position. Changes are greatest for the 4- and 4½-year-olds with above-average ability and for the 4¾- to 6½-year-olds with below-average ability.

15. Changes from the WPPSI to the WPPSI-R include extending the age range (changed from 4 to 6½ to 3 to 7¼), adding the Object Assembly subtest, renaming Animal House as Animal Pegs and making it an optional subtest, eliminating retest norms for Animal Pegs, modifying scoring guidelines and administrative procedures, placing a greater emphasis on speed in scoring, and increasing the IQ range to from 41 to 160 at the upper ages of the test.

16. The administrative considerations that apply to the WISC-III generally apply to the WPPSI-R. Because the WPPSI-R is used with a younger age group than is the WISC-III, there are some problems in adapting the subtests to alternative sensory modalities for children with sensory or motor handicaps.

17. Table H-6 in Appendix H shows the best short-form combinations of two, three, four, and five WPPSI-R subtests, and

Tables H-7, H-8, and H-9 show the IQs for the sum of the scaled scores for the 10 best combinations of two-, three-, and four-subtest short forms.

18. Research is needed to determine whether the WPPSI-R or the WISC-R is more valid at the overlapping ages of 6 to 7¼ years.

19. The interpretive rationale, factor analytic findings, reliability and subtest correlations, and administrative and interpretive considerations for each of the WPPSI-R subtests are presented in the chapter. The proposed interpretive rationales and possible implications of high and low scores are summarized in Table C-24 in Appendix C.

20. The rationale for the WISC-III Object Assembly subtest probably applies to the WPPSI-R Object Assembly subtest. The subtest is a fair measure of *g*, but it contributes to the Performance factor. Its subtest specificity is inadequate at every age, and reliability is marginal ($r_{xx} = .63$). Administrative procedures differ somewhat from those in the WISC-III.

21. Geometric Design is considered to measure perceptual recognition and discrimination in younger children and visual-motor ability, visual construction, and eye-hand coordination in older children. It is a fair measure of *g* and contributes to the Performance factor. Subtest specificity is ample or adequate at five of the nine age groups, and reliability is relatively good ($r_{xx} = .79$). Although improvements have been made in the scoring procedure, the subtest still may be difficult to score.

22. The rationale for the WISC-III Block Design subtest probably applies to the WPPSI-R Block Design subtest. The subtest is a fair measure of *g* and contributes to the Performance factor. Subtest specificity is ample or adequate at seven of the nine age groups, and reliability is good ($r_{xx} = .85$). The subtest requires skill to administer.

23. The rationale for the WISC-III Mazes subtest probably applies to the WPPSI-R Mazes subtest. The subtest is a fair measure of *g*, but it contributes to the Performance factor. Subtest specificity is ample at six of the nine age groups, and reliability is relatively good ($r_{xx} = .77$). Scoring requires considerable judgment. Administrative procedures differ from those used on the WISC-III.

24. The rationale for the WISC-III Picture Completion subtest probably applies to the WPPSI-R Picture Completion subtest. The subtest is a fair measure of *g* and contributes to both the Performance and Verbal factors. Subtest specificity is ample at all ages, and reliability is good ($r_{xx} = .85$). Administration is relatively easy.

25. Animal Pegs is an optional subtest on the WPPSI-R. It is believed to measure memory, attention span, goal awareness, concentration, and finger and manual dexterity. It is a fair measure of *g*, but it contributes to the Performance factor. Subtest specificity is ample at five of the nine groups, and reliability is marginal ($r_{xx} = .66$). Administration is relatively easy.

26. The rationale for the WISC-III Information subtest probably applies to the WPPSI-R Information subtest, although WPPSI-R questions may be related more to the child's experiences than to formal education. The subtest is overall the best

measure of *g* in the scale and contributes to the Verbal factor. Subtest specificity is adequate at only two of the nine age groups, and reliability is good ($r_{xx} = .84$). Judgment is required in scoring responses.

27. The rationale for the WISC-III Comprehension subtest probably applies to the WPPSI-R Comprehension subtest, although linguistic skill and logical reasoning may play a more significant role on the WPPSI-R. The subtest is a good measure of *g* and contributes to the Verbal factor. Subtest specificity is adequate at three of the nine age groups, and reliability is good ($r_{xx} = .83$). Scoring requires considerable judgment.

28. The rationale for the WISC-III Arithmetic subtest probably applies to the WPPSI-R Arithmetic subtest, although formal education probably has less influence on the WPPSI-R. The subtest is a good measure of *g* and contributes to both the Verbal *and* Performance factors. Subtest specificity is ample or adequate at six of the nine age groups, and reliability is good ($r_{xx} = .83$). Scoring is easy.

29. The rationale for the WISC-III Vocabulary subtest probably applies to the WPPSI-R Vocabulary subtest, although formal education probably has less influence on the WPPSI-R. The subtest is a good measure of *g* and contributes to the Verbal factor. Subtest specificity is ample or adequate at four of the nine age groups, and reliability is good ($r_{xx} = .84$). Scoring requires considerable judgment.

30. The WPPSI-R Similarities subtest appears to measure logical thinking to a greater extent than does the WISC-III Similarities subtest, especially at the early ages. The subtest is a good measure of *g* and contributes to the Verbal factor. Subtest specificity is ample or adequate at seven of the nine age groups, and reliability is good ($r_{xx} = .86$). Judgment is required in scoring the last eight items.

31. Sentences is an optional subtest on the WPPSI-R. It is a memory test, measuring immediate recall and attention. The subtest is a fair measure of *g* and contributes to the Verbal factor. Subtest specificity is ample or adequate at five of the nine age groups, and reliability is good ($r_{xx} = .82$). Scoring requires considerable skill.

32. Although the same considerations that apply to profile analysis on the WISC-R apply to profile analysis on the WPPSI-R, more care should be taken in using profile analysis with the WPPSI-R because less is known about the scale.

33. Although the WPPSI-R has some limitations—such as long administration time, inadequate floor, and difficult scoring on some subtests—it is, overall, a well-standardized, carefully developed instrument that is a valuable tool for the assessment of young children's intelligence.

## KEY TERMS, CONCEPTS, AND NAMES

WPPSI-R standardization (p. 978)
WPPSI-R reliability (p. 979)
WPPSI-R validity (p. 981)
WPPSI-R factor analysis (p. 984)
WPPSI-R subtest specificity (p. 985)
Testing-of-limits (p. 994)
WPPSI-R short forms (p. 994)
Yudin's WPPSI-R short form (p. 996)
WPPSI-R Object Assembly (p. 997)
WPPSI-R Geometric Design (p. 997)
WPPSI-R Block Design (p. 998)
WPPSI-R Mazes (p. 999)
WPPSI-R Picture Completion (p. 1000)
WPPSI-R Animal Pegs (p. 1000)
WPPSI-R Information (p. 1001)
WPPSI-R Comprehension (p. 1002)
WPPSI-R Arithmetic (p. 1002)
WPPSI-R Vocabulary (p. 1003)
WPPSI-R Similarities (p. 1004)
WPPSI-R Sentences (p. 1005)
Profile analysis (p. 1006)

## STUDY QUESTIONS

1. Describe the WPPSI-R and then discuss its standardization, reliability, and validity.

2. Describe WPPSI-R factor analytic findings.

3. Discuss some general administrative considerations for the WPPSI-R.

4. Discuss WPPSI-R short forms.

5. Discuss the rationale, factor analytic findings, reliability and correlational highlights, and administrative and interpretive considerations for each of the following WPPSI-R Performance Scale subtests: Object Assembly, Geometric Design, Block Design, Mazes, Picture Completion, and Animal Pegs.

6. Discuss the rationale, factor analytic findings, reliability and correlational highlights, and administrative and interpretive considerations for each of the following WPPSI-R Verbal Scale subtests: Information, Comprehension, Arithmetic, Vocabulary, Similarities, and Sentences.

7. Briefly describe profile analysis on the WPPSI-R.

8. Discuss the assets and limitations of the WPPSI-R.

# APPENDIX H

## TABLES FOR THE WPPSI-R

See also Table C-23, "WPPSI Structure of Intellect Classifications (page 834); Table C-24, "Interpretive Rationales and Implications of High and Low Scores for WPPSI-R and WPPSI Subtests" (page 836): Table C-41, "Percentile Ranks and Suggested Qualitative Descriptions for Scaled Scores on the WISC-R, WPPSI-R, WPPSI, and WAIS-R" (page 855); Table C-42, "Interpretive Rationales, Implications of High and Low Scores, and Instructional Implications for Wechsler Scales and Factor Scores" (page 856); and Table C-43, "Suggested Remediation Activities for Combinations of Wechsler Subtests" (page 858).

**Table H-1**
**Confidence Intervals for WPPSI-R Scales**

| Age level | Scale | Confidence level | | | | |
|---|---|---|---|---|---|---|
| | | 68% | 85% | 90% | 95% | 99% |
| **3** (2-11-16 through 3-5-15) | Performance Scale IQ | ± 4 | ± 6 | ± 7 | ± 8 | ± 10 |
| | Verbal Scale IQ | ± 3 | ± 5 | ± 5 | ± 6 | ± 8 |
| | Full Scale IQ | ± 3 | ± 4 | ± 5 | ± 6 | ± 7 |
| **3½** (3-5-16 through 3-11-15) | Performance Scale IQ | ± 4 | ± 6 | ± 7 | ± 8 | ± 10 |
| | Verbal Scale IQ | ± 3 | ± 5 | ± 5 | ± 6 | ± 8 |
| | Full Scale IQ | ± 3 | ± 4 | ± 5 | ± 6 | ± 7 |
| **4** (3-11-16 through 4-5-15) | Performance Scale IQ | ± 4 | ± 6 | ± 7 | ± 8 | ± 11 |
| | Verbal Scale IQ | ± 3 | ± 4 | ± 5 | ± 6 | ± 8 |
| | Full Scale IQ | ± 3 | ± 4 | ± 5 | ± 6 | ± 7 |
| **4½** (4-5-16 through 4-11-15) | Performance Scale IQ | ± 4 | ± 6 | ± 7 | ± 8 | ± 11 |
| | Verbal Scale IQ | ± 3 | ± 5 | ± 5 | ± 6 | ± 8 |
| | Full Scale IQ | ± 3 | ± 4 | ± 5 | ± 6 | ± 8 |
| **5** (4-11-16 through 5-5-15) | Performance Scale IQ | ± 4 | ± 6 | ± 7 | ± 9 | ± 11 |
| | Verbal Scale IQ | ± 3 | ± 5 | ± 5 | ± 7 | ± 9 |
| | Full Scale IQ | ± 3 | ± 4 | ± 5 | ± 6 | ± 8 |
| **5½** (5-5-16 through 5-11-15) | Performance Scale IQ | ± 5 | ± 7 | ± 8 | ± 9 | ± 12 |
| | Verbal Scale IQ | ± 4 | ± 5 | ± 6 | ± 7 | ± 9 |
| | Full Scale IQ | ± 3 | ± 5 | ± 5 | ± 6 | ± 8 |
| **6** (5-11-16 through 6-5-15) | Performance Scale IQ | ± 4 | ± 6 | ± 7 | ± 9 | ± 11 |
| | Verbal Scale IQ | ± 4 | ± 5 | ± 6 | ± 7 | ± 10 |
| | Full Scale | ± 3 | ± 5 | ± 5 | ± 6 | ± 8 |
| **6½** (6-5-16 through 6-11-15) | Performance Scale IQ | ± 5 | ± 7 | ± 8 | ± 9 | ± 12 |
| | Verbal Scale IQ | ± 4 | ± 6 | ± 7 | ± 8 | ± 10 |
| | Full Scale IQ | ± 3 | ± 5 | ± 7 | ± 7 | ± 9 |
| **7** (6-11-16 through 7-3-15) | Performance Scale IQ | ± 5 | ± 7 | ± 8 | ± 10 | ± 13 |
| | Verbal Scale IQ | ± 5 | ± 7 | ± 8 | ± 10 | ± 13 |
| | Full Scale IQ | ± 4 | ± 6 | ± 6 | ± 8 | ± 10 |

*Note.* See the Note in Table C-1, page 813, for an explanation of method used to obtain confidence intervals.

**Table H-2**
**Significant Differences Between Scaled Scores and Between IQs at Each of the Nine Age Levels of the WPPSI-R (.05/.01 significance levels)**

| Age level | | OA | GD | BD | MA | PC | AP | I | C | A | V | S |
|---|---|---|---|---|---|---|---|---|---|---|---|---|
| **3** | GD | 4/6 | — | | | | | | | | | |
| (2-11-16 | BD | 4/6 | 3/4 | — | | | | | | | VSIQ | |
| through | MA | 4/6 | 3/4 | 3/4 | — | | | | | | PSIQ 10/13 | |
| 3-5-15) | PC | 4/5 | 3/4 | 3/4 | 3/4 | — | | | | | | |
| | AP | 5/7 | 4/5 | 4/6 | 4/5 | 4/5 | — | | | | | |
| | I | 4/5 | 3/4 | 3/4 | 3/4 | 3/4 | 4/5 | — | | | | |
| | C | 4/5 | 3/4 | 3/4 | 3/4 | 3/4 | 4/5 | 3/4 | — | | | |
| | A | 5/6 | 4/5 | 4/5 | 4/5 | 3/4 | 4/6 | 3/4 | 3/5 | — | | |
| | V | 4/6 | 3/4 | 3/4 | 3/4 | 3/4 | 4/5 | 3/4 | 3/4 | 4/5 | — | |
| | S | 4/5 | 3/4 | 3/4 | 3/4 | 3/4 | 4/5 | 3/4 | 3/4 | 3/5 | 3/4 | — |
| | Se | 4/5 | 3/4 | 3/4 | 3/4 | 3/4 | 4/5 | 3/4 | 3/4 | 3/5 | 3/4 | 3/4 |
| **3½** | GD | 4/6 | — | | | | | | | | | |
| (3-5-16 | BD | 4/6 | 3/4 | — | | | | | | | VSIQ | |
| through | MA | 4/6 | 3/4 | 3/5 | — | | | | | | PSIQ 10/13 | |
| 3-11-15) | PC | 4/5 | 3/4 | 3/4 | 3/4 | — | | | | | | |
| | AP | 5/7 | 4/5 | 4/5 | 4/6 | 4/5 | — | | | | | |
| | I | 4/5 | 3/4 | 3/4 | 3/4 | 3/4 | 4/5 | — | | | | |
| | C | 4/5 | 3/4 | 3/4 | 3/4 | 3/4 | 4/5 | 3/4 | — | | | |
| | A | 4/6 | 3/5 | 3/5 | 4/5 | 3/4 | 4/6 | 3/4 | 3/4 | — | | |
| | V | 4/6 | 3/4 | 3/4 | 3/5 | 3/4 | 4/5 | 3/4 | 3/4 | 3/5 | — | |
| | S | 4/5 | 3/4 | 3/4 | 3/4 | 3/4 | 4/5 | 3/4 | 3/4 | 3/4 | 3/4 | — |
| | Se | 4/6 | 3/4 | 3/4 | 3/4 | 3/4 | 4/5 | 3/4 | 3/4 | 3/5 | 3/4 | 3/4 |
| **4** | GD | 4/5 | — | | | | | | | | | |
| (3-11-16 | BD | 4/5 | 3/4 | — | | | | | | | VSIQ | |
| through | MA | 4/6 | 4/5 | 4/5 | — | | | | | | PSIQ 10/13 | |
| 4-5-15) | PC | 4/5 | 3/4 | 3/4 | 4/5 | — | | | | | | |
| | AP | 5/6 | 4/6 | 4/5 | 5/6 | 4/5 | — | | | | | |
| | I | 4/5 | 3/4 | 3/4 | 4/5 | 3/4 | 4/5 | — | | | | |
| | C | 4/5 | 3/4 | 3/4 | 4/5 | 3/4 | 4/5 | 3/4 | — | | | |
| | A | 4/5 | 4/5 | 3/4 | 4/5 | 3/4 | 4/6 | 3/4 | 3/4 | — | | |
| | V | 4/5 | 3/4 | 3/4 | 4/5 | 3/4 | 4/5 | 3/4 | 3/4 | 3/4 | — | |
| | S | 4/5 | 3/4 | 3/4 | 4/5 | 3/4 | 4/5 | 3/4 | 3/4 | 3/4 | 3/4 | — |
| | Se | 4/5 | 3/4 | 3/4 | 4/5 | 3/4 | 4/5 | 3/4 | 3/4 | 3/4 | 3/4 | 3/4 |
| **4½** | GD | 5/6 | — | | | | | | | | | |
| (4-5-16 | BD | 4/6 | 3/4 | — | | | | | | | VSIQ | |
| through | MA | 5/6 | 4/5 | 4/5 | — | | | | | | PSIQ 10/13 | |
| 4-11-15) | PC | 4/6 | 3/4 | 3/3 | 3/4 | — | | | | | | |
| | AP | 5/7 | 4/5 | 4/5 | 5/6 | 4/5 | — | | | | | |
| | I | 4/6 | 3/4 | 3/4 | 3/5 | 2/3 | 4/5 | — | | | | |
| | C | 4/6 | 3/4 | 3/4 | 4/5 | 3/3 | 4/5 | 3/4 | — | | | |
| | A | 5/6 | 3/5 | 3/4 | 4/5 | 3/4 | 4/6 | 3/4 | 3/4 | — | | |
| | V | 5/6 | 3/4 | 3/4 | 4/5 | 3/4 | 4/6 | 3/4 | 3/4 | 4/5 | — | |
| | S | 4/6 | 3/4 | 3/4 | 4/5 | 2/3 | 4/5 | 3/4 | 3/4 | 3/4 | 3/4 | — |
| | Se | 5/6 | 3/4 | 3/4 | 4/5 | 3/4 | 4/6 | 3/4 | 3/4 | 4/5 | 3/5 | 3/4 |

(*Table continues next page*)

**Table H-2 (cont.)**

| Age level | | OA | GD | BD | MA | PC | AP | I | C | A | V | S |
|---|---|---|---|---|---|---|---|---|---|---|---|---|
| **5** | GD | 5/6 | — | | | | | | | | | |
| (4-11-16 | BD | 4/6 | 4/5 | — | | | | | | | | |
| through | MA | 5/6 | 4/5 | 4/5 | — | | | | | | | |
| 5-5-15) | PC | 4/6 | 4/5 | 3/4 | 4/5 | — | | | | | | |
| | AP | 5/7 | 4/6 | 4/5 | 4/6 | 4/5 | — | | | | | |
| | I | 4/6 | 4/5 | 3/4 | 4/5 | 3/4 | 4/5 | — | | | | |
| | C | 4/6 | 4/5 | 3/4 | 4/5 | 3/4 | 4/5 | 3/4 | — | | | |
| | A | 5/6 | 4/5 | 3/5 | 4/5 | 3/5 | 4/6 | 4/5 | 3/5 | — | | |
| | V | 4/6 | 4/5 | 3/4 | 4/5 | 3/4 | 4/5 | 3/4 | 3/4 | 3/5 | — | |
| | S | 4/6 | 4/5 | 3/4 | 4/5 | 3/4 | 4/5 | 3/4 | 3/4 | 3/5 | 3/4 | — |
| | Se | 5/6 | 4/5 | 3/4 | 4/5 | 3/4 | 4/6 | 3/5 | 3/4 | 4/5 | 3/4 | 3/4 |

VSIQ PSIQ 11/14

| Age level | | OA | GD | BD | MA | PC | AP | I | C | A | V | S |
|---|---|---|---|---|---|---|---|---|---|---|---|---|
| **5½** | GD | 5/7 | — | | | | | | | | | |
| (5-5-16 | BD | 5/6 | 4/5 | — | | | | | | | | |
| through | MA | 5/6 | 4/6 | 4/6 | — | | | | | | | |
| 5-11-15) | PC | 5/6 | 4/5 | 4/5 | 4/5 | — | | | | | | |
| | AP | 5/7 | 5/6 | 4/6 | 4/6 | 4/6 | — | | | | | |
| | I | 5/6 | 4/6 | 4/5 | 4/5 | 4/5 | 5/6 | — | | | | |
| | C | 5/6 | 4/5 | 4/5 | 4/5 | 4/5 | 4/6 | 4/6 | — | | | |
| | A | 5/6 | 4/5 | 4/5 | 4/5 | 4/5 | 4/6 | 4/6 | 4/5 | — | | |
| | V | 4/6 | 4/5 | 3/5 | 4/5 | 3/4 | 4/5 | 4/5 | 3/4 | 3/4 | — | |
| | S | 4/6 | 4/5 | 3/5 | 4/5 | 3/4 | 4/5 | 4/5 | 3/4 | 3/4 | 3/4 | — |
| | Se | 5/6 | 4/6 | 4/6 | 4/5 | 4/5 | 4/6 | 4/5 | 4/5 | 4/5 | 4/5 | 4/5 |

VSIQ PSIQ 12/15

| Age level | | OA | GD | BD | MA | PC | AP | I | C | A | V | S |
|---|---|---|---|---|---|---|---|---|---|---|---|---|
| **6** | GD | 4/6 | — | | | | | | | | | |
| (5-11-16 | BD | 4/5 | 4/5 | — | | | | | | | | |
| through | MA | 4/6 | 4/5 | 4/5 | — | | | | | | | |
| 6-5-15) | PC | 4/6 | 4/5 | 4/5 | 4/5 | — | | | | | | |
| | AP | 5/6 | 4/6 | 4/5 | 4/6 | 4/6 | — | | | | | |
| | I | 4/6 | 4/5 | 4/5 | 4/5 | 4/5 | 5/6 | — | | | | |
| | C | 4/6 | 4/5 | 4/5 | 4/5 | 4/5 | 4/6 | 4/5 | — | | | |
| | A | 4/5 | 4/5 | 4/5 | 4/5 | 4/5 | 4/6 | 4/5 | 4/5 | — | | |
| | V | 4/5 | 4/5 | 3/5 | 4/5 | 4/5 | 4/6 | 4/5 | 4/5 | 4/5 | — | |
| | S | 4/5 | 4/5 | 3/4 | 3/5 | 4/5 | 4/5 | 4/5 | 4/5 | 3/5 | 3/4 | — |
| | Se | 4/6 | 4/5 | 4/5 | 4/5 | 4/5 | 4/6 | 4/5 | 4/5 | 4/5 | 4/5 | 4/5 |

VSIQ PSIQ 11/14

| Age level | | OA | GD | BD | MA | PC | AP | I | C | A | V | S |
|---|---|---|---|---|---|---|---|---|---|---|---|---|
| **6½** | GD | 5/6 | — | | | | | | | | | |
| (6-5-16 | BD | 4/6 | 4/5 | — | | | | | | | | |
| through | MA | 5/6 | 4/6 | 4/5 | — | | | | | | | |
| 6-11-15) | PC | 4/6 | 4/6 | 4/5 | 4/5 | — | | | | | | |
| | AP | 5/6 | 5/6 | 4/6 | 5/6 | 5/6 | — | | | | | |
| | I | 4/6 | 4/5 | 4/5 | 4/5 | 4/5 | 4/6 | — | | | | |
| | C | 5/6 | 4/6 | 4/5 | 4/6 | 4/6 | 5/6 | 4/5 | — | | | |
| | A | 4/6 | 4/5 | 4/5 | 4/5 | 4/5 | 4/6 | 4/5 | 4/5 | — | | |
| | V | 4/5 | 4/5 | 3/5 | 4/5 | 4/5 | 4/6 | 4/5 | 4/5 | 4/5 | — | |
| | S | 4/6 | 4/6 | 4/5 | 4/5 | 4/5 | 4/6 | 4/5 | 4/6 | 4/5 | 4/5 | — |
| | Se | 5/6 | 4/6 | 4/5 | 4/6 | 4/6 | 5/6 | 4/5 | 4/6 | 4/5 | 4/5 | 4/6 |

VSIQ PSIQ 12/16

(*Table continues next page*)

**Table H-2 (cont.)**

| Age level | | OA | GD | BD | MA | PC | AP | I | C | A | V | S |
|---|---|---|---|---|---|---|---|---|---|---|---|---|
| **7** | GD | 5/7 | — | | | | | | | | | |
| (6-11-16 | BD | 5/6 | 4/5 | — | | | | | | | | |
| through | MA | 5/7 | 5/6 | 4/5 | — | | | | | | | |
| 7-3-15) | PC | 5/7 | 5/6 | 4/5 | 5/6 | — | | | | | | |
| | AP | 5/7 | 5/6 | 4/5 | 5/6 | 5/6 | — | | | | | |
| | I | 5/7 | 5/6 | 4/6 | 5/7 | 5/6 | 5/7 | — | | | | |
| | C | 5/7 | 5/7 | 4/6 | 5/7 | 5/6 | 5/7 | 5/7 | — | | | |
| | A | 5/7 | 5/6 | 4/5 | 5/6 | 5/6 | 5/6 | 5/7 | 5/7 | — | | |
| | V | 5/7 | 4/6 | 4/5 | 5/6 | 4/6 | 5/6 | 5/6 | 5/6 | 5/6 | — | |
| | S | 6/7 | 5/7 | 5/6 | 5/7 | 5/7 | 5/7 | 5/7 | 5/7 | 5/7 | 5/7 | — |
| | Se | 5/6 | 4/6 | 4/5 | 5/6 | 4/6 | 4/6 | 5/6 | 5/6 | 4/6 | 4/5 | 5/6 |

VSIQ
PSIQ 16/21

*Note.* Abbreviations: OA = Object Assembly, GD = Geometric Design, BD = Block Design, MA = Mazes, PC = Picture Completion, AP = Animal Pegs, I = Information, C = Comprehension, A = Arithmetic, V = Vocabulary, S = Similarities, Se = Sentences.

Sample reading: At age 3, a difference of 4 points between scaled scores on the Object Assembly and Geometric Design subtests is significant at the 5 percent level; a difference of 6 points is significant at the 1 percent level. The small box shows that at age 3 years a 10-point difference between the Performance Scale IQ and Verbal Scale IQ is needed for the 5 percent level, and a 13-point difference is needed for the 1 percent level.

The values in this table for the subtest comparisons are overly liberal when more than one comparison is made. They are more accurate when a priori planned comparisons are made, such as Object Assembly vs. Block Design or Information vs. Vocabulary.

See Chapter 8, Exhibit 8-1, page 168, for an explanation of the method used to arrive at magnitude of differences.

Silverstein (personal communication, February 1990) suggests that the following formula be used to obtain the value of the significant difference at the .05 level between the highest and lowest subtest scores on the profile that allows for making individual subtest comparisons:

$$D = q\sqrt{\Sigma SEM^2/k}$$

where $D$ is the significant difference, $q$ is the critical value of the studentized range statistic, $SEM$ is the standard error of measurement of a particular subtest, and $k$ is the number of subtests. For the WPPSI-R, the $q$ value is 4.62 for 12 and $\infty$ degrees of freedom and $k$ is 12. The sum of the $SEM^2$ for the 12 subtests is 3.31 + 1.88 + 1.35 + 2.07 + 1.35 + 3.06 + 1.44 + 1.54 + 1.80 + 1.44 + 1.25 + 1.61 = 22.10. $D = 4.62 \times \sqrt{22.10/12} = 4.62 \times \sqrt{1.8417} = 4.62 \times 1.3571 = 6$. Thus, a difference of 6 points between the highest and lowest subtest scaled scores represents a significant difference at the .05 level.

**Table H-3**
**Differences Required for Significance When Each Subtest Scaled Score Is Compared to the Mean Scaled Score for Any Individual Child at Each of the Nine Age Levels of the WPPSI-R**

| Age level | Subtest | Mean of 5 Performance Scale subtests[a] | | Mean of 6 Performance Scale subtests | | Mean of 5 Verbal Scale subtests[b] | | Mean of 6 Verbal Scale subtests | |
|---|---|---|---|---|---|---|---|---|---|
| | | .05 | .01 | .05 | .01 | .05 | .01 | .05 | .01 |
| **3** | Object Assembly | 3.96 | 4.72 | 4.12 | 4.92 | – | – | – | – |
| (2-11-16 | Geometric Design | 2.85 | 3.40 | 2.93 | 3.50 | – | – | – | – |
| through | Block Design | 2.91 | 3.47 | 3.00 | 3.58 | – | – | – | – |
| 3-5-15) | Mazes | 2.78 | 3.32 | 2.86 | 3.42 | – | – | – | – |
| | Picture Completion | 2.65 | 3.16 | 2.72 | 3.24 | – | – | – | – |
| | Animal Pegs | – | – | 3.97 | 4.74 | – | – | – | – |
| | Information | – | – | – | – | 2.30 | 2.75 | 2.37 | 2.82 |
| | Comprehension | – | – | – | – | 2.45 | 2.93 | 2.54 | 3.02 |
| | Arithmetic | – | – | – | – | 3.10 | 3.70 | 3.26 | 3.88 |
| | Vocabulary | – | – | – | – | 2.66 | 3.18 | 2.78 | 3.30 |
| | Similarities | – | – | – | – | 2.45 | 2.93 | 2.54 | 3.02 |
| | Sentences | – | – | – | – | – | – | 2.57 | 3.02 |

| Subtest | Mean of 10 subtests[a,b] | | Mean of 11 subtests[a] | | Mean of 11 subtests[b] | | Mean of 12 subtests | |
|---|---|---|---|---|---|---|---|---|
| | .05 | .01 | .05 | .01 | .05 | .01 | .05 | .01 |
| Object Assembly | 4.72 | 5.49 | 5.22 | 5.60 | 4.80 | 5.58 | 4.90 | 5.68 |
| Geometric Design | 3.21 | 3.73 | 3.55 | 3.80 | 3.25 | 3.78 | 3.32 | 3.85 |
| Block Design | 3.30 | 3.84 | 3.65 | 3.91 | 3.34 | 3.89 | 3.41 | 3.95 |
| Mazes | 3.12 | 3.63 | 3.45 | 3.70 | 3.16 | 3.67 | 3.22 | 3.74 |
| Picture Completion | 2.93 | 3.41 | 3.24 | 3.47 | 2.97 | 3.45 | 3.02 | 3.51 |
| Animal Pegs | – | – | 5.02 | 5.38 | – | – | 4.70 | 5.46 |
| Information | 2.62 | 3.05 | 2.90 | 3.11 | 2.65 | 3.08 | 2.70 | 3.13 |
| Comprehension | 2.83 | 3.30 | 3.13 | 3.36 | 2.87 | 3.33 | 2.92 | 3.39 |
| Arithmetic | 3.70 | 4.31 | 4.10 | 4.39 | 3.76 | 4.37 | 3.83 | 4.45 |
| Vocabulary | 3.12 | 3.63 | 3.45 | 3.70 | 3.16 | 3.67 | 3.22 | 3.74 |
| Similarities | 2.83 | 3.30 | 3.13 | 3.36 | 2.87 | 3.33 | 2.92 | 3.39 |
| Sentences | – | – | – | – | 2.87 | 3.33 | 2.92 | 3.39 |

*(Table continues next page)*

**Table H-3 (cont.)**

| Age level | Subtest | Mean of 5 Performance Scale subtests[a] | | Mean of 6 Performance Scale subtests | | Mean of 5 Verbal Scale subtests[b] | | Mean of 6 Verbal Scale subtests | |
|---|---|---|---|---|---|---|---|---|---|
| | | .05 | .01 | .05 | .01 | .05 | .01 | .05 | .01 |
| 3½ (3-5-16 through 3-11-15) | Object Assembly | 3.95 | 4.72 | 4.21 | 5.01 | – | – | – | – |
| | Geometric Design | 2.71 | 3.23 | 2.85 | 3.39 | – | – | – | – |
| | Block Design | 2.77 | 3.31 | 2.92 | 3.48 | – | – | – | – |
| | Mazes | 3.02 | 3.61 | 3.20 | 3.80 | – | – | – | – |
| | Picture Completion | 2.50 | 2.99 | 2.62 | 3.12 | – | – | – | – |
| | Animal Pegs | – | – | 4.06 | 4.83 | – | – | – | – |
| | Information | – | – | – | – | 2.37 | 2.83 | 2.46 | 2.93 |
| | Comprehension | – | – | – | – | 2.45 | 2.92 | 2.55 | 3.03 |
| | Arithmetic | – | – | – | – | 2.98 | 3.55 | 3.13 | 3.73 |
| | Vocabulary | – | – | – | – | 2.73 | 3.25 | 2.86 | 3.40 |
| | Similarities | – | – | – | – | 2.37 | 2.83 | 2.46 | 2.93 |
| | Sentences | – | – | – | – | – | – | 2.71 | 3.22 |

| | Subtest | Mean of 10 subtests[a,b] | | Mean of 11 subtests[a] | | Mean of 11 subtests[b] | | Mean of 12 subtests | |
|---|---|---|---|---|---|---|---|---|---|
| | | .05 | .01 | .05 | .01 | .05 | .01 | .05 | .01 |
| | Object Assembly | 4.71 | 5.48 | 4.81 | 5.59 | 4.80 | 5.58 | 4.89 | 5.68 |
| | Geometric Design | 3.02 | 3.52 | 3.08 | 3.58 | 3.07 | 3.56 | 3.12 | 3.62 |
| | Block Design | 3.12 | 3.63 | 3.18 | 3.69 | 3.16 | 3.67 | 3.22 | 3.74 |
| | Mazes | 3.46 | 4.03 | 3.53 | 4.11 | 3.52 | 4.09 | 3.58 | 4.16 |
| | Picture Completion | 2.73 | 3.17 | 2.78 | 3.23 | 2.76 | 3.21 | 2.81 | 3.26 |
| | Animal Pegs | – | – | 4.63 | 5.37 | – | – | 4.70 | 5.46 |
| | Information | 2.73 | 3.17 | 2.78 | 3.23 | 2.76 | 3.21 | 2.81 | 3.26 |
| | Comprehension | 2.83 | 3.29 | 2.89 | 3.35 | 2.86 | 3.33 | 2.92 | 3.39 |
| | Arithmetic | 3.54 | 4.12 | 3.62 | 4.20 | 3.60 | 4.18 | 3.67 | 4.26 |
| | Vocabulary | 3.21 | 3.73 | 3.27 | 3.80 | 3.25 | 3.78 | 3.31 | 3.85 |
| | Similarities | 2.73 | 3.17 | 2.78 | 3.23 | 2.76 | 3.21 | 2.81 | 3.26 |
| | Sentences | – | – | – | – | 3.07 | 3.56 | 3.12 | 3.62 |

(Table continues next page)

**Table H-3 (cont.)**

| Age level | Subtest | Mean of 5 Performance Scale subtests[a] | | Mean of 6 Performance Scale subtests | | Mean of 5 Verbal Scale subtests[b] | | Mean of 6 Verbal Scale subtests | |
|---|---|---|---|---|---|---|---|---|---|
| | | .05 | .01 | .05 | .01 | .05 | .01 | .05 | .01 |
| **4** | Object Assembly | 3.63 | 4.34 | 3.86 | 4.59 | — | — | — | — |
| (3-11-16 | Geometric Design | 3.10 | 3.70 | 3.27 | 3.89 | — | — | — | — |
| through | Block Design | 2.66 | 3.18 | 2.79 | 3.32 | — | — | — | — |
| 4-5-15) | Mazes | 3.38 | 4.03 | 3.58 | 4.26 | — | — | — | — |
| | Picture Completion | 2.66 | 3.18 | 2.79 | 3.32 | — | — | — | — |
| | Animal Pegs | — | — | 4.07 | 4.84 | — | — | — | — |
| | Information | — | — | — | — | 2.44 | 2.92 | 2.54 | 3.02 |
| | Comprehension | — | — | — | — | 2.52 | 3.00 | 2.62 | 3.11 |
| | Arithmetic | — | — | — | — | 2.97 | 3.55 | 3.13 | 3.72 |
| | Vocabulary | — | — | — | — | 2.52 | 3.00 | 2.62 | 3.11 |
| | Similarities | — | — | — | — | 2.37 | 2.83 | 2.45 | 2.92 |
| | Sentences | — | — | — | — | — | — | 2.54 | 3.02 |

| | Subtest | Mean of 10 subtests[a,b] | | Mean of 11 subtests[a] | | Mean of 11 subtests[b] | | Mean of 12 subtests | |
|---|---|---|---|---|---|---|---|---|---|
| | | .05 | .01 | .05 | .01 | .05 | .01 | .05 | .01 |
| | Object Assembly | 4.27 | 4.97 | 4.36 | 5.07 | 4.35 | 5.05 | 4.43 | 5.14 |
| | Geometric Design | 3.55 | 4.13 | 3.62 | 4.21 | 3.60 | 4.18 | 3.67 | 4.26 |
| | Block Design | 2.93 | 3.41 | 2.99 | 3.48 | 2.97 | 3.45 | 3.02 | 3.51 |
| | Mazes | 3.93 | 4.57 | 4.01 | 4.66 | 3.99 | 4.64 | 4.07 | 4.72 |
| | Picture Completion | 2.93 | 3.41 | 2.99 | 3.48 | 2.97 | 3.45 | 3.02 | 3.51 |
| | Animal Pegs | — | — | 4.63 | 5.38 | — | — | 4.70 | 5.46 |
| | Information | 2.83 | 3.30 | 2.89 | 3.36 | 2.87 | 3.33 | 2.92 | 3.39 |
| | Comprehension | 2.93 | 3.41 | 2.99 | 3.48 | 2.97 | 3.45 | 3.02 | 3.51 |
| | Arithmetic | 3.55 | 4.13 | 3.62 | 4.21 | 3.60 | 4.18 | 3.67 | 4.26 |
| | Vocabulary | 2.93 | 3.41 | 2.99 | 3.48 | 2.97 | 3.45 | 3.02 | 3.51 |
| | Similarities | 2.73 | 3.18 | 2.79 | 3.24 | 2.76 | 3.21 | 2.81 | 3.26 |
| | Sentences | — | — | — | — | 2.87 | 3.33 | 2.92 | 3.39 |

(*Table continues next page*)

**Table H-3 (cont.)**

| Age level | Subtest | Mean of 5 Performance Scale subtests[a] | | Mean of 6 Performance Scale subtests | | Mean of 5 Verbal Scale subtests[b] | | Mean of 6 Verbal Scale subtests | |
|---|---|---|---|---|---|---|---|---|---|
| | | .05 | .01 | .05 | .01 | .05 | .01 | .05 | .01 |
| **4½** (4-5-16 through 4-11-15) | Object Assembly | 4.28 | 5.10 | 4.56 | 5.42 | — | — | — | — |
| | Geometric Design | 2.80 | 3.35 | 2.94 | 3.50 | — | — | — | — |
| | Block Design | 2.60 | 3.11 | 2.72 | 3.24 | — | — | — | — |
| | Mazes | 3.38 | 4.04 | 3.58 | 4.26 | — | — | — | — |
| | Picture Completion | 2.23 | 2.67 | 2.31 | 2.74 | — | — | — | — |
| | Animal Pegs | — | — | 4.07 | 4.85 | — | — | — | — |
| | Information | — | — | — | — | 2.29 | 2.79 | 2.38 | 2.83 |
| | Comprehension | — | — | — | — | 2.44 | 2.97 | 2.55 | 3.04 |
| | Arithmetic | — | — | — | — | 2.91 | 3.54 | 3.07 | 3.66 |
| | Vocabulary | — | — | — | — | 2.79 | 3.39 | 2.93 | 3.49 |
| | Similarities | — | — | — | — | 2.37 | 2.88 | 2.47 | 2.94 |
| | Sentences | — | — | — | — | — | — | 2.93 | 3.49 |

| | Subtest | Mean of 10 subtests[a,b] | | Mean of 11 subtests[a] | | Mean of 11 subtests[b] | | Mean of 12 subtests | |
|---|---|---|---|---|---|---|---|---|---|
| | | .05 | .01 | .05 | .01 | .05 | .01 | .05 | .01 |
| | Object Assembly | 5.12 | 5.96 | 5.23 | 6.08 | 5.22 | 6.07 | 5.32 | 6.18 |
| | Geometric Design | 3.12 | 3.63 | 3.19 | 3.70 | 3.17 | 3.68 | 3.23 | 3.74 |
| | Block Design | 2.84 | 3.30 | 2.89 | 3.36 | 2.87 | 3.34 | 2.93 | 3.39 |
| | Mazes | 3.93 | 4.57 | 4.01 | 4.66 | 4.00 | 4.65 | 4.07 | 4.73 |
| | Picture Completion | 2.28 | 2.65 | 2.32 | 2.70 | 2.30 | 2.67 | 2.34 | 2.71 |
| | Animal Pegs | — | — | 4.63 | 5.38 | — | — | 4.71 | 5.46 |
| | Information | 2.63 | 3.06 | 2.68 | 3.11 | 2.66 | 3.09 | 2.71 | 3.14 |
| | Comprehension | 2.84 | 3.30 | 2.89 | 3.36 | 2.87 | 3.34 | 2.93 | 3.39 |
| | Arithmetic | 3.47 | 4.04 | 3.54 | 4.11 | 3.52 | 4.09 | 3.59 | 4.16 |
| | Vocabulary | 3.30 | 3.84 | 3.67 | 3.91 | 3.35 | 3.89 | 3.41 | 3.96 |
| | Similarities | 2.73 | 3.18 | 2.79 | 3.24 | 2.77 | 3.22 | 2.82 | 3.27 |
| | Sentences | — | — | — | — | 3.35 | 3.89 | 3.41 | 3.96 |

(Table continues next page)

**Table H-3 (cont.)**

| Age level | Subtest | Mean of 5 Performance Scale subtests[a] | | Mean of 6 Performance Scale subtests | | Mean of 5 Verbal Scale subtests[b] | | Mean of 6 Verbal Scale subtests | |
|---|---|---|---|---|---|---|---|---|---|
| | | .05 | .01 | .05 | .01 | .05 | .01 | .05 | .01 |
| **5** (4-11-16 through 5-5-15) | Object Assembly | 4.19 | 3.36 | 4.45 | 5.29 | — | — | — | — |
| | Geometric Design | 3.38 | 3.92 | 3.56 | 4.23 | — | — | — | — |
| | Block Design | 2.79 | 3.21 | 2.91 | 3.46 | — | — | — | — |
| | Mazes | 3.32 | 3.86 | 3.50 | 4.16 | — | — | — | — |
| | Picture Completion | 2.79 | 3.21 | 2.91 | 3.46 | — | — | — | — |
| | Animal Pegs | — | — | 4.10 | 4.88 | — | — | — | — |
| | Information | — | — | — | — | 2.76 | 3.30 | 2.89 | 3.44 |
| | Comprehension | — | — | — | — | 2.63 | 3.14 | 2.75 | 3.27 |
| | Arithmetic | — | — | — | — | 3.01 | 3.60 | 3.17 | 3.77 |
| | Vocabulary | — | — | — | — | 2.70 | 3.22 | 2.82 | 3.36 |
| | Similarities | — | — | — | — | 2.63 | 3.14 | 2.75 | 3.27 |
| | Sentences | — | — | — | — | — | — | 3.04 | 3.61 |

| | Subtest | Mean of 10 subtests[a,b] | | Mean of 11 subtests[a] | | Mean of 11 subtests[b] | | Mean of 12 subtests | |
|---|---|---|---|---|---|---|---|---|---|
| | | .05 | .01 | .05 | .01 | .05 | .01 | .05 | .01 |
| | Object Assembly | 4.97 | 5.78 | 5.07 | 5.89 | 5.06 | 5.88 | 5.16 | 5.98 |
| | Geometric Design | 3.88 | 4.51 | 3.95 | 4.59 | 3.94 | 4.58 | 4.01 | 4.66 |
| | Block Design | 3.06 | 3.56 | 3.11 | 3.62 | 3.10 | 3.60 | 3.15 | 3.65 |
| | Mazes | 3.80 | 4.43 | 3.88 | 4.51 | 3.86 | 4.49 | 3.93 | 4.57 |
| | Picture Completion | 3.06 | 3.56 | 3.11 | 3.62 | 3.10 | 3.60 | 3.15 | 3.65 |
| | Animal Pegs | — | — | 4.64 | 5.40 | — | — | 4.72 | 5.48 |
| | Information | 3.24 | 3.77 | 3.30 | 3.83 | 3.28 | 3.82 | 3.34 | 3.88 |
| | Comprehension | 3.06 | 3.56 | 3.11 | 3.62 | 3.10 | 3.60 | 3.15 | 3.65 |
| | Arithmetic | 3.57 | 4.16 | 3.64 | 4.23 | 3.63 | 4.21 | 3.69 | 4.28 |
| | Vocabulary | 3.15 | 3.66 | 3.21 | 3.73 | 3.19 | 3.71 | 3.25 | 3.77 |
| | Similarities | 3.06 | 3.56 | 3.11 | 3.62 | 3.10 | 3.60 | 3.15 | 3.65 |
| | Sentences | — | — | — | — | 3.46 | 4.02 | 3.52 | 4.08 |

(Table continues next page)

**Table H-3 (cont.)**

| Age level | Subtest | Mean of 5 Performance Scale subtests[a] | | Mean of 6 Performance Scale subtests | | Mean of 5 Verbal Scale subtests[b] | | Mean of 6 Verbal Scale subtests | |
|---|---|---|---|---|---|---|---|---|---|
| | | .05 | .01 | .05 | .01 | .05 | .01 | .05 | .01 |
| **5½** (5-5-16 through 5-11-15) | Object Assembly | 4.32 | 5.16 | 4.57 | 5.44 | — | — | — | — |
| | Geometric Design | 3.69 | 4.41 | 3.88 | 4.61 | — | — | — | — |
| | Block Design | 3.28 | 3.92 | 3.42 | 4.07 | — | — | — | — |
| | Mazes | 3.44 | 4.11 | 3.60 | 4.28 | — | — | — | — |
| | Picture Completion | 3.05 | 3.64 | 3.62 | 3.77 | — | — | — | — |
| | Animal Pegs | — | — | 4.14 | 4.92 | — | — | — | — |
| | Information | — | — | — | — | 3.40 | 4.06 | 3.59 | 4.27 |
| | Comprehension | — | — | — | — | 3.01 | 3.59 | 3.16 | 3.75 |
| | Arithmetic | — | — | — | — | 3.01 | 3.59 | 3.16 | 3.75 |
| | Vocabulary | — | — | — | — | 2.69 | 3.21 | 2.81 | 3.34 |
| | Similarities | — | — | — | — | 2.69 | 3.21 | 2.81 | 3.34 |
| | Sentences | — | — | — | — | — | — | 3.47 | 4.13 |

| | Subtest | Mean of 10 subtests[a,b] | | Mean of 11 subtests[a] | | Mean of 11 subtests[b] | | Mean of 12 subtests | |
|---|---|---|---|---|---|---|---|---|---|
| | | .05 | .01 | .05 | .01 | .05 | .01 | .05 | .01 |
| | Object Assembly | 5.10 | 5.94 | 5.21 | 6.05 | 5.20 | 6.04 | 5.29 | 6.14 |
| | Geometric Design | 4.25 | 4.95 | 4.33 | 5.04 | 4.33 | 5.03 | 4.40 | 5.11 |
| | Block Design | 3.68 | 4.28 | 3.75 | 4.35 | 3.74 | 4.34 | 3.80 | 4.41 |
| | Mazes | 3.91 | 4.54 | 3.98 | 4.62 | 3.97 | 4.61 | 4.04 | 4.68 |
| | Picture Completion | 3.36 | 3.91 | 3.41 | 3.97 | 3.41 | 3.96 | 3.46 | 4.01 |
| | Animal Pegs | — | — | 4.66 | 5.42 | — | — | 4.74 | 5.50 |
| | Information | 4.05 | 4.71 | 4.12 | 4.79 | 4.12 | 4.78 | 4.19 | 4.86 |
| | Comprehension | 3.52 | 4.10 | 3.58 | 4.16 | 3.58 | 4.15 | 3.63 | 4.22 |
| | Arithmetic | 3.52 | 4.10 | 3.58 | 4.16 | 3.58 | 4.15 | 3.63 | 4.22 |
| | Vocabulary | 3.09 | 3.60 | 3.14 | 3.65 | 3.13 | 3.64 | 3.18 | 3.69 |
| | Similarities | 3.09 | 3.60 | 3.14 | 3.65 | 3.13 | 3.64 | 3.18 | 3.69 |
| | Sentences | — | — | — | — | 3.97 | 4.61 | 4.04 | 4.68 |

(Table continues next page)

**Table H-3 (cont.)**

| Age level | Subtest | Mean of 5 Performance Scale subtests[a] | | Mean of 6 Performance Scale subtests | | Mean of 5 Verbal Scale subtests[b] | | Mean of 6 Verbal Scale subtests | |
|---|---|---|---|---|---|---|---|---|---|
| | | .05 | .01 | .05 | .01 | .05 | .01 | .05 | .01 |
| **6** (5-11-16 through 6-5-15) | Object Assembly | 3.67 | 4.38 | 3.89 | 4.62 | – | – | – | – |
| | Geometric Design | 3.26 | 3.89 | 3.43 | 4.08 | – | – | – | – |
| | Block Design | 2.91 | 3.47 | 3.04 | 3.62 | – | – | – | – |
| | Mazes | 3.20 | 3.82 | 3.37 | 4.01 | – | – | – | – |
| | Picture Completion | 3.37 | 4.02 | 3.55 | 4.22 | – | – | – | – |
| | Animal Pegs | – | – | 4.10 | 4.87 | – | – | – | – |
| | Information | – | – | – | – | 3.37 | 4.03 | 3.55 | 4.22 |
| | Comprehension | – | – | – | – | 3.27 | 3.90 | 3.43 | 4.08 |
| | Arithmetic | – | – | – | – | 3.10 | 3.70 | 3.24 | 3.85 |
| | Vocabulary | – | – | – | – | 2.98 | 3.55 | 3.11 | 3.70 |
| | Similarities | – | – | – | – | 2.73 | 3.25 | 2.82 | 3.36 |
| | Sentences | – | – | – | – | – | – | 3.37 | 4.00 |

| | Subtest | Mean of 10 subtests[a,b] | | Mean of 11 subtests[a] | | Mean of 11 subtests[b] | | Mean of 12 subtests | |
|---|---|---|---|---|---|---|---|---|---|
| | | .05 | .01 | .05 | .01 | .05 | .01 | .05 | .01 |
| | Object Assembly | 4.31 | 5.01 | 4.39 | 5.10 | 4.38 | 5.10 | 4.46 | 5.18 |
| | Geometric Design | 3.74 | 4.36 | 3.81 | 4.43 | 3.80 | 4.42 | 3.87 | 4.49 |
| | Block Design | 3.26 | 3.79 | 3.31 | 3.85 | 3.30 | 3.84 | 3.36 | 3.89 |
| | Mazes | 3.67 | 4.27 | 3.74 | 4.34 | 3.73 | 4.33 | 3.79 | 4.40 |
| | Picture Completion | 3.89 | 4.53 | 3.97 | 4.61 | 3.96 | 4.60 | 4.03 | 4.67 |
| | Animal Pegs | – | – | 4.66 | 5.41 | – | – | 4.73 | 5.49 |
| | Information | 3.97 | 4.61 | 4.04 | 4.70 | 4.03 | 4.69 | 4.10 | 4.76 |
| | Comprehension | 3.82 | 4.44 | 3.89 | 4.52 | 3.88 | 4.51 | 3.95 | 4.58 |
| | Arithmetic | 3.59 | 4.18 | 3.66 | 4.25 | 3.65 | 4.24 | 3.71 | 4.30 |
| | Vocabulary | 3.43 | 3.99 | 3.49 | 4.05 | 3.48 | 4.04 | 3.54 | 4.10 |
| | Similarities | 3.08 | 3.58 | 3.13 | 3.64 | 3.12 | 3.62 | 3.17 | 3.68 |
| | Sentences | – | – | – | – | 3.80 | 4.42 | 3.87 | 4.49 |

(*Table continues next page*)

**Table H-3 (cont.)**

| Age level | Subtest | Mean of 5 Performance Scale subtests[a] | | Mean of 6 Performance Scale subtests | | Mean of 5 Verbal Scale subtests[b] | | Mean of 6 Verbal Scale subtests | |
|---|---|---|---|---|---|---|---|---|---|
| | | .05 | .01 | .05 | .01 | .05 | .01 | .05 | .01 |
| **6½** (6-5-16 through 6-11-15) | Object Assembly | 3.87 | 4.62 | 4.08 | 4.85 | – | – | – | – |
| | Geometric Design | 3.63 | 4.33 | 3.82 | 4.54 | – | – | – | – |
| | Block Design | 3.10 | 3.70 | 3.22 | 3.83 | – | – | – | – |
| | Mazes | 3.53 | 4.21 | 3.71 | 4.41 | – | – | – | – |
| | Picture Completion | 3.48 | 4.15 | 3.65 | 4.34 | – | – | – | – |
| | Animal Pegs | – | – | 4.13 | 4.91 | – | – | – | – |
| | Information | – | – | – | – | 3.06 | 3.66 | 3.21 | 3.81 |
| | Comprehension | – | – | – | – | 3.55 | 4.24 | 3.75 | 4.46 |
| | Arithmetic | – | – | – | – | 3.06 | 3.66 | 3.21 | 3.81 |
| | Vocabulary | – | – | – | – | 2.95 | 3.52 | 3.07 | 3.66 |
| | Similarities | – | – | – | – | 3.35 | 3.99 | 3.52 | 4.18 |
| | Sentences | – | – | – | – | – | – | 3.69 | 4.39 |

| | Subtest | Mean of 10 subtests[a,b] | | Mean of 11 subtests[a] | | Mean of 11 subtests[b] | | Mean of 12 subtests | |
|---|---|---|---|---|---|---|---|---|---|
| | | .05 | .01 | .05 | .01 | .05 | .01 | .05 | .01 |
| | Object Assembly | 4.52 | 5.26 | 4.61 | 5.35 | 4.60 | 5.35 | 4.68 | 5.43 |
| | Geometric Design | 4.20 | 4.88 | 4.27 | 4.96 | 4.27 | 4.96 | 4.34 | 5.04 |
| | Block Design | 3.45 | 4.02 | 3.51 | 4.08 | 3.50 | 4.07 | 3.56 | 4.13 |
| | Mazes | 4.06 | 4.72 | 4.13 | 4.80 | 4.13 | 4.79 | 4.19 | 4.87 |
| | Picture Completion | 3.99 | 4.64 | 4.06 | 4.72 | 4.05 | 4.71 | 4.12 | 4.78 |
| | Animal Pegs | – | – | 4.67 | 5.43 | – | – | 4.75 | 5.51 |
| | Information | 3.53 | 4.11 | 3.59 | 4.18 | 3.59 | 4.17 | 3.64 | 4.23 |
| | Comprehension | 4.20 | 4.88 | 4.27 | 4.96 | 4.27 | 4.96 | 4.34 | 5.04 |
| | Arithmetic | 3.53 | 4.11 | 3.59 | 4.18 | 3.59 | 4.17 | 3.64 | 4.23 |
| | Vocabulary | 3.37 | 3.92 | 3.42 | 3.98 | 3.42 | 3.97 | 3.47 | 4.03 |
| | Similarities | 3.92 | 4.56 | 3.98 | 4.63 | 3.98 | 4.62 | 4.04 | 4.69 |
| | Sentences | – | – | – | – | 4.20 | 4.88 | 4.27 | 4.95 |

(*Table continues next page*)

**Table H-3 (cont.)**

| Age level | Subtest | Mean of 5 Performance Scale subtests[a] | | Mean of 6 Performance Scale subtests | | Mean of 5 Verbal Scale subtests[b] | | Mean of 6 Verbal Scale subtests | |
|---|---|---|---|---|---|---|---|---|---|
| | | .05 | .01 | .05 | .01 | .05 | .01 | .05 | .01 |
| 7 (6-11-16 through 7-3-15) | Object Assembly | 4.50 | 5.37 | 4.75 | 5.65 | — | — | — | — |
| | Geometric Design | 3.90 | 4.66 | 4.08 | 4.86 | — | — | — | — |
| | Block Design | 2.96 | 3.53 | 3.02 | 3.60 | — | — | — | — |
| | Mazes | 4.04 | 4.82 | 4.23 | 5.04 | — | — | — | — |
| | Picture Completion | 3.71 | 4.43 | 3.87 | 4.61 | — | — | — | — |
| | Animal Pegs | — | — | 4.18 | 4.98 | — | — | — | — |
| | Information | — | — | — | — | 4.25 | 5.08 | 4.42 | 5.26 |
| | Comprehension | — | — | — | — | 4.38 | 5.23 | 4.56 | 5.42 |
| | Arithmetic | — | — | — | — | 4.08 | 4.87 | 4.23 | 5.03 |
| | Vocabulary | — | — | — | — | 3.71 | 4.43 | 3.81 | 4.53 |
| | Similarities | — | — | — | — | 4.58 | 5.47 | 4.78 | 5.69 |
| | Sentences | — | — | — | — | — | — | 3.70 | 4.40 |

| | Subtest | Mean of 10 subtests[a,b] | | Mean of 11 subtests[a] | | Mean of 11 subtests[b] | | Mean of 12 subtests | |
|---|---|---|---|---|---|---|---|---|---|
| | | .05 | .01 | .05 | .01 | .05 | .01 | .05 | .01 |
| | Object Assembly | 5.34 | 6.22 | 5.44 | 6.32 | 5.43 | 6.31 | 5.52 | 6.40 |
| | Geometric Design | 4.54 | 5.28 | 4.61 | 5.36 | 4.60 | 5.35 | 4.67 | 5.42 |
| | Block Design | 3.22 | 3.75 | 3.25 | 3.78 | 3.24 | 3.76 | 3.27 | 3.79 |
| | Mazes | 4.72 | 5.50 | 4.80 | 5.58 | 4.79 | 5.57 | 4.87 | 5.65 |
| | Picture Completion | 4.28 | 4.98 | 4.34 | 5.05 | 4.34 | 5.04 | 4.40 | 5.10 |
| | Animal Pegs | — | — | 4.74 | 5.50 | — | — | 4.80 | 5.57 |
| | Information | 4.90 | 5.70 | 4.98 | 5.79 | 4.98 | 5.78 | 5.05 | 5.86 |
| | Comprehension | 5.07 | 5.90 | 5.16 | 5.99 | 5.15 | 5.99 | 5.23 | 6.07 |
| | Arithmetic | 4.66 | 5.43 | 4.74 | 5.50 | 4.73 | 5.50 | 4.80 | 5.57 |
| | Vocabulary | 4.15 | 4.83 | 4.21 | 4.89 | 4.20 | 4.88 | 4.26 | 4.94 |
| | Similarities | 5.34 | 6.22 | 5.44 | 6.32 | 5.43 | 6.31 | 5.52 | 6.40 |
| | Sentences | — | — | — | — | 4.05 | 4.71 | 4.11 | 4.77 |

*Note.* Table H-3 shows the minimum deviations from an individual's average subtest scaled score that are significant at the .05 and .01 levels. See the Note in Table C-3 for an explanation of how the deviations were obtained.

[a] Animal Pegs excluded.
[b] Sentences excluded.

**Table H-4**
**Probability of Obtaining Designated Differences Between Individual WPPSI-R Performance and Verbal IQs**

| Probability of obtaining given or greater discrepancy by chance | Age level | | | | | | | | | |
|---|---|---|---|---|---|---|---|---|---|---|
| | 3 | 3½ | 4 | 4½ | 5 | 5½ | 6 | 6½ | 7 | Av.[a] |
| .50 | 3.43 | 3.56 | 3.56 | 3.56 | 3.68 | 4.08 | 3.82 | 4.21 | 3.68 | 5.49 |
| .25 | 6.03 | 6.03 | 6.03 | 6.03 | 6.22 | 6.90 | 6.45 | 7.11 | 6.22 | 9.29 |
| .20 | 6.71 | 6.71 | 6.71 | 6.71 | 6.92 | 7.68 | 7.18 | 7.92 | 6.92 | 10.34 |
| .10 | 8.65 | 8.65 | 8.65 | 8.65 | 8.92 | 9.90 | 9.26 | 10.20 | 8.92 | 13.33 |
| .05 | 10.27 | 10.27 | 10.27 | 10.27 | 10.60 | 11.76 | 11.00 | 12.12 | 10.60 | 15.83 |
| .02 | 12.21 | 12.21 | 12.21 | 12.21 | 12.60 | 13.98 | 13.07 | 14.41 | 12.60 | 18.82 |
| .01 | 13.52 | 13.52 | 13.52 | 13.52 | 13.95 | 15.48 | 14.48 | 15.96 | 13.95 | 20.84 |
| .001 | 17.30 | 17.30 | 17.30 | 17.30 | 17.84 | 19.80 | 18.51 | 20.41 | 17.84 | 26.66 |

*Note.* To use Table H-4: Find the column appropriate to the examinee's age. Locate the discrepancy that is *just less* than the discrepancy obtained by the examinee. The first column in that same row gives the probability of obtaining the given (or a greater) discrepancy by chance. For example, the hypothesis that a 3-year-old examinee obtained a Performance-Verbal discrepancy of 14 by chance can be rejected at the .01 level of significance. Table H-4 is two-tailed. See Chapter 8, Exhibit 8-1, page 168, for an explanation of the method used to arrive at magnitude of differences.
[a]Av. = Average of the nine age groups.

**Table H-5**
**Percentage of Population Obtaining Discrepancies Between WPPSI-R Performance and Verbal IQs**

| Percentage obtaining given or greater discrepancy in either direction | Age level | | | | | | | | | | Percentage obtaining given or greater discrepancy in a specific direction |
|---|---|---|---|---|---|---|---|---|---|---|---|
| | 3 | 3½ | 4 | 4½ | 5 | 5½ | 6 | 6½ | 7 | Av.[a] | |
| 50 | 8.41 | 8.90 | 8.78 | 8.78 | 9.82 | 10.45 | 10.14 | 9.14 | 10.76 | 9.37 | 25 |
| 25 | 14.01 | 14.84 | 14.64 | 14.64 | 16.36 | 17.42 | 16.90 | 15.23 | 17.93 | 15.62 | 12.5 |
| 20 | 15.60 | 16.52 | 16.29 | 16.29 | 18.21 | 19.39 | 18.81 | 16.96 | 19.95 | 17.39 | 10 |
| 10 | 20.11 | 21.29 | 21.00 | 21.00 | 23.48 | 25.00 | 24.25 | 21.86 | 25.72 | 22.41 | 5 |
| 5 | 23.88 | 25.29 | 24.95 | 24.95 | 27.89 | 29.69 | 28.81 | 25.97 | 30.55 | 26.62 | 2.5 |
| 2 | 28.39 | 30.07 | 29.66 | 29.66 | 33.16 | 35.30 | 34.24 | 30.87 | 36.32 | 31.65 | 1 |
| 1 | 31.44 | 33.29 | 32.84 | 32.84 | 36.71 | 39.09 | 37.92 | 34.18 | 40.22 | 35.04 | .5 |
| .1 | 39.85 | 42.19 | 41.62 | 41.62 | 46.53 | 49.54 | 48.06 | 43.32 | 50.97 | 44.42 | .05 |

*Note.* To use Table H-5: Find the column appropriate to the examinee's age. Locate the discrepancy that is *just less* than the one obtained by the examinee. The first column in the same row gives the percentage of the standardization population obtaining discrepancies as large or larger than the located discrepancy. For example, a 3-year-old examinee with a Performance-Verbal discrepancy of 15 will be found in between 20 and 25 percent of the standardization population. See Table C-9 for an explanation of the method used to arrive at magnitude of differences.
[a]Av. = Average of the nine age groups.

**Table H-6**
**Reliability and Validity Coefficients of Proposed WPPSI-R Short Forms**

| Dyad | | | Triad | | | | Tetrad | | | | | Pentad | | | | | |
|---|---|---|---|---|---|---|---|---|---|---|---|---|---|---|---|---|---|
| Short form | $r_{tt}$ | $r$ | Short form | | | $r_{tt}$ | $r$ | Short form | | | | $r_{tt}$ | $r$ | Short form | | | | | $r_{tt}$ | $r$ |

| Short form | $r_{tt}$ | $r$ | Short form | | $r_{tt}$ | $r$ | Short form | | | $r_{tt}$ | $r$ | Short form | | | | $r_{tt}$ | $r$ |
|---|---|---|---|---|---|---|---|---|---|---|---|---|---|---|---|---|---|
| BD I | .890 | .859 | BD I S | | .921 | .894 | BD PC I S | | | .936 | .914 | BD PC I A S | | | | .945 | .929 |
| PC I | .895 | .837 | BD I A | | .914 | .892 | BD PC I Se | | | .930 | .914 | BD PC I A Se | | | | .941 | .929 |
| BD C | .881 | .835 | BD PC I | | .919 | .888 | BD PC I A | | | .932 | .914 | BD PC I A V | | | | .943 | .929 |
| I A | .887 | .835 | BD I V | | .918 | .887 | BD I A S | | | .934 | .913 | GD BD I V S | | | | .940 | .928 |
| BD S | .894 | .829 | BD I Se | | .912 | .885 | BD PC I C | | | .933 | .912 | BD PC C A S | | | | .942 | .927 |
| GD I | .865 | .826 | BD A V | | .909 | .883 | BD PC C A | | | .927 | .911 | GD BD I C S | | | | .939 | .927 |
| BD V | .886 | .826 | BD I C | | .918 | .882 | GD BD I V | | | .924 | .911 | BD PC I C A | | | | .943 | .927 |
| BD A | .880 | .824 | BD C A | | .908 | .881 | BD PC I V | | | .934 | .911 | GD BD I A V | | | | .937 | .927 |
| PC A | .879 | .822 | BD PC C | | .912 | .881 | BD I A V | | | .932 | .910 | BD PC I S Se | | | | .944 | .927 |
| I S | .904 | .820 | PC I A | | .915 | .881 | GD BD I S | | | .927 | .910 | GD BD PC I C | | | | .938 | .927 |

*Note.* Abbreviations: BD = Block Design, GD = Geometric Design, PC = Picture Completion, I = Information, C = Comprehension, A = Arithmetic, V = Vocabulary, S = Similarities, Se = Sentences.

It is recommended that short-form combinations involving Animal Pegs or Sentences not be used because these two subtests were not used in the construction of the IQ tables. The best two-subtest short-form combination for screening children who have severe hearing problems is Block Design and Picture Completion ($r_{tt}$ = .897 and $r$ = .793) followed by Geometric Design and Block Design ($r_{tt}$ = .879 and $r$ = .746). For screening children with severe visual deficits, any of the short-form combinations shown in the table involving subtests in the Verbal Scale can be used, such as Information and Arithmetic or Information and Similarities. Tables H-7, H-8, and H-9 provide estimated IQs associated with the ten best dyads, triads, and tetrads.

This table was constructed using a computer program developed by L. Atkinson and G. Yoshida (1989), "A BASIC Program for Determining Reliability and Validity of Subtest Combination Short Forms," *Educational and Psychological Measurement, 49*, 141–143. The program is based on formulas provided by Tellegen and Briggs (1967).

**Table H-7**
**Estimated WPPSI-R Full Scale IQ Equivalents for Sum of Scaled Scores for Ten Best Short-Form Dyads**

| Sum of scaled scores | Combination | | | | Sum of scaled scores | Combination | | | |
|---|---|---|---|---|---|---|---|---|---|
| | BD+C | BD+A PC+A PC+I | I+A I+S | BD+V BD+I BD+S GD+I | | BD+C | BD+A PC+A PC+I | I+A I+S | BD+V BD+I BD+S GD+I |
| 1 | 41 | 45 | 47 | 43 | 21 | 103 | 103 | 103 | 103 |
| 2 | 44 | 48 | 50 | 46 | 22 | 106 | 106 | 106 | 106 |
| 3 | 47 | 51 | 52 | 49 | 23 | 109 | 109 | 108 | 109 |
| 4 | 50 | 54 | 55 | 52 | 24 | 112 | 112 | 111 | 112 |
| 5 | 54 | 57 | 58 | 55 | 25 | 116 | 115 | 114 | 115 |
| 6 | 57 | 59 | 61 | 58 | 26 | 119 | 117 | 117 | 118 |
| 7 | 60 | 62 | 64 | 61 | 27 | 122 | 120 | 120 | 121 |
| 8 | 63 | 65 | 66 | 64 | 28 | 125 | 123 | 122 | 124 |
| 9 | 66 | 68 | 69 | 67 | 29 | 128 | 126 | 125 | 127 |
| 10 | 69 | 71 | 72 | 70 | 30 | 131 | 129 | 128 | 130 |
| 11 | 72 | 74 | 75 | 73 | 31 | 134 | 132 | 131 | 133 |
| 12 | 75 | 77 | 78 | 76 | 32 | 137 | 135 | 134 | 136 |
| 13 | 78 | 80 | 80 | 79 | 33 | 140 | 138 | 136 | 139 |
| 14 | 81 | 83 | 83 | 82 | 34 | 143 | 141 | 139 | 142 |
| 15 | 85 | 86 | 86 | 85 | 35 | 147 | 144 | 142 | 145 |
| 16 | 88 | 88 | 89 | 88 | 36 | 150 | 146 | 145 | 148 |
| 17 | 91 | 91 | 92 | 91 | 37 | 153 | 149 | 148 | 151 |
| 18 | 94 | 94 | 94 | 94 | 38 | 156 | 152 | 150 | 154 |
| 19 | 97 | 97 | 97 | 97 | 39 | 159 | 155 | 153 | 157 |
| 20 | 100 | 100 | 100 | 100 | 40 | 162 | 158 | 156 | 160 |

*Note.* Abbreviations: BD = Block Design, C = Comprehension, A = Arithmetic, PC = Picture Completion, I = Information, S = Similarities, V = Vocabulary, GD = Geometric Design.

Reliability and validity coefficients associated with each short-form combination are shown in Table H-6. See Exhibit 6-3, page 138, for an explanation of the procedure used to obtain the estimated IQs.

**Table H-8**
**Estimated WPPSI-R Full Scale IQ Equivalents for Sum of Scaled Scores for Ten Best Short-Form Triads**

| | Combination | | | | Combination | | |
|---|---|---|---|---|---|---|---|
| Sum of scaled scores | BD+ I +S<br>BD+ I +A<br>BD+PC+I<br>BD+ I +V<br>BD+ I +Se<br>BD+ A +V<br>BD+ I +C<br>BD+ C +A | BD+PC+C | PC+I+A | Sum of scaled scores | BD+ I +S<br>BD+ I +A<br>BD+PC+I<br>BD+ I +V<br>BD+ I +Se<br>BD+ A +V<br>BD+ I +C<br>BD+ C +A | BD+PC+C | PC+I+A |
| 1 | 39 | 36 | 42 | 31 | 102 | 102 | 102 |
| 2 | 41 | 38 | 44 | 32 | 104 | 104 | 104 |
| 3 | 43 | 41 | 46 | 33 | 106 | 107 | 106 |
| 4 | 45 | 43 | 48 | 34 | 108 | 109 | 108 |
| 5 | 48 | 45 | 50 | 35 | 111 | 111 | 110 |
| 6 | 50 | 47 | 52 | 36 | 113 | 113 | 112 |
| 7 | 52 | 49 | 54 | 37 | 115 | 115 | 114 |
| 8 | 54 | 52 | 56 | 38 | 117 | 118 | 116 |
| 9 | 56 | 54 | 58 | 39 | 119 | 120 | 118 |
| 10 | 58 | 56 | 60 | 40 | 121 | 122 | 120 |
| 11 | 60 | 58 | 62 | 41 | 123 | 124 | 122 |
| 12 | 62 | 60 | 64 | 42 | 125 | 126 | 124 |
| 13 | 64 | 63 | 66 | 43 | 127 | 129 | 126 |
| 14 | 66 | 65 | 68 | 44 | 129 | 131 | 128 |
| 15 | 69 | 67 | 70 | 45 | 132 | 133 | 130 |
| 16 | 71 | 69 | 72 | 46 | 134 | 135 | 132 |
| 17 | 73 | 71 | 74 | 47 | 136 | 137 | 134 |
| 18 | 75 | 74 | 76 | 48 | 138 | 140 | 136 |
| 19 | 77 | 76 | 78 | 49 | 140 | 142 | 138 |
| 20 | 79 | 78 | 80 | 50 | 142 | 144 | 140 |
| 21 | 81 | 80 | 82 | 51 | 144 | 146 | 142 |
| 22 | 83 | 82 | 84 | 52 | 146 | 148 | 144 |
| 23 | 85 | 85 | 86 | 53 | 148 | 151 | 146 |
| 24 | 87 | 87 | 88 | 54 | 150 | 153 | 148 |
| 25 | 90 | 89 | 90 | 55 | 153 | 155 | 150 |
| 26 | 92 | 91 | 92 | 56 | 155 | 157 | 152 |
| 27 | 94 | 93 | 94 | 57 | 157 | 159 | 154 |
| 28 | 96 | 96 | 96 | 58 | 159 | 162 | 156 |
| 29 | 98 | 98 | 98 | 59 | 161 | 164 | 158 |
| 30 | 100 | 100 | 100 | 60 | 163 | 166 | 160 |

*Note.* Abbreviations: BD = Block Design, I = Information, S = Similarities, A = Arithmetic, PC = Picture Completion, V = Vocabulary, Se = Sentences, C = Comprehension.

Reliability and validity coefficients associated with each short-form combination are shown in Table H-6. See Exhibit 6-3, page 138, for an explanation of the procedure used to obtain the estimated IQs.

**Table H-9**
**Estimated WPPSI-R Full Scale IQ Equivalents for Sum of Scaled Scores for Ten Best Short-Form Tetrads**

| Sum of scaled scores | Combination | | Sum of scaled scores | Combination | |
|---|---|---|---|---|---|
| | $BD+PC+I+S$ $BD+PC+I+Se$ $GD+BD+I+V$ $GD+BD+I+S$ | $BD+PC+I+A$ $BD+I+A+S$ $BD+PC+I+C$ $BD+PC+C+A$ $BD+PC+I+V$ $BD+I+A+V$ | | $BD+PC+I+S$ $BD+PC+I+Se$ $GD+BD+I+V$ $GD+BD+I+S$ | $BD+PC+I+A$ $BD+I+A+S$ $BD+PC+I+C$ $BD+PC+C+A$ $BD+PC+I+V$ $BD+I+A+V$ |
| 1 | 34 | 38 | 39 | 98 | 98 |
| 2 | 35 | 39 | 40 | 100 | 100 |
| 3 | 37 | 41 | 41 | 102 | 102 |
| 4 | 39 | 42 | 42 | 103 | 103 |
| 5 | 41 | 44 | 43 | 105 | 105 |
| 6 | 42 | 46 | 44 | 107 | 106 |
| 7 | 44 | 47 | 45 | 109 | 108 |
| 8 | 46 | 49 | 46 | 110 | 110 |
| 9 | 47 | 50 | 47 | 112 | 111 |
| 10 | 49 | 52 | 48 | 114 | 113 |
| 11 | 51 | 54 | 49 | 115 | 114 |
| 12 | 52 | 55 | 50 | 117 | 116 |
| 13 | 54 | 57 | 51 | 119 | 118 |
| 14 | 56 | 58 | 52 | 120 | 119 |
| 15 | 58 | 60 | 53 | 122 | 121 |
| 16 | 59 | 62 | 54 | 124 | 122 |
| 17 | 61 | 63 | 55 | 126 | 124 |
| 18 | 63 | 65 | 56 | 127 | 126 |
| 19 | 64 | 66 | 57 | 129 | 127 |
| 20 | 66 | 68 | 58 | 131 | 129 |
| 21 | 68 | 70 | 59 | 132 | 130 |
| 22 | 69 | 71 | 60 | 134 | 132 |
| 23 | 71 | 73 | 61 | 136 | 134 |
| 24 | 73 | 74 | 62 | 137 | 135 |
| 25 | 75 | 76 | 63 | 139 | 137 |
| 26 | 76 | 78 | 64 | 141 | 138 |
| 27 | 78 | 79 | 65 | 143 | 140 |
| 28 | 80 | 81 | 66 | 144 | 142 |
| 29 | 81 | 82 | 67 | 146 | 143 |
| 30 | 83 | 84 | 68 | 148 | 145 |
| 31 | 85 | 86 | 69 | 149 | 146 |
| 32 | 86 | 87 | 70 | 151 | 148 |
| 33 | 88 | 89 | 71 | 153 | 150 |
| 34 | 90 | 90 | 72 | 154 | 151 |
| 35 | 92 | 92 | 73 | 156 | 153 |
| 36 | 93 | 94 | 74 | 158 | 154 |
| 37 | 95 | 95 | 75 | 160 | 156 |
| 38 | 97 | 97 | 76 | 161 | 158 |

*Note.* Abbreviations: BD = Block Design, PC = Picture Completion, I = Information, S = Similarities, Se = Sentences, GD = Geometric Design, V = Vocabulary, A = Arithmetic, C = Comprehension.

Reliability and validity coefficients associated with each short-form combination are shown in Table H-6. See Exhibit 6-3, page 138, for an explanation of the procedure used to obtain the estimated IQs.

# APPENDIX I

## WECHSLER INTELLIGENCE SCALE FOR CHILDREN—III (WISC-III): DESCRIPTION

*Mind is the great lever of all things; human thought is the process by which human ends are ultimately answered.*

—Daniel Webster

This chapter describes the Wechsler Intelligence Scale for Children—Third Edition (WISC-III), the latest version of the Wechsler scales for children ages 6 through 16 years (Wechsler, 1991[R][1]; see Figure I-1). The Psychological Corporation published the WISC-III in 1991, 17 years after the previous edition of the test, called the WISC-R (Wechsler, 1974). The primary reason for revising the test was to update the norms. Wechsler developed the earliest version of this test, known as the WISC (Wechsler, 1949), as a downward extension of the adult intelligence test, the Wechsler-Bellevue Intelligence Scale. To make the original adult scale more suitable for children, Wechsler added easier items to the beginnings of the subtests.

The WISC-III contains 13 subtests, 6 in the Verbal Scale and 7 in the Performance Scale. Five subtests in each scale are designated as standard subtests. In the Verbal Scale they are Information, Similarities, Arithmetic, Vocabu-

[1] References followed by an [R] are cited in this appendix; all other references are cited in the Reference section.

lary, and Comprehension. In the Performance Scale they are Picture Completion, Coding, Picture Arrangement, Block Design, and Object Assembly. The remaining three subtests—Digit Span in the Verbal Scale and Symbol Search and Mazes in the Performance Scale—are supplementary. Exhibit I-1 shows items similar to those on the WISC-III. About 73 percent of the WISC-R items are retained in the WISC-III (not including the Coding subtest), either in the original or slightly modified form. Symbol Search is a new subtest.

## STANDARDIZATION

The WISC-III was standardized on 2,200 children, 100 boys and 100 girls in each of 11 age groups from 6 through 16 years. The sample was stratified on age, race/ethnicity, geographic region, and parent education (used as a measure of socioeconomic status). For race/ethnic membership, children were classified as White, Black, Hispanic, or Other (composed of Native American, Eskimo, Aleut,

**Figure I-I.  Wechsler Intelligence Scale for Children—III.** Courtesy of The Psychological Corporation.

■ **Exhibit I-I**

**WISC-III–Like Items**

### Information (30 questions)

How many legs do you have?
What must you do to make water freeze?
Who discovered the North Pole?
What is the capital of France?

### Similarities (19 questions)

In what way are pencil and crayon alike?
In what way are tea and coffee alike?
In what way are inch and mile alike?
In what way are binoculars and microscope alike?

### Arithmetic (24 questions)

If I have one piece of candy and get another one, how many pieces will I have?
At 12 cents each, how much will 4 bars of soap cost?
If a suit sells for ½ of the regular price, what is the cost of a $120 suit?

### Vocabulary (30 words)

ball    summer    poem    obstreperous

### Comprehension (18 questions)

Why do we wear shoes?
What is the thing to do if you see someone dropping his packages?
In what two ways is a lamp better than a candle?
Why are we tried by a jury of our peers?

### Digit Span (15 items; 8 in Digits Forward, 7 in Digits Backward)

The task is to repeat digits presented by the examiner in a forward direction in one part (2 to 9 digits in length; example: 1-8) and in a backward direction in the other part (2 to 8 digits in length; example: 6-4-9).

### Picture Completion (30 items)

The task is to identify the essential missing part of the picture, such as (a) a car without a wheel, (b) a dog without a leg, and (c) a telephone without numbers on the dial (see below).

Courtesy of The Psychological Corporation.

### Coding (59 items in Coding A and 119 items in Coding B)

The task is to copy symbols from a key (see below).

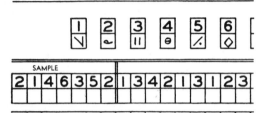

Courtesy of The Psychological Corporation.

### Picture Arrangement (14 items)

The task is to arrange a series of pictures into a meaningful sequence (see below).

Courtesy of The Psychological Corporation.

### Block Design (12 items)

The task is to reproduce stimulus designs using four or nine blocks (see below).

### Object Assembly (5 items)

The task is to arrange pieces into a meaningful object (see below).

Courtesy of The Psychological Corporation.

*(Exhibit continues next page)*

## Exhibit I-I (cont.)

**Symbol Search** (45 items in Part A and 45 items in Part B)

The task is to decide whether a stimulus figure (a symbol) appears in an array (see below).

Courtesy of The Psychological Corporation.

**Mazes** (10 items)

The task is to complete a series of mazes (see below).

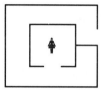

Courtesy of The Psychological Corporation.

Note. The questions resemble those that appear on the WISC-III but are not actually from the test, except for the sample items shown for Symbol Search and Mazes. Appendix J describes each subtest in more detail.

Asian, and Pacific Islander categories). The four geographical regions sampled were Northeast, North Central, South, and West. Within each age group, children were selected so that they matched as closely as possible the proportions found in the 1988 U.S. census data according to race/ethnicity, geographic region, and parent education.

Table I-1 shows the educational status and geographic location by race/ethnic group of the standardization sam-

ple. Parents in the White and Other classifications had the most education—51.5 percent of the White group and 57.2 percent of the Other group had some college education, whereas 27.9 percent of the Black group and 19.9 percent of the Hispanic group had some college education. The majority of the White and Black samples came from the North Central and South regions, whereas the majority of the Hispanic and Other samples came from the South and

**Table I-I**
**Demographic Characteristics of WISC-III Standardization Sample: Education and Geographic Region by Race/Ethnic Group**

| Demographic variable | Race/ethnic group (percent) | | | |
| --- | --- | --- | --- | --- |
| | White | Black | Hispanic | Other[a] |
| *Amount of education* | | | | |
| Eight years or less | 1.6 | 7.1 | 30.0 | 5.7 |
| Some high school | 8.6 | 22.7 | 23.6 | 8.6 |
| High school graduate | 38.4 | 42.2 | 26.4 | 28.6 |
| Some college | 29.4 | 18.8 | 14.5 | 22.9 |
| College graduate | 22.1 | 9.1 | 5.4 | 34.3 |
| Total | 100.1 | 99.9 | 99.9 | 100.1 |
| *Geographic region* | | | | |
| Northeast | 20.5 | 12.3 | 9.1 | 17.1 |
| North Central | 31.2 | 20.8 | 6.4 | 14.3 |
| South | 30.0 | 60.4 | 43.6 | 20.0 |
| West | 18.3 | 6.5 | 40.9 | 48.6 |
| Total | 100.0 | 100.0 | 100.0 | 100.0 |

*Note.* Race/ethnic distribution in total group was as follows: White = 70.1%, Black = 15.4%, Hispanic = 11.0%, Other = 3.5%.
[a] Other represents the following groups: Native American, Eskimo, Aleut, Asian, and Pacific Islander.
*Source:* Adapted from Wechsler (1991[R]).

West. The race/ethnic proportions in the sample were 70.1 percent White, 15.4 percent Black, 11.0 percent Hispanic, and 3.5 percent Other.

Tables 2.2 through 2.5 in the WISC-III manual (pages 23 to 26) indicate that parent education level was stratified within race, that race was stratified within geographic region, and that these variables match the census data with remarkable accuracy. The WISC-III sampling procedure is notably superior to that used on the WISC-R, which stratified race by White v. Non-white categories only. In addition, actual cases were used, without weighting for any demographic variable, to obtain the normative data. This sampling methodology was excellent.

## DEVIATION IQS, SCALED SCORES, AND TEST-AGE EQUIVALENTS

The WISC-III, like the WPPSI-R and WAIS-R, uses the Deviation IQ ($M = 100$, $SD = 15$) for the Verbal, Performance, and Full Scale IQs and scaled scores ($M = 10$, $SD = 3$) for the 13 individual subtests. An IQ is computed by comparing the examinee's scores with the scores earned by a representative sample of his or her age group. After each subtest is scored, raw scores are converted to scaled scores within the examinee's own age group through use of Table A.1 in the WISC-III manual (pages 217–249). Age groups are divided into four-month intervals between 6-0-0 (years, months, days) and 16-11-30.

The table in the WISC-III manual used to obtain IQs (Table A.4, pages 253–254) is based on the 10 standard subtests. The three supplementary subtests are *excluded* from the calculation of the IQ unless a standard subtest is either spoiled or not given. When a supplementary subtest is substituted for a standard subtest, little is known about the reliability and validity of the IQs generated by the altered combination of subtests, because none of the supplementary subtests were used in the construction of the tables used to generate IQs. In fact, there is no information at all in the WISC-III manual about what happens to the reliability and validity of the test when supplementary subtests are used to compute the IQ. There is one statement in the manual (page 5), however, that says that when a supplementary subtest was substituted for a standard subtest, mean changes ranged from .1 to .3 point. Nevertheless, be cautious when using supplementary subtests to compute an IQ.

The WISC-III manual provides guidelines for use of the three supplementary subtests. These guidelines, in part, state that Digit Span may substitute for any Verbal subtest, Mazes may substitute for any Performance subtest, and Symbol Search may substitute for Coding *only*. Unfortunately, the manual fails to discuss the manner in which these recommendations were reached. Why is it improper to substitute both Mazes and Symbol Search for other Performance subtests? It would have been helpful if The Psychological Corporation cited research findings to support its recommendations. [According to Aurelio Prifitera from The Psychological Corporation, this rule was designed to prevent the Performance IQ from being too heavily weighted with subtests that have relatively low $g$ loadings (personal communication, January 1992).]

### Prorating Procedure

When fewer than 10 subtests are administered, you can compute IQs either by prorating or by using a special short-form procedure designed to estimate the Verbal, Performance, and Full Scale IQs. Although the WISC-III manual provides a table (Table A.8, page 258) for prorating sums of scaled scores when you administer four subtests in each scale, I recommend that you use the Tellegen and Briggs (1967) procedure described in Exhibit I-4 in this chapter. The Tellegen and Briggs procedure considers the intercorrelations between the specific subtests administered to the child; prorating does not take this factor into account.

### Test-Age Equivalents

When David Wechsler first developed the WISC, he believed that the mental-age concept was potentially misleading and therefore decided not to use it in calculating IQs. (See pages 20–21 and 75–76 for criticisms associated with the mental-age concept.) Wechsler rejected the notion that mental age represents an absolute level of mental capacity or that the same mental age in different children represents identical intelligence levels. Soon after the initial publication of the WISC, however, he recognized that mental-age or test-age equivalents (the average age associated with a score on a subtest) would be useful. Therefore, in subsequent publications of the WISC, WISC-R, and WISC-III, test-age equivalents are provided (see Table A.9, page 259 in the WISC-III manual). Test-age equivalents are essentially mental age (MA) scores.

Test ages are obtained directly from the raw scores on each subtest. Because a scaled score of 10 represents the mean, the test-age equivalents of the raw scores shown in Table A.9 of the WISC-III manual can be understood as reflecting the average score for each particular age group. To obtain an *average* test-age equivalent, sum the individual subtest age equivalents and divide the sum by the number of subtests you added. To obtain a *median* test age, rank order test ages from high to low and locate the middle-most test age.

The WISC-III test-age equivalent scores can be compared with mental-age or test-age scores from other tests. They also can be used to help parents, teachers, and other individuals better understand the child's level of functioning. Research with the WISC-R suggests that test ages have adequate validity, based on high correlations with the Stanford-Binet: Form L-M mental age ($r = .88$) (Sutton, Koller, & Christian, 1982) and the Peabody Individual Achievement Test ($r = .82$) (Huberty & Koller, 1984). Similar studies are needed with the WISC-III.

**Table I-2**
**Average Internal Consistency Reliability Coefficients, Test-Retest Reliability Coefficients, and Standard Errors of Measurement for WISC-III Subtests and Scales**

| Subtest or scale | Average internal consistency $r_{xx}$ | Average test-retest $r_{tt}$ | Average $SE_m$ |
|---|---|---|---|
| Information | .84 | .85 | 1.23 |
| Similarities | .81 | .81 | 1.30 |
| Arithmetic | .78 | .74 | 1.41 |
| Vocabulary | .87 | .89 | 1.08 |
| Comprehension | .77 | .73 | 1.45 |
| Digit Span | .85 | .73 | 1.17 |
| Picture Completion | .77 | .81 | 1.44 |
| Coding | .79 | .77 | 1.42 |
| Picture Arrangement | .76 | .64 | 1.48 |
| Block Design | .87 | .77 | 1.11 |
| Object Assembly | .69 | .66 | 1.67 |
| Symbol Search | .76 | .74 | 1.48 |
| Mazes | .70 | .57 | 1.64 |
| Verbal Scale IQ | .95 | .94 | 3.53 |
| Performance Scale IQ | .91 | .87 | 4.54 |
| Full Scale IQ | .96 | .94 | 3.20 |

*Note.* Reliabilities for 11 of the 13 subtests (except Coding and Symbol Search) are split-half correlations. For Coding and Symbol Search, the reliability coefficients are test-retest coefficients obtained on a sample of about 60 children in six different age groups (retest interval not given in WISC-III manual). Verbal, Performance, and Full Scale reliability coefficients are based on a formula for computing the reliability of a composite group of tests. Digit Span, Mazes, and Symbol Search were not included in calculating the reliability coefficients for the Verbal, Performance, and Full Scale IQs.
*Source:* Adapted from Wechsler (1991[R]).

# RELIABILITY

The WISC-III has outstanding reliability. The three scales have internal consistency reliability coefficients of .89 or above over the entire age range covered in the standardization group. Average internal consistency reliability coefficients, based on the 11 age groups, are .96 for the Full Scale IQ, .95 for the Verbal Scale IQ, and .91 for the Performance Scale IQ (see Table I-2). The reliability coefficients for ages 6 to 16 years range from .94 to .97 for the Full Scale IQ, .92 to .96 for the Verbal Scale IQ, and .89 to .94 for the Performance Scale IQ. The lowest reliability coefficient is at 14 years for the Performance Scale IQ.

## Subtest Reliabilities

The internal consistency reliabilities for the subtests are lower than those for the three scales (see Table I-2). The average subtest internal consistency reliabilities range from a low of .69 for Object Assembly to a high of .87 for Vocabulary and Block Design. For the 11 age groups, median subtest reliabilities range from .76 at 13 years to .83 at 8 years (see Table I-3). Thus there are no sharp differences in subtest internal consistency reliabilities as a function of age.

## Standard Errors of Measurement

The average standard errors of measurement ($SE_m$) in IQ points are 3.20 for the Full Scale, 3.53 for the Verbal Scale, and 4.54 for the Performance Scale (see Table I-2). Thus,

**Table I-3**
**Range and Median Internal Consistency Reliabilities of WISC-III Subtests at 11 Age Groups**

| Age | Range of $r_{xx}$ | Median $r_{xx}$ |
|---|---|---|
| 6 | .69–.82 | .79 |
| 7 | .65–.84 | .77 |
| 8 | .65–.88 | .83 |
| 9 | .66–.85 | .80 |
| 10 | .69–.89 | .79 |
| 11 | .65–.88 | .79 |
| 12 | .66–.89 | .81 |
| 13 | .70–.90 | .76 |
| 14 | .60–.91 | .77 |
| 15 | .61–.92 | .82 |
| 16 | .67–.90 | .82 |
| Average | .69–.87 | .78 |

*Source:* Adapted from Wechsler (1991[R]).

as with all Wechsler scales, you can place more confidence in IQs based on the Full Scale than in those based on either the Verbal or the Performance Scale. In addition, you can place more confidence in IQs obtained from the Verbal Scale than in those obtained from the Performance Scale.

The average standard errors of measurement for the subtests in scaled-score points range from 1.08 to 1.45 for the Verbal Scale subtests and from 1.11 to 1.67 for the Performance Scale subtests. Within the Verbal Scale, Vocabulary has the smallest $SE_m$ (1.08), and Comprehension, the largest $SE_m$ (1.45). Within the Performance Scale, Block Design has the smallest $SE_m$ (1.11), and Object Assembly, the largest $SE_m$ (1.67).

## Test-Retest Reliability

In the standardization sample, the stability of the WISC-III was assessed by having 353 children from six age groups (6, 7, 10, 11, 14, 15 years) retested after an interval ranging from 12 to 63 days (*Mdn* = 23 days; Wechsler, 1991[R]). The six age groups were then combined to form three age groups for statistical analysis (6–7, 10–11, 14–15 years). In the three age groups, the stability coefficients were, respectively, .92, .95, and .94 for the Full Scale IQ; .90, .94, and .94 for the Verbal Scale IQ; and .86, .88, and .87 for the Performance Scale IQ. Thus, the WISC-III provides stable IQs for the Full Scale and Verbal Scale, but somewhat less stable IQs for the Performance Scale.

The stability coefficients for the subtests ranged from a low of .54 for Mazes at 14–15 years to a high of .93 for Vocabulary at these same ages. Average test-retest reliabilities for the subtests ranged from .57 for Mazes to .89 for Vocabulary (see Table I-2). As expected, internal consistency reliabilities are somewhat higher than average test-retest reliabilities (*Mdn* $r_{xx}$ = .78 versus *Mdn* $r_{xx}$ = .74).

**Changes in IQs.**    Table I-4 shows the mean test-retest IQs and standard deviations for the Verbal, Performance, and Full Scales for the three combined age groups. *On the average, from the first to the second testing, the Full Scale IQ increased by 7.0 to 8.4 points, the Verbal Scale IQ by 1.7 to 3.3 points, and the Performance Scale IQ by 11.5 to 13.5 points.* These increases, which likely result from practice effects, are therefore 4 to 6 times greater for the Performance Scale than for the Verbal Scale. Statistical tests that I performed indicated that all retest gains were significantly greater than chance. Studies will be needed to evaluate the stability of the WISC-III with other samples of children and over longer periods. Studies with the WISC-R (Haynes & Howard, 1986; Naglieri & Pfeiffer, 1983a) reported relatively stable IQs over a two-year interval (mean Verbal, Performance, and Full Scale IQ changes were less than 3 points).

The following may help to explain, in part, why there are greater gains on retest on the Performance subtests than on the Verbal subtests (Kaufman, 1990[R]). When children

**Table I-4**
**Test-Retest WISC-III IQs for Three Groups of Children**

| Age | Scale | First testing Mean IQ | First testing SD | Second testing Mean IQ | Second testing SD | Change |
|---|---|---|---|---|---|---|
| 6–7 | Verbal | 100.8 | 12.7 | 102.5 | 12.3 | + 1.7* |
| (*N* = 111) | Performance | 102.7 | 14.8 | 114.2 | 17.6 | +11.5** |
| | Full | 101.6 | 13.0 | 108.6 | 14.3 | + 7.0** |
| 10–11 | Verbal | 100.3 | 13.7 | 102.2 | 13.8 | + 1.9** |
| (*N* = 119) | Performance | 99.0 | 13.1 | 112.0 | 15.2 | +13.0** |
| | Full | 99.6 | 13.1 | 107.3 | 14.4 | + 7.7** |
| 14–15 | Verbal | 99.4 | 13.8 | 102.7 | 14.5 | + 3.3** |
| (*N* = 123) | Performance | 99.6 | 15.3 | 112.1 | 16.7 | +12.5** |
| | Full | 99.2 | 14.5 | 107.6 | 15.5 | + 8.4** |

*Note.* Test-retest intervals ranged from 12 to 63 days, with a median retest interval of 23 days. Table I-5 shows the *t*-test formula used to evaluate the mean changes.
  * $p < .01$.
 ** $p < .001$.
*Source:* Reprinted, with a change in notation, with permission from the publisher, from *WISC-III Manual* (Wechsler, 1991[R]), pages 170–172, copyright by The Psychological Corporation 1991.

are administered the Performance subtests on a second occasion, they may be able to recall the types of items they were given as well as the strategies they used on the tasks. Initially, the Performance subtests are more novel than the Verbal subtests, but this novelty diminishes on retesting. On retest, the Performance items become less novel, and perhaps more a test of long-term memory and ability to apply learning sets than a test of "adaptability and flexibility when faced with new problem-solving situations" (Kaufman, 1990[R], p. 205).

The large retest gains on the Performance Scale are of major concern when you readminister the WISC-III to children after a period of 2 to 9 weeks. For longer periods of time, however, gains on retest are likely to be lower because practice effects tend to diminish over time. The gains for the short time period were over $\frac{2}{3}$ of a standard deviation on the Performance Scale and about $\frac{1}{2}$ of a standard deviation on the Full Scale, on the average. This means that children are likely to do much better on a second administration of the WISC-III, especially on the Performance Scale. The gain may have nothing to do with their increased ability per se and may simply reflect exposure to the test materials (or practice effects).

Research is needed to determine how much children improve on retest over a longer period of time. Until such research is available, *you should carefully consider whether you want to use the WISC-III for repeated evaluations, especially if you plan to use the results obtained on the retest for placement, eligibility, or diagnostic decisions*. If you decide not to use the WISC-III for a reevaluation when you have given it on a prior occasion, consider using another individually administered well-standardized test of cognitive ability for the reexamination.

**Changes in subtest scores.** Table I-5 shows the changes in subtest scaled scores from the first to the second testing. The largest gains were for Picture Arrangement (increases of 2.7 to 3.3 scaled-score points), and the smallest gains were for Vocabulary (increases of 0 to .2 scaled-score point) and Comprehension (increases of 0 to .5 scaled-score point). In 34 of the 39 $t$ tests that I conducted to evaluate changes in subtest scores, the changes were significantly greater than chance. It is difficult to know why Picture Arrangement scores were higher by almost 1 standard deviation on retest, especially since its internal consistency reliability coefficient is at the median reliability of the Performance subtests. Perhaps, aided by the color of the pictures, the children retained a clear memory of the story elements of the pictures. On the second testing they then may have been able to solve the arrangements more quickly and accurately and gain bonus points.

**Table I-5**
**Test-Retest Gains on WISC-III Subtests for Three Groups of Children**

| | Ages | | |
| --- | --- | --- | --- |
| Subtest | 6–7 (N = 111) | 10–11 (N = 119) | 14–15 (N = 123) |
| Information | .4* | .3* | .7*** |
| Similarities | .5** | .7*** | 1.2*** |
| Arithmetic | .1 | .4* | .4* |
| Vocabulary | 0 | .2 | .2* |
| Comprehension | .5* | 0 | .3 |
| Digit Span | .6** | .7*** | .9*** |
| Picture Completion | 1.2*** | 2.0*** | 2.1*** |
| Coding | 1.8*** | 2.2*** | 1.9*** |
| Picture Arrangement | 3.3*** | 2.9*** | 2.7*** |
| Block Design | .9*** | 1.2*** | 1.0*** |
| Object Assembly | 1.5*** | 1.5*** | 1.7*** |
| Symbol Search | 1.8*** | 1.4*** | 1.4*** |
| Mazes | 1.1*** | 1.0*** | 1.0*** |

*Note.* Test-retest intervals range from 12 to 63 days, with a median retest interval of 23 days. The $t$ test used to evaluate the mean changes on each subtest employed a repeated measures formula:

$$t = \frac{M_1 - M_2}{\sqrt{\left(\frac{SD_1}{\sqrt{N_1}}\right)^2 + \left(\frac{SD_2}{\sqrt{N_2}}\right)^2 - 2r_{12}\left(\frac{SD_1}{\sqrt{N_1}}\right)\left(\frac{SD_2}{\sqrt{N_2}}\right)}}$$

* $p < .05$.
** $p < .01$.
*** $p < .001$.
*Source:* Means and standard deviations obtained from Wechsler (1991[R]), pages 170–172.

The relationship between the gain scores on the subtests and the internal consistency reliabilities of the subtests also is helpful in evaluating the gain scores (personal communication, Leslie Atkinson, January 1992). The moderately negative relationship that was found between these variables (Spearman rank-order correlation of $-.50$, $p < .05$, one-tailed test) suggests that practice effects acted on error variance in such a way as to increase scores on the subtests in inverse proportion to their reliability — there was a tendency for the more reliable subtests to have somewhat smaller gain scores.

**Confidence Intervals**

This text provides two types of confidence intervals. The first type is based solely on the child's obtained score (or IQ) and uses the conventional standard error of measurement. The second type is based on the estimated true score (soon to be discussed) and the standard error of measurement associated with the estimated true score (also referred to as the *standard error of estimation*). The WISC-III manual, in contrast, provides confidence intervals based on the estimated true score only. The following guidelines will help you to select which type of confidence interval to use.

Although confidence intervals can be used for every score obtained by the child, I recommend that you use them primarily for the Full Scale IQ because it is this score that is usually used to make diagnostic and classification decisions. *Individuals who use the test findings need to know that the primary score used to make decisions about the child is not perfectly accurate because it has some inherent measurement error.* Consequently, it is important to give confidence intervals when you report the test results.

**Confidence interval for obtained score without reference to the estimated true score.**   When the confidence interval is based solely on the obtained score, without reference to the estimated true score, the standard error of measurement for obtained scores is used. The formula for obtaining the standard error of measurement (also shown in Chapter 2, page 28) is as follows:

$$SE_m = SD\sqrt{1 - r_{xx}}$$

Confidence intervals associated with the 68, 85, 90, 95, and 99 percent levels of confidence can be obtained by multiplying the standard error of measurement by the appropriate z value (namely, 1.00, 1.44, 1.65, 1.96, and 2.58, respectively). (See pages 28 and 29 for further discussion of confidence intervals using the conventional method.)

Glutting, McDermott, and Stanley (1987[R]) pointed out that if you want to answer the question "What is the best measure of an examinee's *current* functioning in the performance area assessed by a specific test?" (p. 613), then the proper score to interpret is the obtained score, without recourse to the estimated true score. They base their recommendation on the following line of reasoning:

The obtained score is the proper score to interpret . . . because the question pertains exclusively to a single examinee on a given test at a particular point in time. Moreover, long-standing conventions in clinical practice, contemporary social policy, and law require that psychologists use obtained scores for diagnostic and classificatory decisions. . . .

In instances where a single examinee is tested alone, and not as a member of an explicit group, the expected error of measurement (in the statistical sense) is zero because the examinee's score

is the mean of the group ($N = 1$) and the obtained score "regresses" toward this mean because of error of measurement. For the lone-tested individual, confidence limits must be constructed around the obtained score by using the standard error of measurement procedure. . . . The standard error of measurement is a *personal* statistic that, theoretically, is computable for a single examinee and independent of a test's reliability and mean. It yields confidence limits that are applicable when the psychologist does not know to which specific subgroup of the general population the examinee belongs. In diagnostic classification, because one cannot presume to know beforehand the resultant assignment of an examinee to a specific clinical or exceptional subgroup, psychologists are compelled to use scores and confidence limits that are personally focused. (pp. 612–613)

Table L-1 in Appendix L shows the confidence intervals, by age, for the Verbal, Performance, and Full Scale WISC-III IQs based on the obtained score and the conventional standard error of measurement—that is, without recourse to the estimated true score or the standard error of estimation. Use of the child's specific age group allows you to obtain the most accurate confidence interval.

**Confidence limits for obtained scores with reference to the estimated true score.**   Glutting et al. (1987[R]) also pointed out that if you are interested in answering the question "What is the best *long-run* (stable) measure of an examinee's functioning in the performance area assessed by a specific test *relative to other examinees in a particular reference group*?" (p. 612), then the proper score to interpret is the estimated true score. They go on to note that

the "reference group" could include all examinees in the standardization sample for the test, or some independent clinical subgroup of those examinees (e.g., the gifted or mentally retarded), or examinees comprising subsets similar to the examinee in age, sex, score level, and other relevant characteristics. In this situation, the estimated true score . . . is the appropriate score for interpretation, as it considers the mean and reliability for the specific reference group in question and corrects for mean regression on that basis. (p. 613)

Table L-2 in Appendix L shows the confidence intervals, by age, for the WISC-III Full Scale, Verbal, and Performance IQs based on the estimated true score and the appropriate standard error of measurement. The confidence intervals in Table L-2, as noted below, are applied to the obtained score just as they are in Table L-1. You can also use this table for the WPPSI-R and WAIS-R, and for any test with $M = 100$ and $SD = 15$ that has a reliability coefficient of .85 to .98. The formula used to obtain the estimated true score is as follows:

$$T = r_{xx}X + (1 - r_{xx})\overline{X}$$

where  $T$ = estimated true score
$r_{xx}$ = reliability of the test
$X$ = obtained score
$\overline{X}$ = mean of test.

The formula used to obtain the standard error of estimation ($SE_E$) is as follows:

$$SE_E = r_{xx}SE_m$$

where  $SE_E$ = standard error of estimation (or standard error of measurement of the true score)
$r_{xx}$ = reliability of the test
$SE_m$ = standard error of measurement of the test.

Thus the estimated true score for an obtained WISC-III Full Scale IQ of 60 (where $r_{xx}$ = .96) would be $T$ = .96(60) + .04(100) = 57.60 + 4 = 62. And the standard error of estimation would be $SE_E$ = .96(3.20) = 3.07.

Because the confidence intervals are centered around the estimated true score, the intervals become asymmetrical when applied to the obtained score. The asymmetry is greatest for values farthest from the mean because regression to the mean is greater at the extremes of the distribution than at the center of the distribution. In fact, for scores at the mean, there is no asymmetry at all—the confidence intervals are equal around the mean (see Figure I-2, Section L). The procedure used to obtain the confidence intervals in Table L-2 is the same as that used in the construction of the confidence intervals in the WISC-III manual.

To use Table L-2 in Appendix L, follow this procedure. First, use the chart at the beginning of the table to find which section of the table represents the examinee's age, the appropriate test (WISC-III, WPPSI-R, or WAIS-R), and the appropriate scale (that is, Full Scale, Verbal Scale, or Performance Scale). Then select one confidence level from the columns labeled 68%, 85%, 90%, 95%, and

**K. WISC-III—Verbal Scale—Ages 10, 11, 12, 14, 16, and Average; WISC-III—Full Scale—Ages 6, 9, 11, 13, and 14; WPPSI-R—Performance Scale—Age 5; WPPSI-R—Verbal Scale—Average; WPPSI-R—Full Scale—Ages 5½, 6, and 6½; WAIS-R—Verbal Scale—Ages 16–17 ($r_{xx}$ = .95)**

| 68% | | | 85% | | | 90% | | | 95% | | | 99% | | |
|---|---|---|---|---|---|---|---|---|---|---|---|---|---|---|
| IQ | L | U | IQ | L | U | IQ | L | U | IQ | L | U | IQ | L | U |
| 40–46 | 0 | 6 | 40–41 | − 2 | 8 | 40–44 | − 2 | 8 | 40–45 | − 3 | 9 | 40–45 | − 5 | 11 |
| 47–53 | − 1 | 6 | 42–58 | − 2 | 7 | 45–55 | − 3 | 8 | 46–54 | − 4 | 9 | 46–54 | − 6 | 11 |

**L. WISC-III—Verbal Scale—Ages 8 and 15; WISC-III—Full Scale—Ages 8, 10, 12, 16, and Average; WPPSI-R—Performance Scale—Ages 3, 3½, 4, and 4½; WPPSI-R—Full Scale—Age 5 and Average; WAIS-R—Verbal Scale—Ages 18–19 and 20–24; WAIS-R—Full Scale—Ages 16–17 and 18–19 ($r_{xx}$ = .96)**

| 68% | | | 85% | | | 90% | | | 95% | | | 99% | | |
|---|---|---|---|---|---|---|---|---|---|---|---|---|---|---|
| IQ | L | U | IQ | L | U | IQ | L | U | IQ | L | U | IQ | L | U |
| 91–109 | − 3 | 3 | 92–108 | − 4 | 4 | 94–106 | − 5 | 5 | 97–103 | − 6 | 6 | 99–101 | − 7 | 7 |
| 110–115 | − 3 | 2 | 109–116 | − 5 | 4 | 107–118 | − 5 | 4 | 104–121 | − 6 | 5 | 102–123 | − 8 | 7 |

**M. WISC-III—Full Scale—Age 15; WPPSI-R—Full Scale—Ages 3, 3½, 4, and 4½; WAIS-R—Verbal Scale—Ages 25–34, 35–44, 45–54, 55–64, 65–69, 70–74, and Average; WAIS-R—Full Scale—Ages 20–24, 45–54, 55–64, 70–74, and Average ($r_{xx}$ = .97)**

| 68% | | | 85% | | | 90% | | | 95% | | | 99% | | |
|---|---|---|---|---|---|---|---|---|---|---|---|---|---|---|
| IQ | L | U | IQ | L | U | IQ | L | U | IQ | L | U | IQ | L | U |
| 133–134 | − 4 | 2 | 130–137 | − 5 | 3 | 144–155 | − 6 | 3 | 148–152 | − 6 | 3 | 101–133 | − 7 | 6 |
| 135–160 | − 4 | 1 | 138–160 | − 5 | 2 | 156–160 | − 6 | 2 | 153–160 | − 7 | 3 | 134–160 | − 8 | 5 |

**Figure I-2.** Part of Table L-2 in Appendix L showing WISC-III confidence intervals based on the estimated true score.

99%. The absolute values in the table under the appropriate confidence level will allow you to calculate the lower (L) and upper (U) limits of the confidence interval for the obtained IQ. If the sign is *positive* before the absolute value (no sign precedes the value and the + sign is understood), *add* the absolute value to the obtained IQ. If the sign is *negative* before the absolute value (a − sign precedes the absolute value), *subtract* the absolute value from the obtained IQ. In most cases, the lower limits are found by subtracting an absolute value from the obtained IQ, and the upper limits are found by adding an absolute value to the obtained IQ.

Here are three examples of how to calculate the confidence intervals.

1. To calculate the confidence interval for a 6-year-old child who obtains a WISC-III Full Scale IQ of 46, see Table L-2, Section K, in Appendix L. Section K shows that the absolute values for the lower and upper limits of the confidence interval are 0 and 6 at the 68 percent confidence level, respectively. (Figure I-2 shows the parts of Table L-2 that relate to the three examples in this section.) Because both signs are positive, you can obtain the lower and upper limits of the confidence interval by adding these absolute values to the obtained IQ. The resulting confidence interval is 46 to 52 (lower limit is 46 + 0 = 46; upper limit is 46 + 6 = 52).

2. For a 10-year-old child who obtains a WISC-III Full Scale IQ of 100, see Table L-2, Section L, in Appendix L. Section L shows that the absolute values at the 90 percent confidence level are 5 (preceded by a − sign) and 5 (preceded by a + sign) for the lower and upper limits of the confidence interval, respectively (see Figure I-2). To find the lower limit, subtract the absolute value in the column labeled "L" from the obtained IQ (100 − 5 = 95). To find the upper limit, add the absolute value in the column labeled "U" to the obtained IQ (100 + 5 = 105). Thus the confidence interval is 95 to 105.

3. For a 15-year-old child who obtains a WISC-III Full Scale IQ of 155, see Table L-2, Section M, in Appendix L. At the 99 percent confidence level, Section M shows that the appropriate absolute values are 8 (preceded by a − sign) and 5 (preceded by a + sign) for the lower and upper limits of the confidence interval, respectively (see Figure I-2). To find the lower limit, subtract the absolute value in the column labeled "L" from the obtained IQ (155 − 8 = 147). To find the upper limit, add the absolute value in the column labeled "U" to the obtained IQ (155 + 5 = 160). The confidence interval then is 147 to 160.

Note that although the values for the confidence intervals are obtained for the estimated true score, they are applied to the obtained score. Also note that the estimated true score is not given in the report. It is used only to generate the confidence interval.

Table L-2 in Appendix L is based on the child's age and not on average values for the total sample; this is in contrast to the WISC-III manual, where the confidence intervals are based on the total sample. *Use of the child's specific age group allows you to obtain the most accurate confidence interval.*

**Comment on confidence intervals.**    In clinical and psychoeducational assessments, questions usually center on how the child is functioning at the time of the referral. Therefore, I recommend that you use the confidence interval based on the child's obtained score, without recourse to the child's estimated true score. If you follow this recommendation, use the confidence intervals for the obtained score and the conventional standard error of measurement—Table L-1 in Appendix L; the WISC-III manual does not provide a similar table. However, when you want to provide information about how the child might perform over a longer period of time in relation to a specific reference group, then use the confidence interval based on the estimated true score—Table L-2 in Appendix L. Again, the confidence intervals shown in Table L-2 are more appropriate than those shown in the WISC-III manual because they are based on the child's specific age.

## VALIDITY

Because the WISC-III is a newly published test, little is known about its validity, aside from the studies reported in the WISC-III manual. Although approximately 27 percent of the items on the WISC-III are new, much of the research on the validity of the WISC-R probably applies to the WISC-III. Studies related to the validity of the WISC-R, reviewed on pages 123–125 of this text, indicate that the WISC-R has adequate construct, concurrent, and predictive validity for many different types of normal and handicapped children in the age range covered by the test. Let us now look at the studies reported in the WISC-III manual.

### Concurrent Validity

The concurrent validity studies cited below of the WISC-III with the WISC-R, WAIS-R, and WPPSI-R do not allow us to determine with precision how WISC-III IQs compare with those on the other Wechsler tests. This is because the WISC-III was administered in counterbalanced order with another Wechsler test (that is, the two test administrations were alternated). The resulting scores on the second test are thus confounded by practice effects – the second test was influenced by the child's exposure to the first test. In order to know whether scores on two tests differ, we need to have data from independent test administrations. In the studies reported in the WISC-III manual, the independent test data would be from the first test administration *only*; however, these data were not reported. Therefore, you must interpret cautiously the tables in the WISC-III manual that show the means and standard deviations for the WISC-III and other Wechsler tests (that is, Tables 6.8, 6.10, and 6.12); all mean scores in these tables are based on the average of the two orders of administration. The means in these tables are probably a bit higher because of practice effects.

1. *WISC-III and WISC-R.* Two studies are reported in the WISC-III manual regarding concurrent validity between the WISC-III and WISC-R. In the first study, a sample of 206 normal children between the ages of 6 and 16 years (*Mdn* = 11 years) were administered the WISC-III and WISC-R in counterbalanced order. The interval between the two tests ranged from 12 to 70 days (*Mdn* = 21 days). The correlations were .90 for the Verbal Scale, .81 for the Performance Scale, and .89 for the Full Scale.

Full Scale IQs on the WISC-III were 5.3 points *lower*, on the average, than those on the WISC-R (WISC-III *M* IQ = 102.9, *SD* = 14.7; WISC-R *M* IQ = 108.2, *SD* = 15.1). Similarly, IQs on the Verbal Scale and Performance Scale were *lower* on the WISC-III than on the WISC-R by 2.4 and 7.4 points, respectively, on the average. These results agree with previous findings that individuals almost invariably score lower on newer tests than on older ones (Flynn, 1984[R], 1987[R]).

For the 12 subtests that the WISC-III and the WISC-R have in common, correlations ranged from a low of .42 for Picture Arrangement to a high of .80 for Information (*Mdn r* = .685). Correlations between subtests on the Verbal Scale were slightly higher (range of .67 to .80, *Mdn r* = .725) than those on the Performance Scale (range of .42 to .76, *Mdn r* = .575). This pattern suggests that the Verbal subtests on the WISC-III and WISC-R have more in common than do the Performance subtests. It is not clear why the correlations between the subtests on the two tests were not higher, given that approximately 73 percent of the items are the same on both tests.

In the second study, a sample of 104 children, composed primarily of children with learning difficulties, reading difficulties, or attention deficit hyperactivity disorders, were administered the WISC-III and WISC-R in counterbalanced order. The correlations were .86 for the Verbal

Scale, .73 for the Performance Scale, and .86 for the Full Scale. Full Scale IQs on the WISC-III were 5.9 points *lower*, on the average, than those on the WISC-R. Similarly, IQs on the Verbal and Performance Scales were *lower* on the WISC-III than on the WISC-R by 5.4 and 5.1 points, respectively, on the average.

2. *WISC-III and WAIS-R.* Because the WISC-III and WAIS-R overlap at ages 16 to 17 years, it is important to know the relationship between the two tests for this age group. In a sample of 189 16-year-old normal adolescents, the WISC-III and WAIS-R were administered in counterbalanced order. The interval between the two tests ranged from 12 to 70 days (*Mdn* = 21 days). The correlations were .90 for the Verbal Scale, .80 for the Performance Scale, and .86 for the Full Scale.

Full Scale IQs on the WISC-III were 3.9 points *lower*, on the average, than those on the WAIS-R (WISC-III *M* IQ = 101.4, *SD* = 15; WAIS-R *M* IQ = 105.3, *SD* = 14.9). Similarly, IQs on the Verbal and Performance Scales were *lower* on the WISC-III than on the WAIS-R by 1.5 and 5.9 points, respectively, on the average.

For the 11 subtests that the WISC-III and the WAIS-R have in common, correlations ranged from a low of .35 for Picture Arrangement to a high of .85 for Vocabulary (*Mdn r* = .67). Correlations between subtests on the Verbal Scale were higher (range of .51 to .85, *Mdn r* = .72) than those on the Performance Scale (range of .35 to .79, *Mdn r* = .52). This pattern, like that for the WISC-III and WISC-R, suggests that WISC-III and WAIS-R Verbal subtests have more in common than do the Performance subtests.

3. *WISC-III and WPPSI-R.* Because the WISC-III overlaps with the WPPSI-R in the age range of 6 to 7-3 years, it is important to know the relationship between the two tests for this age group. The WISC-III and WPPSI-R were administered in counterbalanced order to 188 normal 6-year-old children. The interval between the two tests ranged from 12 to 62 days (*Mdn* = 21 days). The correlations were .85 for the Verbal Scale, .73 for the Performance Scale, and .85 for the Full Scale. These correlations are somewhat inflated because the two tests have as many as 35 items in common.

Full Scale IQs on the WISC-III were 4.0 points *higher* than those on the WPPSI-R. Similarly, IQs on the Verbal and Performance Scales were *higher* on the WISC-III than on the WPPSI-R by 1.9 and 5.9 points, respectively.

4. *WISC-III and other measures of ability and achievement.* Table I-6 summarizes correlations between the WISC-III and seven different measures of ability or achievement. The WISC-III Full Scale correlates highly with the Total Index of the Otis-Lennon School Ability Test

**Table I-6**
**Summary of WISC-III Criterion Validity Studies Cited in the WISC-III Manual**

| | WISC-III | | |
| | Verbal Scale | Performance Scale | Full Scale |
|---|---|---|---|
| Criterion | | | |
| *Otis-Lennon School Ability Test* | | | |
| Verbal Index | .69 | .59 | .73 |
| Nonverbal Index | .44 | .59 | .58 |
| Total Index | .64 | .65 | .73 |
| *Differential Ability Scales* | | | |
| Verbal | .87 | .31 | .71 |
| Nonverbal | .58 | .78 | .81 |
| Spatial | .66 | .82 | .86 |
| General Conceptual | .82 | .80 | .92 |
| Basic Number | .55 | .34 | .54 |
| Spelling | .54 | .29 | .51 |
| Word Reading | .54 | .41 | .58 |
| *Wide Range Achievement Test—Revised* | | | |
| Reading | .62 | .29 | .53 |
| Spelling | .41 | .11 | .28 |
| Arithmetic | .61 | .40 | .58 |
| *Halstead-Reitan Neuropsychological Battery* | | | |
| Tactual Performance Test—Memory | .19 | .45 | .37 |
| Finger Tapping | −.40 | −.37 | −.45 |
| *Benton Revised Visual Retention Test* | .15 | .47 | .37 |
| *Group-administered achievement tests*[a] | | | |
| Total | .74 | .57 | .74 |
| Reading | .70 | .43 | .66 |
| Mathematics | .63 | .58 | .68 |
| Written Language | .56 | .46 | .57 |
| *School grades* | | | |
| GPA | .42 | .39 | .47 |
| Mathematics | .35 | .35 | .41 |
| English | .36 | .31 | .40 |
| Reading | .44 | .39 | .48 |
| Spelling | .28 | .32 | .36 |

*Note.* The WISC-III manual presents means, standard deviations, and other statistical information about the studies in this table.
[a] See the WISC-III manual for a description of these tests.
*Source*: Adapted from Wechsler (1991[R]).

($r = .73$) and with the General Conceptual Ability score of the Differential Ability Scales ($r = .92$). Correlations between the WISC-III Full Scale and the Wide Range Achievement Test—Revised (WRAT-R) and the Differential Ability Scales achievement tests are for the most part in the .50s. The one exception is the .28 correlation between the WISC-III Full Scale and WRAT-R Spelling. Correlations between the WISC-III Full Scale and the reading, mathematics, and written language sections of group-administered achievement tests are in the high .50s and .60s. Correlations between the WISC-III Full Scale and measures of visual-motor speed or copying are usually in the .30s to .40s. Finally, correlations between the WISC-III Full Scale and school grades are in the .30s and .40s.

## Predictive Validity

Two predictive validity studies are reported in the WISC-III manual. In the first study, the WISC-III was compared with the WISC-R, which had been administered about 13 months earlier (range of 5 to 20 months) to a sample of 23 gifted children (ages and IQs not reported). Full Scale IQs on the WISC-III were 4.9 points *lower*, on the average, than those on the WISC-R. Similarly, IQs on the Verbal and Performance Scales were *lower* on the WISC-III than on the WISC-R by 5.8 and 1.1 points, respectively, on the average.

In the second study, the WISC-III was compared with the WISC-R, which had been administered about 26 months earlier (range of 14 to 37 months), on the average, to a sample of 28 mentally retarded children (ages and IQs not reported). Full Scale IQs on the WISC-III were 8.9 points *lower*, on the average, than those on the WISC-R. Similarly, IQs on the Verbal Scale and Performance Scale were *lower* on the WISC-III than on the WISC-R by 8.9 and 6.8 points, respectively.

The results of these two predictive validity studies with small samples of exceptional children suggest, if replicated, that children will obtain *lower* scores on the WISC-III than on the WISC-R. In fact, after a 2-year interval, mentally retarded children may obtain Full Scale IQs on the WISC-III that are approximately *9 points lower* than those they obtained on the WISC-R. Similarly, after a 1-year interval, gifted children may obtain Full Scale IQs on the WISC-III that are about *5 points lower* than those they had on the WISC-R. You should not consider decrements of these magnitudes to reflect meaningful changes in the child's ability. Rather, interpret the changes simply as scores on two different tests that, although highly similar, have different norms. Nevertheless, large differences between scores on the WISC-III and the WISC-R may reflect meaningful changes in the child's ability.

## Construct Validity

The maximum-likelihood factor analysis and the principal components analysis cited later in this chapter, as well as the factor analyses cited in the WISC-III manual, indicate that the test adequately measures two factors that correspond to the Verbal and Performance Scales of the test. In addition, the test provides a fair measure of general intelligence. Thus, there is support for the construct validity of the WISC-III.

## Comment on the Validity of the WISC-III

The validity studies in the WISC-III manual suggest that the WISC-III has adequate concurrent and construct validity. The validity coefficients reported in the WISC-III manual are similar to those reported for the WISC-R. Thus, there is every reason to believe that studies using such criteria as other intelligence tests, achievement tests, and school grades will find the WISC-III to be a valid instrument.

You should not consider either the WISC-III and WAIS-R or the WISC-III and WPPSI-R to be parallel forms in the overlapping age groups. The WISC-III yields *lower* Full Scale IQs than the WAIS-R by about 4 points and *higher* Full Scale IQs than the WPPSI-R by about 4 points. We do not know to what extent these generalizations hold for handicapped children or exceptional children, and particularly for children at the lower or upper levels of the IQ distribution.

If you administer either the WAIS-R or the WPPSI-R *after* the WISC-III (or vice versa), small changes on the second test may have nothing to do with any intervening events in the child's life. Rather, the changes are likely to be associated with errors of measurement, different norm groups, or practice effects. For example, almost 11 years separate the standardization of the WISC-III and WAIS-R, and 2 years separate the standardization of the WISC-III and WPPSI-R. We do not know why the WISC-III yields *higher* IQs than the WPPSI-R and *lower* IQs than the WAIS-R.

Investigators need to replicate and extend all results reported in the WISC-III manual to different samples of children. Investigators also need to study how the WISC-III compares to the Stanford-Binet Intelligence Scale—4th Edition, K-ABC, and other individually administered measures of intellectual ability and to study how handicapped or exceptional children perform on the WISC-III.

## INTERCORRELATIONS BETWEEN SUBTESTS AND SCALES

Inspection of the intercorrelations between WISC-III subtests and scales (see Table C.12, page 281 in the WISC-III manual) indicates that in the total group, correlations between the 13 subtests range from a low of .14 (Mazes and Digit Span) to a high of .70 (Vocabulary and Information; *Mdn r* = .355). The six highest subtest average intercorrelations are between Vocabulary and Information (.70), Vocabulary and Similarities (.69), Similarities and Information (.66), Comprehension and Vocabulary (.64), Comprehension and Similarities (.59), and Arithmetic and Information (.57). The seven lowest subtest average intercorrelations are between Mazes and Digit Span (.14), Mazes and Coding (.15), Mazes and Vocabulary (.17), Mazes and Comprehension (.17), Mazes and Similarities (.18), Mazes and Information (.18), and Coding and Picture Completion (.18). (Seven are given instead of six because of tied ranks.)

In the total group, the Verbal Scale subtests correlate more highly with each other (*Mdn r* = .55) than do the Performance Scale subtests (*Mdn r* = .33). Average correlations between the Verbal Scale subtests and the Verbal Scale range from .42 to .78 (*Mdn r* = .72); those between the Performance Scale subtests and the Performance Scale range from .32 to .65 (*Mdn r* = .45). Thus, the Verbal subtests have more in common with each other than do the Performance subtests (see Table I-7).

Average correlations between the 13 individual subtests and the Full Scale range from .31 to .74 (*Mdn r* = .58). Vocabulary has the highest correlation with the Full Scale (.74), followed by Information (.72), Similarities (.72), Block Design (.66), Arithmetic (.65), Comprehension (.64), Picture Completion (.58), Object Assembly (.58), Symbol Search (.56), Picture Arrangement (.52), Digit Span (.43), Coding (.33), and Mazes (.31). These findings indicate that the five standard Verbal subtests plus Block Design correlate more highly with the Full Scale than do the other subtests (see Table I-7). Vocabulary has the highest correlation with the Verbal Scale (.78), and Block Design has the highest correlation with the Performance Scale (.65).

**Table I-7**
**Average Correlations Between WISC-III Subtests and Scales**

| Subtest | Verbal Scale | Performance Scale | Full Scale |
|---|---|---|---|
| Information | .75 | .55 | .72 |
| Similarities | .75 | .55 | .72 |
| Arithmetic | .62 | .54 | .65 |
| Vocabulary | .78 | .56 | .74 |
| Comprehension | .67 | .49 | .64 |
| Digit Span | .42 | .35 | .43 |
| Picture Completion | .52 | .54 | .58 |
| Coding | .29 | .32 | .33 |
| Picture Arrangement | .45 | .49 | .52 |
| Block Design | .57 | .65 | .66 |
| Object Assembly | .48 | .60 | .58 |
| Symbol Search | .44 | .58 | .56 |
| Mazes | .23 | .35 | .31 |

*Source:* Adapted from Wechsler (1991[R]), Table C.12 (page 281).

## WISC-III AND PARENT EDUCATION

Table I-8 shows the relationship between WISC-III IQs and level of parent education reported in a study by Granier and O'Donnell (1991[R]). Their sample consisted of 1,194 children, ages 6 through 16 years, who were part of the WISC-III standardization group. Children whose parents had a college education had higher IQs (*M* IQ = 106.01) than children whose parents had a ninth grade education or less (*M* IQ = 86.38), a difference of about 20 points. These findings are similar to those found on the WISC-R

**Table I-8**
**Relationship Between Parent Education Level and WISC-III IQs**

| Parent education level | Verbal IQ | Performance IQ | Full Scale IQ |
|---|---|---|---|
| Less than 9th grade | 85.60 | 89.80 | 86.38 |
| 9th through 11th grade | 91.63 | 94.04 | 92.10 |
| High school diploma | 97.82 | 98.33 | 97.72 |
| Some college | 100.84 | 100.92 | 100.82 |
| College graduate | 106.03 | 105.17 | 106.01 |

*Source:* Reprinted with permission of the authors, M. Granier and L. O'Donnell (1991[R]), *Children's WISC-III scores: Impact of parent education and home environment.* Copyright 1991 by The Psychological Corporation.

(see pages 126 and 128 of this text), even though parent occupation – instead of parent education – was used on the WISC-R as a stratification variable.

## FACTOR ANALYSIS

I performed a maximum-likelihood factor analysis of the standardization group for each age group and for the total sample for 2, 3, and 4 factor solutions using BMDP4M (version 1990). The results suggested that a three-factor model best characterizes the WISC-III (see Table I-9). These factors may be labeled Verbal Comprehension, Perceptual Organization, and Processing Speed. The three factors account for 25, 16, and 10 percent of the variance, respectively. Thus the Processing Speed factor accounts for less variance than do the Verbal Comprehension and Perceptual Organization factors.

The term *Verbal Comprehension* describes the hypothesized ability underlying the factor for both item content (verbal) and mental process (comprehension). This factor appears to measure a variable common to most of the Verbal Scale subtests. For the total sample, Vocabulary, Information, Comprehension, and Similarities have the highest loadings on the Verbal Comprehension factor, followed by Arithmetic, which has a moderate loading, and Digit Span, which has a minimal loading. Three Performance Scale subtests – Picture Completion, Picture Arrangement, and Block Design – also have minimal loadings on the Verbal Comprehension factor. It may be that verbal processing is involved in successful performance on Picture Completion and Picture Arrangement and that the high *g* loadings associated with Block Design (see below) explain its correlation with Verbal Comprehension. It also may be that these three Performance Scale subtests, together with the Verbal Scale subtests, are highly related to a more general cognitive factor.

The term *Perceptual Organization* describes the hypothesized ability underlying the factor for both item content (perceptual) and mental process (organization). This factor appears to measure a variable common to several of the Performance Scale subtests. For the total sample, Block Design and Object Assembly have high loadings on the Perceptual Organization factor, followed by Picture Completion, which has a moderate loading, and Mazes, Picture Arrangement, and Symbol Search, which have minimal loadings.

The term *Processing Speed* describes the hypothesized ability underlying the factor for both item content (perceptual processing) and mental process (speed). This factor appears to reflect the ability to employ a high degree of

**Table I-9**
**Factor Loadings of WISC-III Subtests for II Age Groups Following Maximum-Likelihood Factor Analysis (Varimax Rotation)**

| Subtest | 6 | 7 | 8 | 9 | 10 | 11 | 12 | 13 | 14 | 15 | 16 | Av.[a] |
|---|---|---|---|---|---|---|---|---|---|---|---|---|
| | | | | | | Age | | | | | | |
| **Factor A – Verbal Comprehension** | | | | | | | | | | | | |
| Information | 70 | 72 | 77 | 70 | 74 | 69 | 79 | 79 | 74 | 82 | 82 | 75 |
| Similarities | 76 | 66 | 79 | 77 | 80 | 70 | 74 | 68 | 75 | 73 | 77 | 75 |
| Arithmetic | 59 | 41 | 56 | 46 | 63 | 35 | 58 | 46 | 64 | 51 | 58 | 55 |
| Vocabulary | 65 | 75 | 76 | 87 | 88 | 79 | 84 | 82 | 87 | 81 | 83 | 82 |
| Comprehension | 58 | 72 | 70 | 60 | 69 | 63 | 73 | 65 | 71 | 58 | 70 | 68 |
| Digit Span | 50 | 29 | 36 | 31 | 38 | 24 | 24 | 25 | 36 | 36 | 28 | 34 |
| Picture Completion | 37 | 22 | 38 | 43 | 48 | 42 | 36 | 30 | 47 | 51 | 36 | 39 |
| Coding | 00 | 06 | 12 | 16 | 16 | 13 | 14 | 13 | 16 | 13 | 07 | 13 |
| Picture Arrangement | 41 | 33 | 40 | 25 | 36 | 34 | 32 | 27 | 34 | 44 | 37 | 34 |
| Block Design | 46 | 19 | 38 | 33 | 28 | 22 | 36 | 29 | 42 | 35 | 45 | 33 |
| Object Assembly | 28 | 25 | 23 | 37 | 30 | 29 | 27 | 18 | 11 | 35 | 33 | 28 |
| Symbol Search | 32 | 23 | 34 | 21 | 27 | 20 | 20 | 08 | 25 | 29 | 20 | 23 |
| Mazes | 22 | 04 | 20 | 02 | 07 | 02 | 08 | 15 | 01 | 14 | 00 | 09 |
| **Factor B – Perceptual Organization** | | | | | | | | | | | | |
| Information | 18 | 29 | 33 | 30 | 22 | 24 | 34 | 30 | 34 | 30 | 21 | 29 |
| Similarities | 23 | 26 | 33 | 31 | 19 | 29 | 30 | 37 | 18 | 31 | 28 | 30 |
| Arithmetic | 35 | 21 | 43 | 34 | 25 | 28 | 27 | 43 | 30 | 49 | 31 | 37 |
| Vocabulary | 31 | 20 | 34 | 14 | 13 | 22 | 19 | 28 | 15 | 27 | 17 | 22 |
| Comprehension | 19 | 08 | 22 | 15 | 19 | 22 | 25 | 17 | 07 | 41 | 12 | 19 |
| Digit Span | 24 | 25 | 23 | 12 | 19 | 19 | 22 | 18 | 11 | 38 | 20 | 22 |
| Picture Completion | 55 | 55 | 54 | 45 | 39 | 54 | 54 | 60 | 49 | 55 | 58 | 53 |
| Coding | 21 | 15 | 12 | 10 | 11 | 37 | 09 | 00 | 09 | 21 | 04 | 12 |
| Picture Arrangement | 40 | 29 | 20 | 29 | 34 | 40 | 38 | 33 | 48 | 40 | 33 | 36 |
| Block Design | 53 | 71 | 60 | 73 | 86 | 73 | 74 | 77 | 58 | 76 | 62 | 73 |
| Object Assembly | 71 | 65 | 78 | 60 | 66 | 59 | 77 | 61 | 73 | 62 | 64 | 67 |
| Symbol Search | 17 | 26 | 37 | 26 | 29 | 54 | 31 | 31 | 27 | 40 | 35 | 35 |
| Mazes | 43 | 32 | 32 | 28 | 50 | 23 | 34 | 39 | 20 | 44 | 48 | 36 |
| **Factor C – Processing Speed** | | | | | | | | | | | | |
| Information | 18 | 21 | 18 | 22 | 14 | 27 | 08 | 07 | 09 | 12 | 10 | 11 |
| Similarities | 04 | 30 | 09 | 10 | 10 | 31 | 17 | 14 | 17 | 09 | 09 | 10 |
| Arithmetic | 20 | 48 | 27 | 32 | 12 | 89 | 21 | 28 | 14 | 15 | 36 | 23 |
| Vocabulary | 09 | 21 | 16 | 15 | 23 | 23 | 17 | 16 | 08 | 33 | 14 | 16 |
| Comprehension | 10 | 07 | 16 | 18 | 19 | 22 | 21 | 27 | 19 | 31 | 19 | 19 |
| Digit Span | 11 | 26 | 25 | 22 | 22 | 44 | 19 | 38 | 13 | 13 | 35 | 22 |
| Picture Completion | 17 | 14 | 07 | 18 | 10 | 09 | 08 | 04 | 07 | 04 | 02 | 09 |
| Coding | 45 | 42 | 93 | 76 | 92 | 14 | 77 | 90 | 62 | 94 | 74 | 74 |
| Picture Arrangement | 24 | 46 | 23 | 35 | 27 | -09 | 26 | 26 | 14 | 19 | 29 | 25 |
| Block Design | 29 | 30 | 21 | 15 | 12 | 26 | 20 | 32 | 26 | 23 | 29 | 19 |
| Object Assembly | 20 | 19 | 16 | 09 | 12 | 14 | 18 | 22 | 26 | 22 | 19 | 15 |
| Symbol Search | 93 | 67 | 54 | 75 | 53 | 13 | 61 | 56 | 71 | 48 | 77 | 62 |
| Mazes | 25 | 19 | 19 | 13 | 14 | 09 | 08 | 03 | 23 | 19 | 13 | 14 |

*Note.* Decimal points omitted.
[a] Av. = average of 11 age groups.

concentration and attention in processing information rapidly by scanning an array. For the total sample, Coding and Symbol Search have high loadings on the Processing Speed factor.

The factor analytic results give strong empirical support to interpretation of the Verbal and Performance IQs as separately functioning entities in the WISC-III. *The factor structure of the WISC-III closely agrees with the actual organization of the subtests.*

### Factor Analytic Findings Related to Age

Although the findings of the maximum-likelihood factor analysis suggest that a three-factor model best characterizes the WISC-III, the model is somewhat weak at ages 6 and 15 years, where only two factors emerged using as a criterion eigenvalues of 1 or above. (Eigenvalues refer to the proportion of variance that a given factor can account for; it is a mathematical value obtained from the factor analysis.) In addition, the third factor, Processing Speed, is usually represented by Coding and Symbol Search, but not at all ages. For example, Arithmetic and Digit Span largely represent the third factor at 11 years, and Symbol Search, Arithmetic, Picture Arrangement, and Coding primarily represent the third factor at 7 years. However, for the entire group, Coding and Symbol Search, as noted previously, have substantial loadings on Processing Speed.

Three of the Performance subtests—Picture Completion, Picture Arrangement, and Block Design—correlate (.30 or above) with the Verbal Comprehension factor at almost every age. However, it is difficult to explain why the pattern of correlations was not consistent at all ages. For example, Block Design loaded on Verbal Comprehension at only 7 of the 11 ages. Similarly, Picture Completion loaded on the Verbal Comprehension factor at all ages, except for age 7 years. Another way to look at the findings is to note that 8, 9, or 10 subtests load on Verbal Comprehension at 9 of the 11 ages and at the average of the 11 age groups. Why these specific nine ages? The pattern of factor loadings may simply be a function of measurement error and may not be a reflection of any underlying developmental trends.

Several Verbal subtests also load (.30 or above) on the Perceptual Organization factor. These usually include Arithmetic, Similarities, and Information. Again, the fact that all subtests are related to *g* may explain these correlations. At 4 of the 11 ages, 8 or more subtests load on Perceptual Organization.

The two Verbal subtests that also load (.30 or above) on Processing Speed at some ages are Arithmetic and Digit Span. Arithmetic involves a speed factor to some extent, but not Digit Span. However, Arithmetic, Digit Span, Coding, and Symbol Search do have in common the need for attention and concentration, perhaps to a greater extent than do the other subtests. Overall, however, Arithmetic and Digit Span do not make a substantial contribution to the Processing Speed factor. Table I-10 summarizes the major trends of the maximum-likelihood factor analysis by age level.

### Comment on Maximum-Likelihood Factor Analysis

The findings of the maximum-likelihood factor analysis reported in this text differ from those reported in the WISC-III manual. The Psychological Corporation also performed a maximum-likelihood factor analysis, but used four age-group clusters (6–7, 8–10, 11–13, and 14–16 years) instead of the 11 separate age groups for the analysis. Consequently, the WISC-III manual reports no factor analytic data for the 11 individual age groups. The WISC-III manual suggests that a four-factor model best describes the WISC-III. The fourth factor is the Freedom from Distractibility factor composed of Arithmetic and Digit Span.

I believe that the four-factor model is inappropriate. I also conducted a maximum-likelihood factor analysis using a four-factor solution, as noted earlier, for each separate age group. At each age group and for the total sample, the eigenvalues were below 1 for the fourth factor. But even more telling was the finding that the so-called Freedom from Distractibility factor did not emerge in 4 of the 11 age groups. At ages 6, 8, 10, and 16 years, the loadings on Arithmetic and Digit Span for the proposed Freedom from Distractibility factor were as follows: age 6: .17 and .15, respectively; age 8: .01 and −.22, respectively; age 10: .16 and −.09, respectively; age 16: .20 and .09, respectively. When a subtest has a loading below .30 on a factor, it suggests that the subtest fails to make a contribution to that factor. A principal components analysis provided essentially similar findings. A four-factor solution never emerged in the principal components analysis. These results suggest that the Freedom from Distractibility factor on the WISC-III should be disregarded until there is further evidence to support its use. If you do choose to interpret the Freedom from Distractibility factor as recommended in the WISC-III manual, do so with caution because of the relative weakness of this factor.

### WISC-III Manual Cautions for Factor Score Interpretations

The WISC-III manual on page 210 makes a curious state-

**Table 1-10**
**Summary of Major Trends of Maximum-Likelihood Factor Analysis by Age Level and for the Average of the Total Sample on WISC-III**

| Age | Number of factors | Subtests with loadings of .30 or higher on Verbal Comprehension | Subtests with loadings of .30 or higher on Perceptual Organization | Subtests with loadings of .30 or higher on Processing Speed |
|---|---|---|---|---|
| 6 | 3[a] | All 6 Verbal subtests, PC, PA, BD, SS | PC, PA, BD, OA, MA, A, V | CD, SS |
| 7 | 3 | I, S, A, V, C, PA | PC, BD, OA, MA | S, A, CD, PA, BD, SS |
| 8 | 3 | All 6 Verbal subtests, PC, PA, BD, SS | PC, BD, OA, SS, MA, I, S, A, V | CD, SS |
| 9 | 3 | All 6 Verbal subtests, PC, BD, OA | PC, BD, OA, I, S, A | A, CD, PA, SS |
| 10 | 3 | All 6 Verbal subtests, PC, PA, OA | PC, PA, BD, OA, MA | CD, SS |
| 11 | 3 | I, S, A, V, C, PC, PA | PC, CD, PA, BD, OA, SS | S, A, DS |
| 12 | 3 | I, S, A, V, C, PC, PA, BD | PC, PA, BD, OA, SS, MA, I, S | CD, SS |
| 13 | 3 | I, S, A, V, C, PC | PC, PA, BD, OA, SS, MA, I, S, A | DS, CD, BD, SS |
| 14 | 3 | All 6 Verbal subtests, PC, PA, BD | PC, PA, BD, OA, I, A | CD, SS |
| 15 | 3[a] | All 6 Verbal subtests, PC, PA, BD, OA | PC, PA, BD, OA, SS, MA, I, S, A, C, DS | V, C, CD, SS |
| 16 | 3 | I, S, A, V, C, PC, PA, BD, OA | PC, PA, BD, OA, SS, MA, A | A, DS, CD, SS |
| Av. | 3 | All 6 Verbal subtests, PC, PA, BD | PC, PA, BD, OA, SS, MA, S, A | CD, SS |

*Note.* Abbreviations: I = Information, S = Similarities, A = Arithmetic, V = Vocabulary, C = Comprehension, DS = Digit Span, PC = Picture Completion, CD = Coding, PA = Picture Arrangement, BD = Block Design, OA = Object Assembly, SS = Symbol Search, MA = Mazes, Av. = Average of 11 age groups.
[a] The eigenvalue for the third factor is less then 1.00 at age 6 years (namely, .87) and at age 15 years (namely, .86). This means that the third factor is weak at these two ages.

ment about the Processing Speed and Freedom from Distractibility factor scores. The statement (italicized below) was made in the context of a study of 38 gifted children who were administered the WISC-III. The children obtained higher scores on the Verbal Comprehension, Perceptual Organization, and Freedom from Distractibility factors than on the Processing Speed factor ($Ms$ = 126.9, 125.8, 123.0, and 110.2, respectively). These findings were interpreted to mean that

The Freedom from Distractibility and the Processing Speed scales are not as highly related to general intellectual ability as the Verbal Comprehension and Perceptual Organization scales. *Scores on these scales can be expected to vary independently of FSIQ* [Full Scale IQ] *scores* [italics added]. This finding empha-

sizes the reason that the index scores are not referred to as IQ scores. (Wechsler, 1991[R], p. 210)

The statement that "Scores on these scales can be expected to vary independently of FSIQ scores" is misleading. First, the WISC-III manual did not present any data to support this assertion, except for the means on each factor score. In fact, the mean on the Freedom from Distractibility factor was almost as high as the means on the Verbal Comprehension and Perceptual Organization factors. Second, the subtests that make up the third and fourth factors cited in the WISC-III manual all correlate significantly with the Full Scale (Symbol Search $r$ = .56, $p$ < .001; Coding $r$ = .33, $p$ < .001; Arithmetic $r$ = .65, $p$ < .001; Digit Span $r$ = .43, $p$ < .001; all correlations based on the total group). In some cases, these subtests have as high or higher a correlation with the Full Scale than do other subtests. For example, the correlations between Picture Completion and Picture Arrangement with the Full Scale are .58 and .52, respectively. Furthermore, Arithmetic, Digit Span, and Symbol Search are either good or fair measures of $g$. Until further data are available, I believe that it is misleading to say that Processing Speed and Freedom from Distractibility scores "vary independently of FSIQ scores."

(In a telephone conversation on November 4, 1991 with Aurelio Prifitera, who was the Project Director in The Psychological Corporation for the WISC-III, Dr. Prifitera indicated that they included this statement in the WISC-III manual to emphasize that examiners should never use the Freedom from Distractibility or Processing Speed factor scores as independent estimates of a child's Full Scale IQ. I agree fully with this recommendation.)

### WISC-III Subtests as Measure of $g$

Examination of the loadings on the first unrotated factor—in either a principal components analysis or a factor analysis—allows us to determine the extent to which the WISC-III subtests measure general intelligence, or $g$. In this section the results are based on a principal components analysis. Overall, the WISC-III is a fair measure of $g$, with 43 percent of its variance attributed to $g$.

The WISC-III subtests form three clusters with respect to the measurement of $g$: (a) Vocabulary, Information, Similarities, Block Design, Arithmetic, and Comprehension are good measures of $g$; (b) Object Assembly, Picture Completion, Symbol Search, Picture Arrangement, and Digit Span are fair measures of $g$; and (c) Coding and Mazes are poor measures of $g$ (see Table I-11). The subtests

in the Verbal Scale have higher $g$ loadings than those in the Performance Scale (52 percent, on the average, for the Verbal subtests; 36 percent, on the average, for the Performance subtests). Highest loadings are for Vocabulary, Information, and Similarities in the Verbal Scale and Block Design, Object Assembly, and Picture Completion in the Performance Scale. Any of the five standard Verbal subtests may serve as a good measure of $g$, but only Block Design in the Performance Scale may serve as a good measure of $g$.

### Subtest Specificity

Subtest specificity refers to the proportion of a subtest's variance that is both reliable (that is, not due to measurement errors) and distinctive to the subtest (see pages 32–34 of this text for further information about subtest specificity). Although the individual subtests on the WISC-III overlap in their measurement properties (that is, the majority of the reliable variance for most subtests is common factor variance), many possess sufficient specificity at some ages to justify interpretation of specific subtest functions (see Table I-12).

Throughout the age range covered by the WISC-III, Digit Span, Picture Arrangement, and Block Design have ample specificity. In addition, Picture Completion, Coding, and Mazes have ample specificity at 10 of the 11 age levels. Each of the seven remaining subtests shows a unique pattern of specificity—that is, the ages at which each has ample, adequate, or inadequate specificity differ. Similarities, Arithmetic, Comprehension, and Object Assembly have inadequate specificity for at least five ages.

Subtests with inadequate specificity should not be interpreted as measuring specific functions. These subtests, however, can be interpreted as (a) good, fair, or poor

**Table I-II**
**WISC-III Subtests as Measures of $g$**

| Good measure of g | | | Fair measure of g | | | Poor measure of g | | |
|---|---|---|---|---|---|---|---|---|
| *Subtest* | *Average loading of g* | *Proportion of variance attributed to g (%)* | *Subtest* | *Average loading of g* | *Proportion of variance attributed to g (%)* | *Subtest* | *Average loading of g* | *Proportion of variance attributed to g (%)* |
| Vocabulary | .79 | 62 | Object Assembly | .66 | 44 | Coding | .44 | 20 |
| Information | .78 | 61 | Picture Completion | .66 | 44 | Mazes | .37 | 13 |
| Similarities | .78 | 60 | Symbol Search | .62 | 38 | | | |
| Block Design | .74 | 56 | Picture Arrangement | .60 | 36 | | | |
| Arithmetic | .74 | 54 | Digit Span | .51 | 26 | | | |
| Comprehension | .70 | 50 | | | | | | |

**Table I-12**
**Amount of Specificity in WISC-III Subtests for 11 Ages and Average**

| Subtest | Ages with ample specificity | Ages with adequate specificity | Ages with inadequate specificity |
|---|---|---|---|
| Information | 11, Av. | 8–10, 12–16 | 6–7 |
| Similarities | 6, 14 | 11–12, 15–16, Av. | 7–10, 13 |
| Arithmetic | 6–7, 10, 13, 15, Av. | 16 | 8–9, 11–12, 14 |
| Vocabulary | 6, 11 | 7–8, 12–16, Av. | 9–10 |
| Comprehension | 6, 8–11, Av. | 12 | 7, 13–16 |
| Digit Span | 6–16, Av. | — | — |
| Picture Completion | 6–11, 13–16, Av. | — | 12 |
| Coding | 6–7, 9–16, Av. | — | 8 |
| Picture Arrangement | 6–16, Av. | — | — |
| Block Design | 6–16, Av. | — | — |
| Object Assembly | 9, 13, 15 | 6 | 7–8, 10–12, 14, 16, Av. |
| Symbol Search | 7, 10–16, Av. | — | 6, 8–9 |
| Mazes | 6–14, 16, Av. | — | 15 |

*Note.* Av. = average of the 11 age groups. Kaufman's (1975a) rule of thumb was used to classify the amount of specificity in each subtest. Subtests with ample specificity have specific variance that (a) reflects 25 percent or more of the subtest's total variance (100%) and (b) exceeds the subtest's error variance. Subtests with adequate specificity have specific variance that (a) reflects between 15 and 24 percent of the subtest's total variance and (b) exceeds the subtest's error variance. Subtests with inadequate specificity have specific variance that either (a) is less than 15 percent of the subtest's total variance or (b) is equal to or less than the subtest's error variance.

Specific variance is obtained by subtracting the squared multiple correlation (from the maximum-likelihood factor analysis with varimax rotation) from the subtest's reliability ($r_{xx}$ − SMC) (A. Silverstein, personal communication, October 1991). Error variance is obtained by subtracting the subtest's reliability from 1.00 ($1 − r_{xx}$).

measures of *g* (see Table I-11) and (b) representing a specific factor (that is, Verbal Comprehension, Perceptual Organization, or Processing Speed; see Table I-9), where appropriate.

You should also determine which subtest scaled scores are significantly different from the mean of their scale and, in some cases, from one another, and analyze performance on all relevant subtests before drawing any conclusions about unusual ability or weakness; we refer to this as *profile analysis*. (See Chapter 8 and Appendix K for a discussion of profile analysis.) For example, low scores on Coding and Symbol Search and average or high scores on the other subtests may indicate that the child is having difficulty processing information rapidly. However, high scores on Coding and low scores on Symbol Search do not suggest difficulty in processing information rapidly; the picture is mixed.

**Factor Scores**

You can also obtain factor scores from the WISC-III and thereby identify meaningful psychological dimensions. The Verbal Comprehension factor score measures verbal knowledge and understanding obtained through both informal and formal education and reflects the application of

verbal skills to new situations. The Perceptual Organization factor score, a nonverbal score, reflects the ability to interpret and organize visually perceived material within a time limit. The Processing Speed factor score measures the ability to process visually perceived nonverbal information quickly. Concentration and rapid eye-hand coordination may be important components of the Processing Speed factor.

There are at least three different ways of obtaining factor scores:

1. *Three-factor model focusing on subtests with high loadings on each factor.* The results of the three-factor maximum-likelihood factor analysis suggest that the following combinations would be most robust in forming factor scores:

Verbal
Comprehension = Sum of scaled scores on
Information, Similarities,
Vocabulary, and Comprehension

Perceptual
Organization = Sum of scaled scores on Picture
Completion, Block Design, and
Object Assembly

Processing
Speed       = Sum of scaled scores on Coding
              and Symbol Search

2. *Three-factor model focusing on subtests often said to reflect the two principal factors plus the new factor.* The results of the maximum-likelihood factor analysis provide only weak support for using the same three factors as noted in number 1, with the addition of Picture Arrangement as a fourth subtest in the Perceptual Organization factor. Perceptual Organization is weaker if Picture Arrangement is included because Picture Arrangement has a .36 loading on Perceptual Organization and a .34 loading on Verbal Comprehension. Picture Arrangement, therefore, is not a pure measure of Perceptual Organization, nor does it have a substantial loading on the factor.

3. *Four-factor model as noted in the WISC-III manual.* Based on the results of a four-factor maximum-likelihood factor analysis, the WISC-III manual proposes that the subtests be divided into four factors, as noted previously. This model is similar to that described in number 2, with the addition of Arithmetic and Digit Span to form the Freedom from Distractibility factor. However, the four-factor model needs further empirical support before I can recommend it.

Use of any of the above combinations ensures against subtests' overlapping in any factors. If you decide to follow the procedure recommended in this text, use the following tables to convert the sum of scaled scores into WISC-III Deviation Quotients:

• Table A.5 (page 255) in the WISC-III manual for Verbal Comprehension (Information, Similarities, Vocabulary, and Comprehension)
• Table A.7 (page 257) in the WISC-III manual for Processing Speed (Coding and Symbol Search)
• Table L-13 in Appendix L for Perceptual Organization (Picture Completion, Block Design, and Object Assembly)

If you decide to use Picture Arrangement as part of the Perceptual Organization factor, use Table A.6 (page 256) in the WISC-III manual to obtain the Deviation Quotients. *Do not report factor scores in a psychological report—use them only for evaluating the child's strengths and weaknesses and for generating hypotheses about the child's abilities.*

## RANGE OF SUBTEST SCALED SCORES

The WISC-III provides a range of scaled scores from 1 to 19. However, this range is not possible for all subtests at all

ages of the test. For example, there are minor problems with scaled-score ranges at 6 years and at 11 through 16 years. At 6 years, children receive 2 scaled-score points credit on four subtests—Information, Similarities, Picture Arrangement, and Block Design—*even though they fail all items on these subtests.* At 7 years and afterward, however, children receive only 1 scaled-score point if they fail all items on these four subtests.

After the age of 11 years, the ceiling level drops for one or more subtests; however, the drop is no more than 2 scaled-score points. Table I-13 shows the maximum possible scaled scores for each subtest by age. The failure to have the same maximum scaled score at the upper limits (that is, a scaled score of 19) throughout the test primarily

**Table I-13**
**Maximum WISC-III Subtest Scaled Scores by Age**

| Subtest | Maximum scaled score | Age (in years) |
|---|---|---|
| Information | 19 | 6 to 14 |
|  | 18 | 15 |
|  | 17 | 16 |
| Similarities | 19 | 6 to 16 |
| Arithmetic | 19 | 6 to 15 |
|  | 18 | 16 |
| Vocabulary | 19 | 6 to 16 |
| Comprehension | 19 | 6 to 15 |
|  | 18 | 16 |
| Digit Span | 19 | 6 to 16 |
| Picture Completion | 19 | 6 to 13 |
|  | 18 | 14 to 15 |
|  | 17 | 16 |
| Coding | 19 | 6 to 16 |
| Picture Arrangement | 19 | 6 to 16 |
| Block Design | 19 | 6 to 15 |
|  | 18 | 16 |
| Object Assembly | 19 | 6 to 15 |
|  | 18 | 16 |
| Symbol Search | 19 | 6 to 15 |
|  | 18 | 16 |
| Mazes | 19 | 6 to 10 |
|  | 18 | 11 to 12 |
|  | 17 | 13 to 16 |

affects how you interpret the profiles of bright children aged 14 years and older. (When Mazes is included, there are difficulties in interpreting the profiles of bright children ages 11 through 16 years.)

You can apply profile analysis techniques appropriately at all ages for five subtests only—Similarities, Vocabulary, Digit Span, Coding, and Picture Arrangement. For older gifted children, you can apply profile analysis uniformly only when all scaled scores are 17 or below. *Applying profile analysis uniformly to all subtests would be misleading in some individual cases because the child cannot obtain the same number of scaled-score points on all subtests.* However, the failure to have the same scaled-score range at all age levels and for all subtests is usually only a minor difficulty because all subtests have a scaled-score range of 1 to 17.

## RANGE OF FULL SCALE IQs

The range of Full Scale IQs from 40 to 160 on the WISC-III is insufficient for both severely retarded children and extremely gifted children. This range also is not available at some ages of the test. For example, the highest possible IQ that adolescents who are aged 16-8 years can get is 154; the lowest possible IQ that children who are 6-0 years old can get is 46. The test is designed so that every child receives at least 10 scaled-score points for giving *no* correct answers to any subtest. In fact, 6-year-old children receive 14 scaled-score points even when they fail every item.

The Psychological Corporation recognized that awarding scaled-score points for no successes might be a problem. They therefore recommended that examiners compute IQs on each scale only when the child obtains a raw score greater than 0 on at least three subtests on each scale. Similarly, they recommended that examiners compute a Full Scale IQ only when the child obtains raw scores greater than 0 on three Verbal *and* on three Performance subtests. This is a rule of thumb, rather than an empirically based recommendation, but it does have merit. However, validity data are needed to show that this rule of thumb or other procedures are or are not valid for computing IQs. The WISC-III manual provides no validity data to support this recommendation.

If we follow The Psychological Corporation's recommended procedure, what is the lowest possible IQ that a 6-year-old child can receive? If the child obtained raw scores of 1 on the Information, Similarities, Comprehension, Picture Completion, Picture Arrangement, and Block Design subtests and a raw score of 0 on each of the remaining four subtests, the resulting IQs would be as follows: Verbal Scale IQ = 58 (13 scaled-score points), Performance Scale IQ = 55 (13 scaled-score points), and Full Scale IQ = 53 (26 scaled-score points). Six 1-point successes thus yield an IQ of 53. Therefore, the WISC-III may not provide precise IQs for young children who are functioning at two or more standard deviations below the mean of the scale. The WISC-III does not appear to sample a sufficient range of cognitive abilities for low-functioning children. If a child fails all or most of the items on the WISC-III, consider giving another test that may give you a more accurate estimate of the child's ability.

## COMPARISON OF THE WISC-III AND WISC-R

Although similar to its predecessor, the WISC-III differs from the WISC-R in some important ways.

1. As previously noted, the revision contains a new supplementary subtest, Symbol Search.

2. The Freedom from Distractibility factor does not emerge as a strong factor, if at all. In fact, Coding now unites with Symbol Search to form a new factor called *Processing Speed.*

3. Full-color illustrations are used in the revision.

4. Scoring guidelines and administrative procedures for most subtests have been modified in the revision. For example, changes have been made in the order in which the subtests are administered, order of items, starting points, discontinuance criteria, and allotment of bonus points.

5. Speed (coupled with correct performance) is awarded bonus points on the last six Arithmetic subtest items in the WISC-III.

6. The number of items has been increased on Similarities, Arithmetic, Comprehension, Digit Span, Picture Completion, Coding, Picture Arrangement, Object Assembly, and Mazes and decreased on Vocabulary; the number of items on Information remains the same. Table I-14 highlights the changes in the WISC-III.

## ADMINISTERING THE WISC-III

The general procedures discussed in Chapter 5 for administering psychological tests should help you administer the WISC-III. However, you must master the special procedures developed for the WISC-III, whether or not you are familiar with the WISC-R. You must be careful not to confuse procedures for the WISC-R, WPPSI-R, or WAIS-R with those for the WISC-III—some subtests with the

**Table I-14**
**Highlights of Changes in WISC-III**

| Area or subtest | Changes from WISC-R | Area or subtest | Changes from WISC-R |
|---|---|---|---|
| Age range | No change. | Types of scores | Provides IQs ($M = 100$, $SD = 15$) for Verbal, Performance, and Full Scales; Index Scores ($M = 100$, $SD = 15$) for four factor scores; percentile ranks for IQs and Index Scores; and test-age equivalents of raw scores. WISC-R provided IQs for Verbal, Performance, and Full Scales and test-age equivalents of raw scores only. |
| Standardization | 1988 census data used. | | |
| Number of subtests | 13 instead of 12. | | |
| Number of items | Number of items increased on most subtests. | | |
| Reliability | Reliability coefficients similar to those on WISC-R. | | |
| Validity | Validity seems to be similar to WISC-R. | | |
| Scoring examples | Somewhat expanded and placed with subtest proper instead of in appendixes in back of manual. | Confidence intervals | Confidence intervals presented in manual based on estimated true score method. No confidence intervals presented in the WISC-R manual. |
| General administrative changes | Order of administering subtests changed, item order changed on some subtests, starting points changed on some subtests, samples added on some subtests, discontinuance criteria changed on some subtests, bonus-point allotment changed on some subtests. Manual has a built-in stand. | Factor structure | Manual proposes a four-factor model (Verbal Comprehension, Perceptual Organization, Freedom from Distractibility, Processing Speed) which differs from the three factors found on the WISC-R. However, the four-factor model, as noted in this chapter, is questionable. |
| Computation of IQ | No change (stipulates, as does the WISC-R, that 3 Verbal and 3 Performance subtests must have raw scores greater than 0). | $g$ loading | About the same as on the WISC-R (average loading of $g$ is 43 percent on WISC-III and 42 percent on WISC-R). |
| Intelligence classification | Uses "intellectually deficient" instead of "mental retardation" to classify IQs below 70. | Art work | Color used instead of black and white on all pictures throughout the test, all pictures enlarged, and art work has a more contemporary appearance. |
| Record Form | Front cover changed to include places for calculating factor scores, confidence intervals, and percentile ranks; Coding Response Sheet is a separate pullout sheet in Record Form. More space provided for writing responses on Information, Similarities, Vocabulary, and Comprehension subtests. More space provided on Coding Response Sheet between the key and the stimulus items. Full page provided for recording behavioral observations. | Test-retest changes | Retest changes 3 points greater on WISC-III Performance Scale than on WISC-R Performance Scale (approximately 13 vs. 10 IQ points). |
| | | Ceiling and floor level of IQ | Range of Full Scale IQs is from 40 to 160 on both tests, but this range is not available at all ages on either test. |
| | | Ages at which scaled scores of 1 to 19 are available | More subtests have a range of 1 to 19 scaled-score points on WISC-III than on WISC-R. |

*(Table continues next page)*

**Table I-I4 (cont.)**

| Area or subtest | Changes from WISC-R | Area or subtest | Changes from WISC-R |
|---|---|---|---|
| Information | Same number of items (30), with 21 unchanged or slightly reworded, 2 substantially changed, and 7 new items. Starting point item now counted in reverse sequence. | Picture Completion (cont.) | Two additional starting points added for a total of 4 points. Discontinuance rule changed from 4 to 5 consecutive failures. |
| Similarities | Contains 19 instead of 17 items, with 13 unchanged or slightly reworded and 6 new items. Sample item used. Scoring criteria and sample responses are directly following each item rather than in an appendix. | Coding | Contains 59 items on Coding A, instead of 45, and 119 items on Coding B, instead of 93; additional rows added and additional items added in rows on both parts of the subtest. Symbols enlarged slightly. Black no. 2 pencil required instead of red pencil. Recording form now part of Record Form. |
| Arithmetic | Contains 24 instead of 18 items, with 14 slightly reworded and 10 new items. Starting point item now counted in reverse sequence. Minor changes in scoring and administration. Bonus points given for speed on items 19 to 24. | Picture Arrangement | Contains 14 instead of 12 items, with 7 slightly redrawn, sample item redrawn, and all pictures in color. Slight changes in starting points. Changes in scoring procedure for alternative arrangements and bonus-point allotment. |
| Vocabulary | Contains 30 instead of 32 items, with 19 items the same and 11 new items. Starting point item counted in reverse sequence. Discontinuance rule changed from 5 to 4 consecutive failures. Scoring criteria and sample responses are directly following each item rather than in an appendix. | Block Design | Contains 12 instead of 11 items, with 10 items exactly the same and 2 new items added (one easy and one difficult). Changes in bonus-point allotment. Minor administrative changes. |
| Comprehension | Contains 18 instead of 17 items, with 12 items unchanged or slightly reworded and 6 new items. Eight items (instead of nine) require two responses for full credit. Discontinuance rule changed from 4 to 3 consecutive failures. Scoring criteria and sample responses are directly following each item rather than in an appendix. | Object Assembly | Contains 5 instead of 4 items, with 4 items slightly redrawn and 1 new item; sample item included as in WISC-R. Additional juncture for scoring Face item added. Layout shield is now freestanding. Changes in bonus-point allotment. |
| Digit Span | Contains 15 instead of 14 sets of digits, with one 2-digit set added to Digits Forward. | Symbol Search | New optional subtest with two levels, with each level containing 45 items. |
| Picture Completion | Contains 30 items instead of 26, with 17 slightly modified and 13 new items. All pictures enlarged and in color. Sample item added. | Mazes | Contains 10 instead of 9 mazes, with the new maze at the difficult end of the series. Overall design of the mazes is unchanged, although each is slightly larger. Minor administrative changes, including changes in maximum number of errors and elimination of need for red-lead pencil. |

same name have different instructions and time limits. Appendix J presents guidelines that will help you administer the WISC-III subtests; they supplement those in the WISC-III manual. Appendix D presents special procedures for administering the WISC-R (and WISC-III) Performance subtests to deaf children. Some general administrative issues are discussed below. Finally, the suggestions in Exhibit I-2 and the checklist shown in Exhibit I-3 should also help you learn to administer the WISC-III.

Study the instructions in the WISC-III manual and become familiar with the test materials before you give the test. Although the Verbal subtests are generally easier to administer than the Performance subtests, they are more difficult to score. You will find a stopwatch (or a wristwatch with a digital timer) helpful, if not essential, for administering the timed WISC-III subtests.

The Record Form (see Figure I-3) should be clearly and accurately completed; record all responses relevant to the test and testing situation *verbatim*. You also need to check all calculations carefully, as well as the conversion of raw scores to scaled scores and of scaled scores to IQs. In converting the raw scores to scaled scores, be aware that the order of subtests on the front of the Record Form is not the same as the order of subtests in Table A.1 (pages 217–249) in the WISC-III manual. The order of subtests on the Record Form is the order in which the subtests are administered, whereas the order of subtests in Table A.1 is by scale—the six Verbal subtests in the upper half of the table and the seven Performance subtests in the lower half of the table. Be sure to use the appropriate columns in Table A.1 for converting raw scores to scaled scores. For example, to convert a raw score on Picture Completion (the first subtest administered) to a scaled score, you must use the columns in the lower half of Table A.1 ("Performance Subtests"), which show the raw scores for the Picture Completion subtest and their corresponding scaled scores. Calculate the child's chronological age with care. If you master the administrative procedures early in your testing career, you will be better able to move ahead and focus on learning how to interpret the test results.

### General Problems in Administering the WISC-III

Here are some problems that have been observed when examiners administered the Wechsler tests.

1. Reading questions too quickly or too slowly.
2. Not enunciating clearly.
3. Leaving unessential materials on the table.
4. Not recording all responses.
5. Calculating chronological age incorrectly.
6. Not adhering to guidelines for giving help.
7. Not adhering to directions.
8. Ignoring proper time limits.
9. Not questioning ambiguous or vague responses.
10. Not crediting all responses.
11. Not following starting rule.
12. Not following discontinuance rule.
13. Making errors in converting raw scores to scaled scores.
14. Prorating incorrectly.
15. Giving time-bonus credits incorrectly.
16. Using inappropriate norms.
17. Not giving a score of 0 to an incorrect response.
18. Adding raw scores incorrectly.
19. Adding scaled scores incorrectly.
20. Not checking all Coding subtest responses.
21. Failing to credit items not administered below the starting point.
22. Giving credit to items passed above the discontinuance point.
23. Not giving credit to items missed below the starting point.
24. Not scoring a subtest.
25. Converting scaled scores to IQs incorrectly.
26. Including a supplementary subtest, in addition to the five standard subtests in each scale, to compute an IQ.
27. Using both Coding and Symbol Search to compute an IQ.

One study (Slate & Chick, 1989) found that the most common scoring errors on the WISC-R were on the Vocabulary, Comprehension, and Similarities subtests. The major scoring errors were in assigning 2 points to a 1-point response or 1 point to a 0-point response. Other errors found in the student examiners' test administrations were failing to question responses, failing to record responses verbatim, failing to establish the correct starting points and discontinuance points, and failing to add scores properly. Scoring errors may be due to the examiner's receiving poor instructional preparation; ambiguity in the scoring criteria presented in the test manual; carelessness on the part of the examiner; factors in the examiner-examinee relationship; the examiner's personal stress or fatigue; and the examiner's becoming bored with testing (Slate & Hunnicutt, 1988[R]).

To avoid scoring and administration errors, carefully review how you administer and score each subtest. During the test assign tentative scores, and always rescore each item after you finish administering the entire test. If you are unsure of how to score a response while testing, and the item is involved in establishing a starting point (also re-

**Figure I-3. Cover page of WISC-III Record Form.** Copyright © 1971, 1974, 1991 by The Psychological Corporation, San Antonio, TX. All Rights Reserved.

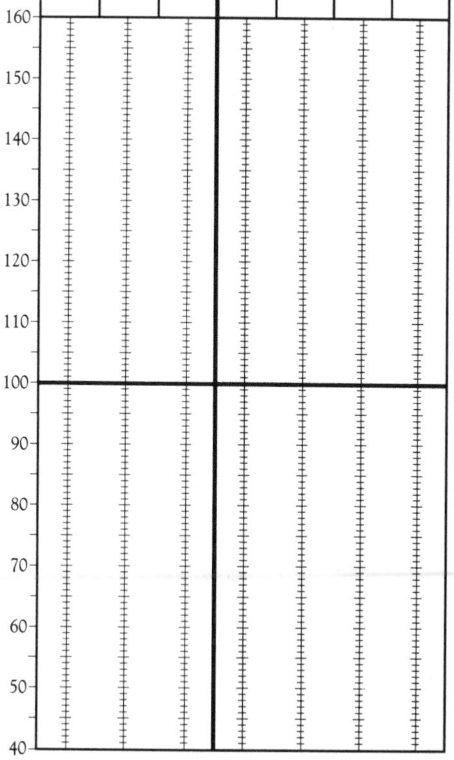

1055

■ **Exhibit I-2** ━━━━━━━━━━━━━━━━━━━━━━━━━━━━━━━

## Supplementary Instructions for Administering the WISC-III

1. Study and practice administering the test before you give it to a child to fulfill a class assignment.

2. Organize your test materials before the child comes into the room. Make sure that all test materials—including stimulus booklets, blocks, cards, puzzle pieces, Record Form, stop watch, and pencils—are in the kit. Arrange the Picture Arrangement cards in numerical sequence. Have extra blank paper to make notes if needed.

3. Complete the top of the Record Form (examinee's name, sex, school, grade, examiner, and handedness).

4. Enter the date tested and date of birth, calculate the chronological age (CA), and put it in the box provided. Months are considered to have 30 days for testing purposes. Check the chronological age by adding the chronological age to the date of birth to obtain the date of testing.

5. Administer the subtests in the order presented in the manual, except in rare circumstances. Do not change the wording on any subtest. Read the directions exactly as shown in the manual. Do not ad lib.

6. Start with the appropriate item on each subtest and follow discontinuance criteria. You must know the scoring criteria *before* you give the test.

7. Write down verbatim all of the child's responses that are pertinent to the test, testing situation, or referral question or are otherwise helpful in understanding the child. Write clearly and do not use unusual abbreviations. Record time accurately in the spaces provided in the Record Form.

8. Question all ambiguous or unscorable responses, writing a (Q) after each questioned response. Question all responses when a (Q) follows the response in the WISC-III manual.

9. Introduce the test by saying something like "We will be doing lots of different things today. Some will be easy and some will be hard. I'd like you to do the best you can. OK?" Make eye contact with the child from time to time, and use the child's first name when possible. Watch for signs that the child needs a break (for example, a stretch, a drink, or a trip to the bathroom). Between subtests say something like "Now we'll do something different." At the end of the test, thank the child for coming and for being cooperative (if appropriate).

10. On Information item 8, if the child first says "5," ask "How many counting the weekend?" If the child then says "2," ask "How many altogether, all week?"

11. On Arithmetic, you may repeat an item only once.

12. On Comprehension, the Record Form is marked with an asterisk next to those items that require you to ask for a second response.

13. On Digits Forward and Digits Backward, always administer both trials of each series. Read the digits at the rate of one per second and at an even pace—that is, no chunking—and drop your voice inflection slightly on the last digit in the sequence.

14. On Picture Completion, place the Stimulus Booklet flat on the table close to the child. Note that the time limit is 20 seconds. If you are not sure whether the child's verbal response is correct, say "Show me where you mean." You must know the cautions (top of page 61 in the WISC-III manual) and when to use them. On item 29, give credit to "rib" or "spoke" (personal communication, Lawrence Weiss, The Psychological Corporation, September 1991). Although the letters are missing on the buttons of the telephone (item 23), The Psychological Corporation advised that you not give credit to a response mentioning this omission because it is an unessential missing part (personal communication, Lawrence Weiss, The Psychological Corporation, January 1992). If this is the first unessential missing part mentioned by the child, say "Yes, but what is the most important part that is missing?" The child can turn the pages of the test booklet if you are sure that he or she will allow you to set the pace.

15. On Picture Arrangement, when you are doing the sample, move each card down to a new row rather than shifting the cards within their original row. Place the cards at least 3 or 4 inches away from the edge of the table.

16. On Block Design, when you demonstrate the samples, put them together slowly. Be careful not to cover the blocks with your hand; the child needs to see what you are doing. Make the designs so that they are in the appropriate direction for the child. This means that you will be making the designs upside down. Don't make a design right side up and then turn the whole thing around to face the child.

17. On Symbol Search, only items that have been attempted within 120 seconds are counted as correct or incorrect (personal communication, Lawrence Weiss, The Psychological Corporation, January 1992).

18. To facilitate the scoring of the Coding subtest, write at the end of each row of the Coding scoring template the cumulative total number of symbols up to and including that row. For the Coding A template, the numbers that should be written at the ends of rows 1 through 8, respectively, are 3, 11, 19, 27, 35, 43, 51, and 59. On the Coding B template, the cumulative totals are 14, 35, 56, 77, 98, and 119; these numbers should be written at the ends of the first through sixth rows. After you write the numbers, laminate the template to prolong its life (cf. Danielson, 1991). (In January 1992, Aurelio Prifitera, from The Psychological Corporation, informed me that the second printing of the templates will include these numbers.)

19. On subtests that receive bonus points for speed, make

*(Exhibit continues next page)*

**Exhibit I-2 (cont.)**

sure that the score you circle on the Record Form corresponds to the time taken by the child to complete the item. In no case give bonus points for 0-point answers.

20. Keep materials, other than those needed for the test, off the table (for example, soda cans, pocketbook, and keys).

21. Carefully score each protocol and recheck your scoring. If you failed to question a response when you should have and the response is obviously not a 0 response, give the child the most appropriate score based on the child's actual response.

22. If a subtest was spoiled, write *spoiled* by the subtest total score and on the front cover of the Record Form next to the name of the subtest. If the subtest was not administered, write *NA* in the margin of the Record Form next to the subtest name and on the front of the Record Form.

23. Add the raw scores for each subtest carefully. Make sure that you give credit for items not administered below the starting-point items. Be sure to add correctly the points associated with the circled numbers on the Record Form for all subtests that have bonus points.

24. Transfer subtest scores to the front of the Record Form under Raw Scores. After transferring all raw scores to the front page of the Record Form, check to see that the raw scores on the front page match those noted inside the Record Form for each subtest.

25. Transform raw scores into scaled scores by using Table A.1 on pages 217 to 249 of the WISC-III manual. Be sure to use the page of Table A.1 that is appropriate for the child's age and the correct row and column for each transformation.

26. Add the scaled scores for the five standard Verbal subtests to compute the sum of the scaled scores. Do not use Digit Span to compute the Verbal score unless you have substituted it for another Verbal subtest. Add the scaled scores for the five standard Performance subtests. Do not include Symbol Search or Mazes to compute the Performance score unless you have substituted Symbol Search for Coding or Mazes for another Performance subtest. You can include both Mazes and Symbol Search to compute the Performance score if you have substituted Symbol Search for Coding and Mazes for some other Performance subtest. Sum the Verbal and the Performance subtest scaled scores to obtain the sum for the Full Scale. Recheck all of your additions.

27. Convert the sums of scaled scores for the Verbal, Performance, and Full Scales by use of the appropriate conversion tables in Appendix A (pages 251 to 254) in the WISC-III manual. Use Table A.2 for the Verbal Scale, Table A.3 for the Performance Scale, and Table A.4 for the Full Scale. Be sure to use the correct table for the appropriate scale. Record the IQs on the front of the Record Form.

28. Recheck all of your work. If the IQ was obtained by use

of a short form, write *SF* beside the appropriate IQ. If IQs were prorated, write *PRO* beside each appropriate IQ.

29. If fewer than five subtests were administered in the Verbal section or fewer than five subtests in the Performance section, use the Tellegen and Briggs short-form procedure described on page 138 of this text to compute the IQ. This procedure is the most reliable one for prorating IQs. You can also consult Table L-12, L-13, L-14, or L-15. These tables provide estimated Full Scale Deviation Quotients for several combinations of short forms based on the Tellegen and Briggs procedure.

30. Make a profile of the examinee's scaled scores on the front of the Record Form by plotting the scores on the graph provided.

31. Look up the confidence intervals for the Full Scale IQ, Verbal Scale IQ, and Performance Scale IQ in Table L-1 or L-2 in Appendix L of this text. Use Table L-1, unless you are making a long-term prediction; in that case use Table L-2. All confidence intervals in Tables L-1 and L-2 are based on the examinee's exact age group as well as on the total sample. Normally, the confidence intervals are not used with the Verbal or Performance IQs, unless these are the only IQs reported. Write the confidence intervals on the front cover of the Record Form in the space provided.

32. Look up the percentile rank and classification for each of the IQs in Tables BC-1 and BC-2 on the inside back cover of this text. You can also use Tables A.2, A.3, and A.4 (pages 251 to 254) in the WISC-III manual for the percentile ranks and Table 2.8 (page 32 in the WISC-III manual) for classifications.

33. If you want to obtain test-age equivalents, use Table A.9 on page 259 of the WISC-III manual. They can be placed (in parentheses) in the right margin of the box that contains the scaled scores. For test-age equivalents *above* those in the table, use the highest test-age equivalent and a plus sign. For test-age equivalents *below* those in the table, use the lowest test-age equivalent and a minus sign.

34. If you want to, you can enter the factor scores on the front cover of the Record Form. The Deviation Quotients associated with the factor scores advocated in this text can be obtained from Tables A.5 and A.7 in the WISC-III manual for Verbal Comprehension and Processing Speed, respectively, and from Table L-13 in Appendix L for Perceptual Organization.

35. In summary, read the directions verbatim, pronounce words clearly, query at the appropriate times, start with the appropriate item, discontinue at the proper place, place items properly before the child, use correct timing, and follow the specific guidelines in the manual for administering the test.

■ **Exhibit I-3** ━━━━━━━━━━━━━

**Administrative Checklist for the WISC-III**

ADMINISTRATIVE CHECKLIST FOR THE WISC-III

*Name of examiner:* _____   *Date:* _____

*Name of examinee:* _____   *Name of observer:* _____

(Note. *If an item is not applicable, mark NA to the left of the number.*)

| Picture Completion | Circle One |
|---|---|
| 1. Reads directions verbatim | Yes No |
| 2. Reads directions clearly | Yes No |
| 3. Pronounces words in queries clearly | Yes No |
| 4. Starts with appropriate item | Yes No |
| 5. Places booklet flat on table, close to child | Yes No |
| 6. Begins timing after last word of instructions | Yes No |
| 7. Gives a maximum of 20 seconds on each item | Yes No |
| 8. Gives correct answer for sample item and items 1 and 2 if child fails these items | Yes No |
| 9. Does not give correct answer on items 3–30 | Yes No |
| 10. Gives the prompt "Yes, but what's missing?" no more than one time | Yes No |
| 11. Gives the prompt "A part is missing in the picture. What is it that is missing?" no more than one time | Yes No |
| 12. Gives the prompt "Yes, but what is the most important part that is missing" no more than one time | Yes No |
| 13. Inquires correctly on items 6, 13, 21, 23, 26, and 28 when certain responses are given | Yes No |
| 14. Gives credit to correct responses made after the prompt | Yes No |
| 15. Administers items in reverse order, when the first or second item administered is failed, to children ages 8 to 16 until they pass two consecutive items | Yes No |
| 16. Gives credit to items not administered when those items precede two consecutive successes | Yes No |
| 17. Gives credit for a correct oral or pointing response | Yes No |
| 18. Gives 1 point credit for each correct response | Yes No |
| 19. Gives no credit for correct responses given after time limit | Yes No |
| 20. Records 0 or 1 point for each item | Yes No |
| 21. Discontinues subtest after 5 consecutive failures | Yes No |

| Picture Completion (cont.) | Circle One |
|---|---|
| 22. Adds points correctly | Yes No |

Comments: _____

_____

| Information | Circle One |
|---|---|
| 1. Reads directions verbatim | Yes No |
| 2. Reads directions clearly | Yes No |
| 3. Reads items verbatim and clearly | Yes No |
| 4. Starts with appropriate item | Yes No |
| 5. Gives sufficient time for child to respond to each question | Yes No |
| 6. Gives correct answer for item 1 if child fails item | Yes No |
| 7. Does not give correct answer for items 2–30 | Yes No |
| 8. Says "Explain what you mean" or "Tell me more about it" for responses that are not clear | Yes No |
| 9. Gives prompts when the child's response suggests that the child has misheard or misunderstood the exact meaning of the question | Yes No |
| 10. Repeats question if child says he (she) does not understand it | Yes No |
| 11. Inquires correctly on items 4, 8, 16, 18, 19, 21, 24, 26, 28, 29, 30 when certain responses are given | Yes No |
| 12. Gives credit to correct responses made after the prompt (or inquiry) | Yes No |
| 13. Administers items in reverse order, when the first or second item administered is failed, to children ages 8 to 16 until they pass two consecutive items | Yes No |
| 14. Does not ask leading questions or spell words | Yes No |
| 15. Gives credit to items not administered when those items precede two consecutive successes | Yes No |
| 16. Gives 1 point credit for each correct response | Yes No |

*(Exhibit continues next page)*

**Exhibit I-3 (cont.)**

| Information (cont.) | *Circle One* | |
|---|---|---|
| 17. Records 0 or 1 point for each item | Yes | No |
| 18. Discontinues subtest after 5 consecutive failures | Yes | No |
| 19. Adds points correctly | Yes | No |

Comments: _____

_____

**Coding**

| | | *Circle One* | |
|---|---|---|---|
| 1. | Reads directions verbatim | Yes | No |
| 2. | Reads directions clearly | Yes | No |
| 3. | Correctly selects either Coding A or B | Yes | No |
| 4. | Provides two no. 2 graphite pencils without erasers | Yes | No |
| 5. | Removes Coding Response Sheet from the Record Form | Yes | No |
| 6. | Provides a smooth work surface | Yes | No |
| 7. | Provides extra Coding Response Sheet for left-handed children | Yes | No |
| 8. | Points to the key while reading the first part of the instructions | Yes | No |
| 9. | Points to the proper forms (e.g., star, ball, triangle, circle, box with two lines) while reading instructions | Yes | No |
| 10. | Follows directions in manual for pointing to sample items while reading directions | Yes | No |
| 11. | Praises child's successes on each sample item by saying "yes" or "right" | Yes | No |
| 12. | Corrects child's mistakes on sample items | Yes | No |
| 13. | Does not begin subtest until child clearly understands the task | Yes | No |
| 14. | Gives proper instructions after child completes the sample items and understands the task | Yes | No |
| 15. | Provides proper caution the first time child omits item or does only one type: "Do them in order. Don't skip any." Then points to the next item and says "Do this one next." | Yes | No |
| 16. | Gives caution about omitting or skipping item only one time | Yes | No |
| 17. | Reminds child to continue until told to stop (when needed) | Yes | No |
| 18. | Does not time the sample items | Yes | No |
| 19. | Begins timing immediately after completing instructions | Yes | No |
| 20. | Allows 120 seconds | Yes | No |
| 21. | Records time accurately | Yes | No |
| 22. | Uses scoring stencil to score subtest | Yes | No |

| Coding (cont.) | *Circle One* | |
|---|---|---|
| 23. Places a mark through each incorrect box | Yes | No |
| 24. Adds number of correct boxes or subtracts number of incorrect boxes from number attempted | Yes | No |
| 25. Gives time-bonus credits appropriately on Coding A | Yes | No |
| 26. Gives no time-bonus credits on Coding B | Yes | No |
| 27. Records correct number of items | Yes | No |

Comments: _____

_____

**Similarities**

| | | *Circle One* | |
|---|---|---|---|
| 1. | Reads directions verbatim | Yes | No |
| 2. | Reads directions clearly | Yes | No |
| 3. | Reads items verbatim and clearly | Yes | No |
| 4. | Begins with sample item and then item 1, regardless of child's age | Yes | No |
| 5. | Gives sufficient time for child to respond to each question | Yes | No |
| 6. | Gives correct answer for items 1 and 2 if child fails items | Yes | No |
| 7. | Does not give correct answer for items 3–19 | Yes | No |
| 8. | Gives an example of a 2-point response if a 1-point response is given on item 6 or item 7 | Yes | No |
| 9. | Queries every response followed in the WISC-III manual by a (Q), even if it is a 0-point response | Yes | No |
| 10. | Queries vague responses | Yes | No |
| 11. | Says "Explain what you mean" or "Tell me more about it" and no other statement to query a response | Yes | No |
| 12. | Does not query a clearcut response, especially one that is not followed in the WISC-III manual by a (Q) | Yes | No |
| 13. | Asks "Now which one is it?" each time a child's response contains both a correct and an incorrect answer | Yes | No |
| 14. | Gives 1 point credit for each correct response to items 1–5 | Yes | No |
| 15. | Gives 1 or 2 points credit for each correct response to items 6–19 | Yes | No |
| 16. | Records 0, 1, or 2 points as appropriate | Yes | No |
| 17. | Discontinues after 4 consecutive failures | Yes | No |
| 18. | Adds points correctly | Yes | No |

Comments: _____

_____

*(Exhibit continues next page)*

**Exhibit I-3 (cont.)**

| Picture Arrangement | Circle One |
|---|---|
| 1. Reads directions verbatim | Yes No |
| 2. Reads directions clearly | Yes No |
| 3. Gives sample item to all children and then item 1 to children aged 6–8 or item 3 to children aged 9–16 | Yes No |
| 4. Has cards arranged in numerical sequence and places all cards in correct numerical order from child's left to child's right | Yes No |
| 5. Rearranges sample item in correct order by moving cards one at a time to a new row and then points to each card as story is told | Yes No |
| 6. Allows child 10 seconds to look at correct arrangement on sample item | Yes No |
| 7. Begins timing after last word of instructions | Yes No |
| 8. Records time in the Record Form | Yes No |
| 9. Stops timing when child is obviously finished with each arrangement | Yes No |
| 10. Gives a second trial when child fails first trial on items 1–2 | Yes No |
| 11. Does not give a second trial on items 1–2 when child passes first trial | Yes No |
| 12. Does not give a second trial on items 4–14 | Yes No |
| 13. Uses correct time limits | Yes No |
| 14. Gives 2 points credit for each correct response given to items 1 and 2 on first trial or 1 point credit for each correct response given on second trial | Yes No |
| 15. Administers items 1 and 2 in that sequence if children between ages 9 and 16 fail item 3 | Yes No |
| 16. Allows child to continue working on arrangement after time limit has expired when child is nearing completion of task | Yes No |
| 17. Records the exact amount of time taken to solve item | Yes No |
| 18. Records child's exact arrangement (in letters) in Record Form | Yes No |
| 19. Gives correct number of points credit, including time-bonus credit, for items 3–14 | Yes No |
| 20. Gives no time-bonus credit to WODAHS arrangement for item 14 | Yes No |
| 21. Discontinues after 3 consecutive failures | Yes No |
| 22. Adds points correctly | Yes No |

Comments: _____

_____

| Arithmetic | Circle One |
|---|---|
| 1. Reads items verbatim | Yes No |
| 2. Reads items clearly | Yes No |
| 3. Starts with appropriate item | Yes No |
| 4. Places booklet properly in front of child for items 1–5 and for items 19–24 | Yes No |
| 5. Uses correct timing | Yes No |
| 6. Gives correct answer for items 1 and 2 if child fails items | Yes No |
| 7. Does not give correct answer for items 3–24 | Yes No |
| 8. Explains the concept of "cover up" without using card for demonstration if child does not understand it on item 3 | Yes No |
| 9. Does not allow child to use pencil and paper | Yes No |
| 10. Allows child to use a finger to "write" on the table | Yes No |
| 11. Administers items in reverse order, when the first or second item administered is failed, to children ages 7 to 16 until they pass two consecutive items | Yes No |
| 12. Reads items 19–24 aloud to children who have visual problems or reading difficulties | Yes No |
| 13. Records the exact amount of time taken to solve each problem | Yes No |
| 14. Begins timing immediately after each problem has been read | Yes No |
| 15. Repeats a problem only once | Yes No |
| 16. Records time from the ending of the first reading of problem to when the response is made, even when problem is read again | Yes No |
| 17. Asks child to select one of two responses when it is not clear which response is the final choice by saying "You said _____ and you said _____. Which one do you mean?" | Yes No |
| 18. Gives no credit for correct responses given after time limit | Yes No |
| 19. Gives 1 point credit for each correct response on items 1–18 | Yes No |
| 20. Gives 2 points credit for each correct response given between 1 and 10 seconds on items 19–24 | Yes No |
| 21. Gives credit for correct numerical quantity even when unit is not given | Yes No |
| 22. Gives credit when child spontaneously corrects an incorrect response within time limit | Yes No |
| 23. Records 0, 1, or 2 points as appropriate | Yes No |

*(Exhibit continues next page)*

**Exhibit I-3 (cont.)**

| Arithmetic (cont.) | *Circle One* | |
|---|---|---|
| 24. Discontinues after 3 consecutive failures | Yes | No |
| 25. Adds points correctly | Yes | No |

Comments: _____

_____

## Block Design

| | | |
|---|---|---|
| 1. Reads directions verbatim | Yes | No |
| 2. Reads directions clearly | Yes | No |
| 3. Turns blocks slowly to show different sides as instructions are read | Yes | No |
| 4. Starts with appropriate item | Yes | No |
| 5. Places blocks and cards properly | Yes | No |
| 6. Constructs model or places Stimulus Booklet approximately 7 inches from the child's edge of the table | Yes | No |
| 7. Places model or Stimulus Booklet somewhat to the left of the child's midline for right-handed children and somewhat to the right of midline for left-handed children | Yes | No |
| 8. Constructs designs 1 and 2 properly | Yes | No |
| 9. Presents pictures in the Stimulus Book with the unbound edge toward the child | Yes | No |
| 10. Lays out blocks so that different colored surfaces face up on different blocks | Yes | No |
| 11. Lays out blocks so that only one block has a red-and-white side facing up for the two- and four-block designs and only two blocks have a red-and-white side facing up for the nine-block designs | Yes | No |
| 12. Scrambles blocks between designs | Yes | No |
| 13. Begins timing after the last word of instructions | Yes | No |
| 14. Records time in the Record Form | Yes | No |
| 15. Uses correct time limits | Yes | No |
| 16. Stops timing when child is obviously finished with design (except for items 1–3) | Yes | No |
| 17. Allows child to continue working on design after time limit when child is nearing completion of task | Yes | No |
| 18. Gives a second trial when child fails first trial on items 1–3 | Yes | No |
| 19. Does not give second trial on items 4–9 | Yes | No |
| 20. Uses the correct number of blocks for each item | Yes | No |
| 21. Says "But, you see, the blocks go this way" and corrects the child's design the first time child rotates a design | Yes | No |
| 22. Gives instructions about need to correct a rotated design only once during the test | Yes | No |

| Block Design (cont.) | *Circle One* | |
|---|---|---|
| 23. Uses the appropriate instructions for item 3 depending on whether the child started the subtest with item 1 or 3 | Yes | No |
| 24. Gives 2 points when child gets items 1–3 correct on the first trial | Yes | No |
| 25. Gives 1 point when child gets items 1–3 correct on the second trial | Yes | No |
| 26. Gives correct number of points, including time-bonus credits, for items 4–12 | Yes | No |
| 27. Gives no credit for correct responses given after time limit | Yes | No |
| 28. Circles on the Record Form a Y (Yes) or N (No) for each item | Yes | No |
| 29. Stops child on items 1–3 when time limit has expired on first trial and gives second trial | Yes | No |
| 30. Records the exact amount of time taken to solve each item | Yes | No |
| 31. Administers items 1 and 2 in normal sequence, when the first or second trial of item 3 is failed, to children ages 8 to 16 | Yes | No |
| 32. Begins the directions for item 1 by assembling the model when child fails either the first or the second trial of item 3 | Yes | No |
| 33. Records 0–7 points as appropriate | Yes | No |
| 34. Discontinues subtest after 2 consecutive failures | Yes | No |
| 35. Adds points correctly | Yes | No |

Comments: _____

_____

## Vocabulary

| | | |
|---|---|---|
| 1. Reads directions verbatim | Yes | No |
| 2. Reads directions clearly | Yes | No |
| 3. Pronounces words clearly | Yes | No |
| 4. Starts with appropriate item | Yes | No |
| 5. Gives sufficient time for child to respond to each word | Yes | No |
| 6. Queries every response followed in the WISC-III manual by a (Q), even if it is a 0-point response | Yes | No |
| 7. Queries vague responses | Yes | No |
| 8. Does not query a clearcut response, especially one that is not followed in the WISC-III manual by a (Q) | Yes | No |
| 9. Gives the 2-point answer for item 1 if child gives a 0- or 1-point response | Yes | No |
| 10. Does not give correct answers for items 2–30 if child misses items | Yes | No |
| 11. Does not give credit to a pointing response | Yes | No |

*(Exhibit continues next page)*

**Exhibit I-3 (cont.)**

| Vocabulary (cont.) | *Circle One* | |
|---|---|---|
| 12. Uses "Listen carefully" prompt for misheard words | Yes | No |
| 13. Does not spell any words | Yes | No |
| 14. Gives credit to items not administered when those items precede perfect (2 point) scores on the first two items administered to children ages 9 to 16 | Yes | No |
| 15. Administers items in reverse order, when the child fails or gives a 1-point response to first or second item administered, to children ages 9 to 16 until they obtain perfect (2 point) scores on two consecutive items | Yes | No |
| 16. Inquires about vague responses, regionalisms, or slang responses | Yes | No |
| 17. Gives 1 or 2 points credit for each correct response | Yes | No |
| 18. Records 0, 1, or 2 points as appropriate | Yes | No |
| 19. Discontinues after 4 consecutive failures | Yes | No |
| 20. Adds points correctly | Yes | No |

Comments: _____

_____

**Object Assembly**

| | *Circle One* | |
|---|---|---|
| 1. Reads directions verbatim | Yes | No |
| 2. Reads directions clearly | Yes | No |
| 3. Starts with sample item | Yes | No |
| 4. Administers all items | Yes | No |
| 5. Uses shield correctly | Yes | No |
| 6. Presents puzzles with pieces arranged properly | Yes | No |
| 7. Begins timing immediately after last word of instructions | Yes | No |
| 8. Stops timing when child is obviously through | Yes | No |
| 9. Records time accurately | Yes | No |
| 10. Records number of junctures correctly completed within time limit | Yes | No |
| 11. Gives no credit for correct responses given after time limit | Yes | No |
| 12. Gives 10-second exposure after assembling sample item (apple) | Yes | No |
| 13. Demonstrates correct arrangement on item 1 (girl) if child's assembly is incomplete | Yes | No |
| 14. Does not demonstrate correct arrangement on items 2–5 even if child's arrangements are incomplete | Yes | No |
| 15. Does not give name of object for items 3–5 | Yes | No |
| 16. Records 0–10 points as appropriate | Yes | No |
| 17. Gives proper time-bonus credit | Yes | No |

| Object Assembly (cont.) | *Circle One* | |
|---|---|---|
| 18. Adds points correctly | Yes | No |

Comments: _____

_____

**Comprehension**

| | *Circle One* | |
|---|---|---|
| 1. Reads items verbatim | Yes | No |
| 2. Reads items clearly | Yes | No |
| 3. Begins with item 1 for all children | Yes | No |
| 4. Repeats question if child has difficulty remembering it or has not responded after 10–15 seconds | Yes | No |
| 5. Encourages a hesitant child to speak | Yes | No |
| 6. Queries every response followed in the WISC-III manual by a (Q), even if it is a 0-point response | Yes | No |
| 7. Queries vague responses | Yes | No |
| 8. Does not query a clearcut response, especially one that is not followed in the WISC-III manual by a (Q) | Yes | No |
| 9. Gives a few 2-point answers to item 1 if child gives a 0- or 1-point response | Yes | No |
| 10. Does not give correct answers to items 2–18 if child fails or does not give a 2-point response | Yes | No |
| 11. Prompts for second response on items 2, 6, 7, 11, 12, 15, 17, and 18, and only when first response is right | Yes | No |
| 12. Prompts for a second response only *once* per designated item | Yes | No |
| 13. Records 0, 1, or 2 points as appropriate | Yes | No |
| 14. Discontinues after 3 consecutive failures | Yes | No |
| 15. Adds points correctly | Yes | No |

Comments: _____

_____

**Symbol Search**

| | *Circle One* | |
|---|---|---|
| 1. Reads directions verbatim | Yes | No |
| 2. Reads directions clearly | Yes | No |
| 3. Correctly selects either Part A or Part B | Yes | No |
| 4. Provides two no. 2 graphite pencils without erasers | Yes | No |
| 5. Proceeds with test items only when child understands the task | Yes | No |
| 6. Points from child's left to right when giving instructions for sample item | Yes | No |
| 7. Offers praise such as "Yes" or "Right" when child marks the correct answer for the two practice items | Yes | No |

*(Exhibit continues next page)*

**Exhibit I-3 (cont.)**

| **Symbol Search (cont.)** | Circle One |
|---|---|

8. Gives correct instructions when child fails practice item — Yes No
9. Opens booklet to page 2 after child completes practice items — Yes No
10. Points to correct part of booklet as instructions are read for subtest items — Yes No
11. Turns page briefly to show child third page of items — Yes No
12. Begins timing after completing instructions — Yes No
13. Reminds child, if needed, to go in order and to continue the task until told to stop — Yes No
14. Discontinues after 120 seconds — Yes No
15. Places a mark through each incorrect item — Yes No
16. Records number of correct and incorrect items properly — Yes No
17. Obtains score by subtracting number of incorrect from number of correct items attempted — Yes No

Comments: _____

_____

**Digit Span**

1. Begins with item 1 — Yes No
2. Reads directions verbatim — Yes No
3. Reads directions clearly — Yes No
4. Administers both trials of each item — Yes No
5. Pronounces digits singly, distinctly, at the rate of one digit per second, and without chunking digits — Yes No
6. Drops voice inflection slightly on last digit — Yes No
7. Pauses after each sequence to allow child to respond — Yes No
8. Gives sample item for Digits Backward — Yes No
9. Gives child the correct answer to sample item if child fails item on Digits Backward — Yes No
10. Gives both trials of each item for Digits Forward and for Digits Backward — Yes No
11. Discontinues Digits Forward after failure on both trials of any item and then gives Digits Backward — Yes No
12. Discontinues Digits Backward after failure on both trials of any item — Yes No
13. Gives 1 point for each trial passed — Yes No
14. Records successes and failures in Record Form — Yes No
15. Adds points correctly — Yes No

Comments: _____

_____

| **Mazes** | Circle One |
|---|---|

1. Reads directions verbatim — Yes No
2. Reads directions clearly — Yes No
3. Begins with appropriate item — Yes No
4. Provides two no. 2 graphite pencils without erasers — Yes No
5. Exposes sheet properly (with arrow pointed toward examiner) — Yes No
6. Folds Mazes Response Booklet so that only one page is exposed — Yes No
7. Provides a smooth work surface — Yes No
8. Demonstrates the correct solution if child fails Maze 1 — Yes No
9. Demonstrates the correct solution if child fails Maze 2 — Yes No
10. Gives credit for all preceding items if child aged 8–16 obtains a perfect score on Maze 4 — Yes No
11. Administers Mazes 1–3 in normal sequence if child aged 8–16 obtains partial credit on Maze 4 — Yes No
12. Demonstrates sample maze and administers Mazes 1–3 in normal sequence if child aged 8–16 fails Maze 4 — Yes No
13. Begins timing after last word of instructions — Yes No
14. Records number of errors in the appropriate column in Record Form — Yes No
15. Uses "pencil point on paper" caution appropriately — Yes No
16. Uses "begins outside center of box" caution appropriately — Yes No
17. Uses "begins at the exit" caution appropriately — Yes No
18. Uses "don't stop" caution appropriately — Yes No
19. Uses "not allowed to start over" caution appropriately — Yes No
20. Uses "not completely clear the exit" caution appropriately — Yes No
21. Does examiner portion of sample appropriately — Yes No
22. Points to boy or girl figure in each maze as instructions are read — Yes No
23. Uses correct timing for each maze — Yes No
24. Records time accurately — Yes No
25. Discontinues after 2 consecutive failures — Yes No
26. Adds points correctly — Yes No

Comments: _____

_____

*(Exhibit continues next page)*

**Exhibit I-3 (cont.)**

| Other Aspects of Test Administration | Circle One | |
|---|---|---|
| 1. Establishes rapport | Yes | No |
| 2. Is well organized | Yes | No |
| 3. Has all needed materials in kit | Yes | No |
| 4. Has extra paper and pencils | Yes | No |
| 5. Makes smooth transition from subtest to subtest | Yes | No |
| 6. Provides support between subtests as needed | Yes | No |
| 7. Focuses child's attention on tasks | Yes | No |
| 8. Handles mild behavior problems appropriately | Yes | No |
| 9. Makes the test experience positive | Yes | No |

**Front Page of Record Form**

| | Circle One | |
|---|---|---|
| 1. Transfers raw scores to front page of Record Form for each subtest correctly | Yes | No |
| 2. Converts raw scores to scaled scores for each subtest correctly | Yes | No |
| 3. Adds scaled scores correctly for Verbal Scale | Yes | No |
| 4. Adds scaled scores correctly for Performance Scale | Yes | No |
| 5. Adds scaled scores correctly for Full Scale | Yes | No |
| 6. Converts sum of scaled scores in Verbal Scale to IQ correctly | Yes | No |

| Front Page of Record Form (cont.) | Circle One | |
|---|---|---|
| 7. Converts sum of scaled scores in Performance Scale to IQ correctly | Yes | No |
| 8. Converts sum of scaled scores in Full Scale to IQ correctly | Yes | No |
| 9. Completes profile of subtest scores correctly | Yes | No |
| 10. Completes identifying information section on front of Record Form correctly; assumes that all months have 30 days for purposes of calculating the chronological age; does not round up age (for example, 8 years–2 months–28 days is not rounded to 8 years, 3 months) | Yes | No |
| 11. Writes child's name, date, and examiner's name on Coding sheet and on Symbol Search and Mazes forms, if given | Yes | No |

**Overall Assessment of Test Administration**

*Circle one*: Excellent  Good  Average  Poor  Failing

Overall strengths: _____

Overall weaknesses: _____

Other comments: _____

_____

ferred to as a *basal level*) or discontinuance point (also referred to as a *ceiling level*), always err on the side of safety: *It is better to administer an item that may (or may not) be critical to a starting point or discontinuance point than to invalidate the subtest!*

If possible, make a videotape of your test administration and have a fellow student review it with you. Be alert to possible sources of error—both covert and overt—in your test administration and take appropriate steps to prevent these errors from occurring. Also check the Record Form to be sure that it is completed accurately. And, again, have a fellow student review the Record Form with you. In many training programs, your instructor or teaching assistant will give you feedback about your testing techniques. The key to proper test administration is to follow standard test procedures and to be an objective, but sensitive and supportive, examiner.

Following are some examples of how examiners were not sensitive to the child's needs or how they influenced the child's performance inappropriately (from Teglasi & Freeman, 1983, pp. 232–234, 239, with changes in wording and comments by me).

*Example 1.* Before administering the WISC-III, the examiner discussed with the child issues connected with the child's stealing. Later, when questioned on the Comprehension subtest about finding someone's wallet, the child looked distressed, but the examiner did not recognize the distress. *Comment.* Be sensitive to nonverbal cues as well as verbal ones. An alert examiner would have said something like "Now, this question has nothing to do with our previous discussion. This is one of the questions I ask everyone." An even more sensitive examiner may have waited to discuss the potentially emotionally arousing "stealing" issue until *after* the test was completed. You should always consider how any discussion may affect rapport.

*Example 2.* The examiner wanted to say something supportive to the examinee after the Digit Span subtest. *Examiner:* "Are you aware that you have a very good memory?" (Child obtained a low score on Digit Span.) *Child:* "No, I have a lousy one. I forget things all the time." *Comment.* Be sure that any reinforcing comments you make are congruent with the examinee's performance and given at appropriate times.

*Example 3*. The examiner watched a 10-year-old assemble the horse on the Object Assembly subtest, leaving one piece out. When the child said "finished," the examiner pointed to the extra piece. The child quickly corrected the error and was given full credit. *Comment*. Do not give nonverbal cues, such as the one in the example. They are not part of the standard procedure, and their use may invalidate the test results.

*Example 4*. Only when the child's arrangement on the Picture Arrangement subtest was correct did the examiner ask "finished?" If the child was still checking an incorrect sequence, the examiner was silent. The child soon caught on. *Comment*. Do not give verbal cues that may alert examinees to how well they are doing.

*Example 5*. The examiner, noting that a child had misplaced only one block in a complicated design on the Block Design subtest, said, "Be sure to check your answer." *Comment*. Do not ad lib directions, especially when your comments may help the examinee obtain higher scores. Stay as close to the directions in the manual as possible.

## Subtest Sequence

Administer the subtests in the order specified in the manual unless you have a compelling reason to use another order. For example, a compelling reason might be giving a child who is extremely bored or frustrated a different subtest or a subtest of his or her choice to motivate him or her. Another reason might be giving a child with a sensory handicap selected subtests. Using the standard sequence of administration provides you with a baseline for evaluating children whom you will test in the future; it also represents an order comparable to that given by other examiners. Following the specified order in the WISC-III manual, which alternates nonverbal and verbal subtests, also may help to maintain the child's interest in the tasks.

The WISC-III manual states that "Picture Completion provides an engaging, nonthreatening task" (p. 14). However, for children who have difficulty with perceptual discrimination, Picture Completion may be neither engaging nor nonthreatening. Similarly, children with test anxiety may feel anxious when they start the test, regardless of what the first subtest is. Therefore, you must always carefully attend to the child's behavior, especially at the beginning of the test session. Do not assume that the order of the subtests will automatically reduce children's anxiety level or help them to feel relaxed. We need research to learn about how the order of administering the subtests affects children's anxiety level.

## Scoring WISC-III Responses

You may find it difficult to score some responses on the Similarities, Vocabulary, and Comprehension subtests, especially those that are ambiguous. To become a skilled examiner, study carefully the scoring criteria, scoring guidelines, and scoring examples in the WISC-III manual. Although the WISC-III manual provides detailed scoring guidelines for each subtest, the sample responses in the manual simply cannot cover all possible responses that children will give. For this reason, you will have to use judgment in scoring responses.

Some examiners are more lenient than others in giving credit, and at times even the same examiners may not consistently adhere to their own relative standards. Thus, for example, they may be strict on some occasions and lenient on others. Studies have reported dramatic differences in the scoring standards of examiners. For example, in one study, 99 school psychologists gave IQs ranging from 63 to 117 to the *same* WISC protocol (Massey, 1964). In other studies with graduate-student examiners (Miller et al., 1970) and with members of the American Psychological Association (Miller & Chansky, 1972), examiners differed by as much as 17 points in scoring the same WISC protocol.

## Starting-Point Scoring Rule

Occasionally, you may have doubts about whether the child passed items at the starting point. (The starting-point items are those that the child must pass before you continue with the subtest.) When this happens, you will need to administer earlier items in the subtest. The WISC-III manual does not provide any guidance in how to score items that the examinee fails *below* the starting point. The WISC-R manual, however, did provide such guidance: *If subsequent scoring of the items indicates that the early items were administered unnecessarily, give the child full credit for these items even if he or she earned only partial or no credit* (cf. Wechsler, 1974, page 59). I recommend that you follow the same procedure on the WISC-III. (Lawrence Weiss from The Psychological Corporation fully supports this recommendation; personal communication, October 1991.) This means that when the child fails one or more items *below* the starting point (or receives partial credit), give *full credit* to these items if further checking indicates that, in fact, the child correctly answered the items at the starting point. This rule usually applies to children aged 7 years and older because they may have starting points above the first item on certain subtests.

Here is an example of the starting-point scoring rule. You administer items 5 and 6 on the Information subtest to an 8-year-old child and are uncertain of how to score the responses. You then administer items 4 and 3, which the child clearly fails, and then items 2 and 1, which the child clearly passes. You follow this procedure because the directions for the subtest state that the child must pass two consecutive items before you administer the rest of the subtest. Because the child passed items 1 and 2, you continue giving the subtest with item 7. After the examination, you decide that the child did indeed pass items 5 and 6. The starting-point scoring rule requires that you give the child full credit for items 3 and 4, even though he or she failed them, because these two items are *below* the starting-point items 5 and 6, which the child passed.

The starting-point scoring rule favors the child by ensuring that you do not penalize him or her for failing items that, as it turned out, need not have been administered. The starting-point scoring rule is an attempt to maintain standardized scoring procedures.

## Discontinuance-Point Scoring Rule

The discontinuance-point scoring rule applies to situations in which you have doubts about whether the child failed the items at the discontinuance point and you then administer additional items in the subtest (see page 43 of the WISC-III manual). (The discontinuance-point items are those that the child must fail before you discontinue the subtest.) The discontinuance-point scoring rule is as follows: *If subsequent scoring of the items indicates that the additional items were administered unnecessarily, do not give the child credit for items that he or she passed after the discontinuance point.*

Here is an example of the discontinuance-point scoring rule. You administer the first 15 words of the Vocabulary subtest, but are uncertain of how to score the child's responses to words 11 through 14. You then administer additional words. The child knows words 15 and 16 but not words 17 to 21. You therefore discontinue the subtest after word 21. After the test is over, you check your scoring and decide that the child's answers were wrong on words 11 to 14. The discontinuance-point scoring rule requires that you *not* give the child credit for words 15 and 16, even though the definitions were correct, because these words occur *after* you should have discontinued the subtest.

In contrast to the starting-point scoring rule, the discontinuance-point scoring rule does not favor the child. This scoring rule prevents the child from receiving credit on items that, as it turned out, need not have been adminis-tered. This rule constitutes another attempt to maintain standardized scoring procedures.

## Repetition of Items

When a child says "I don't know," you must decide whether the response means that the child doesn't know the answer or that the child doesn't want to answer the question. If you decide that it is a motivational issue, encourage the child to attempt an answer. If necessary, repeat the question or ask it again at some later point—especially if the child says "I don't know" to an easy question. Better yet, the first time a child says "I don't know," say something like "I want you to try your hardest on each of these. Try your best to answer each question." Give the child credit if he or she answers the question correctly. However, never repeat items on Digit Span.

## Use of Probing Questions and Queries

The sample response sections of the WISC-III manual indicate that you need to query certain responses. However, you will also need to query responses that are not shown in the manual. For example, negativistic or mis-trustful responses, such as the following, can be acknowl-edged and then probed. If a child responded to the Compre-hension question dealing with freedom of speech with "Freedom of speech is relative so that at times it is improper when it incites people," you could say "Well, try to give some answers that other people think are reasonable." You will have to be alert to recognize responses needing these kinds of probes. You will also need to probe verbal re-sponses that are incomplete, indefinite, or vague. Ask additional questions (that is, use queries or probes) when you are unsure of how to score a response; however, do not ask additional questions to elicit a higher quality response from the child unless the WISC-III manual so indicates. For responses in the WISC-III manual followed by a "Q" in black, the examinee must give the response shown after the "Q" in order to get the appropriate credit. Consequently, the entire response—that is, the initial response plus the response to the query—receives the appropriate credit.

## Spoiled Responses

An explicit scoring rule on the WISC-III is that you give a score of 0 to a spoiled response (see pages 50–51 in the WISC-III manual). A spoiled response is one that initially was partially right, but was spoiled by the child's incorrect elaboration on his or her initial response. For example, a child who says that *clock* means "Goes ticktock," and then says "It's the engine on a motorcycle," in response to a probe, has spoiled his or her response. This elaboration reveals the child's misconception about the meaning of the word *clock*.

## Modifying Standard Procedures

Research with the WISC-R indicated that children are likely to obtain higher scores on some subtests when they are encouraged to talk about their problem-solving procedures, think about their answers before responding, explain their picture arrangements, or solve problems after receiving a series of cues (Herrell & Golland, 1969; Post, 1970; Sattler, 1969; Schwebel & Bernstein, 1970). We would expect similar results on the WISC-III. If you use such modifications, employ them only *after* the standard administration. Modifications may be helpful in clinical assessment of the child's potential for learning, but they may invalidate the scores if they are used during the standard administration.

## Potential Administrative Problems on Arithmetic and Picture Arrangement

There can be subtle administration problems on the Arithmetic and Picture Arrangement subtests that may never arise, but are worth noting. On the Arithmetic subtest, children are requested to read problems 19 through 24. Because timing begins when children finish reading each of these problems, slow readers have more time to solve the problems than fast readers. Some children also may intentionally slow their reading in order to solve the problems before timing begins. What effect reading speed has on the speed of solving the problems is unknown. Because bonus points are awarded for speed on Arithmetic items 19 through 24, differences in reading speed and in problem-solving strategies may affect children's scores.

Another potential problem with Arithmetic is that some children may feel anxious when they read the problems aloud. If children do feel anxious, we do not know how their anxiety will affect their ability to solve the problems. And finally, there seems to be a subtle difference in administration when the examiner reads items 19 through 24 aloud to children who cannot read and when children read the problems aloud by themselves. In the former case, memory plays an important role because the children cannot "see" the questions. In the latter case, memory plays a smaller role because the children see the problems during the entire time that they work on them.

On Picture Arrangement, not all children receive the same type of help. All children start with the sample item, which includes the story elements in the directions. Young children (6 to 8 years) are then administered items 1 and 2 and again are told the story elements as part of the directions. Older children (9 to 16 years), in contrast, are not given any story elements when they begin item 3. We do not know to what extent hearing the story elements on items 1 and 2 helps children on later items.

# SHORT FORMS OF THE WISC-III

Examiners may use short forms of the WISC-III and other Wechsler scales as *screening devices* (when the short form may be followed by administering the remaining subtests), *for research purposes* (to describe the intellectual level of a group), and *for a quick check on a child's intellectual status* (and only when the IQ is peripheral to the referral question) (Silverstein, 1990b[R]). Ideally, you should select a short form based on such criteria as acceptable reliability and validity, the power of the short form to answer the referral question and provide clinically useful information, the examinee's physical capabilities, and the amount of time available for administering the test.

Researchers often evaluate the validity of short forms by correlating the short-form IQ with the Full Scale IQ, evaluating mean differences between the two IQs, and determining the extent of agreement in the intelligence classifications provided by the two IQs. Silverstein (1985a) argued, however, that these three criteria are not useful. First, it is virtually certain that there will be high correlations between short-form and Full Scale IQs. Second, with sufficiently large samples, a significant difference between long and short IQs is likely to occur, making this criterion nearly meaningless. Third, it is virtually certain that the short-form and Full Scale IQs will yield different classifications. [Goh (1978), for example, found that short-form WISC-R IQs misclassified 45 percent of a group of 142 children.] In light of the findings, Silverstein suggested that examiners use other considerations to determine the appropriateness of a short form. *If you must obtain a specific classification for a clinical or psychoeducational purpose, do not use a short form.*

### Selecting the Short Form

Table L-11 in Appendix L shows the 10 best short-form combinations of two, three, four, and five WISC-III subtests. To obtain the reliability and validity coefficients shown in Table L-11, I used the standardization data and the Tellegen and Briggs (1967) procedure, which takes into account the reliabilities of the subtests used in the short form. (Exhibit I-4 shows the formulas used to compute the reliability and validity of the short-form combinations.) An inspection of the coefficients in Table L-11 indicates that all of the four- and five-subtest short-form combinations have reliability coefficients of .93 or higher. Even the three-subtest short-form combinations have reliabilities of .92 to .93. However, 6 of the 10 two-subtest short-form combinations have reliabilities below .90. Therefore, for the combinations shown in Table L-11, the more subtests used in the short form, the higher the reliability will be of the estimated IQ.

Because the reliabilities and validities of the various short forms are high, clinical considerations should also guide you in selecting the short form. For example, if you want to use a four-subtest short form, consider selecting a combination of two Verbal and two Performance Scale subtests, to obtain some representation of both verbal and performance skills in the short form.

An examinee's physical capabilities may also guide you in selecting a short form. Examinees with marked visual impairment or severe motor dysfunction of the upper extremities will have difficulty with Performance Scale tasks. In such cases, the Verbal Scale (or Verbal factor) serves as a useful short form. For hearing-impaired examinees, the Performance Scale (or Performance factor) alone is a useful short form. Administer these short forms by using the child's preferred mode of communication and supplement your evaluation by using other tests designed to accommodate the special physical abilities of the child (see Chapter 12).

## Converting Short-Form Scores into Deviation Quotients

After you administer the short form, you will need to convert the child's scaled scores to a Full Scale IQ estimate. Simple prorating and regression procedures are not applicable in this case because they do not deal adequately with the problem of subtest reliability (Tellegen & Briggs, 1967). The more acceptable procedure is to transform the short-form scores into the familiar Wechsler-type Deviation Quotient, which has a mean of 100 and a standard deviation of 15. Exhibit I-4 shows the procedure for converting the short-form scores into a Deviation Quotient. This procedure holds for all Wechsler tests. Although this approach does not eliminate the many problems associated with short forms, it is statistically appropriate.

I used the Tellegen and Briggs (1967) procedure to obtain estimated WISC-III Deviation Quotients for the 10 best short-form dyads, triads, tetrads, and pentads (see Tables L-12, L-13, L-14, and L-15 in Appendix L, respectively).

The notes in Tables L-12, L-13, and L-14 also describe other short-form combinations, some of which are useful for screening hearing-impaired children.

## Yudin's Abbreviated Procedure

In the Yudin (1966) WISC short-form procedure, which also applies to the WISC-III, you administer every other item on most subtests. Table C-11 of Appendix C describes the specific procedure, as modified by Silverstein (1968a). After the test is administered, scaled scores and IQs are obtained from the manual in the usual way. The Yudin procedure differs from other short-form procedures in that it uses all of the standard subtests. Its advantages are that you administer a representative sample of items, can apply profile analysis, and use about 56 percent of the items.

Although the Yudin procedure has satisfactory reliability (Reid, Moore, & Alexander, 1968; Yudin, 1966), it has shortcomings. These include a moderate loss of validity and reliability, less reliable profile data, and IQs that differ from those obtained on the Full Scale (Dean, 1977f; Erikson, 1967; Finch, Kendall, Spirito, Entin, Montgomery, & Schwartz, 1979; Gayton, Wilson, & Bernstein, 1970; Goh, 1978; Rasbury, Falgout, & Perry, 1978; Satz, Van de Riet, & Mogel, 1967; Tellegen & Briggs, 1967). Silverstein (1990a[R]) reported, for example, that the Yudin procedure yields a reliability coefficient of .905 for the WISC-R Full Scale IQ, whereas the best four-subtest short-form combination yields a reliability coefficient of .942. Silverstein concluded that "reducing the number of items within subtests rather than the number of subtests exacts a steep price in reliability" (p. 196). Consider carefully the assets and liabilities of the Yudin abbreviated procedure before you use it.

Hobby (1980) described a WISC-R short-form procedure, which you also can use with the WISC-III, in which you administer only odd items on most subtests. It is similar to the Yudin procedure, but has more specific basal and ceiling procedures and correction factors.

A major problem with reduced-item short forms that has not been addressed in the research literature is that they represent a violent departure from the standard administration (personal communication, Leslie Atkinson, January 1992). Because half of the items are excluded, the difficulty slope of the items increases much more rapidly than under standard conditions, while the opportunity for practice decreases equally rapidly. Research to date has involved administering the entire scale and generating validity coefficients for the relevant half. This situation is different from simply administering half of the items. For these reasons,

---

**■ Exhibit I-4 ■**

**Obtaining Deviation Quotients for Wechsler Short Forms**

---

### Computing the Deviation Quotient of the Short Form

The following formula is used to compute the Deviation Quotient for a short form:

$$\text{Deviation Quotient} = (15/S_c)(X_c - M_c) + 100$$

where $S_c = S_s\sqrt{n + 2\Sigma r_{jk}}$ (standard deviation of composite score)

$X_c$ = composite score (sum of subtest scaled scores in the short form)

$M_c$ = normative mean, which is equal to $10n$

$S_s$ = subtest standard deviation, which is equal to 3

$n$ = number of component subtests

$\Sigma r_{jk}$ = sum of the correlations between component subtests.

This equation considers the number of subtests in the short form, the correlations between the subtests, and the total scaled-score points obtained on the short form.

A more straightforward computational formula for obtaining the Deviation Quotient is as follows:

$$\text{Deviation Quotient} = (\text{composite score} \times a) + b$$

where $a = 15/S_c$

$b = 100 - n(150)/S_c$.

Table C-36 in Appendix C (page 850) can be used in obtaining the appropriate $a$ and $b$ constants. In using Table C-36, first select the heading corresponding to the number of subtests in the short form. The first column under each heading is $\Sigma r_{jk}$. This term represents the sum of the correlations between the subtests making up the composite score. To obtain $\Sigma r_{jk}$, use the WISC-III correlation table of the group closest in age to the examinee (Tables C.1 through C.12 on pages 270 through 281 of the WISC-III manual). With two subtests in the short form, only one correlation is needed. With three subtests in the short form, three correlations are summed (1 with 2, 1 with 3, and 2 with 3). With four subtests in the short form, six correlations are summed (1 with 2, 1 with 3, 1 with 4, 2 with 3, 2 with 4, and 3 with 4). With five subtests in the short form, 10 correlations are summed (1 with 2, 1 with 3, 1 with 4, 1 with 5, 2 with 3, 2 with 4, 2 with 5, 3 with 4, 3 with 5, and 4 with 5). After $\Sigma r_{jk}$ is calculated, the values for the two constants are obtained under the appropriate heading.

The procedure used to obtain the Deviation Quotient can be summarized as follows:

1. Sum the scaled scores of the subtests in the short form to obtain the composite score.
2. Sum the correlations between the subtests to obtain $\Sigma r_{jk}$.
3. Find the appropriate $a$ and $b$ constants in Table C-36 in Appendix C (page 850) after $\Sigma r_{jk}$ has been obtained.
4. Compute the Deviation Quotient by using the composite score and the $a$ and $b$ constants.

*Example:* A three-subtest short form composed of the Arithmetic, Vocabulary, and Block Design subtests is administered to a 6-year-old child. The child obtains scaled scores of 7, 12, and 13 on the three subtests. The four steps are as follows:

1. The three scaled scores are summed to yield a composite score of 32.
2. The correlations between the three subtests are obtained from Table C.1 (page 270) of the WISC-III manual (Arithmetic and Vocabulary, .50; Arithmetic and Block Design, .51; Vocabulary and Block Design, .53). These are summed to yield 1.54 ($\Sigma r_{jk}$).
3. The appropriate row in Table C-36 in Appendix C is the third one under the heading "3 Subtests." The values for the constants $a$ and $b$ are 2.0 and 40, respectively.
4. The formula

$$\text{Deviation Quotient} = (\text{composite score} \times a) + b$$

is used to obtain a Deviation Quotient of 104 [$(32 \times 2.0) + 40$].

### Computing the Reliability Coefficient of the Short Form

The following formula is used to obtain the reliability of the short form:

$$r_{ss} = \frac{\Sigma r_{ii} + 2\Sigma r_{ij}}{k + \Sigma 2 r_{ij}}$$

where $r_{ss}$ = reliability of the short form

$r_{ii}$ = reliability of subtest $i$

$r_{ij}$ = correlation between any subtests $i$ and $j$

$k$ = number of component subtests.

*Example:* The reliability of the two-subtest combination of Vocabulary and Block Design is calculated in the following way, given $r_{ii}$ (Vocabulary) = .87, $r_{ii}$ (Block Design) = .87, and $r_{ij}$ (Vocabulary and Block Design) = .46.

$$r_{ss} = \frac{1.74 + .92}{2 + .92} = \frac{2.66}{2.92} = .91$$

*(Exhibit continues next page)*

**Exhibit I-4 (cont.)**

**Computing the Validity Coefficient of the Short Form**

The following formula is used to obtain the validity of the short form:

$$r'_{pw} = \frac{\Sigma\Sigma r_{jl}}{\sqrt{k + 2\,\Sigma r_{ij}}\,\sqrt{t + 2\,\Sigma r_{lm}}}$$

where  $r'_{pw}$ = modified coefficient of correlation between the composite part and the composite whole

$r_{jl}$ = correlation between any subtest $j$ included in the part and any subtest $l$ included in the whole, where any included correlation between a subtest and itself is represented by its reliability coefficient

$r_{ij}$ = correlation between subtests $i$ and $j$

$r_{lm}$ = correlation between subtests $l$ and $m$

$k$ = number of component subtests

$t$ = number of subtests included in the whole.

To obtain $\Sigma\Sigma r_{jl}$, total the following three sums: (a) the sum of the reliabilities of the component subtests, (b) twice the sum of the intercorrelations among the component subtests ($2\Sigma r_{ij}$), and (c) the sum of the intercorrelations between any component subtest and any noncomponent subtest.

*Example:* The validity of the two-subtest combination of Vocabulary and Block Design is calculated in the following way, given $r_{ii}$ (Vocabulary) = .87, $r_{ii}$ (Block Design) = .87, and $r_{ij}$ (Vocabulary and Block Design) = .46. In this example, all 13 WISC-III subtests are used. In other cases, only the 10 standard subtests may be used.

$$r'_{pw} = \frac{1.74 + .92 + 9.74}{\sqrt{2 + 2(.46)}\,\sqrt{13 + 2(28.91)}}$$

$$= \frac{12.40}{(1.71)(8.42)} = \frac{12.40}{14.40} = .86$$

*Source:* Adapted from Tellegen & Briggs (1967).

---

Atkinson recommended that reduced-item short forms not be used.

## Vocabulary and Block Design Short Form

A popular screening short form consists of Vocabulary and Block Design. These two subtests have excellent reliability, correlate highly with the Full Scale over a wide age range, and are good measures of g. You can use Table L-12 in Appendix L to convert the sum of scaled scores on these two subtests directly to an estimated Deviation Quotient.

## Information, Vocabulary, Picture Completion, and Block Design

This short-form combination, which contains two Verbal subtests and two Performance subtests, has high reliability ($r_{tt}$ = .935). It takes longer to administer than the Vocabulary and Block Design short form, but provides more clinical and diagnostic information. You can use Table L-14 in Appendix L to convert the sum of scaled scores on these four subtests directly to an estimated Deviation Quotient.

## Other Useful Short Forms

Other short forms discussed in the literature for the WISC-R, which you can also use for the WISC-III, are Similarities and Vocabulary (Fell & Fell, 1982); Similarities and Object Assembly (Fell & Fell, 1982); Similarities, Vocabulary, and Block Design (Karnes & Brown, 1981); Similarities, Vocabulary, Block Design, and Object Assembly (Karnes & Brown, 1981); Similarities, Vocabulary, Block Design, and Picture Completion (Clarizio & Veres, 1984); Similarities, Object Assembly, and Vocabulary (Dirks, Wessels, Quarfoth, & Quenon, 1980); Information, Comprehension, Block Design, Picture Arrangement, and Coding (Kennedy & Elder, 1982); and Arithmetic, Vocabulary, Picture Arrangement, and Block Design (Kaufman, 1976b).

If you want to give a short form that you can administer quickly and score relatively easily, consider the following combinations (reliabilities shown in parentheses): two subtests—Information and Picture Completion ($r_{xx}$ = .87); three subtests—Information, Similarities, and Picture Completion ($r_{xx}$ = .91); four subtests—Information, Similarities, Picture Completion, and Object Assembly ($r_{xx}$ = .91). These short forms, although they do not fall into the 10-best combinations, are effective as screening tools and have in their favor, as noted earlier, quick administration with a minimum of scoring problems. The four subtests have relatively high correlations with the Full Scale ($r$'s of .72, .72, .58, and .56, respectively). You can use Tables L-12, L-13, and L-14, respectively, to convert the sum of scaled scores on these combinations directly to an estimated Deviation Quotient. The footnotes at the bottom of these tables indicate which columns to use for these short-form combinations.

A word of caution is in order, however. Even though the Information and Picture Completion short form is more convenient in terms of time and scoring than Vocabulary and Block Design, you do not get any information about how the child copes with a less-structured task (Vocabulary) or uses problem-solving strategies (Block Design) when you use this short form. For the extra time involved, you will get more valuable clinical information by using Vocabulary and Block Design in a two-subtest short form (or in a longer short-form combination). I recommend that you consider using Vocabulary and Block Design in a short form if you need to use one.

### Comment on Short Forms of the WISC-III (and Short Forms of Other Tests as Well)

Short forms save time and are useful screening devices, but they have many disadvantages. First, you usually obtain less stable IQs with short forms than you do with the full battery of subtests. Second, you lose information about cognitive patterning (that is, the pattern of strengths and weaknesses and the pattern of variability among subtest scores). Third, you lose the opportunity to observe the examinee's problem-solving methods over a range of situations. Fourth, you lose information about nonverbal ability when you administer short forms composed of Verbal subtests only, and you lose information about verbal ability when you administer short forms composed of Performance subtests only. Finally, the internal consistency reliability of the IQ is diminished when you eliminate subtests.

If you are thinking about using a short form, weigh the time saved against the validity lost. In addition, consider what kind of decision you will make on the basis of the short-form scores. The most efficient testing strategy for a particular situation will depend, in part, on the goal of the evaluation—whether it is for a general assessment of intelligence, classification, selection, or screening.

Even when you administer all of the subtests, the IQ you obtain on any intelligence tests is merely an *estimate* of the abilities possessed by a child. When you use a small number of subtests, the estimate may be far less adequate than that provided by the Full Scale. *Additionally, educational and clinical situations call for more, rather than less, extensive cognitive evaluation. Consequently, the Full Scale should be administered to maximize the diagnostic information you can obtain and to minimize placement errors. I encourage you to administer the Full Scale, unless there is some compelling reason to administer a short form.* Included among these reasons would be situations in which the child was ready to quit testing or the physical capabilities of the examinee made some of the subtests inappropriate. *I do not recommend short forms for any placement, educational, or clinical decision-making purpose.*

## CHOOSING BETWEEN THE WISC-III AND THE WPPSI-R AND BETWEEN THE WISC-III AND THE WAIS-R

The WISC-III overlaps with the WPPSI-R for ages 6-0-0 to 7-3-15 and with the WAIS-R for ages 16-0-0 to 16-11-30. The overlap in ages between the WISC-III and the WPPSI-R and between the WISC-III and the WAIS-R is especially helpful in retest situations. For example, you can retest a child first administered the WISC-III at age 6 years with the WPPSI-R at any time during the next 15 months. Similarly, you can retest a 16-year-old adolescent who initially was given the WAIS-R with the WISC-III up until his or her seventeenth birthday. However, because the WISC-III and the WPPSI-R share many items in common, the two tests are not truly independent instruments.

In the overlapping age ranges, Atkinson (personal communication, January 1992) compared the WISC-III with the WPPSI-R and the WISC-III with the WAIS-R on several criteria, including mean subtest reliability, Full Scale reliability, mean subtest floor, mean subtest ceiling, item gradients (refers to number of items needed to reach the mean and the relationship of raw score points to scaled-score points), Full Scale floor, and Full Scale ceiling. His recommendations are discussed below.

### WISC-III vs. WPPSI-R

Age considerations should be taken into account in evaluating the choice of either the WISC-III or WPPSI-R.

a. For *ages 6-0 to 6-11*, the WISC-III and WPPSI-R are comparable in all respects, except for measures of item gradients. Item gradient statistics suggest the following:

- *the WPPSI-R is a better choice for children with below-average ability*
- *the WISC-III is a better choice for children with above-average ability*
- *either test is adequate for children with average ability*

b. For *ages 7-0 to 7-3*, the WISC-III has superior subtest reliabilities, higher subtest ceilings, and better item gradients both above and below the mean. In other respects the two tests are comparable. Therefore,

- *the WISC-III is a better choice for all children at 7-0 to 7-3*

The following example illustrates how you can obtain a more thorough sampling on the WPPSI-R than on the WISC-III for a 6-year-old child with below-average ability. To obtain a scaled score of 5 on Information, a 6-year-child needs a raw score of 16 on the WPPSI-R, but only a raw score of 2 on the WISC-III.

Atkinson's recommendations are summarized in the following chart:

| Recommendations for Selecting WISC-III or WPPSI-R | | | |
|---|---|---|---|
| | Ability level | | |
| Ages | Below average | Average | Above average |
| 6-0 to 6-11 | WPPSI-R | either test | WISC-III |
| 7-0 to 7-3 | WISC-III | WISC-III | WISC-III |

These recommendations differ somewhat from those presented in the WISC-III manual. The WISC-III manual (page 8) recommends that in the overlapping ages you use the WISC-III for children with average or above-average ability and the WPPSI-R for children with below-average ability. I suggest that you follow Atkinson's recommendations.

## WISC-III vs. WAIS-R

For ages 16-0 to 16-11, the WISC-III, in comparison to the WAIS-R, has better subtest reliabilities, lower subtest floors, better item gradients below the mean, a lower Full Scale IQ floor, and a higher Full Scale IQ ceiling. Therefore, Atkinson noted that

* *the WISC-III is a better choice than the WAIS-R*

Atkinson's recommendations are summarized in the following chart:

| Recommendations for Selecting WISC-III or WAIS-R | | | |
|---|---|---|---|
| | Ability level | | |
| Ages | Below average | Average | Above average |
| 16-0 to 16-11 | WISC-III | WISC-III | WISC-III |

The following example illustrates how you can obtain a more thorough sampling on the WISC-III than on the WAIS-R for a 16-year-, 8-month-old adolescent with below-average ability. On Information, to obtain a scaled score of 5, the adolescent needs a raw score of 14 on the WISC-III but only a raw score of 4 on the WAIS-R.

This recommendation differs from that presented in the WISC-III manual. The WISC-III manual recommends that you use the WISC-III for adolescents with below-average ability, but makes no recommendation for adolescents with

average or above-average ability. I suggest that you follow Atkinson's recommendations.

## Comment on Choosing the WISC-III or WPPSI-R and WISC-III or WAIS-R

The previous recommendations were based on internal psychometric data. The issue of validity still needs to be addressed. In the final analysis, the choice of a test in the overlapping ages should depend on the validity of the inferences that you can make from scores on it. To this end, validity studies that compare the WISC-III with the WPPSI-R and the WISC-III with the WAIS-R in their overlapping age ranges, using samples of both normal and exceptional children, would be helpful.

## ADMINISTERING THE WECHSLER TESTS TO HANDICAPPED CHILDREN

For handicapped children, you will need to evaluate the child's sensory-motor abilities before you administer one of the Wechsler tests. If you find that the child has a visual, hearing, or motor problem that may interfere with his or her ability to take one or more subtests, do not administer those subtests.

Table I-15 shows the physical abilities that an examinee needs to take a Wechsler test. Obviously, if you give the directions orally, the child must be able to hear what you say. On most of the Performance subtests, the child must be able to see the items and use his or her hands to solve the problems.

If you want to administer a Wechlser test to a child with a physical disability, you will need to administer the subtests without providing cues to the child. If your modifications go beyond simply permitting the child to respond in a different manner or using alternative procedures to present the items, the results may be invalid.

### Verbal Scale Subtests

You can administer all of the Verbal Scale subtests orally to a child who can hear. If the child cannot hear but can read, you can type the Information, Comprehension, Similarities, and Vocabulary questions on cards and show the cards to the child one at a time. However, visually presenting the Arithmetic and Digit Span items poses more difficulties because of the time limits involved in the Arithmetic subtest and because visual presentation of the items seems drastically different from oral presentation, especially with Digit Span items. Therefore, you may have to omit Digit

**Table I-I5**
**Physical Abilities Necessary and Adaptable for Subtests on the Wechsler Scales**

| Subtest | Physical ability | | | |
|---|---|---|---|---|
| | Vision | Hearing | Oral speech | Arm-hand use |
| Information | S | A | A | W |
| Comprehension | S | A | A | W |
| Arithmetic | S | A | A | W |
| Similarities | S | A | A | W |
| Vocabulary | S | A | A | W |
| Digit Span | N | R | A | W |
| Picture Completion | R | A | O | P or W |
| Coding, Digit Symbol | R | A | N | R |
| Picture Arrangement | R | A | O | A |
| Block Design | R | A | N | R |
| Object Assembly | R | A | N | R |
| Symbol Search | R | A | O | P or W |
| Mazes | R | A | N | R |
| Sentences | S | A | A | W |
| Animal Pegs | R | A | O | A |
| Geometric Design | R | A | N | R |

*Note.* The code is as follows:

A—This ability is required for standard administration, but the subtest is adaptable.

N—This ability is not required.

O—Examinees who are able to speak can say their answers.

P—Examinees who are able to point can point to their answers.

R—This ability is required. Adaptation is not feasible if this function is absent or more than mildly impaired.

S—Examinees who are able to read can be shown the questions. If the examinee cannot read, hearing is necessary. If neither the ability to read nor the ability to hear is present, the subtest should not be administered.

W—Examinees who are able to write can write their answers.

---

Span when you test deaf children. If the child cannot respond orally, you can accept written replies (or those typed on a typewriter or computer) to any of the Verbal Scale subtests.

### Performance Scale Subtests

Adaptations of the Performance Scale subtests center on the child's method of responding. You can give the Picture Completion subtest only to a child who has adequate vision and who can describe the missing part either orally or in writing (or typed on a typewriter or computer) or by pointing to it. You cannot easily adapt Block Design, Object Assembly, Coding, Digit Symbol (WAIS-R), Mazes, Animal Pegs (WPPSI-R), and Geometric Design (WPPSI-R) for a child whose arm-hand use is severely impaired. However, you can adapt the Picture Arrangement subtest for a child who has an arm-hand impairment. In this case, ask the child to tell you in what order he or she wants you to arrange the cards. This can be done orally or

by writing or typing. You can adapt Symbol Search by pointing to each item and having the child say (or type) whether the symbol is or is not in the array. Appendixes D and M provide detailed instructions for administering the Performance Scale subtests to a deaf child.

### Advantages of Two Separate Scales

The division of the Wechsler subtests into Verbal and Performance Scales is helpful in testing handicapped children. You can administer the Verbal Scale to a blind child or to a child with severe motor handicaps. And you can administer the Performance Scale to a hearing-impaired child or to a child who has little or no speech. If you also administer the Verbal Scale to a hearing-impaired child, you can compare the child's performance on the Verbal and Performance Scales to evaluate the child's verbal deficit. *However, in such cases do not include the Verbal Scale in the computation of the IQ; only use the Performance Scale as the best estimate of the hearing-impaired child's intellectual ability.*

## Unknown Effects of Modifications

Without empirical findings, there is no way of knowing how the suggested modifications affect the reliability and validity of the scores. Yet, when you cannot use standard procedures because handicaps prevent the child from comprehending the instructions or manipulating the materials, you may need to use such modifications. *When you use modifications, consider the resulting score only as an approximate estimate of the score that the child might obtain under standardized procedures.*

## Timed Subtests

A study of the WISC-R indicated that speed of correct response on the WISC-R Picture Arrangement, Block Design, and Object Assembly subtests significantly relates to children's chronological age and to their problem-solving ability (Kaufman, 1979b). Older children solve the tasks more quickly than younger children, and those who solve the problems quickly also tend to solve more problems than those who solve them slowly. Because speed plays only a limited role in enabling children below 10 years of age to earn bonus points, it is reasonable to administer these subtests to 6- to 10-year-old orthopedically handicapped children who are able to manipulate the materials; you will not unduly penalize these children for failure to earn bonus points (Kaufman, 1979b). These findings likely hold for the WISC-III, although we need research before we can accept them without question.

## ASSETS OF THE WISC-III

The WISC-III is a well-standardized test, with excellent reliability and adequate concurrent and construct validity. The 13 subtests are divided into a Verbal and Performance section, and the test provides a Verbal, Performance, and Full Scale IQ. The division into a Verbal and Performance section is especially helpful in clinical and psychoeducational work and aids in the assessment of brain-behavior relationships. A valuable feature of the test is that all children take a comparable battery of subtests. For children with sensory impairments, the Verbal Scale can be administered to blind children and the Performance Scale to deaf children. The following are assets of the WISC-III:

1. *Excellent standardization.* The standardization procedures were excellent, sampling four geographical regions, both sexes, White, Black, Hispanic, and other children, and the entire socioeconomic status range. The standardization group well represents the nation as a whole for the age groups covered by the test.

2. *Excellent overall psychometric properties.* The WISC-III has excellent reliability for the IQs generated by the Verbal, Performance, and Full Scales. The few studies available suggest that the WISC-III has adequate concurrent and construct validity, although we need more research to evaluate the validity of the latest edition of the test.

3. *Useful diagnostic information.* The WISC-III provides diagnostic information useful for the assessment of cognitive abilities of elementary- and high-school age children who are functioning within four standard deviations from the mean ($\pm 4$ *SD*). It also furnishes data likely to be helpful in planning special school programs, perhaps tapping important developmental or maturational factors needed for school success, especially in the lower grades.

4. *Good administration procedures.* The procedures described in the WISC-III manual for administering the test are excellent. The examiner actively probes the child's responses to evaluate the breadth of the child's knowledge and determine whether the child really knows the answer. On items that require two reasons for maximum credit, examiners ask the child for another reason when he or she gives only one reason. These procedures ensure that the test does not penalize the child for failing to understand the demands of the questions. The emphasis on probing questions and queries is extremely desirable.

5. *Good manual and interesting test materials.* The WISC-III manual is easy to use; it provides clear directions and tables. Examiners are aided by instructions printed in a color that differs from that of other text material. The manual provides helpful abbreviations for recording the child's responses, such as "P" for Pass, "F" for Fail, "Q" for Query, "DK" for Don't Know, "NR" for No Response, "Inc." for Incomplete, and "R" for Rotation. The test materials are also interesting to children.

6. *Helpful scoring criteria.* Wechsler and The Psychological Corporation carefully prepared the criteria for scoring responses. The Similarities and Vocabulary scoring guidelines, for example, detail the rationale for 2-, 1-, and 0-point scores. Several examples demonstrate the application of the scoring principles. The scoring guidelines present several examples, and those thought to need further inquiry are indicated by a "Q."

7. *Extensive research and clinical literature.* There is a vast amount of research and case material on the WISC-R that you can use to interpret the WISC-III. However, the composition of the WISC-III differs from that of the WISC-R, particularly with regard to factor structure and subtest specificity. These differences mean that the interpretations used for the WISC-R may not always apply to the WISC-III. We also need research to evaluate the validity of hypotheses derived from the WISC-III.

## LIMITATIONS OF THE WISC-III

Although the WISC-III is overall an excellent instrument, some problems do exist.

1. *Limited floor and ceiling.* The test is not applicable for severely retarded or extremely gifted children.

2. *Low reliability of individual subtests.* Reliability coefficients for the individual subtests are lower than .80 at most ages. In these cases, the scores may not be dependable. In addition, during the standardization of the scale, The Psychological Corporation did not obtain test-retest scores for the Coding and Symbol Search subtests for each age level of the test; therefore, we do not know the accuracy of the reliability estimates (based on adjacent ages) for the ages at which the two subtests were not readministered.

3. *Nonuniformity of subtest scaled scores.* Because the range of scaled scores on all subtests is less than 19 at some of the older ages, there may be some minor problems in profile analysis at the upper extremes of scores. All subtests, however, do have a range of 1 to 17 for all ages.

4. *Difficulty in interpreting norms when you substitute a supplementary subtest for a regular subtest.* With the norms based on only the 10 standard subtests, you have no way of knowing precisely what the scores mean when you substitute one of the supplementary subtests (Digit Span, Mazes, or Symbol Search) for a regular subtest. Make a substitution of this kind, therefore, only in unusual circumstances and label the results "tentative" when you report the scores.

5. *Possible difficulties in scoring responses.* Work with the WISC-R suggests that Similarities, Vocabulary, and Comprehension may be difficult to score. The WISC-III manual cites a study in which there was high agreement among examiners in the scores they gave to these subtests (and to the Mazes subtest as well). These results are encouraging, but researchers need to replicate them. I recommend that you consult colleagues when you are having trouble scoring responses.

6. *Large practice effects on the Performance Scale.* The large practice effects on the Performance Scale, close to 1 standard deviation, suggest that the WISC-III may give misleading scores in retest situations. This is especially so when the retest interval is less than 9 weeks. This means that the WISC-III may not be useful to gauge change and progress in children retested within a short time. (See pages 537 and 540 for further discussion of practice effects.) Carefully consider whether you want to use the WISC-III for a retest when you have previously given the test and what the retest results may mean if you use the test.

7. *Lack of independence.* At least 23 items overlap on the WISC-III and WPPSI-R, primarily on the Information, Vocabulary, Picture Completion, and Mazes subtests. This overlap is unfortunate for at least two reasons. First, it means that the WISC-III and WPPSI-R are not independent parallel forms at the overlapping age levels (6-0 to 7-3 years). Second, it means that children tested with the WPPSI-R and then with the WISC-III (or vice versa) have an advantage on the second test because of practice effects. On the next revision of either test, The Psychological Corporation should ensure that there are no overlapping items on the two tests.

8. *Problems for children who do not place a premium on speed.* Because many of the subtests place a premium on speed (all Performance Scale subtests and Arithmetic), the test may penalize children who are from a minority group that does not place a premium on speed (see Chapter 19) or any children who work in a slow, deliberate, and thoughtful manner.

9. *Poor quality of some test materials.* Danielson (1991) pointed out that the Coding and Symbol Search templates are poorly constructed and may rip and disintegrate quickly. He also noted that

the puzzle pieces included in the WISC-III Object Assembly subtest are of much lighter construction than are those in the WISC-R and have a tendency to be jarred apart as additional pieces are added to each puzzle. Care should therefore be taken when dealing with highly compulsive children who may spend an inordinate amount of time trying to make sure that all of the edges touch one another. It is also very unclear why the horse in this subtest is gray on both sides. Certainly, this has to increase degree of confusion and the assembly time for children who inadvertently turn one of the pieces over. One of the features on the WISC-R Object Assembly subtest was that the front and back of each piece was clearly a different color. (p. 23)

## CONCLUDING COMMENT ON THE WISC-III

The WISC-III will likely be well received by those who use tests to evaluate children's intellectual ability. It has excellent standardization, reliability, and concurrent and construct validity, and much care has been taken to provide useful administrative and scoring guidelines. The manual is excellent, and much thought has gone into the revision. A valuable addition to the manual would have been data about the standard errors of measurement of IQ scores on the Verbal, Performance, and Full Scales at IQ levels of 70, 100, and 130 (if not others). The WISC-III will likely serve as a valuable instrument in the assessment of children's intelligence for many years to come.

## THINKING THROUGH THE ISSUES

Although the Wechsler tests were by no means unique when they were developed, they did make a substantial impact on the assessment field. Why do you think the Wechsler tests were so successful as clinical assessment instruments?

The Wechsler tests do not provide interchangeable scores. What problems do you foresee in using different Wechsler tests with children in the overlapping ages where either of the two tests is appropriate?

Here are some other issues that you might want to consider. In what cases would you want to use the WISC-III factor scores? What explanation do you have as to why the WISC-III Verbal Scale subtests are better measures of g than the Performance Scale subtests? What can you do to develop proper WISC-III administrative techniques? When do you think WISC-III short forms would be appropriate to use? How would the limitations of the WISC-III affect its clinical usefulness?

---

Question:　What letter comes after T?
Answer:　Well, that's easy; V.

---

## SUMMARY

1. The Psychological Corporation published the WISC-III in 1991, 17 years after the former edition, the WISC-R. The WISC-III is similar to its predecessor, with 73 percent of the items retained, plus the original Coding subtest, which was slightly modified. Symbol Search, a supplementary subtest, is new. The WISC-III is applicable to children from 6-0-0 to 16-11-30 years of age. Standardization of the scale was excellent and included White, Black, Hispanic, and other children.

2. The WISC-III provides Deviation IQs for the Verbal, Performance, and Full Scales ($M = 100$, $SD = 15$) and standard scores for the 13 subtests ($M = 10$, $SD = 3$).

3. Although Wechsler objected to the use of mental ages in the calculation of IQs, the WISC-III manual includes a table of test-age equivalents for the scaled scores; these are essentially mental-age scores.

4. The internal consistency reliabilities of the Verbal, Performance, and Full Scales are excellent (average $r_{xx}$ of .95, .91, and .96, respectively). Subtest internal consistency reliabilities range from .69 to .87, and test-retest reliabilities range from .57 to .89. Reliabilities for the three scales are higher than those for the individual subtests.

5. Standard errors of measurement are 3.53 for the Verbal Scale, 4.54 for the Performance Scale, and 3.20 for the Full Scale. Most confidence can be placed in the Full Scale, followed by the Verbal Scale and then the Performance Scale.

6. Shifts in IQ due to practice effects (after approximately a three-week interval) were about 8 IQ points higher on the Full Scale, 2 IQ points higher on the Verbal Scale, and 12 IQ points higher on the Performance Scale.

7. Confidence intervals based on the obtained score and its standard error of measurement should be used when you want to describe the measurement error associated with a child's current functioning. Confidence intervals based on the estimated true score and its standard error of estimation should be used when you want to describe the measurement error associated with the best long-term measure of the child's functioning relative to other children in a particular group. The former method produces symmetrical confidence intervals around the obtained score; the latter method produces asymmetrical confidence intervals around the obtained score. The asymmetry is most pronounced for IQs furthest from the mean.

8. Studies in the WISC-III manual suggest that the WISC-III has acceptable concurrent, criterion, and construct validity. Median correlations with measures of achievement and school grades range from the upper .30s to the low .70s. Correlations with the WISC-R, WPPSI-R, and WAIS-R are in the .70s to .90s for the Verbal, Performance, and Full Scale IQs.

9. Based on the limited studies reported in the WISC-III manual, the WISC-III tends to provide *lower* IQs than does the WISC-R by about 5 to 9 points, *lower* IQs than the WAIS-R by about 4 points, and *higher* IQs than the WPPSI-R by about 4 points. The various Wechsler scales do not appear to provide interchangeable IQs.

10. The Verbal Scale subtests correlate more highly with each other (*Mdn r* = .55) than do the Performance Scale subtests (*Mdn r* = .33). Correlations between the Verbal subtests and the Verbal Scale (*Mdn r* = .72) are higher than those between the Performance subtests and the Performance Scale (*Mdn r* = .45). The Verbal subtests also have higher correlations with the Full Scale (*Mdn r* = .68) than do the Performance subtests (*Mdn r* = .56).

11. A factor analysis of the WISC-III standardization data indicated that three factors account for the test's structure: Verbal Comprehension, Perceptual Organization, and Processing Speed. The best measures of g are Vocabulary, Information, Similarities, Arithmetic, Comprehension, and Block Design.

12. Because several WISC-III subtests have an adequate degree of subtest specificity, interpretation of profiles of subtest scores generally is on firm ground.

13. You can use the Deviation IQs associated with the Verbal and Performance Scale IQs as factor scores. You can obtain somewhat purer factor scores by using (a) Information, Similarities, Vocabulary, and Comprehension for Verbal Comprehension; (b) Picture Completion, Block Design, and Object Assembly for Perceptual Organization; and (c) Coding and Symbol Search for Processing Speed.

14. The subtest scaled-score range is from 1 to 19, but not at all ages. After 11 years, the ceiling level ranges from 17 to 19 scaled-score points, depending on the subtest and age.

15. The WISC-III does not adequately assess the cognitive ability of children who are either severely retarded or exceptionally gifted. Although the WISC-III manual shows a range of Full Scale IQs from 40 to 160, the range of the test is more limited at some ages.

16. The WISC-III differs from the WISC-R in both major and minor ways. The most noticeable changes are the addition of a new subtest (Symbol Search), a new factor (Processing Speed) in place of the Freedom from Distractibility factor, and full color illustrations for all pictures. New items have been added or changed on every subtest, and numerous administrative changes have been made.

17. Developing proper administrative procedures early in your testing career is an important step in becoming a competent clinician.

18. Beginning examiners tend to make administrative errors. These include failing to follow the scoring rules, to complete the Record Form properly, to adhere to directions, to probe ambiguous responses, and to follow starting point and discontinuance procedures.

19. Follow the standard order of administering the subtests in all but the most exceptional circumstances.

20. To ensure that scoring is standardized at the starting and discontinuance points, credit any items failed below the starting-point items when the child passes the starting-point items and do not credit any items passed above the discontinuance-point items when the child fails the discontinuance-point items.

21. The WISC-III requires the use of many probing questions and queries. Give spoiled responses a score of 0.

22. Certain modifications in test procedures have been found to increase children's scores on the WISC-R. Similar modifications probably will affect WISC-III scores. Use such modifications only *after* the standard administration.

23. Scoring WISC-III Similarities, Vocabulary, and Comprehension subtests requires considerable skill. A careful study of the scoring criteria can help to reduce scoring errors.

24. Short forms of the WISC-III, although practical, have serious disadvantages. Short-form IQs may be less stable, impede profile analysis, and result in misclassifications. Do not use short forms for any placement, education, or clinical decision-making purpose. If you need to use a short form for screening purposes, follow the procedures advocated by Tellegen and Briggs to determine Deviation IQs. Table L-11 in Appendix L shows the best short-form combinations of two, three, four, and five WISC-III subtests. Appendixes L-12, L-13, L-14, and L-15 show the estimated IQs associated with these short-form combinations. The best two-subtest short-form combination is Vocabulary and Block Design.

25. Although you can view the WISC-III and the WPPSI-R as alternative forms for children aged 6-0 to 7-3 years, the two tests are not independent because many items overlap. You can give both the WISC-III and the WAIS-R to adolescents aged 16-0 to 16-11 years. I recommend that for children aged 6-0 to 6-11 you give the WPPSI-R to those with below-average ability, the WISC-III to those with above-average ability, and either test to children with average ability. For *all* children aged 7-0 to 7-3, give the WISC-III. I recommend that you give the WISC-III to *all* adolescents aged 16-0 to 16-11.

26. Children must be able to hear to take most WISC-III (and WPPSI-R and WAIS-R) Verbal subtests, although they may use vision as a substitute modality for some subtests. Arm-hand use is a prerequisite for most of the Performance subtests, although some adaptations are possible. Testing handicapped children is facilitated by the arrangement of subtests into a Verbal Scale and a Performance Scale. You usually will need to use special procedures, described in Appendixes D and M, to administer the Performance Scale to deaf children.

27. The assets of the WISC-III include its excellent standardization, excellent reliability, and good validity; usefulness as a diagnostic instrument; good administrative procedures; good manual and interesting test materials; helpful scoring criteria; and extensive research and clinical literature with the prior edition.

28. The limitations of the WISC-III include limited range of IQs (40 to 160), low reliability of individual subtests, nonuniformity of scaled scores, difficulty in interpreting norms when you substitute a supplementary subtest for a standard subtest, difficulty in scoring some subtests, large practice effects for the Performance Scale subtests, overlap of items with the WPPSI-R, problems for children who do not place a premium on speed, and quality of some test materials.

29. Overall, the WISC-III represents a major contribution to the field of intelligence testing of children. It serves as an important instrument for this purpose.

## KEY TERMS, CONCEPTS, AND NAMES

## STUDY QUESTIONS

1. Discuss the WISC-III. Include in your discussion the following issues: standardization, Deviation IQs, test-age equivalents, reliability, and validity.

2. Discuss two procedures for developing confidence intervals.

3. Describe and interpret the intercorrelations between WISC-III subtests and scales.

4. Describe and interpret WISC-III factor analytic findings.

5. Discuss WISC-III administrative considerations.

6. Discuss WISC-III short forms, including their values and limitations.

7. For overlapping ages, how would you go about choosing between the WISC-III and the WPPSI-R, and between the WISC-III and the WAIS-R?

8. Identify the most important factors to consider in administering the WISC-III (and other Wechsler tests) to handicapped children.

9. Discuss the assets and limitations of the WISC-III.

## REFERENCES

Danielson, G. I. (1991). An initial reaction to the WISC-III. *Communiqué, 20*(4), 23.

Flynn, J. R. (1984). The mean IQ of Americans: Massive gains 1932 to 1978. *Psychological Bulletin, 95,* 29–51.

Flynn, J. R. (1987). Massive IQ gains in 14 nations: What IQ tests really measure. *Psychological Bulletin, 101,* 192–212.

Glutting, J. J., McDermott, P. A., & Stanley, J. C. (1987). Resolving differences among methods of establishing confidence limits for test scores. *Educational and Psychological Measurement, 45,* 607–614.

Granier, M. J., & O'Donnell, L. (1991). Children's WISC-III scores: Impact of parent education and home environment. Paper presented at a poster session of the 99th Annual Convention of the American Psychological Association, San Francisco, CA.

Kaufman, A. S. (1990). *Assessing adolescent and adult intelligence.* Needham, MA: Allyn and Bacon.

Silverstein, A. B. (1990a). Notes on the reliability of Wechsler short forms. *Journal of Clinical Psychology, 46,* 194–196.

Silverstein, A. B. (1990b). Short forms of individual intelligence tests. *Psychological Assessment: A Journal of Consulting and Clinical Psychology, 2,* 3–11.

Slate, J. R., & Chick, D. (1989). WISC-R examiner errors: Cause for concern. *Psychology in the Schools, 26,* 78–84.

Slate, J. R., & Hunnicutt, L. C., Jr. (1988). Examiner errors on the Wechsler Scales. *Journal of Psychoeducational Assessment, 6,* 280–288.

Wechsler, D. (1991). *Manual for the Wechsler Intelligence Scale for Children – Third Edition.* San Antonio: The Psychological Corporation.

# APPENDIX J

## WISC-III SUBTESTS

*Order and simplification are the first steps toward the mastery of a subject — the actual enemy is the unknown.*
—Thomas Mann

This appendix provides information that will help you administer, score, and interpret the 13 WISC-III subtests. It gives the rationale, factor analytic findings, reliability and correlational highlights, administrative suggestions, and interpretive suggestions for each subtest. The factor analytic findings and reliability and correlational data discussed in this appendix are based on the WISC-III standardization sample (as presented in the WISC-III manual). (See Appendix I for information about the factor analysis.) Reliabilities for the Coding and Symbol Search subtests are test-retest correlations, whereas those for the remaining 11 subtests are split-half correlations corrected by the Spearman-Brown formula.

For the 12 subtests that are common to both the WISC-III and WISC-R, Table C-13 in Appendix C summarizes those abilities measured by each subtest, background factors influencing performance, implications of high and low scores, and instructional suggestions to improve a child's abilities. Table L-16 in Appendix L summarizes similar information for the WISC-III Symbol Search subtest. Therefore, both Table C-13 and Table L-16 are useful references for report writing and deserve careful study. If you are interested in the WISC-III Structure-of-Intellect classifications for the Arithmetic, Vocabulary, Comprehension, Digit Span, Picture Completion, Picture Arrangement, Block Design, Object Assembly, Coding, and Mazes subtests, see Table C-12 in Appendix C (page 822); these classifications are based on Guilford's model of intelligence (see Chapter 3). When you consider the abilities measured by the subtests, recognize that all of the subtests require the child to pay attention, to hear, to listen, to understand directions, and to retain these directions in mind while solving problems.

Many of the WISC-III subtests have enough subtest specificity at most ages (see Table I-12 in Appendix I) to provide reliable estimates of specific abilities, or at least to permit development of hypotheses about the underlying cognitive functions that may be measured by a subtest. The subtests that have sufficient specificity at most ages are Information, Similarities, Vocabulary, Digit Span, Picture Completion, Picture Arrangement, Block Design, Symbol Search, and Mazes. The other subtests have ample or adequate specificity only at a few ages.

Combinations of subtests provide the best estimates of specific abilities. For example, the Verbal Scale IQ, derived from a combination of five subtests, yields more accurate data about a child's verbal skills than does a single subtest, such as Vocabulary. Similarly, Coding and Symbol Search together provide more information about speed of processing than does either subtest alone.

For each subtest, this chapter poses questions to help you observe and interpret the child's performance. The answers to these questions will serve as a database for testing any clinical hypotheses you may form. After the test is administered, you will often have questions about the child's performance. For example, you may have questions about the quality of the child's responses, the pattern of failures, or how close to a solution the child was. By recording the child's performance carefully, you will be in a better position to answer any such questions that arise later.

This appendix provides suggestions for testing-of-limits for several of the WISC-III subtests. Testing-of-limits should be done *after* you administer the entire test following standard procedures. Testing-of-limits is useful for several purposes, including following up leads about the child's functioning obtained during the standard administration, testing clinical hypotheses, and evaluating how the child performs when he or she receives additional cues.

This appendix, unlike the WISC-III manual, uses the term "mental retardation" instead of the term "intellectual deficiency" to describe children who may be significantly below average in their intellectual ability. "Mental retardation" is the term used in *DSM III-R* and by the American Association on Mental Retardation. Consequently, I believe that "mental retardation" is the preferred term for describing children who are functioning two or more standard deviations below the mean. Let us now turn to a discussion of each of the 13 WISC-III subtests.

## INFORMATION

The Information subtest requires the child to answer a broad range of questions dealing with factual information. The subtest contains 30 questions. Included are questions about names of objects, dates, a literary figure, and historical and geographical facts. The child's age determines which item is used to start testing. Children 6 to 7 years old (and older children suspected of mental retardation) start with item 1, 8 to 10 years old with item 5, 11 to 13 years old with item 8, and 14 to 16 years old with item 11. All items are scored 1 or 0 (pass-fail). The subtest is not timed and is discontinued after five consecutive failures.

Children can usually answer the questions correctly with a brief, simply stated fact. They need only demonstrate that they know specific facts; they need not find relationships between these facts.

### Rationale

The amount of knowledge a child possesses may depend on his or her natural endowment, the extent of his or her education (both formal and informal), and his or her cultural opportunities and predilections. In general, the Information subtest samples the knowledge that average children with average opportunities should be able to acquire through normal home and school experiences. The child's responses and comments provide clues about the child's general range of information, alertness to the environment, social or cultural background, and attitudes toward school and school-like tasks (for example, the child may say "Those questions are hard, just like my teacher asks").

You should not necessarily interpret high scores as indications of mental efficiency and competence. Children may have acquired isolated facts but not know how to use them appropriately or effectively. However, intellectual drive may contribute to higher scores. Successful performance on the Information subtest requires memory for habitual, overlearned material (that is, information that the child has likely been exposed to over and over), especially in older children. Thus Information provides clues about the child's ability to store and retrieve old data.

## Factor Analytic Findings

The Information subtest is the second-best measure of $g$ in the test (61 percent of its variance may be attributed to $g$ — range of 50 to 69 percent in the 11 age groups). The subtest contributes substantially to the Verbal Comprehension factor (Average loading = .75). Specificity is either ample or adequate at 9 of the 11 ages; at ages 6 and 7 it is inadequate.

## Reliability and Correlational Highlights

Information is a reliable subtest ($r_{xx}$ = .84), with reliability coefficients above .70 at each of the 11 age groups (range of .73 to .88). The subtest correlates more highly with Vocabulary ($r$ = .70) and Similarities ($r$ = .66) than with other subtests. It correlates moderately with both the Full Scale ($r$ = .72) and the Verbal Scale ($r$ = .75) and to a lesser degree with the Performance Scale ($r$ = .55).

## Administrative Suggestions

The Information subtest is easy to administer. The questions are simple and direct. Scoring is usually straightforward: a correct response receives 1 point and an incorrect response, 0. If the child gives two or more answers to a question, ask the child to choose the best answer. Answers should be recorded verbatim. Encourage a child who is hesitant to respond or guess or take a chance. Give the child credit if he or she answers Information questions correctly at any time during the entire test.

## Interpretive Suggestions

Note the quality of a child's answers.

• Is the child thinking the questions through or simply guessing?

• Does the child give answers confidently or hesitantly?

• Does the child give peculiar responses? If so, what does your inquiry reveal?

• Are the child's answers imprecise and roundabout? Difficulty in giving precise answers, such as "When it is hot" for *summer* or "When it is cold" for *winter*, may suggest word-retrieval difficulties.

• Are the child's answers wordy? Overly long responses or responses filled with extraneous information may suggest an obsessive-compulsive orientation — a child with this orientation sometimes feels compelled to prove how much he or she knows. Alternatively, excessive responses may simply reflect the child's desire to impress you. The child's entire test protocol, plus other relevant information, should be considered in interpreting such behavior.

• Does the child seem to be inhibited in making responses? Inability to recall an answer may suggest that the question is associated with conflict-laden material. For example, a child may not be able to recall the number of legs on a dog because of a traumatic experience with dogs.

Examine the pattern of successes and failures. Failures on easy items coupled with successes on more difficult ones may suggest poor motivation, anxiety, temporary inefficiency, boredom, or an environment that has not been consistent. Alternatively, this pattern may indicate a problem with retrieval of information from long-term memory. When you suspect such a problem, analyze the content of the failed items — do they deal with numerical information, history, science, or geography? Content analysis may provide clues about the child's interests or areas that you might want to inquire about after you complete the test.

If you think the child may have word-retrieval problems, you can use a multiple-choice testing-of-limits procedure (Holmes, 1988[R][1]). This procedure may help you differentiate deficits associated with word retrieval from those associated with lack of knowledge. After you complete the test, go back to the item (or items) for which the child seemed to have difficulty in retrieving the correct answer. Then give the child three choices. For example, for item 13 you might say "Was he a king or an explorer or a writer?"

---

[1] References followed by an [R] are cited in this appendix; all other references are cited in the Reference section.

Be sure to vary randomly the position of the correct answer in the series (that is, sometimes put the correct answer as the first choice, sometimes second, and sometimes third). If the child answers the multiple-choice questions correctly but not the open-ended questions, you may infer that he or she has a word-finding difficulty and not a lack of knowledge.

The range of scaled scores from 1 to 19 at ages 6-0 to 13-11 years aids in profile analysis for children in this age range. However, profile analysis is somewhat hindered at ages 14-0 to 15-11 years and 16-0 to 16-11 years, where the scaled scores range from 1 to 18 and 1 to 17, respectively.

---

Question: What are the four seasons?
Answer: Football, basketball, baseball, and hockey.

---

## SIMILARITIES

The Similarities subtest requires the child to answer questions about how objects or concepts are alike. The subtest contains 19 pairs of words; the child must state the similarity between the two items in each pair. All children start with the sample item and then are administered the first item. The first five items are scored 1 or 0 (pass-fail), and items 6 through 19 are scored 2, 1, or 0, depending on the conceptual quality of the response. The subtest is not timed and is discontinued after four consecutive failures.

### Rationale

On the Similarities subtest, in addition to perceiving the common elements of the paired terms, the child must bring these common elements together in a concept to answer the questions. Thus the Similarities subtest may measure verbal concept formation – the ability to place objects and events together into a meaningful group or groups. To do this, the child may need to organize, abstract, and find relationships that are not at first obvious. Although concept formation can be a voluntary, effortful process, it can also reflect well-automatized verbal conventions (Rapaport, Gill, & Schafer, 1968). Performance on the Similarities subtest may be related to cultural opportunities and interest patterns. Memory may also be involved. Success initially depends on the child's ability to comprehend the meaning of the task.

### Factor Analytic Findings

The Similarities subtest is the third-best measure of $g$ in the test (60 percent of its variance may be attributed to $g$ – range of 52 to 65 percent in the 11 age groups). The subtest contributes substantially to the Verbal Comprehension factor (Average loading = .75) and to a limited extent to the Perceptual Organization factor (Average loading = .30). Specificity is either ample or adequate at 6 ages (6, 11, 12, 14, 15, 16); at 5 ages (7, 8, 9, 10, 13) it is inadequate.

### Reliability and Correlational Highlights

Similarities is a reliable subtest ($r_{xx}$ = .81), with reliability coefficients above .70 at each of the 11 age groups (range of .77 to .84). The subtest correlates most highly with Vocabulary ($r$ = .69) and Information ($r$ = .66). It correlates moderately with the Full Scale ($r$ = .72) and the Verbal Scale ($r$ = .75) and to a lesser degree with the Performance Scale ($r$ = .55).

### Administrative Suggestions

Note whether the child understands the task. On items 1 and 2, give the child the correct response if he or she fails to provide an acceptable response to these items. If a child states that he or she does not know the answer, encourage the child to try to answer the question, but do not press him or her unreasonably. When a child gives multiple acceptable responses to an item, score his or her best response. When a child gives both a correct and an incorrect response to an item, say "Now which one is it?" Base your score on the answer to this question. If the child gives a 1-point answer to item 6 or 7, tell the child the 2-point answer; this is done to help the child give 2-point responses on later items.

Responses to the first five questions are generally easy to score, but you will find the scoring of items 6 to 19 more difficult. On these items (6–19), a conceptual response, such as a general classification, receives a score of 2; a more concrete response, such as a specific property of the item, receives a score of 1; and an incorrect response receives a score of 0.

A careful study of the scoring guide in the WISC-III manual will help you become more proficient in scoring Similarities responses. Study carefully the sample responses that follow each item. These sample responses also list responses that you need to probe [as shown by a "(Q)"]. Also master the general scoring principles, which elucidate the rationale for 2, 1, and 0 scores (see page 84 in the WISC-III manual).

If research with the WISC-R holds for the WISC-III, many Similarities responses are likely to be difficult to score. For example, when a group of 110 psychologists and graduate students scored WISC-R Similarities, Vocabulary, and Comprehension subtest responses, the raters achieved a level of 80 percent agreement in scoring for only 51 percent of the ambiguous Similarities responses (95 out of 187 responses) (Sattler, Andres, Squire, Wisely, & Maloy, 1978). In practice, however, it is unlikely that any one protocol would include many ambiguous responses. Scoring difficulties arise in part from the relatively few examples in the manual and the difficulty of establishing precise criteria that apply to all responses, including idiosyncratic ones.

### Interpretive Suggestions

You may gain insight into the logical character of the child's thinking processes by studying his or her responses to the items on the Similarities subtest. Observe the child's typical level of conceptualization throughout the subtest. Are the child's answers on a concrete, functional, or abstract level? Concrete answers typically refer to qualities of the objects (or stimuli) that can be seen or touched (apple-banana: "Both have a skin"). Functional answers typically concern a function or use of the objects (apple-banana: "You eat them"). Finally, abstract answers typically refer to a more universal property or to a common classification of the objects (apple-banana: "Both are fruits").

You can tell, in part, whether the child's response style is concrete, functional, or abstract by the numbers of 0-, 1-, and 2-point responses. Responses that are scored 0 or 1 point suggest a more concrete and functional conceptualization style, whereas 2-point responses suggest an abstract conceptualization style. However, a 2-point response does not necessarily reflect abstract thinking ability. It may simply be an overlearned response. For example, there may be a difference between the 2-point response "Both fruits" for apple-banana and the 2-point response "Artistic expressions" for painting-statue. The former, even though it receives 2 points, may be an overlearned response, whereas the latter may reflect a more abstract level of conceptual ability. Furthermore, if the child earns 1 point on a number of items, the child may have a good breadth of knowledge but not depth. If the child generally earns 2 points for each correct response but responds correctly to only a few items, the child may have a good depth of knowledge but less breadth.

Also note whether the child gives *overinclusive responses*. Overinclusive responses are those that are so general that many objects are included in the concept. For example, the reply "Both contain molecules" to a question asking for the similarity between an apple and a banana is overinclusive because it does not delimit the particular characteristics of these two objects. Overinclusive responses may be a subtle indication of disturbed thinking.

Observe how the child handles any frustration induced by the subtest questions. When the child has difficulty answering the questions, does he or she become negativistic and uncooperative, or does the child still try to answer the questions? A child who responds with "They are not alike" may be displaying negativism, avoidance of the task demands, suspiciousness, or a coping mechanism or may just not know the answer. To determine which of these may account for the child's response, compare the child's style of responding to the Similarities questions with his or her style on other subtests.

The range of scaled scores from 1 to 19 at all ages aids in profile analysis.

---

Question: In what way are an orange and a pear alike?
Answer: Both give me hives.

---

## ARITHMETIC

The Arithmetic subtest requires the child to answer simple to complex problems involving arithmetical concepts and numerical reasoning. The subtest contains 24 problems, with 5 presented on picture cards, 13 presented orally, and 6 presented in written form. The first five and the last six Arithmetic items are in the Stimulus Booklet, which also contains the Picture Completion and Block Design stimuli. Many of the arithmetic problems are similar to those commonly encountered by children in school, although the child cannot use paper and pencil to solve the problems.

Children 6 years old (and older children suspected of mental retardation) start with item 1, 7 to 8 years old with item 6, 9 to 12 years old with item 12, and 13 to 16 years old with item 14. All items are timed, with items 1 to 17 having a 30-second time limit; item 18, a 45-second time limit; and items 19 to 24, a 75-second time limit. Items 1 to 18 are scored 1 or 0 and do not have time-bonus points. Items 19 to 24 are scored 2, 1, or 0 (a score of 2 includes a 1-point bonus for answering the item correctly within the first 10 seconds). The subtest is discontinued after three consecutive failures.

Arithmetic subtest problems test various skills. Problems 1 and 2 require direct counting of discrete objects.

Reprinted with special permission of North America Syndicate, Inc.

Problems 3, 4, and 5 require subtraction using objects as the stimuli. Problems 6 and 17 require simple division. Problems 7 through 14 and problem 16 require simple addition or subtraction. Problem 15 involves multiplication (or addition). Problems 18 through 24 require the use of automatized number facts and subtle mathematical reasoning operations, such as identifying relevant relationships at a glance, understanding task requirements, and understanding probability.

### Rationale

The problems on the Arithmetic subtest require the child to follow verbal directions, concentrate on selected parts of questions, and use numerical operations. The child must have knowledge of addition, subtraction, multiplication, and/or division operations, depending on the problem. The emphasis of the problems is not on mathematical knowledge per se, but on mental computation and concentration. Concentration is especially important for the more complex problems.

The Arithmetic subtest measures numerical reasoning—the ability to solve arithmetical problems. It requires the use of noncognitive functions (concentration and attention) in conjunction with cognitive functions (knowledge of numerical operations). Success on the subtest is influenced by education, interests, fluctuations of attention, and transient emotional reactions such as anxiety. Like the Vocabulary and Information subtests, Arithmetic taps memory and prior learning; however, it also requires concentration and the active application of select skills to new and unique situations (Blatt & Allison, 1968).

Information-processing strategies as well as mathematical skills may underlie performance on the Arithmetic subtest (Stewart & Moely, 1983). These strategies may include rehearsal (in order to remember the information presented in the task) and recognition of an appropriate response (in order to change incorrect patterns or strategies). The mathematical skills include the ability to comprehend and integrate verbal information presented in a mathematical context, together with numerical ability.

### Factor Analytic Findings

The Arithmetic subtest is a good measure of $g$ (54 percent of its variance may be attributed to $g$—range of 47 to 61 percent in the 11 age groups). The subtest contributes moderately to the Verbal Comprehension factor (Average loading = .55) and to a limited extent to the Perceptual Organization factor (Average loading = .37). Specificity is either ample or adequate at 6 ages (6, 7, 10, 13, 15, 16); at 5 ages (8, 9, 11, 12, 14 years) it is inadequate.

### Reliability and Correlational Highlights

Arithmetic is a relatively reliable subtest ($r_{xx} = .78$), with reliability coefficients above .70 at each of the 11 age groups (range of .71 to .82). The subtest correlates more highly with Information ($r = .57$) and Similarities ($r = .55$) than with the other subtests. It correlates moderately with the Full Scale ($r = .65$) and Verbal Scale ($r = .62$) and to a lesser degree with the Performance Scale ($r = .54$).

### Administrative Suggestions

You may need to be especially reassuring to a child who is anxious about his or her arithmetical skills. Although the child is not permitted to use pencil and paper to solve the problems, writing with fingers is permitted. If a child seems to be on the verge of solving a problem and the time limit has been reached, give the child additional time to complete the problem. This will give you information about the child's ability to solve the problem. Even though the child receives no credit for a correct response made after the time limit, record the response and the amount of time the child took to respond.

### Interpretive Suggestions

Observe the child's reactions to the items.

- Is the child anxious?
- What approach does the child use to solve problems?
- Does the child show temporary inefficiencies?
- Does the child recognize failures?
- Does the child attempt to correct perceived errors?
- Does the child ask to have questions repeated?

After you complete the standard administration, you might want to learn about the reasons for the child's failure by asking the child about his or her performance. You might say, for example, "Let's try this one again. Tell me how you solved the problem." If necessary, you can tell the child that he or she can think out loud. This may help you see how the child went about solving the problem. Failure may be caused, for example, by poor knowledge of arithmetical operations, inadequate conceptualization of the problem, temporary inefficiency or anxiety, poor concentration, or carelessness.

Allowing the child to use paper and pencil is another testing-of-limits procedure that may help you find out whether the child has poor arithmetical knowledge or attention and concentration difficulties. If the child can solve the problems with pencil and paper, the failure is not associated with lack of arithmetical knowledge; the errors may be associated with attention or concentration difficulties that inhibit mental computation. If the child fails the items in both situations, the failures more likely reflect difficulties with arithmetical knowledge, although attention and concentration difficulties may be interfering with the child's ability to solve written arithmetic problems. Inspect the written work to see whether the child misaligns numbers, sequences computational steps incorrectly, or has poor mastery of basic arithmetical operations. If the child misaligns numbers while working, spatial difficulties may be indicated.

The information you obtain from testing-of-limits may help you to differentiate between failures due to temporary inefficiency and those due to limited knowledge. Successful delayed performance, for example, may indicate temporary inefficiency or a slow, painstaking approach to problem solving. During testing-of-limits, note whether the child passes or fails the items. Of course, do not give the child credit on the test for answering any items correctly during testing-of-limits.

The range of scaled scores from 1 to 19 at ages 6-0 to 15-11 years aids in profile analysis. However, from 16-0 to 16-11 years, profile analysis is somewhat hindered because the scaled scores range from only 1 to 18.

---

Question: If I cut a pear in thirds, how many pieces will I have?

Answer: One.

Question: (Testing-of-limits) Are you sure I will have only one piece?

Answer: Yes, and I will have the other two pieces.

---

DRABBLE reprinted by permission of UFS, Inc.

# VOCABULARY

The Vocabulary subtest requires the child to listen as the examiner reads words aloud and then to define the words. The subtest contains 30 words arranged in order of increasing difficulty. The child is asked to explain the meaning of each word (for example, "What is a _____?" or "What does _____ mean?"). Children 6 to 8 years old (and older children suspected of mental retardation) start with item 1, 9 to 10 years old with item 3, 11 to 13 years old with item 5, and 14 to 16 years old with item 7. All items are scored 2, 1, or 0. The subtest is not timed, and it is discontinued after four consecutive failures.

## Rationale

The Vocabulary subtest, a test of word knowledge, may tap cognition-related factors—including the child's learning ability, fund of information, richness of ideas, memory, concept formation, and language development—that may be closely related to his or her experiences and educational environments. Because the number of words known by a child correlates with his or her ability to learn and to accumulate information, the subtest provides an excellent estimate of intellectual ability. Performance on the subtest is stable over time and relatively resistant to neurological deficit and psychological disturbance (Blatt & Allison, 1968). Scores on Vocabulary therefore provide a useful index of the child's general mental ability.

## Factor Analytic Findings

The Vocabulary subtest is the best measure of $g$ in the test (62 percent of its variance may be attributed to $g$—range of 51 to 71 percent in the 11 age groups). The subtest contributes substantially to the Verbal Comprehension factor (Average loading = .82). Specificity is either ample or adequate at 9 of the 11 age groups; at ages 9 and 10 it is inadequate.

## Reliability and Correlational Highlights

Vocabulary is the most reliable subtest ($r_{xx}$ = .87) in the Verbal Scale. Reliability coefficients are above .70 in each of the 11 age groups (range of .79 to .91). It correlates more highly with Information ($r$ = .70), Similarities ($r$ = .69), and Comprehension ($r$ = .64) than with the other subtests. It correlates moderately with the Full Scale ($r$ = .74) and the Verbal Scale ($r$ = .78) and to a lesser degree with the Performance Scale ($r$ = .56).

## Administrative Suggestions

Be sure to pronounce each word clearly and correctly. Be especially careful about how you pronounce the words, because you are not allowed to show the words to the child or to spell them. When you suspect that the child has not heard a word correctly, have the child repeat it to you. If the child heard the word incorrectly, say the word again. Carefully record the child's definitions.

The scoring system (2, 1, or 0 for all items) considers the quality of the response. Award 2 points for good synonyms, major uses, or general classifications, and award one point for vague responses, less pertinent synonyms, or minor uses. Do not consider the child's elegance of expression in scoring the response.

Vocabulary is one of the more difficult subtests to score, and it may not always be easy to implement the scoring criteria in the WISC-III manual. In the study by Sattler et al. (1978), 80 percent of the raters gave the same score to only 38 percent of 352 ambiguous WISC-R Vocabulary responses. Probing borderline responses and studying carefully the scoring guidelines in the WISC-III manual will help you resolve some of the scoring problems that arise as you give the subtest. Do the best job possible with the guidelines given in the WISC-III manual. Consulting with a colleague may be helpful in scoring ambiguous responses.

When young children (or older children who may be mentally retarded) give a 0- or 1-point response to the first word of the Vocabulary subtest, tell them the 2-point answer. Use this procedure, which is designed to encourage 2-point responses, only on the first item.

Probe responses that suggest regionalisms or slang (for example, "Give me another meaning for _____"). The scoring guidelines following each item in the WISC-III manual list many responses that you should query [as shown by a "(Q)"]; study these guidelines carefully so that you can recognize responses that need to be probed.

The nature of the response should determine whether the inquiry occurs during or after the standard administration. For example, if the answer clearly defines a homonym of the test item, repeat the question by saying "What else does _____ mean?" However, if the response is possibly indicative of a thought disorder, delay probing until you have completed the test. During the testing-of-limits phase, you might say "To the word _____ you said _____. Tell me more about your answer."

## Interpretive Suggestions

The following guidelines are useful for observing and evaluating Vocabulary responses (Taylor, 1961).

• Write down all of the child's responses, whether they are correct or not.

• Note whether the child is definitely familiar with the word or only vaguely familiar with it. If the child explains a word, is the explanation precise and brief, roundabout, or vague and lengthy? Are the child's responses objective, or do they relate to personal experiences?

• Note whether the child confuses the word with another one that sounds like it. If the child does not know the meaning of a word, does he or she guess? Does the child readily say "I don't know" and shake off further demands, or does the child pause, ponder, or think aloud about the item?

• If you show the child the words during testing-of-limits, note whether seeing the printed word helps the child.

• Watch for possible hearing difficulties by listening carefully to how the child repeats words. Has the child heard the words correctly or with some distortion?

• Note how the child expresses himself or herself. Does the child find it easy or difficult to say what he or she means? Does the child have mechanical difficulties pronouncing words properly? Does the child seem uncertain about how best to express what he or she thinks? Does the child use gestures to illustrate his or her statements or even depend on them exclusively?

• Note also the content of definitions. Are the words chosen synonyms for the stimulus word (thief: "A burglar"), or do they describe an action (thief: "Takes stuff")? Does the child describe some particular feature of the object (donkey: "It has four legs"), or does the child try to fit it into some category (donkey: "A living creature that is kept in a barn")?

• Note any emotional overtones or reference to personal experiences (alphabet: "I hate to write").

The child's responses to the Vocabulary subtest may reveal something about his or her language skills, background, cultural milieu, social development, life experiences, responses to frustration, and thought processes. See if you can determine the basis for incorrect responses. It is important to distinguish among guesses, clang associations (that is, responses that appear to be based on the sound of the stimulus word rather than on its meaning), idiosyncratic associations, and bizarre associations. Whenever a child gives peculiar responses, mispronounces words, or has peculiar inflections, inquire further. You can occasionally see language disturbances in the word definitions of children with schizophrenia or with other severe forms of mental disorder.

The range of scaled scores from 1 to 19 at all ages aids in profile analysis.

| Question: | What is a chisel? |
| Answer: | When you are cold you get the chisels. |
| | (Flumen & Flumen, 1979) |

PEANUTS reprinted by permission of UFS, Inc.

## COMPREHENSION

The Comprehension subtest requires the child to explain situations, actions, or activities that relate to events familiar to most children. The questions cover several content areas, including knowledge of one's body, interpersonal relations, and social mores. The subtest contains 18 questions. All children start with the first item. All items are scored 2, 1, or 0. The subtest is not timed, and it is discontinued after three consecutive failures.

### Rationale

On the Comprehension subtest, the child must understand given situations and provide answers to specific problems. Success depends on the child's possession of practical information, plus an ability to draw on previous experiences. Responses may reflect the child's knowledge of conventional standards of behavior, extensiveness of cultural opportunities, and level of development of conscience or moral sense. Success suggests that the child has social judgment, common sense, and a grasp of social conventionality. These characteristics imply an ability to use facts in a pertinent, meaningful, and emotionally appropriate manner. Success is based on the ability to verbalize acceptable actions, as well.

### Factor Analytic Findings

The Comprehension subtest is a good measure of $g$ (50 percent of its variance may be attributed to $g$ – range of 35 to 63 percent in the 11 age groups). The subtest contributes substantially to the Verbal Comprehension factor (Average loading = .68). Specificity is adequate at 6 of the 11 age groups (6, 8, 9, 10, 11, 12); at 5 ages (7, 13, 14, 15, 16) it is inadequate.

### Reliability and Correlational Highlights

Comprehension is a reasonably reliable subtest ($r_{xx} = .77$), with reliability coefficients above .70 at all ages (range of .72 to .85 in the 11 age groups). The subtest correlates more highly with Vocabulary ($r = .64$), Similarities ($r = .59$), and Information ($r = .56$) than with the other subtests. It correlates moderately with the Full Scale ($r = .64$) and the Verbal Scale ($r = .67$) and to a lesser degree with the Performance Scale ($r = .49$).

### Administrative Suggestions

The Comprehension subtest is difficult to score because children may give responses that differ from those pro-

vided in the manual. In the Sattler et al. (1978) study, 80 percent of the raters gave the same score to only 49 of the 187 ambiguous WISC-R Comprehension responses.

On the first item, tell the child the correct 2-point response if the child gives a less adequate response (that is, a response scored 1 or 0). This procedure is meant to encourage the child to give 2-point responses and is allowed only on the first item. On the eight items (2, 6, 7, 11, 12, 15, 17, and 18) that require two ideas for full credit (2 points), ask the child for a second idea when he or she gives only one correct idea, so that you do not penalize the child automatically for not giving two reasons. However, on the other items, for which an adequate one-idea answer receives 2 points, do not probe obvious 1-point responses in an attempt to improve the child's score.

The most complete or best response receives a score of 2; a less adequate response, 1; and an incorrect response, 0. Carefully study the examples following each item in the manual so that you will know which response types need further inquiry [these are labeled "(Q)"]. The examples indicate that you should query many 0- and 1-point responses. If, in response to your query, the child alters his or her response, score the response given to your query rather than the initial response. Additional queries offer you an opportunity to evaluate more thoroughly the extensiveness of the child's knowledge.

When a child gives unusual responses, ask him or her to explain the responses. Although your inquiry may give you insight into what the child is thinking, do not routinely inquire after every response. You can conduct an extensive inquiry as part of testing-of-limits *after* you complete the test. Record the child's responses verbatim during the initial presentation of the items and during the inquiry phase so that you have a complete record with which to evaluate the responses.

### Interpretive Suggestions

Responses to the Comprehension questions may provide valuable information about the child's personality style, ethical values, and social and cultural background. Unlike the Information questions, which usually elicit precise answers, the Comprehension questions may elicit more complex and idiosyncratic replies. Because the questions involve judgment of social situations, answers may reflect the child's attitudes. Some responses reveal understanding *and* acceptance of social mores, whereas others reveal understanding *but not* acceptance of social mores. A child may know the right answers but not practice them. Some children may maintain that they do not have to abide by social conventions, believing that such matters do not pertain to them personally.

A child's replies can reveal initiative, self-reliance, independence, self-confidence, helplessness, indecisiveness, inflexibility, and other traits. For example, a child with a dependent personality style may say that he or she would seek help from his or her mother or others when faced with problem situations. Replies to question 8, which asks the child what should be done if a much smaller child starts a fight with him or her, may reveal independence, manipulative tendencies, naïve perceptions of problems, cooperative solutions, hostility, or aggression (Robb, Bernardoni, & Johnson, 1972).

Note *how* the child responds to the questions (Taylor, 1961):

• Do the child's failures indicate misunderstanding of the meaning of a word or the implications of a particular phrase?
• Does the child give complete answers or just part of a phrase?
• Does the child respond to the entire question or only to a part of it?
• Does the child seem to be objective, seeing various possibilities and choosing the best way?
• Is the child indecisive—unable to come to firm answers?
• Are the child's responses too quick, indicating failure to consider the questions in their entirety?
• Does the child recognize when his or her answers are sufficient?

Because Comprehension requires considerable verbal expression, the subtest may be sensitive to mild language impairments and to disordered thought processes. Be alert to language deficits (such as word-finding difficulties), circumstantial or tangential speech, or other expressive difficulties.

The range of scaled scores from 1 to 19 at ages 6-0 to 15-11 years aids in profile analysis. However, at 16-0 to 16-11 years, profile analysis is somewhat hindered because the scaled scores range only from 1 to 18.

Question: Why should children who are sick stay home?
Answer: To take their antibionics.
(Flumen & Flumen, 1979)

## DIGIT SPAN

The Digit Span subtest, a supplementary subtest, requires the child to repeat a series of digits given orally by the examiner. The subtest has two parts: Digits Forward, which contains series ranging in length from two to nine digits, and Digits Backward, which contains series ranging in length from two to eight digits. There are two series of digits for each sequence length. Digits Forward is administered first, followed by Digits Backward. The subtest is untimed.

Digit Span is not used in the computation of the IQ when the five standard Verbal Scale subtests are administered. All children start with the first trial of Digits Forward, and with the sample item of Digits Backward after Digits Forward is completed. All items are scored 2, 1, or 0. On both Digits Forward and Digits Backward, the subtest is discontinued when the child fails both trials on any one item.

Although Digit Span is a supplementary subtest, administering it may give you useful diagnostic information. Considering the small investment of time and energy required to give it, I recommend that you administer Digit Span routinely.

### Rationale

Digit Span is a measure of the child's short-term auditory memory and attention. Performance may be affected by the child's ability to relax, as a child who is calm and relaxed may achieve a higher score on the subtest than one who is excessively anxious. The task assesses the child's ability to retain several elements that have no logical relationship to one another. Because the child must recall auditory information and repeat the information orally in proper sequence, the task also involves sequencing.

Digits Forward primarily involves rote learning and memory, whereas Digits Backward requires transformation of the stimulus input prior to responding. Not only must the child hold the mental image of the numerical sequence longer (usually) than in the Digits Forward sequence, but he or she must also manipulate the sequence before restating it. High scores on Digits Backward may indicate flexibility, good tolerance for stress, and excellent concentration. Digits Backward involves more complex cognitive processing than does Digits Forward and has higher loadings on $g$ than does Digits Forward (Jensen & Osborne, 1979).

Because of differences between the two tasks, it is useful to consider Digits Forward and Digits Backward separately. Digits Forward appears to involve primarily sequential processing, whereas Digits Backward appears to involve both planning ability and sequential processing. Additionally, Digits Backward may involve the ability to form mental images and the ability to scan an internal visual display formed from an auditory stimulus. However, more research is needed to support the hypothesis about the role of visualization in Digits Backward performance.

## Factor Analytic Findings

The Digit Span subtest is a fair measure of $g$ (26 percent of its variance may be attributed to $g$—range of 18 to 35 percent in the 11 age groups). The subtest contributes minimally to the Verbal Comprehension factor (Average loading = .34). Specificity is ample at all ages.

## Reliability and Correlational Highlights

Digit Span is a reliable subtest ($r_{xx}$ = .85), with reliability coefficients above .70 at each age (range of .79 to .91 in the 11 age groups). The subtest correlates more highly with Arithmetic ($r$ = .43) than with any other subtest. It has a low correlation with the Full Scale ($r$ = .43), Verbal Scale ($r$ = .42), and Performance Scale ($r$ = .35).

## Administrative Suggestions

Be sure that the child cannot see the digits in the manual or on the Record Form. Read the digits clearly at the rate of one per second, and drop your inflection on the last digit in the series. Practice reading speed with a stopwatch. Never repeat any of the digits on either trial of a series during the subtest proper.

Always administer both trials of each series. Give the child credit for each trial that he or she passes. On Digits Backward, if the child passes the sample two-digit series (on either the first or the second trial), proceed to the two-digit series in the subtest proper. If the child fails the sample series, read the specific directions in the manual that explain how the series should be repeated. Whenever there is any doubt about the child's auditory acuity, an audiological examination should be requested. Because this subtest contains no cues (that is, you only present several random series of digits), hard-of-hearing examinees may be especially prone to failure.

You can record the number of digits correctly recalled in each series by placing in the Record Form either a mark designating a correct answer above each digit correctly recalled or a mark designating an incorrect answer on each digit missed. An even better procedure is to record the exact sequence given by the child in the available space. A

good record can help you evaluate the child's performance. A child who consistently misses the last digit in the first series and then successfully completes the second series differs from one who fails to recall any of the digits in the first series but successfully completes the second. Similarly, a child who responds to the sequence 3-4-1-7 with "3-1-4-7" is quite different from the child who says "9-8-5-6."

The scoring system does not distinguish among failure patterns. For example, a child who misses one digit in the eight-digit sequence obtains the same score as a child who misses all eight digits, even though the second child's performance is more inefficient than the first child's performance—perhaps because the second child had lapses in attention associated with anxiety or other factors.

## Interpretive Suggestions

Observe whether the child's failures involve leaving out one or more digits, transposing digits, interjecting incorrect digits, producing more digits than were given, or giving a series of digits in numerical order (for example, 6-7-8-9). The child who recalls the correct digits but in an incorrect sequence is more likely to have a deficit in auditory sequential memory than in auditory memory. The child who fails the first trial but passes the second trial may be displaying a learning-to-learn pattern or a need for a warm-up to achieve success.

Consider the following questions:

• Is the child's performance effortless, or does the child seem to use much concentration?

• Does the child view the task as interesting, boring, or difficult?

• Does the child notice his or her errors, or does the child think that his or her answers are always correct?

• Does the child understand the difference between Digits Backward and Digits Forward?

• Are the errors the child makes on Digits Backward similar to or different from those he or she made on Digits Forward?

• As the Digits Backward series proceeds, does the child become stimulated and encouraged or tense, anxious, and frustrated?

• Does the child do much better on Digits Forward than on Digits Backward? (If so, the child may be overwhelmed by the more complex operations required on Digits Backward.)

• Does the child make more errors on Digits Forward than on Digits Backward? (This may mean that the child sees Digits Backward as more of a challenge and therefore

**Table J-1**
**Median Number of Digits Recalled on Digits Forward and Digits Backward by Age**

| | Median | |
|---|---|---|
| Age | Forward | Backward |
| 6 | 5 | 3 |
| 7 | 5 | 3 |
| 8 | 5 | 3 |
| 9 | 6 | 4 |
| 10 | 6 | 4 |
| 11 | 6 | 4 |
| 12 | 6 | 4 |
| 13 | 6 | 4 |
| 14 | 6 | 5 |
| 15 | 7 | 5 |
| 16 | 7 | 5 |
| All ages | 6 | 4 |

*Note.* There were 200 children at each age level.
*Source:* Adapted from Wechsler (1991[R]), Table B.6 (page 267).

mobilizes more of his or her resources — for example, giving added concentration and attention — to cope with Digits Backward.)

The child may use various methods to recall the digits. For example, the child may simply repeat what he or she has heard; visualize the digits; say the digits to himself or herself; use a finger to write the digits; or group the digits. Some grouping techniques introduce meaning into the task so separate digits become numbers grouped into hundreds, tens, or other units (for example, 3-1-7 becomes three hundred seventeen). If the child uses grouping, the function underlying the task may be changed from one of attention to one of concentration. After you complete the subtest, you might ask the child how he or she went about remembering the numbers. If you do, record the child's response.

The WISC-III manual does not provide separate scaled scores for Digits Forward and Digits Backward. However, there are two useful tables in the WISC-III manual that show how the standardization group performed on Digits Forward and on Digits Backward. Table B.6 (page 267 of the WISC-III manual) shows the longest Digits Forward span and the longest Digits Backward span recalled by children. Across all age groups, children had a median Digits Forward span of 6 (range of 5 to 7) and a median Digits Backward span of 4 (range of 3 to 5) (see Table J-1).

Table B.7 (page 268 of the WISC-III manual) shows the extent to which children recalled more digits forward than backwards and vice versa. In all age groups and in the total sample, children recalled more digits forward than backward (*Mdn* difference = 2 at 10 of the 11 age groups and in the total sample, except at age 15, where *Mdn* difference = 1). Thus, raw score differences of 3 points (or more) between Digits Forward and Digits Backward may be considered noteworthy. The percentage of children in the standardization group who recalled more digits backward than forward was less than 4 percent in the total group, about 1 percent at 6 to 8 years, less than 3 percent at 9 to 11 years, between 4 and 6 percent at 12 to 14 years, 10.5 percent at 15 years, and 9 percent at 16 years (see Table J-2).

The range of scaled scores from 1 to 19 at all ages aids in profile analysis.

---

Question: Now I am going to say some more numbers, but this time when I stop I want you to say them backwards. For example, if I said "8-4-6-5-9-1-7," what would you say?
Answer: I'd say "You've got to be kidding!"
(Adapted from Flumen & Flumen, 1979)

---

**Table J-2**
**Percentage of Children in Standardization Group Who Recalled More Digits Backward than Digits Forward by Age**

| Age | Percent |
|---|---|
| 6 | 1.0 |
| 7 | 1.0 |
| 8 | .5 |
| 9 | 1.5 |
| 10 | 2.5 |
| 11 | 2.5 |
| 12 | 4.0 |
| 13 | 4.0 |
| 14 | 6.0 |
| 15 | 10.5 |
| 16 | 9.0 |
| All ages | 3.8 |

*Note.* There were 200 children at each age level.
*Source:* Adapted from Wechsler (1991[R]), Table B.7 (page 268).

## PICTURE COMPLETION

The Picture Completion subtest requires the child to identify the single most important missing detail in 30 drawings of common objects, animals, or people, such as a box, cat, and face. The child's task is to name or point to the essential missing portion of the incomplete picture within the 20-second time limit. The pictures are shown one at a time.

All children start with the sample item. Children 6 to 7 years old (and older children suspected of mental retardation) are then given item 1; 8 to 9 years old, item 5; 10 to 13 years old, item 7; and 14 to 16 years old, item 11. All items are scored 1 or 0 (pass-fail). The subtest is discontinued after five consecutive failures.

### Rationale

On the Picture Completion subtest, the child must recognize the object depicted, appreciate its incompleteness, and determine the missing part. It is a test of visual discrimination—the ability to differentiate essential from nonessential details. Picture Completion requires concentration, reasoning (or visual alertness), visual organization, and long-term visual memory (as the items require the child to have stored information about the complete figure).

Picture Completion may also measure perceptual and conceptual abilities involved in visual recognition and identification of familiar objects. Perception, cognition, judgment, and delay of impulse all may influence performance. The time limit on the subtest places additional demands on the child. The richness of the child's life experiences also may affect his or her performance on the subtest.

### Factor Analytic Findings

The Picture Completion subtest is a fair measure of $g$ (44 percent of its variance may be attributed to $g$—range of 32 to 47 percent in the 11 age groups). The subtest contributes moderately to the Perceptual Organization factor (Average loading = .53) and to a lesser extent to the Verbal Comprehension factor (Average loading = .39). These results suggest that verbal reasoning may help children to detect the missing part of the pictures. Subtest specificity is either ample or adequate at 10 of the 11 age groups; at age 12 it is inadequate.

### Reliability and Correlational Highlights

Picture Completion is a relatively reliable subtest ($r_{xx}$ = .77), with reliability coefficients *above* .70 at all age groups (range of .72 to .84 in the 11 age groups). The subtest correlates more highly with Block Design ($r$ = .52), Object Assembly ($r$ = .49), and Information ($r$ = .47) than with the other subtests. It has low correlations with the Full Scale ($r$ = .58), Performance Scale ($r$ = .54), and Verbal Scale ($r$ = .52).

### Administrative Suggestions

Picture Completion is easy to administer. Simply leave the booklet flat on the table and turn the cards over to show each consecutive picture. If the child has speech difficulties, such as those that occur in aphasia, you can administer the subtest by having the child point to the place where the part is missing.

The child should be aware that he or she is being timed, because it is important for the child to realize that speed is expected. Usually, allowing the child to see the stopwatch is all that is necessary. However, you should not tell the child that he or she is being timed.

The WISC-III manual indicates that, if necessary, you may give each of three guiding statements *once* to help the child understand the requirements of this subtest: (a) If the child names the object pictured, ask the child what is missing in the picture. (b) If the child names a part that is not on the card, ask the child what part *in* the picture is missing. (c) If the child mentions a nonessential missing part, ask the child for the most important part that is missing.

On five items (6, 13, 21, 23, 28), ask the child to point to the missing part on the card if he or she gives an ambiguous response. In other cases as well, whenever there is any doubt about the child's verbal or pointing response, ask the child for clarification.

### Interpretive Suggestions

As you administer the subtest, consider the following:

- Does the child understand the task?
- Does the child say anything that comes to mind, or does the child search for the right answer?
- When the child fails, does he or she find fault with himself or herself or with the picture?
- What is the child's rate of response—for example, quick and impulsive, or slow and deliberate?
- Is the child fearful of making an error, hesitant, or suspicious?
- Is the child aware of being timed? If so, does the timing make the child anxious or prompt the child to change the pace of his or her responding?

• Does the child give roundabout definitions of parts (sometimes referred to as *circumlocutions*)? [Such responses may suggest word-retrieval difficulties. For example, to item 1 (correct response is "Ear"), a roundabout response would be "The thing you hear with."]

• Does the child point excessively? A child who points excessively or responds with circumlocutions may have word-finding problems (*dysnomia*).

If the child's performance leaves any doubt about his or her visual skills, request a visual examination.

Observe whether perseveration occurs. A child displays perseveration, for example, when he or she says "Ear" for each picture portraying an animal (pictures 1, 3, 5). "Ear" is the correct answer for picture 1, but not for the subsequent pictures depicting animals.

Comparing Picture Completion scores with those on Block Design and Object Assembly may help you distinguish between visuospatial difficulties and visual-motor difficulties. Picture Completion is the only task on the WISC-III Performance Scale that does not have a motor component.

Record each incorrect response verbatim as well as the time the child takes to make the response. The child who usually responds in less than five seconds may be more impulsive, more confident, and, if correct, brighter than the child who takes more time. A child who responds correctly *after* the time limit (for which he or she does not receive credit) may be brighter than the child who fails the item even with additional time. Because the pass-fail scoring makes no provision for such qualitative factors, carefully evaluate individual variations in each case and discuss these qualitative factors in the report. Delayed correct responses may suggest temporary inefficiency, depression, or simply a slow and diligent approach, whereas extremely quick but incorrect responses may reflect impulsivity.

After you administer the subtest, you can inquire about the child's perceptions of the task: "How did you go about coming up with the answer?" or "How did you decide when to give an answer?" Query any peculiar answers. The child's behavior during this subtest may provide insight into how the child reacts to time pressure. As a testing-of-limits procedure, you can ask the child to look again at those pictures that he or she missed. You might say "Look at this picture again. Before, you said that _____ was missing. That's not the part that's missing. Look for something else." In some cases, you may ask the child to name the picture, especially when he or she missed many items.

The range of scaled scores from 1 to 19 at ages 6-0 to 13-11 years aids in profile analysis. However, profile analysis is somewhat hindered at ages 14-0 to 15-11 years and

16-0 to 16-11 years, where the scaled scores range from 1 to 18 and 1 to 17, respectively.

---

Question:  What are 2, 4, and 6?
Answer:  That's easy; CBS, NBC, and ABC.

---

## CODING

The Coding subtest requires that the child copy symbols paired with other symbols. The subtest consists of two separate and distinct parts. Each part uses a sample, or key. In Coding A, the sample (or key) consists of five shapes—star, circle, triangle, cross, and square. Within each sample shape, there is a special mark (a vertical line, two horizontal lines, a horizontal line, a circle, and two vertical lines, respectively). The child must place within each test shape (which is empty) the mark that is within the sample shape. There are 5 practice shapes, followed by 59 shapes in the subtest proper.

In Coding B, the sample (or key) consists of boxes containing one of the numbers 1 through 9 in the upper part and a symbol in the lower part. Each number is paired with a different symbol. The test stimuli are boxes containing a number in the upper part and an empty box in the lower part. The child must write in the empty box the symbol that is paired with the number in the sample. There are 7 practice boxes, followed by 119 boxes in the subtest proper. The time limit for each Coding task is 120 seconds.

Coding A is given to children under 8 years of age, and Coding B is given to children 8 years of age and older. On Coding A, 1 point is given for each correct item, and up to 6 additional time-bonus points are given for a perfect score. On Coding B, 1 point is given for each correct item, but there are no time-bonus points.

### Rationale

Coding taps the child's ability to learn an unfamiliar task. The subtest involves speed and accuracy of visual-motor coordination, attentional skills, visual scanning and tracking (repeated visual scanning between the code key and answer spaces), short-term memory or new learning (paired-associate learning of an unfamiliar code), cognitive flexibility (in shifting rapidly from one pair to another), handwriting speed, and, possibly, motivation. The subtest also involves speed of mental operation (psychomotor speed) and, to some extent, visual acuity. Success depends not only on comprehending the task, but also on using pencil and paper skillfully. The subtest is sensitive to visuoperceptual difficulties.

Coding B may also involve a verbal-encoding process if the child attaches verbal descriptions to the symbols. For example, a child may label a "+" symbol as a "plus sign" or "cross" and the "V" symbol as the letter "V." A child may improve his or her performance when he or she uses verbal labels to recode the symbols. Consequently, Coding B can also be described as measuring the ability to learn combinations of symbols and shapes and the ability to make associations quickly and accurately. Coding A can also involve a verbal-encoding process, but to a lesser degree. Coding A and Coding B thus may involve separate information-processing modes.

The speed and accuracy with which the child performs the task are a measure of the child's intellectual ability.

At each step in the task the [child] must inspect the next digit, go to the proper location in the table, code the information distinguishing the symbol found, and carry this information in short-term memory long enough to reproduce the symbol in the proper answer box. (Estes, 1974, p. 745)

Coding thus can be conceptualized as an information-processing task involving the discrimination and memory of visual pattern symbols.

### Factor Analytic Findings

The Coding subtest is a poor measure of $g$ (20 percent of its variance may be attributed to $g$ — range of 10 to 30 percent in the 11 age groups). The subtest contributes substantially to the Processing Speed factor (Average loading = .74). Specificity is ample at 10 of the 11 age groups; at age 8 it is inadequate.

### Reliability and Correlational Highlights

Coding is a relatively reliable subtest ($r_{xx}$ = .79). Reliability coefficients are above .70 at 6 ages (6, 7, 10, 11, 14, 15) reported in the WISC-III manual (range of .70 to .90 in the 6 age groups). Unfortunately, there are no reliability coefficients shown in the WISC-III manual for 5 age groups (8, 9, 12, 13, 16) because no children were retested at these ages. The subtest correlates more highly with Symbol Search ($r$ = .53) than with any other subtest. It has a low correlation with the Full Scale ($r$ = .33), Performance Scale ($r$ = .32), and Verbal Scale ($r$ = .29).

### Administrative Suggestions

The Coding subtest items are located in the Record Form. Administer the subtest on a smooth drawing surface, and tear the page out of the Record Form. Be sure to put the child's name, the date, and your name at the top of the Coding Response Sheet to identify it if it is misplaced. You and the child should each use a no. 2 graphite pencil without an eraser.

A child with visual defects or specific motor disabilities may be penalized on this subtest. Generally, do not give the subtest to a child with either of these disabilities. If you give it, do not count it in the final score.

A left-handed child also may be penalized on the Coding subtest. If the way the child writes causes the child to cover the sample immediately above the line of writing, the child will have to lift his or her hand repeatedly during the task to view the key. If the child is left handed, the WISC-III manual suggests that you place an extra Coding Response Sheet to the right of the child's sheet and have the child work with the separate key both during the sample items and during the subtest proper.

### Interpretive Suggestions

Useful observational guidelines are as follows:

- Is the child impulsive or meticulous?
- Does the child display tremor?
- Does the child's speed increase or decrease as he or she proceeds?
- Are the child's symbol marks well executed, barely recognizable, or wrong?
- Do the child's symbol marks show any distortions?
- If the child's symbols marks do show distortions, do the distortions appear only once, occasionally, or each time the child draws the symbol mark? How many different symbols are distorted?
- Does the child draw the same symbol over and over again even though the numbers change (perseveration)?
- Is the child being penalized for lack of speed, for inaccuracy, or for both?
- Does the child understand the task?
- Does the child understand and proceed correctly after you give an explanation?

• Are the child's failures due to inadequate form perception or to poor attention?

• Does the child check each symbol with the sample, or does he or she seem to remember the symbols?

• Does the child recheck every symbol before moving on to the next one?

• Does the child pick out one number only and skip the others?

• Does the child work smoothly, or does he or she seem confused at times?

• Is the child aware of any errors?

• Do the child's errors occur in some regular manner?

• How does the child react to making errors?

• Is the child persistent?

• Does the child need repeated urging?

• Is the child bored with the task?

Answers to the above questions will provide information about the child's attention span, method of working, and other behaviors. An increase in speed, coupled with correct copying of symbols, suggests that the child is adjusting to the task well. A decrease in speed, coupled with incorrect copying of symbols, suggests that the child may be showing fatigue.

Coding is particularly useful for evaluating the child's attention when you suspect attentional difficulties, such as in cases of learning disability or after a head injury. If other tests indicate that the child has adequate response speed and visual acuity, then poor scores on Coding are likely to be associated with attentional deficits and not visuoperceptual difficulties per se. A slow and deliberate approach may suggest depressive features.

Distortion of forms may mean that the child has difficulties with perceptual functioning. Ask the child about any symbol that is peculiarly written to find out whether it has some symbolic meaning to him or her.

Perseveration may suggest neurological difficulties that should be investigated further.

Boredom might be present with a bright child who does not appear to be challenged by the task.

The range of scaled scores from 1 to 19 at all ages aids in profile analysis.

---

Question:  What is celebrated on Thanksgiving Day?
Answer:  My cousin's birthday.

---

# PICTURE ARRANGEMENT

The Picture Arrangement subtest requires the child to place a series of pictures in logical order. The subtest contains 14 series, or items, similar to short comic strips. Individual cards, each containing a picture, are placed in a specified disarranged order, and the child is asked to rearrange the pictures in the "right" order to tell a story that makes sense. The number of pictures per set ranges from three to six. One set of cards is given at a time to the child. Each item is timed, with 45 seconds for items 1 to 11 and 60 seconds for items 12 to 14. The only motor action required is for the child to change the position of the pictures.

All children are started with the sample item, after which children 6 to 8 years old (and older children suspected of mental retardation) are given item 1 and children 9 to 16 years are given item 3. There are two trials for items 1 and 2. Items 1 and 2 are scored 2, 1, or 0. Items 3 to 14 are scored 5, 4, 3, 2, or 0, with 2 points for the correct arrangement and up to 3 additional time-bonus points for quick execution. An alternative arrangement on item 14 receives 1 point only, with no time-bonus points. The subtest is discontinued after three consecutive failures.

## Rationale

The Picture Arrangement subtest measures the child's ability to comprehend and evaluate a situation. To accomplish the task, the child must grasp the general idea of a story. Although a child may sometimes use trial-and-error experimentation on the subtest, the child usually needs to appraise the total situation depicted in the cards in order to succeed.

The subtest may be viewed as a measure of nonverbal reasoning that involves planning ability, anticipation, visual organization, and temporal sequencing. The subtest measures the ability to anticipate the consequences of initial acts or situations, as well as the ability to interpret social situations. Some children may generate covert, analytical, verbal descriptions of alternative story sequences to guide them in arranging the stimulus cards. In such cases, the subtest may measure verbal sequencing processes as well. The capacity to anticipate, judge, and understand the possible antecedents and consequences of events is important in lending meaningful continuity to everyday experiences (Blatt & Allison, 1968).

## Factor Analytic Findings

The Picture Arrangement subtest is a fair measure of $g$ (36 percent of its variance may be attributed to $g$ – range of 23 to 46 percent in the 11 age groups). The subtest contributes minimally both to the Perceptual Organization factor (Average loading = .36) and to the Verbal Comprehension factor (Average loading = .34). Specificity is ample at all ages.

## Reliability and Correlational Highlights

Picture Arrangement is a relatively reliable subtest ($r_{xx}$ = .76), with reliability coefficients of .70 or above at all the ages (range of .70 to .84 in the 11 age groups). The subtest correlates more highly with Block Design ($r$ = .41), Information ($r$ = .40), Vocabulary ($r$ = .40), and Similarities ($r$ = .39) than with other subtests. It has a relatively low correlation with the Full Scale ($r$ = .52), Performance Scale ($r$ = .49), and Verbal Scale ($r$ = .45).

## Administrative Suggestions

Arrange the Picture Arrangement items from the child's left to right in the order given in the manual. As you present the demonstration items to the child (that is, the sample item and trial 2 of items 1 and 2), be sure not to cover the pictures with your hand inadvertently – the child should be able to see all the pictures and follow your movements when you are rearranging the pictures. Record the child's Picture Arrangement sequence as soon as you pick up the cards. Coach the child (as indicated in the WISC-III manual) if he or she fails either item 1 or item 2.

The child can earn bonus points for speed on items 3 through 14. To help the child understand the importance of speed, encourage him or her to work quickly. If the child does not tell you when he or she is finished, ask him or her. When the child is perfectionistic, tell the child that the cards do not have to be perfectly straight (or aligned), so that the child does not lose time-bonus points for his or her neatness.

## Interpretive Suggestions

The Picture Arrangement subtest gives you the opportunity to observe how the child approaches performance tasks involving planning ability.

• Does the child examine the cards, come to some decision, and then reassess his or her decision while he or she arranges the cards (Taylor, 1961)?

• Does the child proceed quickly without stopping to reconsider his or her decision?

• Are the child's failures due to lack of understanding of the task? (For example, does the child leave the pictures in their original order?)

• What errors does the child make? (For example, are cards placed in a perfunctory or random manner, or is one card always moved to the same position?)

• Is the child persistent, discouraged, impulsive, or rigid?

• What types of trial-and-error patterns does the child use?

• How does the child's approach to the Picture Arrangement items compare with his or her approach to the Block Design and Object Assembly items?

• Does the child employ the same patterns consistently in searching for solutions?

• If the child does not employ the same patterns, what might account for the differences?

• How do task content, fatigue, and mood changes influence the child's approach to the items?

• If you coach the child on trial 2 of items 1 and 2, does the coaching help the child grasp the point of the arrangement, story, or task requirements (cf. Zimmerman & Woo-Sam, 1985)?

It may be useful to ask the child to explain or describe his or her arrangements. If you do so, *wait until you have finished administering the entire test in order to follow standard procedures.* Select items that you think may help you understand the child's thought patterns better. You may want to focus on items that the child failed. However, you can also use items that the child passed, because even correct arrangements do not necessarily mean that the child interpreted the series correctly. Because the last two items attempted are likely to be the most complex for the child, you can select them if you have no other specific choices. Arrange the Picture Arrangement cards for each item separately, in the order given by the child. Then ask the child to "Tell what is happening in the pictures" or to "Make up a story" or to "Tell what the pictures show."

Consider the following in evaluating the stories:

• Are the child's stories logical, fanciful, confused, or bizarre?

• Are the child's stories creative or conventional?

• Does the child reveal any attitudes in the stories, such as self-oriented or socially oriented themes?

• Are the child's incorrect arrangements a consequence of incorrect perceptions of details in the pictures or of failure to consider some details?

• Does the child consider all the relationships in the pictures?

• Are the child's sequences *correct* but the point of the stories not grasped?

• Are the child's sequences *incorrect* but the point of the story grasped?

Useful testing-of-limits procedures include giving the child additional time to complete the arrangement and giving the child cues on items that he or she missed. The latter can be done by placing the first card before the child and saying "Here is the first picture. What goes next?" If one card does not help the child, place the second correct card next to the first one and say "What picture goes next?" In some cases you may need to arrange even more cards to help the child. The child who solves the problems with cues may have more ability than the child who fails in spite of additional guidance. *Introduce graded help only after you have completed the standard examination because such help during testing can raise Picture Arrangement scores* (Sattler, 1969). You may also ask the child to arrange the stories in an alternative sequence.

The range of scaled scores from 1 to 19 at all ages aids in profile analysis.

---

Question: What is a nuisance?
Answer: My little brother.
(Flumen & Flumen, 1979)

---

## BLOCK DESIGN

The Block Design subtest requires the child to reproduce designs using three-dimensional blocks with a red surface, a white surface, and a surface that is cut diagonally into half red and half white. The subtest contains 12 items. The child uses blocks to assemble a design identical to a model constructed by the examiner (items 1 and 2) or to a two-dimensional, red-and-white picture (items 3 through 12). Children 6 to 7 years old (and older children suspected of mental retardation) start with item 1 and children 8 to 16 years old with item 3. The patterns are arranged in order of increasing difficulty. Two blocks are used for the first design, four blocks for designs 2 to 9, and nine blocks for designs 10 through 12.

All items are timed. Item 1 has a maximum of 30 seconds; items 2 to 5, 45 seconds; items 6 to 9, 75 seconds; and items 10 to 12, 120 seconds. Items 1 to 3 are scored 2, 1,

or 0. Items 4 to 12 are scored 7, 6, 5, 4, or 0, with 4 points for a correct completion and up to 3 additional time-bonus points for quick execution. The subtest is discontinued after two consecutive failures.

### Rationale

On the Block Design subtest, the child must perceive and analyze forms by breaking down a whole (the design) into its component parts and then assembling the components into the identical design. This process is referred to as analysis and synthesis. To succeed, the child must use visual organization and visual-motor coordination. Success also involves the application of logic and reasoning to spatial relationship problems. Consequently, Block Design can be considered to be a nonverbal concept formation task requiring perceptual organization, spatial visualization, and abstract conceptualization. It can also be viewed as a constructional task involving spatial relations and figure-ground separation.

A child's performance on Block Design may be affected by his or her rate of motor activity, as well as vision. Do not interpret inadequate performance as direct evidence of inadequate visual form and pattern perception, because the ability to discriminate block designs (that is, to perceive the designs accurately at a recognition level) may be intact even though the ability to reproduce them is impaired. Scores on Picture Completion may help you determine the proper explanation.

### Factor Analytic Findings

The Block Design subtest is the best measure of $g$ among the Performance Scale subtests, and it is the fourth-best measure of $g$ in the test (56 percent of its variance may be attributed to $g$—range of 46 to 64 percent in the 11 age groups). The subtest contributes substantially to the Perceptual Organization factor (Average loading = .73) and to a lesser extent to the Verbal Comprehension factor (Average loading = .33). Specificity is ample at all ages.

### Reliability and Correlational Highlights

Block Design is a reliable subtest ($r_{xx} = .87$), with reliability coefficients above .70 at all ages (range of .77 to .92 in the 11 age groups). The subtest correlates more highly with Object Assembly ($r = .61$), Picture Completion ($r = .52$), and Arithmetic ($r = .52$) than with the other subtests. It correlates moderately with the Full Scale ($r = .66$) and the Performance Scale ($r = .65$) and to a lesser degree with the Verbal Scale ($r = .57$). It correlates more highly with the Verbal Scale than do the other subtests on the Performance Scale.

## Administrative Suggestions

Be sure that the area you use to arrange the blocks is clear of other blocks and materials. Construct the design for item 1 by laying out the two blocks from the child's left to right. Construct design 2 by completing, from the child's left to right, the first row (that is, the top row of the design from the child's perspective) and then the second row. Be careful that your hand does not block the child's view. Scramble the blocks before you administer each new design and place before the child the exact number of blocks needed for the item.

Instruct the child to tell you when he or she has completed items 1, 2, 3, 10, 11, and 12, if you have any doubt about when the child is finished. In such cases, say "Tell me when you have finished." Give this instruction routinely on items 4 through 9, as indicated in the WISC-III manual, but also give it on the other items as needed.

## Interpretive Suggestions

Block Design is an excellent subtest for observing the child's problem-solving approach. Consider the following issues:

• Is the child hasty and impulsive or deliberate and careful?
• Does the child slowly and methodically check each block with the design?
• Does the child give up easily or become frustrated when faced with possible failure, or does the child persist and keep on working even after he or she reaches the time limit?
• Does the child use only one kind of approach, or does the child alter his or her approach as the need arises?
• Does the child use a slow approach or a rapid trial-and-error approach?
• Does the child study the designs first?
• Does the child appear to have a plan when executing the items?
• Does the child construct the design in units of blocks, or does the child work in a piecemeal fashion?
• Does the child understand the principle of using individual blocks to construct the designs?
• Does the child express concerns about differences between blocks?

• Does the child say that his or her designs are correct when, in fact, they are not?
• Is the child able to succeed even on the more complex block designs (for example, those requiring nine blocks)?

Excessive fumbling or failure to check the pattern suggests anxiety. Visuoperceptual difficulties may be indicated if the child twists his or her body to improve his or her perspective on the design or if the child leaves space between the blocks in the assembled design. Try to differentiate between excessive cautiousness as a personality style and excessive slowness as a possible indication of depression or boredom.

Conduct testing-of-limits *after* you have administered the entire test. Research has shown that children benefit from receiving cues during the standard administration of the Block Design subtest (Sattler, 1969). A useful testing-of-limits procedure is to select one (or more) design(s) that the child failed. Show the child the Block Design card (or assembled design). As you give the directions, place one row or block in its correct position. Say "Let's try some of these again. I'm going to put together some of the blocks. I will make the top row [or arrange the first block]. Now you go ahead and finish it. Now make one like this. Tell me when you have finished." If the child still fails, arrange additional blocks. Record the amount of help the child needs to reproduce the designs accurately. A child who needs many cues may have weaker spatial reasoning ability than a child who needs few cues. In some cases, the additional cues may not help the child reproduce the designs.

The range of scaled scores from 1 to 19 at ages 6-0 to 15-11 years aids in profile analysis. However, at 16-0 to 16-11 years, profile analysis is somewhat hindered because scaled scores range only from 1 to 18.

*Cautionary note.* Prior experience with the commercial game Trac 4, which uses block design patterns, increased bright 10-year-old children's WISC-R Block Design scores by about 3 scaled-score points (Dirks, 1982). However, scores did not increase on the other subtests. These results, which likely apply to the WISC-III, suggest that you should avoid using the Block Design subtest in short forms if children have played Trac 4, because the scores are likely to be inflated. Standard IQs may also be slightly inflated on the WISC-III if children have played this game.

---

Question:  In what direction does the sun rise?
Answer:  Near Kansas City.

# OBJECT ASSEMBLY

The Object Assembly subtest requires the child to put jigsaw pieces together to form common objects: a girl (seven pieces), a car (seven pieces), a horse (six pieces), a ball (six pieces), and a face (nine pieces). There is one sample item: an apple (four pieces). Items are given one at a time, and the pieces are presented in the specified disarranged pattern indicated in the WISC-III manual. Every item is administered to all children, beginning with the sample item and continuing with items 1 through 5.

All items are timed. The first item has a maximum of 120 seconds; the next two items, 150 seconds each; and the last two items, 180 seconds each. For perfect performance, the scores are 6 points for the girl, 5 points each for the car and the horse, and 7 points each for the ball and the face. Bonuses of up to 3 points are given for quick performance. The girl, car, and horse items each have a maximum score of 8, and the ball and face items, 10. Points are also given for partially correct assemblies on all items.

## Rationale

The Object Assembly subtest is mainly a test of the child's skill at synthesis—putting things together to form familiar objects. It requires visual-motor coordination, with motor activity guided by visual perception and sensorimotor feedback. Object Assembly is also a test of visual organizational ability, for visual organization is needed to produce an object out of parts that may not be immediately recognizable. To solve the jigsaw puzzles, the child must be able to grasp an entire pattern by anticipating the relationships among its individual parts. The tasks require some constructive ability as well as perceptual skill—the child must recognize individual parts and place them correctly in the incomplete figure. Performance may also be related to rate and precision of motor activity; persistence, especially when much trial and error is required; and long-term visual memory (having stored information about the object to be formed).

## Factor Analytic Findings

The Object Assembly subtest is a fair measure of $g$ (44 percent of its variance may be attributed to $g$—range of 46 to 64 percent in the 11 age groups). The subtest contributes substantially to the Perceptual Organization factor (Average loading = .67). Specificity is ample or adequate at 4 of the 11 age groups (6, 9, 13, 15); at 7 age groups (7, 8, 10, 11, 12, 14, 16) it is inadequate.

## Reliability and Correlational Highlights

Object Assembly is a marginally reliable subtest ($r_{xx} = .69$), with reliability coefficients above .70 in only 5 of the 11 age groups (6, 9, 13, 15, 16) and between .60 and .69 in the other age groups (range of .60 to .76 over the 11 age groups). The subtest correlates more highly with Block Design ($r = .61$) than with any other subtest. It has a somewhat low correlation with the Full Scale ($r = .58$), a moderate correlation with the Performance Scale ($r = .60$), and a low correlation with the Verbal Scale ($r = .48$).

## Administrative Suggestions

Make sure that the child does not see the pages of the WISC-III manual that contain pictures of the correctly assembled objects. You can use the Object Assembly Layout Shield, not only to set up the individual puzzle parts, but to shield the manual as well. Place the pieces close to the child so that the child does not have to waste time reaching for them. As in other subtests, you may have to ask the child to tell you when he or she is finished—"Tell me when you have finished." You may need to give this instruction on items 2 through 5 because the directions in the WISC-III manual do not include it. Do not give any cues to the child that indicate approval or disapproval of his or her performance.

Because all items are given to all children, young school-aged children may experience some frustration on Object Assembly. If so, it would be useful to investigate what effects a discontinuance criterion would have on Object Assembly. Would it reduce young children's anxiety level without affecting the reliability and validity of the subtest? This, of course, is a proposal for research. The subtest should still be administered following the exact procedures stated in the WISC-III manual.

## Interpretive Suggestions

Object Assembly is an especially good subtest for observing the child's thinking and work habits. Some children envision the complete object almost from the start and either recognize the relations of the individual parts to the whole or have an imperfect understanding of the relations between the parts and the whole. Others merely try to fit the pieces together by trial-and-error methods. Still others may have initial failure, followed by trial and error and then sudden insight and recognition of the object.

Observe how the child responds to errors and how the child handles frustration.

• Does the child demand to know what the object is before he or she constructs it, or insist that pieces are missing, or say that the object doesn't make sense (Zimmerman & Woo-Sam, 1985)?

• If the child has low scores, are they due to temporary inefficiency, such as reversal of two parts, which results in loss of time-bonus credits?

• Does the child spend a long time with one piece, trying to position it in an incorrect location? (If so, this behavior may indicate anxiety or rigidity.)

After you administer the subtest, ask the child about any constructions that may be peculiar or unusual (such as pieces placed on top of each other). You can use testing-of-limits procedures similar to those described for the Picture Arrangement and Block Design subtests *after* you have administered the entire test. For example, you can introduce a series of graduated cues, such as placing one or more pieces in the correct location. Note the amount of help the child needs to complete the task successfully. The child who needs only a few cues to complete the object may have underlying perceptual organization skills not evident during the standard administration of the subtest and may have better perceptual organization skills than the child who needs many cues.

Another testing-of-limits approach is to ask the child to visualize the object in his or her mind before you lay out the puzzle pieces. For example, say "Think of how a horse looks" and give the child the horse item. See if this instruction helps the child to assemble the puzzle.

The range of scaled scores from 1 to 19 at ages 6-0 to 15-11 years aids in profile analysis. However, at ages 16-0 to 16-11 years, profile analysis is somewhat hindered because scaled scores range only from 1 to 18.

---

Question:  What is gasoline?
  Answer:  To put on the thing what takes your temperature so it don't hurt you.
        (Flumen & Flumen, 1979)

---

## SYMBOL SEARCH

The Symbol Search subtest, a supplementary subtest, requires the child to look at a symbol (or symbols) and then decide whether the symbol(s) is(are) present in an array of symbols. Symbol Search is not used in the computation of the IQ when the five standard Performance Scale subtests are administered. The subtest consists of two separate parts. Part A is administered to children 6 to 7–11 years old, and Part B to children between 8 and 16 years old.

In Part A there is one target symbol and three symbols in the array. The child is told to draw a slash (/) through the box labeled YES if the target symbol is also in the array. If the target symbol is not in the array, the child should draw a slash (/) through the box labeled NO. The target symbols usually are nonsense shapes and designs, as are the symbols in the array. There are 2 demonstration (sample) items and 2 practice items. Part A contains 45 items in addition to the 2 sample and 2 practice items.

In Part B there are two target symbols and five symbols in the array. As in Part A, the child is told to draw a slash (/) through the box labeled YES if either of the target symbols is also in the array. If neither one of the target symbols is in the array, the child should draw a slash (/) through the box labeled NO. The target symbols, like those in Part A, are usually nonsense shapes and designs, as are the symbols in the array. There are 2 demonstration (sample) items and 2 practice items. Part B contains 45 items in addition to the 2 sample and 2 practice items. Some of the symbols in Part A and Part B are the same. Each part has a time limit of 120 seconds.

The score on each part is the number of correct items minus the number of incorrect items. There are no time-bonus credits on either Part A or Part B.

### Rationale

On the Symbol Search subtest, the child looks at a stimulus figure (target stimulus), scans an array, and decides whether the stimulus figure appears in the array. The task involves perceptual discrimination, speed and accuracy, attention and concentration, short-term memory, and cognitive flexibility (in shifting rapidly from one array to the next). Visual-motor coordination plays a role, albeit minor, because the only motor movement is that of drawing a slash. Part B is more complex than Part A because there are two target stimulus figures instead of one (as in Part A) and five symbols in the array instead of three (as in Part A).

Most of the symbols used in the Symbol Search subtest will be difficult to encode verbally. However, some symbols may be verbally encoded if children attach verbal descriptions to them. These include, for example, $\pm$ (plus or minus), $\mathsf{L}$ (L shape), $>$ (greater than sign), $\cap$ (inverted U), and $\vdash$ (a T on its side). Research is needed to learn whether children verbally encode these or other symbols and whether the encoding affects their performance.

As in the Coding subtest, the speed and accuracy with which the child performs the task are a measure of the child's intellectual ability. For each item, the child must inspect the target stimulus, go to the array, look at the array items and determine whether the target stimulus is present, and then mark the appropriate box (YES or NO) once he or she makes the decision. You can thus conceptualize Symbol Search as a task involving visual discrimination and visuoperceptual scanning.

### Factor Analytic Findings

The Symbol Search subtest is a fair measure of $g$ (38 percent of its variance may be attributed to $g$ — range of 27 to 48 percent in the 11 age groups). The subtest contributes substantially to the Processing Speed factor (Average loading = .62) and to a lesser degree to the Perceptual Organization factor (Average loading = .35). Subtest specificity is ample at 8 of the 11 age groups (7, 10, 11, 12, 13, 14, 15, 16); at 3 ages (6, 8, 9) it is inadequate.

### Reliability and Correlational Highlights

Symbol Search is a relatively reliable subtest ($r_{xx}$ = .76), with reliability coefficients above .70 at 5 of the 6 age groups reported (7, 10, 11, 14, 15); the one exception is at age 6, where the reliability coefficient is .69 (range of .69 to .82 in the 6 age groups). As with Coding, reliability coefficients are not given for 5 age groups (8, 9, 12, 13, 16) because no children were retested at these ages. The subtest correlates more highly with Coding ($r$ = .53) than with any of the other subtests. It has low correlations with the Full Scale ($r$ = .56), Performance Scale ($r$ = .58), and Verbal Scale ($r$ = .44).

### Administrative Suggestions

The Symbol Search subtest is in a separate booklet (WISC-III Symbol Search Response Booklet). You and the child should each use a no. 2 graphite pencil without an eraser. Write the child's name, the date, and your name in the space provided on the Symbol Search Response Booklet. Administer the subtest on a smooth drawing surface.

A child with visual defects or specific motor disabilities may be penalized on this subtest. Generally, do not give the subtest to a child with either of these handicaps. If you do give it to a child with these handicaps, do not count it in the final score, even when it replaces a standard Performance Scale subtest. Other types of children also may be penalized on this subtest, including those who are unable to make quick decisions; those who respond slowly and care-

fully; those who are compulsive and need to constantly check the stimulus figure(s) against those in the array; and those who are impulsive and fail to check the array figures against the stimulus figure(s).

Observe the child's work methods. Tell the child who stops working after the first line to "Continue on the next line." Tell the child who fails to turn the page to "Go to the next page." Count these instructions as part of the 2-minute time limit. If the child skips lines, tell him or her to do the lines in order.

### Interpretive Suggestions

Useful observational guidelines are as follows:

• Does the child carefully check the target symbol with those in the array?
• Does the child draw the slash (/) mark slowly or quickly?
• Does the child respond impulsively?
• Is the child penalized for working slowly?
• Does the child make many errors?
• Does the child understand the task?
• Does the child work smoothly, or does he or she seem confused at times?
• Does the child seem to be aware of any errors?

Answers to the above questions may provide valuable information about attention, persistence, impulsive tendencies, compulsive tendencies, and depressive features. It will be of interest to compare children who obtain the same score in different ways. For example, two children may get a score of 10, but one child has 10 correct responses and zero errors and the other child has 20 correct responses and 10 errors. These two children likely have different styles of working. The first child may be a careful and diligent worker, but unwilling (or unable) to work quickly, whereas the second child may be a quick worker, but rather careless and impulsive.

After the test is over, for children who make many errors, you may want to go over each item on which an error occurred. You can point to an item on which an error occurred and say "Tell me about your answer" or "Tell me about why you marked a 'No' (or 'Yes')."

Compare the child's response style on Symbol Search with that on other subtests. If there are differences, try to determine what might account for them. Consider, for example, the nature of the tasks, the child's motivation, the child's scores on all tasks, and when the tasks were administered — that is, at the beginning, middle, or end of the examination.

The range of scaled scores from 1 to 19 at ages 6–0 to

15–11 years aids in profile analysis. However, at ages 16–0 to 16–11 years, profile analysis is somewhat hindered because scaled scores range only from 1 to 18.

---

Question:   In what way are a computer and TV alike?
Answer:   They both go on the blink when you need them.

---

## MAZES

The Mazes subtest, a supplementary subtest, requires the child to solve paper-and-pencil mazes that differ in level of complexity. Mazes is not used in the computation of the IQ when the five standard Performance Scale subtests are administered. Mazes consists of 1 sample problem and 10 problems in the subtest proper. The child is asked to draw a line from the center of each maze to the outside without crossing any of the lines that indicate walls. Each maze is presented separately. Children 6 to 7 years (and older children suspected of mental retardation) start with the sample maze followed by item 1, whereas children 8 to 16 years start with item 4.

All items are timed. The first four mazes are given a maximum of 30 seconds each; the fifth maze, 45 seconds; the sixth maze, 60 seconds; the seventh and eighth mazes, 120 seconds; and the ninth and tenth mazes, 150 seconds. The number of errors made determines the child's score. Scores range from 0 to 5 points, with mazes 1 to 6 having a maximum score of 2; maze 7, a maximum score of 3; mazes 8 and 9, a maximum score of 4; and maze 10, a maximum score of 5. The subtest is discontinued after two consecutive failures. Although you do not have to administer Mazes routinely, administering it to children who are either language-impaired or from a different culture, in particular, may give you useful information.

### Rationale

To complete the Mazes subtest successfully, the child must (a) attend to the directions, which include locating a route from the entrance to the exit, avoiding blind alleys, crossing no lines, and holding the pencil on the paper, and (b) execute the task, which involves remembering and following the directions, displaying visual-motor coordination, and resisting the disruptive effect of an implied need for speed (Madden, 1974). The Mazes subtest appears to measure the child's planning ability and perceptual organizational ability—that is, the ability to follow a visual pat-

tern. To succeed, a child must have visual-motor control combined with speed and accuracy.

### Factor Analytic Findings

The Mazes subtest is the poorest measure of $g$ in the test (13 percent of its variance may be attributed to $g$—range of 5 to 30 percent in the 11 age groups). The subtest contributes minimally to the Perceptual Organization factor (Average loading = .36). Subtest specificity is ample at 10 of the 11 age groups; at age 15 it is inadequate.

### Reliability and Correlational Highlights

Mazes is a relatively reliable subtest ($r_{xx}$ = .70), with reliability coefficients above .70 in 6 of the 11 age groups (6, 7, 8, 10, 13, 14) and between .61 and .68 in the other 5 age groups (9, 11, 12, 15, 16; range of .61 to .80 in the 11 age groups). The subtest correlates more highly with Block Design ($r$ = .31) than with any other subtest. It has a low correlation with the Full Scale ($r$ = .31), Performance Scale ($r$ = .35), and Verbal Scale ($r$ = .23).

### Administrative Suggestions

The Mazes subtest is in a separate booklet (WISC-III Mazes Response Booklet). Administer the subtest on a smooth drawing surface. Use a no. 2 graphite pencil without an eraser to demonstrate the sample item, and give a no. 2 pencil without an eraser to the child. Write the child's name, the date, and your name in the space provided on the Mazes Response Booklet.

When a child makes certain errors, give the child the cues described in the WISC-III manual. The first time these errors occur, tell the child that he or she has made an error and give the child the appropriate cue. The cues are designed to help the child, especially if he or she does not fully understand what to do. A table in the WISC-III manual (page 159) shows how to score the child's performance. The sample responses that illustrate the scoring criteria should be carefully studied (see pages 160–164 in the WISC-III manual).

In the first printing of the WISC-III manual, there is an incorrect direction on page 157 for maze 3. The sentence says, "If the child completes the maze within the time limit with no more than one error, proceed to Maze 4." *Disregard this direction because it conflicts with the discontinuance rule.* The discontinuance rule states that Mazes should be discontinued after two consecutive failures. Therefore, you should proceed to maze 4 if the child passes maze 1 and maze 2, regardless of the number of errors he or she makes on maze 3. (On October 28, 1991 I notified The Psychological Corporation of this error. Lawrence Weiss acknowledged that the sentence is incorrect in the manual and that it will be changed in the next printing.)

**Interpretive Suggestions**

Consider the following questions as you observe the child's performance.

• Does the child understand the task?
• Does the child study the mazes extensively and plan a route before proceeding?
• Does the child show signs of tremor, difficulty in controlling the pencil, or difficulty in drawing uniform lines?
• Does the child solve the mazes correctly after the time limit has expired?
• Does the child cross lines?
• If the child crosses lines, is this tendency related to poor visual-motor coordination or to impulsivity?
• Does the child say anything that suggests anxiety (for example, "The little boy is trapped in the center of the maze")?

These observations (and the overall success rate) will give you information about the child's motor planning, speed, execution, impulsivity, and sustained attention.

The range of scaled scores from 1 to 19 at ages 6-0 to 10-11 years aids in profile analysis. However, profile analysis is somewhat hindered at 11-0 to 12-11 years and 13-0 to 16-11 years, where the scaled scores range from 1 to 18 and 1 to 17, respectively.

---

Question: Listen, say just what I say: "Eating too much cake and ice cream can give you a stomach ache."
Answer: So you have to take an Alka Seltzer, right? (Adapted from Flumen & Flumen, 1979)

---

# THINKING THROUGH THE ISSUES

In evaluating the 13 WISC-III subtests, consider the following: Which WISC-III subtests are the most reliable? In what ways do the WISC-III subtests share common properties, and in what ways do they differ? What other kinds of subtests would you like to see incorporated in the WISC-III? Why?

If you were evaluating a child who had both language and motor impairments, which WISC-III subtests would be most useful? Which ones might be least useful? Why?

# SUMMARY

1. Information measures the child's available information acquired as a result of native ability and early cultural experience. Memory is an important aspect of performance on the subtest. The subtest is the second-best measure of $g$ and contributes to the Verbal Comprehension factor. Subtest specificity is ample or adequate at most ages. Information is a reliable subtest ($r_{xx} = .84$). It is easy to administer and score.

2. Similarities measures verbal concept formation. The subtest is the third-best measure of $g$. Subtest specificity is ample or adequate at 6 of the 11 ages. Similarities is a reliable subtest ($r_{xx} = .81$). It is easy to administer but difficult to score.

3. Arithmetic measures numerical reasoning ability. The subtest is a good measure of $g$ and contributes to the Verbal Comprehension factor and the Perceptual Organization factor. Subtest specificity is ample or adequate at 6 of the 11 ages. Arithmetic is a reasonably reliable subtest ($r_{xx} = .78$). It is easy to administer and score.

4. Vocabulary measures language development, learning ability, and fund of information. The subtest is an excellent measure of $g$ and contributes to the Verbal Comprehension factor. Subtest specificity is adequate at 9 of the 11 ages. Vocabulary is a reliable subtest ($r_{xx} = .87$). It is relatively easy to administer but difficult to score.

5. Comprehension measures social judgment: the ability to use facts in a pertinent, meaningful, and emotionally appropriate manner. The subtest is a good measure of $g$ and contributes to the Verbal Comprehension factor. Subtest specificity is adequate at 6 of the 11 ages. Comprehension is a relatively reliable subtest ($r_{xx} = .77$). It is easy to administer but difficult to score.

6. Digit Span is a supplementary subtest that measures short-term memory and attention. The subtest is a fair measure of $g$ and contributes to the Verbal Comprehension factor. Subtest specificity is ample at all ages. Digit Span is a reliable subtest ($r_{xx} = .85$). It is easy to administer and score. Administer it routinely, even though it is not used to compute the IQ when the five standard Verbal subtests are administered.

7. Picture Completion measures the ability to differentiate essential from nonessential details. It requires concentration, visual organization, and visual memory. The subtest is a fair measure of $g$. It contributes to the Perceptual Organization factor and to the Verbal Comprehension factor. Subtest specificity is ample or adequate at 10 of the 11 ages. Picture Completion is a reasonably reliable subtest ($r_{xx} = .77$). It is easy to administer and relatively easy to score.

8. Coding measures visual-motor coordination, speed of mental operation, and short-term memory. The subtest is a poor measure of $g$ and contributes to the Processing Speed factor.

Subtest specificity is adequate at 10 of the 11 ages. Coding is a relatively reliable subtest ($r_{xx} = .79$). It is easy to administer and score.

9. Picture Arrangement measures nonverbal reasoning ability. It may be viewed as a measure of planning ability – that is, the ability to comprehend and evaluate a total situation. The subtest is a fair measure of $g$ and contributes to the Perceptual Organization factor and to the Verbal Comprehension factor. Subtest specificity is ample at all ages. Picture Arrangement is a relatively reliable subtest ($r_{xx} = .76$). It is easy to administer and score.

10. Block Design measures spatial visualization ability and nonverbal concept formation. The subtest is the best measure of $g$ among the Performance Scale subtests. It contributes to the Perceptual Organization factor and to the Verbal Comprehension factor. Subtest specificity is ample at all ages. Block Design is a reliable subtest ($r_{xx} = .87$). It is somewhat difficult to administer but easy to score.

11. Object Assembly measures visual organizational ability. The subtest is a fair measure of $g$ and contributes to the Perceptual Organization factor. Specificity is ample or adequate at 4 of the 11 ages. Object Assembly is a marginally reliable subtest ($r_{xx} = .69$). It is somewhat difficult to administer but relatively easy to score.

12. Symbol Search is a supplementary subtest that measures visual discrimination and visuoperceptual scanning. The subtest is a fair measure of $g$ and contributes to the Processing Speed factor and to the Perceptual Organization factor. Subtest specificity is ample at 8 of the 11 ages. Symbol Search is a relatively reliable subtest ($r_{xx} = .76$). It is easy to administer and score.

13. Mazes is a supplementary subtest that measures planning ability and perceptual organization. The subtest is the poorest measure of $g$ in the test and contributes to the Perceptual Organization factor. Subtest specificity is ample at 10 of the 11 ages. Mazes is a relatively reliable subtest ($r_{xx} = .70$). It is easy to administer but difficult to score.

## KEY TERMS, CONCEPTS, AND NAMES

WISC-III Information (p. 1080)
WISC-III Similarities (p. 1082)
WISC-III Arithmetic (p. 1083)
WISC-III Vocabulary (p. 1086)
WISC-III Comprehension (p. 1088)
WISC-III Digit Span (p. 1089)
WISC-III Picture Completion (p. 1092)
WISC-III Coding (p. 1093)
WISC-III Picture Arrangement (p. 1095)
WISC-III Block Design (p. 1097)
WISC-III Object Assembly (p. 1099)
WISC-III Symbol Search (p. 1100)
WISC-III Mazes (p. 1102)

## STUDY QUESTION

Discuss the rationale, factor analytic findings, reliability and correlational highlights, and administrative and interpretive considerations for each of the following WISC-III subtests: Information, Similarities, Arithmetic, Vocabulary, Comprehension, Digit Span, Picture Completion, Coding, Picture Arrangement, Block Design, Object Assembly, Symbol Search, and Mazes.

## REFERENCES

Holmes, J. M. (1988). Testing. In R. G. Rudel, *Assessment of developmental learning disorders* (pp. 166–201). New York: Basic Books.

Wechsler, D. (1991). *Manual for the Wechsler Intelligence Scale for Children – Third Edition*. San Antonio: The Psychological Corporation.

# APPENDIX K

## INTERPRETING THE WISC-III

*The gifts of nature are infinite in their variety, and mind differs from mind almost as much as body from body.*
—Quintilian

Appendix K presents guidelines for interpreting the WISC-III and for writing reports. *The appendix must be used in conjunction with Chapters 8 and 23, because these chapters present more detailed guidelines for interpreting all of the Wechsler tests and for writing reports.* Because the methods of interpreting the WISC-III—such as the successive level approach, profile analysis, Performance/Verbal Scale comparisons, and subtest comparisons—are essentially the same for both the WISC-R and the WISC-III, study carefully the contents of Chapter 8 that pertain to these issues. Appendix K complements these chapters by focusing on the WISC-III. Appendix K also includes a training exercise designed to sharpen your report writing skills (Exhibit K-3) and two illustrative reports (Exhibits K-1 and K-4).

Appendix L contains tables specifically designed to help you interpret the WISC-III. Other tables that can assist you in interpreting the WISC-III and in writing reports are as follows: Table C-13 (page 824), which summarizes the abilities thought to be measured by 12 of the WISC-III subtests (with some minor exceptions, as noted in the footnote to the table; Table L-16 in Appendix L presents similar information for Symbol Search); Table C-42 (pages 856–857), which summarizes the interpretive rationales for the Full Scale, Verbal Scale, and Performance Scale of the Wechsler batteries; and Table C-43 (page 858), which presents activities to improve children's skills based on Wechsler subtests.

On the inside back cover of this text, Table BC-2 shows the classifications associated with WISC-III IQs, and Table BC-1 shows the percentile ranks for the WISC-III Full Scale, Performance Scale, and Verbal Scale IQs. Percentile ranks for the three IQs also can be obtained directly from the WISC-III manual in Tables A.2, A.3, and A.4 (pages 251–254). Table C-41 in Appendix C (page 855) shows the percentile ranks associated with subtest scaled scores. Table C-12 in Appendix C (page 822), which gives the Structure of Intellect classifications for the subtests on the WISC-R, also can be used for the following WISC-III subtests: Arithmetic, Vocabulary, Comprehension, Digit Span, Picture Completion, Picture Arrangement, Block Design, Object Assembly, Coding, and Mazes.

## PROFILE ANALYSIS

The seven primary approaches to profile analysis of the WISC-III described below are essentially the same as those described for the WISC-R (see pages 166–171). However, there are some differences.

First, for profile analysis you should use the tables in Appendix L, which cover the WISC-III, instead of those in Appendix C, which cover the WISC-R.

Second, the critical values in Appendix L for the WISC-III are based on the child's specific age group rather than an average value (as in the WISC-R).

Third, factor scores on the WISC-III (see Appendix I) differ from those on the WISC-R (see Chapter 6) in the following ways: Although the Verbal Comprehension factor is the same on both tests (Information, Similarities, Vocabulary, and Comprehension), the Perceptual Organization factor is not (Picture Completion, Block Design, and Object Assembly on the WISC-III and Picture Completion, Block Design, Object Assembly, and Picture Arrangement on the WISC-R). In addition, the WISC-III has a Processing Speed factor (composed of Coding and Symbol Search) that is not present on the WISC-R, and the WISC-R has a Freedom from Distractibility factor (Arithmetic, Digit Span, and Coding) that is not present on the WISC-III. On the WISC-III, Arithmetic, Digit Span, Picture Arrangement, and Mazes are not included in a factor score.

Let us now examine the seven primary approaches to profile analysis.

1. *Comparing Verbal and Performance Scale IQs.* Table L-3 in Appendix L provides the critical values for comparing the Verbal and Performance IQs for the 11 age groups of the WISC-III. These values range from 10 to 13 at the .05 level and from 13 to 17 at the .01 level. Thus, an average critical value based on the entire standardization group would be misleading. Therefore, use the values for the child's specific age group to evaluate differences between the child's Verbal and Performance IQs. (Table L-7 in Appendix L shows the probabilities associated with various differences between the WISC-III Verbal and Performance Scale IQs.)

2. *Comparing each Verbal subtest scaled score to the mean Verbal scaled score.* Table L-4 in Appendix L provides the critical values for each of the 11 age groups of the WISC-III. Typical values for 6-year-old children on the five standard Verbal subtests, for example, range from 3.01 to 3.51 at the .05 level and from 3.60 to 4.20 at the .01 level.

3. *Comparing each Performance subtest scaled score to the mean Performance scaled score.* Table L-4 in Appendix L provides the critical values for each of the 11 age groups of the WISC-III. Typical values for 6-year-old children for the five standard Performance subtests, for example, range from 3.03 to 3.62 at the .05 level and from 3.62 to 4.34 at the .01 level.

4. *Comparing each subtest scaled score to the mean subtest scaled score.* Table L-4 in Appendix L provides the

critical values for each of the 11 age groups in the WISC-III for 10, 11, 12, and 13 subtests. Typical values for 6-year-old children for the 10 standard subtests, for example, range from 3.43 to 4.25 at the .05 level and from 4.02 to 4.97 at the .01 level. This approach to profile analysis tends to be used less often than Methods 2 and 3.

5. *Comparing pairs of individual subtest scores.* Table L-3 in Appendix L provides the critical values for comparing pairs of subtest scores for each of the 11 age groups of the WISC-III. They range from 3 to 5 at the .05 level and from 4 to 7 at the .01 level. The values in Table L-3 are overly liberal (that is, lead to too many significant differences) when you make more than one comparison. They are most accurate when you make a priori planned comparisons, such as Comprehension versus Information or Block Design versus Object Assembly. Pages 174 to 179 provide additional information about making comparisons between subtests.

Before making multiple comparisons, determine the difference between the highest and lowest subtest scores. If this difference is 6 scaled-score points or more, a significant difference at the .05 level is indicated. You can then interpret differences between subtests that are 6 scaled-score points or greater. If the difference between the highest and lowest subtest scaled scores is less than 6 scaled-score points, do not make multiple comparisons between individual subtest scores. (The *Note* to Table H-2 in Appendix H shows the formula used to compute the significant difference. The formula considers the average standard error of measurement for each of the 13 subtests and the studentized range statistic.)

6. *Comparing the Verbal Comprehension, Perceptual Organization, and Processing Speed factor scores.* Table L-3 in Appendix L presents the differences between sets of Verbal Comprehension, Perceptual Organization, and Processing Speed factor scores (in the form of Deviation IQs) needed to reach the .05 and .01 significance levels. (Table L-10 in Appendix L shows the probabilities associated with various differences between WISC-III factor score Deviation Quotients.)

7. *Comparing subtest scaled scores in each factor with their respective factor scores.* Table L-5 in Appendix L provides the critical values for the total WISC-III sample for the Verbal Comprehension, Perceptual Organization, and Processing Speed factors. Typical values for Verbal Comprehension range from 2.48 to 2.99 at the 5 percent level and 3.00 to 3.62 at the 1 percent level. For Perceptual Organization, they range from 2.60 to 3.12 at the 5 percent level and from 3.19 to 3.82 at the 1 percent level. For Processing Speed, they are 2.30 at the 5 percent level and 2.88 at the 1 percent level. The procedure used for this method is similar to that used in Methods 2 and 3 described above.

Supplementary approaches to profile analysis (referred to as *base rate approaches*) examine the kinds of variability found in the normative group, allowing features of an individual child's profile to be compared with those of the normative group. The three base rate approaches described below can be used for examining different kinds of variability.

### Base Rate Subtest Scaled-Score Ranges

A descriptive statistic that provides information about the variability, or spread, of a child's subtest scores (also referred to as *scatter*) is the *range* (see Chapter 2, page 15). The scaled-score range indicates the distance between the two most extreme scaled scores in a child's profile. It is obtained by subtracting the lowest scaled score from the highest scaled score. Thus, in a profile where the highest scaled score is 14 and the lowest scaled score is 5, the range is 9 ($14 - 5 = 9$).

In the standardization group, the median scaled-score range was 7 points for the 10 standard subtests on the Full Scale, 4 points for the 5 standard subtests on the Verbal Scale, and 6 points for the 5 standard subtests on the Performance Scale (see Table B.5, page 266 in the WISC-III manual). The scaled-score range is not a very helpful measure of variability because it is difficult to interpret and little research is available to guide its interpretation. It deals with only 2 scores and therefore fails to take into account the variability among all 10 (or 11, 12, or 13) subtest scores. The range index should not be discarded, however, because it provides base rate information about what occurred in the standardization sample.

### Base Rate Verbal-Performance Differences
### (The Probability-of-Occurrence Approach)

Determining how frequently a Verbal-Performance IQ difference of a given magnitude occurred in the standardization sample is referred to as the probability-of-occurrence approach. The frequencies with which several Verbal-Performance discrepancies are estimated to have occurred in the normative standardization sample are given in the expectancy table in Table L-8 of Appendix L. The table shows, for example, that a 10-point difference in either direction between the Verbal and Performance IQs was estimated to occur among 25 to 50 percent of the children in each age group of the standardization sample. Table L-10 in Appendix L presents a similar table – but only for the total group – for the Deviation Quotients associated with the Verbal Comprehension, Perceptual Organization, and Processing Speed factor scores.

For the total sample, Table B.2 in the WISC-III manual (page 262) shows the actual cumulative percentages of the total standardization sample that obtained various Verbal-Performance IQ discrepancies. (Table B.2 also shows similar information for the factor scores as proposed in the WISC-III manual.) The mean discrepancy was 10.0, and the median discrepancy was 8.0. Twenty-five percent of the sample had a discrepancy of 14 points or higher, and 75 percent of the sample had a discrepancy of 4 points or higher.

### Base Rate Differences Between Each Subtest Scaled Score and an Average Subtest Scaled Score in the WISC-III Standardization Sample

Table L-6 in Appendix L gives the estimated frequencies with which various differences occurred in the standardization sample between a child's scaled score on each subtest and his or her average WISC-III Verbal, Performance, or overall scaled score. The table shows, for example, that a difference of 3.12 points between the scaled score on Information and the Verbal Scale average, composed of the five standard subtests, was obtained by 5 percent of the standardization sample. Use this table only for differences that have first been shown to be reliable. (See Methods 2, 3, and 4 above.) Differences of approximately 2.94 to 4.96 points between each subtest scaled score and the respective average Verbal Scale or Performance Scale score were obtained by 5 percent of the standardization sample.

## GUIDELINES FOR INTERPRETING AND COMMUNICATING WISC-III FINDINGS IN THE PSYCHOLOGICAL REPORT

The guidelines in this section, used with other material in this appendix and with Appendixes I and J and Chapters 8 and 23, will help you interpret the WISC-III (and other intelligence tests) and write better reports. This section somewhat overlaps with the material in Chapter 23, but any redundancy is intended to emphasize some of the more subtle principles of test interpretation and report writing.

### Interpreting Individual Subtests

*Scores on individual subtests should not be used as a means of describing specific cognitive skills with precision;*

*rather, they should be used to generate hypotheses about the child's abilities.* You can derive the most reliable estimates of *specific abilities* from the Verbal Scale IQ (verbal or verbal comprehension abilities) and the Performance Scale IQ (performance, perceptual organization, or nonverbal abilities), not from individual subtest scores. Factor scores also provide more reliable information about abilities than do individual subtest scores. In fact, of the 133 separate reliability coefficients for the 13 subtests at the 11 age groups of the test, less than half (65) are .80 or above. Of these, only 7 are .90 or above—Vocabulary at ages 14 and 15, Digit Span at age 15, and Block Design at ages 13, 14, 15, and 16. The remaining 68 reliability coefficients are below .80 and are not sufficiently reliable for decision-making or classification purposes (see Table 5.1 on page 166 of the WISC-III manual). However, reliability coefficients of .70 or above are useful for generating hypotheses.

### Integrating Quantitative and Qualitative Aspects of Performance

*In interpreting the child's overall performance, look at the level of performance, quality of performance, relationship between level of performance and quality of performance, and problem-solving strategies used by the child to reach a solution* (Holmes, 1988[R][1]).

• Level of performance refers to whether the child's scores reflect strengths, weaknesses, or average ability.

• Quality of performance depends on such factors as the child's language, affect, level of attention, and approach to the tasks (for example, systematic or unsystematic), as well as the examiner-examinee interactions.

• Problem-solving strategies refer to such things as the child's verbalizations to himself or herself and whether child checked solutions, repeated key elements of problems, recognized when the solutions were correct or incorrect, found alternative ways of solving problems, and formulated plans to solve problems.

You may sometimes observe that the examinee has difficulty completing tasks. For example, tasks requiring speed and quick execution, such as Coding or Symbol Search, may be taxing for depressed children. Although depressed children's performance on these tasks may not reflect their level of cognitive ability, the tasks are still valuable because

---

[1] References followed by an [R] are cited at the end of this appendix; all other references are cited in the Reference section.

they provide information not readily obtained from interviews or observations conducted in natural settings. Coding, for example, gives you clues about the child's ability to follow a complex set of instructions, visual scanning processes, and learning ability. And Symbol Search gives you clues about visual scanning and the ability to shift rapidly. You may not want to report a score for these tasks for children who are depressed, but you can use such results to develop hypotheses to guide your clinical judgments.

Here is an illustration of how quantitative and qualitative information were woven into a report, along with a discussion of the profile. The report, only parts of which are shown below, is based on the administration of a WISC-III to a 16-year-, 11-month-old female. Her scores were as follows: Information 12, Similarities 12, Arithmetic 8, Vocabulary, 10, Comprehension 9, Digit Span 6, Picture Completion 9, Coding 11, Picture Arrangement 5, Block Design 9, Object Assembly 9, Verbal IQ 101, Performance IQ 91, and Full Scale IQ 94.

...Her short-term sequential memory is relatively less well developed than her overall verbal skills. The subtest measuring short-term auditory memory involves repeating a sequence of digits from immediate memory. Her weakness in short-term auditory sequential memory may be due to temporary inefficiency caused by anxiety or inattention. However, it is important to note that neither anxiety nor inattention appeared to affect her performance on other subtests adversely. It is more likely that her weakness in short-term auditory memory for digit sequences indicated difficulty forming in memory an adequate mental image of the correct digit sequence. Helen was often able to recall the correct digits but in the wrong sequence, indicating specific weakness in auditory sequential memory rather than in general auditory memory.

. . . Her visual sequencing ability is relatively less developed than her other nonverbal skills. Her average attention to visual detail, coupled with her below average visual sequencing ability, indicates that although her perception of visual details is adequate, her ability to organize and sequence these details is poor. Moreover, it is important to note that both her verbal and her nonverbal weaknesses lie in her sequencing ability in different domains — auditory sequencing and visual sequencing. This may indicate an inefficiency in her general sequential processing abilities, although further testing would be needed to substantiate this hypothesis. It is unclear how her weakness in auditory and visual sequencing has affected her academic performance at school; this needs to be investigated. However, her overall average verbal and nonverbal skills indicate that she has the ability to perform adequately in school.

## Steps in Analyzing a Wechsler Protocol

Here are some steps that you may find useful in analyzing a Wechsler protocol. They are by no means the only ones you

should consider, but they do cover several important areas that will help you interpret a child's performance.

1. Evaluate the reliability of the test scores.

2. Evaluate the validity of the test scores.

3. Look at the Full Scale IQ and its percentile rank and evaluate the implications of this score.

4. Look at the Verbal Scale IQ and its percentile rank and evaluate the implications of this score.

5. Look at the Performance Scale IQ and its percentile rank and evaluate the implications of this score.

6. Determine whether there is a significant discrepancy between the Verbal and Performance IQs. If there is, which IQ is higher? What is the base rate for the discrepancy? What are the implications of the discrepancy?

7. Determine whether there are any significant discrepancies between subtest scores and the means of their respective scaled scores. If there is a significant discrepancy, is the subtest score lower or higher than the mean? What is the base rate for the discrepancy? What are the implications of the discrepancy? Note the absolute level of each subtest score that differs significantly from its respective mean score.

8. Are there any subtest scores that differ significantly? If so, which ones are they? What are the implications of each discrepancy? Note which subtest score is higher or lower than the other and the absolute level of each score.

9. Consider the child's factor scores. Are there any significant discrepancies among the factor scores? If so, which factor scores differ significantly? Note which factor score is higher or lower than the others and the absolute level of each score. Do any of the subtest scores on a factor differ significantly from the mean factor score? If so, is the subtest score lower or higher than the mean? What are the base rates for the discrepancies? What are the implications of any significant discrepancies?

10. Were there any qualitative features of the child's performance that were especially noteworthy? Is so, what were they? What are the implications of these features by themselves and in relation to the test scores?

---

**Guideline 1. Describe carefully the behaviors you observe. Make inferences about underlying traits or processes only with extreme caution, if at all.**

## Discussion of Guideline 1

It is tempting to interpret and explain an examinee's behavior. However, be extremely cautious in making interpretations based on a limited sample of behavior. You should, of course, describe the child's behavior in the report. And when you have information that you believe supports an interpretation, go ahead and make it.

## Examples of Statements That Do Not Meet Guideline 1

1. "Jean was careless and erratic when she was sure she could perform a task." This statement is questionable because we don't know how the examiner knew that the child "was *sure* she could perform a task." Suggestion: "Jean was careless and erratic on nonverbal tasks. However, on verbal tasks she was more systematic and organized and seemed to be more confident."

2. "From the start, Derek had a tendency either to repeat questions to himself or to ask the examiner to repeat the questions for him. This appeared to be an attempt by Derek to structure or clarify the questions for himself." This behavior pattern may mean one or more things. It could reflect the examinee's attempt to structure the question, but it is not clear how repeating the question helped him to clarify it. It could also be a means of controlling the situation, or it could suggest inattention. In addition, the behavior may reflect a way of holding on, a delay reaction, a need for additional support, or a coping pattern associated with a possible hearing deficit. Examine the entire performance to arrive at the best interpretation. Suggestion: Leave out the second sentence unless other information supports one or more of the above interpretations or some other interpretation.

3. "As the test progressed, he had a tendency to sit with his arms folded or to pick at and scratch his arm when answering questions. Though at first these behaviors made John seem less interested, it appears that he was compensating for his lowered self-confidence." This interpretation seems to have little merit. In what way does folding and scratching arms reflect compensation for lowered self-confidence? Could these actions simply be a habit or a response to frustration? Suggestion: Keep the first sentence and eliminate the second one. Then describe what comments the examinee made about his performance, if any, and note how cooperative he was.

4. "She responded impulsively on the verbal subtests. On the nonverbal subtests, she was more attentive and careful. This behavior may simply reflect an impulsive personality." This interpretation may or may not be correct.

Performing impulsively on one part of the test but not on the other may *not* be an indication of an impulsive personality. Perhaps there are tendencies in this direction, but the generalization may be inappropriate. You should also consider whether there was anything about the verbal items that led her to respond impulsively. Suggestion: Keep the first two sentences and eliminate the third one. Then describe her scores on the verbal and nonverbal parts of the test.

5. "Harry's statements about his inadequacies resulted in an increase in feelings of inferiority and self-deprecating behavior, as demonstrated by an increase in nervous laughter and by impulsive answers." This inference is conjectural. It implies a cause-and-effect relationship between verbal expressions and behavior. There is no way of knowing what the examinee's statements led to. Suggestion: Limit the statements to a description of his verbalizations and behavior. For example, "On difficult items, Harry answered impulsively, laughed anxiously, and made self-deprecatory remarks."

6. "Rachel also showed a tendency to ignore specific directions by giving information that was not asked for. For example, in the Picture Completion subtest, she tended to say what was in the picture rather than what was missing." The examinee's way of responding to the task may have been her way of coping with a difficult situation rather than a case of "ignoring" directions. Suggestion: "On a task requiring her to give the missing details of pictures, Rachel tended to say what was in the picture rather than what was missing." Then state how she performed on the subtest.

7. "The inconsistency in her performance during certain periods of time may have been due to her medical diagnosis of hyperactivity." This statement has at least two difficulties. First, the term *inconsistency* is unclear. It could be a description of her behavior (qualitative information) or a description of her test scores (quantitative information). Second, a diagnosis can't cause an inconsistency. Suggestion: Describe the inconsistency clearly. Note whether it was in behavior, test performance, or both; where it occurred (that is, on what subtests or items); and when it occurred (that is, during the early, middle, or later part of the test session). After you describe the inconsistency, you might want to point out that the inconsistency and her hyperactivity may be related.

8. "On the performance tasks, he seemed to be hampered by the inability to manipulate the pieces easily." This description is ambiguous because *manipulate* can refer to motor dexterity or to the cognitive operations required by the task (for example, planning and organizing). Note that in the following suggested sentence an inference is made ("seemed to be frustrated") that is supported by a reference to the examinee's behavior. Suggestion (assuming these

behaviors were noted): "When assembling puzzle-like pieces, he seemed to be frustrated, slamming pieces down when he could not complete the object correctly."

9. The following interpretation was based on a Verbal IQ of 98: "Her anxious laughter and quick replies of 'I don't know' seem to suggest that overall Mary was less comfortable with verbal tasks than with nonverbal tasks. Whether it is a deficiency of skills in verbal interactions that causes the anxiousness and subsequent poor performance or whether it is the anxiousness that causes a subsequent deficiency in verbal skills is unknown." It is helpful to tie together observations and subtest scores. However, the second sentence is misleading because the examinee does not have a *deficiency* in verbal skills – she obtained an average score. The statement about causality is unnecessary because it is almost impossible to know what is cause and what is effect simply on the basis of performance on an intelligence test. In addition, the expression *verbal interactions* is ambiguous. Suggestion: Leave the second sentence out of the report.

10. The following statement was based on average IQs on the three scales: "Her quick performance on both verbal and nonverbal tasks seemed to lower her scores." This statement may be correct, but it is also possible that even with additional time the examinee would have failed the items or that the examinee worked quickly in order to avoid frustration. Suggestion: "She responded quickly, and often incorrectly, on both verbal and nonverbal tasks. However, it is not known to what extent her performance would have improved if she had taken more time before answering the questions."

---

> **Guideline 2. Provide clear descriptions of abilities thought to be measured by the subtests, and use factor loadings, if you want to, to guide your interpretations of the subtests.**

---

### Discussion of Guideline 2

Clinical lore has given us several possibilities for describing or interpreting the abilities measured by the WISC-III subtests. These abilities are summarized in Table C-13 on page 824. You will have to decide which description best characterizes the child's performance. Whichever one (or ones) you choose, describe the child's ability clearly. The factor analytic findings also can guide your interpretations. For example, although the WISC-III subtests are grouped into Verbal and Performance Scales, factor analytic findings suggest that Coding and Symbol Search are best interpreted as measuring sustained attention and the ability to process nonmeaningful information rapidly. This would seem to be a more appropriate interpretation than referring to Coding or Symbol Search simply as measures of performance ability.

When you describe the functions thought to be measured by a subtest, try to be as specific as possible. For example, if you are writing about Digit Span, identify the type of short-term memory being evaluated (auditory) and the type of content (nonmeaningful). Furthermore, recognize that every subtest provides only a *sampling* of abilities – no one subtest samples the entire ability domain. Subtests such as Arithmetic, for example, do not measure the entire range of mathematical ability. In fact, the Arithmetic subtest may not reliably and systematically measure skills involving addition, subtraction, multiplication, and division. To measure these skills, select a test that is specifically designed to do so, such as the Key Math Diagnostic Arithmetic Test (see page 340).

Profiles can be analyzed from two frames of reference. In one method, you compare the examinee's scores to the norm group; we refer to this as an *interindividual comparison*. In the other method, you compare the examinee's scores to his or her own unique profile; we refer to this as an *intraindividual comparison* (see below). In either case, you will always be using the scaled scores based on the norm group. Let us now focus on the interindividual approach to profile analysis.

**Interindividual comparison.** The simplest way to approach a profile is to evaluate the scores in reference to the norm group. The following three categories will be useful for describing the subtest scaled scores:

| Scaled score | Description |
|---|---|
| 1 to 7 | Weakness or below average |
| 8 to 12 | Average |
| 13 to 19 | Strength or above average |

You can also add to your description the percentiles associated with each qualitative description of the subtest function. The percentiles (or percentile ranks) provide a more precise description of the child's level of functioning (see Table C-41, page 855).

Here are some illustrations of how to describe scaled scores:

• "She has strengths in abstract reasoning (91st percentile) and word knowledge (84th percentile)."

• "His weaknesses are in spatial visualization organization (5th percentile) and sustained attention for auditory information (9th percentile)."

• "She has average ability in ..., all between the 25th and 75th percentiles. . . ."

• "His abilities are above average (in the 84th to 98th percentiles) in . . . ."

Other statements useful in describing profiles are as follows. These statements were based on Verbal scaled scores of 7 to 12:

• "His verbal skills range from below average to average."

• "Within the verbal domain, his skills range from below average to average. His range of knowledge, concept formation, . . . are all average for his age." The key phrase "are all average for his age" reflects a comparison with the norm group.

You can also use a finer gradation—five categories instead of three—to describe the subtest scaled scores. The five categories are as follows:

| Scaled score | Description |
|---|---|
| 1 to 4 | Exceptional weakness or very poorly developed or far below average or very poor |
| 5 to 7 | Weakness or poorly developed or below average or poor |
| 8 to 12 | Average |
| 13 to 15 | Strength or well developed or above average or good |
| 16 to 19 | Exceptional strength or very well developed or superior or excellent |

Either the three- or the five-level category system can be used to describe subtest scaled scores, depending on your preferences or the preferences of your instructor. For different reports, you may prefer different systems. As you study the qualitative descriptions of the subtest scaled scores, *notice that scaled scores of 8 or above are never described as weaknesses and scaled scores of 7 or below are never described as strengths.*

**Intraindividual comparison.**   When you evaluate the profile from the vantage point of the examinee's own specific pattern of abilities, you are making an *intraindividual comparison* (or using an *ipsative* approach). The focus is on describing areas that are better or more poorly developed for the specific examinee. As noted above, the absolute values of the scaled scores are still used to guide you in the way you describe the examinee's performance. That is,

scores of 13 to 19 are always strengths; 8 to 12, average; and 1 to 7, weaknesses.

• This statement was based on Verbal scaled scores of 3 to 7: "Relative to her own level of verbal ability, her social comprehension is her best developed ability, but still at a below-average level (16th percentile)." The key phrase "relative to her own level of verbal ability" reflects a comparison based on the examinee's individual profile. Note, however, that the absolute values of the scaled scores are still used for an intraindividual profile analysis. Her scaled score of 7 does not indicate a strength, even if it is the highest score in the profile. Also note that in this example the phrase "but still at a below-average level" helps the reader understand that, although social comprehension is the examinee's best ability, it is still at a level that is below average for her peer group.

• This statement was based on scaled scores of 7 to 15 over the 10 standard subtests and a Full Scale IQ of 113: "Within his overall above-average level of functioning, his command of word knowledge is a considerable strength (95th percentile)." The key phrase "within his overall above-average level of functioning" prepares the reader for some comment related to the child's individual profile.

**Abilities common to more than one subtest.**   Descriptions of abilities that apply to more than one subtest, such as verbal comprehension, must be carefully used. For example, if a child has a scaled score of 13 on Vocabulary, you must also consider the child's scores on the other subtests that measure verbal comprehension (Information, Comprehension, Similarities) before you say that the child has a strength in verbal comprehension. For example, if this same child obtained a scaled score of 7 on Information, do not say that verbal comprehension is a strength. Instead use a phrase that refers to Vocabulary but not Information. The same guideline holds for the subtests that measure perceptual organization (Picture Completion, Block Design, Object Assembly) and for those that measure the ability to sustain attention (Coding and Symbol Search).

**Examples of Statements That Do Not Meet Guideline 2**

1. The following statement was based on a Picture Completion scaled score of 7: "She displayed a weakness in her ability to perceive significant features." The phrase "to perceive significant features" is vague. Suggestion: "She displayed a weakness in her ability to perceive missing details of pictures."

2. The following statement was based on a Picture Arrangement scaled score of 9: "She was average in her ability to anticipate and sequence cause-and-effect social interactions." The phrase "ability to anticipate and sequence cause-and-effect social interactions" is difficult to follow. Suggestion: "Her ability to anticipate in a meaningful way the results that might be expected from various acts of behavior is average (37th percentile)."

3. "His average score in Arithmetic suggests that he has no difficulties in mathematics." This generalization is too broad. Suggestion: "His numerical reasoning ability is average."

4. The following statement was based on a scaled score of 10 on Digit Span: "Short-term memory is adequate." Although this description is satisfactory, it could be more precise. Suggestion: "Short-term auditory memory for nonmeaningful material is average (50th percentile)."

5. "He is average in number reasoning." *Numerical reasoning* is the preferred terminology.

6. "Her WISC-III performance suggests that Helen likes and does well in spelling." There is little, if any, information obtained from the WISC-III that would support this statement.

7. The following statement was based on Profile 2.7 in Table K-1: "Henry showed a strength on a test of perceptual organization." The statement as such is accurate for the Object Assembly subtest, but it fails to consider that Picture Completion and Block Design also measure perceptual organization. Scores on Picture Completion and Block Design were average and not above average. Suggestion: "Henry showed a strength in his ability to synthesize concrete parts into meaningful wholes."

8. The following statement was based on a Similarities scaled score of 6: "She has difficulties in forming verbal concepts that pertain to creativity." There is no way of knowing to what extent Similarities involves creativity. There may be some relationship, but I am not aware of data that support this interpretation. Suggestion: "She has difficulties in forming verbal concepts."

9. The child obtained a Digit Span score of 15, which was the highest score in the profile: "His highest scaled score was on Digit Span, which is a verbal task." Although this statement is technically accurate, it can be improved in two ways. First, instead of listing the name of the subtest, describe what the subtest may measure. Second, use a qualitative description for a scaled score of 15. Suggestion: "His attention span is well developed, as noted by his ability to recall digits."

10. "Jill has ability in the area of perceptual-motor organization, but is less able in numerical reasoning." This sentence doesn't tell the reader about the child's level of performance. The terms "has ability" and "less able" are vague. Suggestion: "Jill's strength is in the area of perceptual-motor organization (84th percentile). She is at an average level in numerical reasoning (50th percentile)."

**Table K-I**
**WISC-III Profiles Cited in Examples in Guidelines**

| Subtest | Profile | | | | | | |
|---|---|---|---|---|---|---|---|
| | 2.7 | 3.3 | 3.9 | 4.1 | 4.7 | 5.0 | 8.8 |
| Information | – | 9 | – | 8 | 15 | 6 | 7 |
| Similarities | – | 10 | – | 4 | 14 | 5 | 12 |
| Arithmetic | – | 14 | – | 7 | 13 | 3 | 12 |
| Vocabulary | – | 9 | – | 9 | 14 | 6 | 9 |
| Comprehension | – | 10 | – | 8 | 13 | 7 | 10 |
| Digit Span | – | 12 | – | 7 | 9 | 8 | 12 |
| Picture Completion | 8 | 12 | 16 | 6 | 16 | 5 | 10 |
| Coding | 9 | 15 | 13 | 9 | 13 | 10 | 14 |
| Picture Arrangement | 7 | 13 | 14 | 11 | 14 | 5 | 7 |
| Block Design | 9 | 9 | 12 | 6 | 12 | 5 | 14 |
| Object Assembly | 13 | 8 | 13 | 7 | 13 | 4 | 10 |
| Symbol Search | – | – | – | – | – | – | – |
| Mazes | – | – | 16 | – | 16 | – | – |
| Verbal IQ | – | 102 | – | 84 | 123 | 74 | 100 |
| Performance IQ | – | 110 | – | 86 | 125 | 74 | 107 |
| Full Scale IQ | – | 106 | – | 84 | 126 | 72 | 104 |

> **Guideline 3. Relate inferences based on subtest scores or IQs to the cognitive processes measured (or thought to be measured) by the subtests and scales.**

### Discussion of Guideline 3

Although every effort should be made to discuss the implications of the child's test performance, stay close to the cognitive operations measured by the subtests or scales. If you have information about the child's achievements in school, case history information, behavioral observations, and other test data, you will be in a better position to make generalizations about your findings.

Generalizations about how examinees will perform in school, on a job, or in other settings based solely or primarily on the results of an intelligence test must be made with caution. Although scores on intelligence tests correlate significantly with school grades, the correlations tend to run in the .30s and .40s (see Appendix I, page 1042). These correlations mean that intelligence test scores account for only 10 to 20 percent of the variance in school grades. We simply do not know what specific Wechsler scores (or scores on other intelligence tests) are needed in order to do average, above-average, or superior work in school. We also do not know with certainty what scores should be considered deficits. For example, should an IQ of 80 be considered a deficit? If this score is adequate for the examinee to achieve his or her goals, it may not be a deficit.

Other types of generalizations also should be made with caution. For example, the statement "His strengths in immediate auditory memory, numerical reasoning, and visual-motor spatial integration will help him in his understanding of historical events and their link with today's society" may or may not be accurate. Because there is limited, if any, indication in the literature of a relationship between these skills and the understanding of historical events, it is better not to make this type of inference.

How do we discuss the results of an evaluation when they differ from our expectations of how the examinee should have performed? For example, if an examinee obtains an IQ of 150, but is making grades of C, D, and F in school, do we say that the intelligence test scores are invalid? Or is it better to say that the examinee's poor school performance is probably associated not with cognitive difficulties but with other factors? Conversely, if an examinee with an IQ of 80 achieves a B or A average in school, do we say that the IQ is inconsistent with the examinee's school grades? Grading practices are highly variable, and grades also depend on course content, subject matter, and student effort. Unless you have information about grading practices, course content, curriculum, and the child's study habits, be careful about the inferences you make about the relationship between test scores and school grades. When you discuss the examinee's occupational goals or academic performance or potential, consider the examinee's IQ as well as motivation, temperament, interpersonal skills, and other characteristics that may be needed for successful performance.

Recommendations that intelligence test scores could be improved by having the examinee engage in certain activities should be based on research findings or at least on relevant clinical or psychoeducational theories. For example, there is little, if any, evidence that participating in sports aids an examinee in developing the motor coordination needed for successful performance on intelligence tests, as athletics primarily involves gross motor skills. How will involvement in sports improve such nonverbal cognitive skills as eye-hand coordination (Coding) and manipulating materials in an analytic manner (Block Design and Object Assembly)? It is doubtful that participation in athletics leads to better developed nonverbal cognitive skills, as measured by the Performance Scale subtests of the Wechsler tests.

Always use the absolute level of the scaled scores to guide your analysis. Scaled scores of 13 to 19 always indicate strengths — they are in the 84th to 99th percentile rank. For example, if there is one scaled score of 13 in a profile, it still represents a strength, even if the other scores are all 18 or 19. You don't want to imply that a scaled score of 13 indicates limited ability or a weakness or deficit. *It is the absolute score, not a comparison with any other scores, that is used to determine the examinee's level of ability in the areas measured by the subtest or test.* However, in a profile that ranges from 13 to 19, you can identify the scaled score of 13 as a strength that is less well developed than the examinee's other strengths.

Be careful when you discuss cause-and-effect relationships. For example, did the examinee do well in an area because he or she likes the area, or does the examinee like the area because he or she does well in it? In some cases examinees may like an area that they do not do well in or dislike an area that they do well in. Also, to what extent does the examinee's level of performance relate to what happens in the family? Research does suggest that what is emphasized in the home is related to children's cognitive development, but the relationship is far from perfect (see Chapter 4). Therefore, a statement such as "His high nonverbal skills are related to the emphasis on sports in his family" may or may not be accurate. In addition, as noted above, the motor skills involved in sports are not the same as those involved in the performance subtests of the Wechsler tests or other individually administered tests of intelligence.

## Examples of Statements That Do Not Meet Guideline 3

Here are examples of questionable inferences made on the basis of test scores:

1. "Dean performed in the low average range. His cognitive deficits during this examination are inconsistent with his reported B average in school." The terms *deficits* and *inconsistent* may not be appropriate, as noted previously. Suggestion: Leave out the terms *deficit* and *inconsistent*, but comment on the examinee's test performance and report that the examinee has above-average school performance.

2. "She demonstrated below-average performance in visual discrimination tasks and nonverbal reasoning tasks. Despite these skills, she exhibited average performance in analyzing and synthesizing nonverbal information." Why are the words "despite these skills" used to begin the second sentence? Does the writer mean to say "In contrast with these below-average skills, her skills. . ."? The writer seems to imply that visual discrimination skills and nonverbal reasoning skills may also be involved in analyzing and synthesizing nonverbal information. This implication may be appropriate, but it is not adequately developed in the presentation.

3. The following interpretations were based on Profile 3.3 in Table K-1 (page 1113) for a 16-year-, 0-month-old female: "Helen demonstrated abilities overall in the Average range, with strengths in nonverbal social intelligence, numerical reasoning, and symbol association skills. Her performance indicates that she may have trouble with her studies at school." The second sentence does not follow from the first one. Why should average overall ability and skills in specific areas lead to a prediction that the examinee may have trouble in school? It is risky to make such predictions based on a profile of subtest scores that has no absolute weakness and is in the Average range for the Verbal, Performance, and Full Scales.

4. "Debbie's career goals appear to be realistic, based on her IQ of 110." This statement would be more accurate if the examinee also had other characteristics needed for successful performance in a specific career. Suggestion: "Based on her IQ of 110 and her overall motivation and enthusiasm for. . . ."

5. "The low concentration and attention scores may indicate that Jane's inability to ignore distractions (i.e., nervousness, examiner's note taking, etc.) is indicative of a tendency to give up when items get more difficult (i.e., saying 'I don't know' quickly before thinking about an appropriate response to a test item)." This is a confusing sentence. It is not clear how nervousness is related to an inability to ignore distractions. Saying "I don't know" quickly may have been realistic. If not, what factors suggested to the examiner that the examinee had the ability to solve the problems?

6. "Low scores on Information and Arithmetic may indicate weakness in the ability to assimilate given material and then provide a solution for the designated problem." This description attempts to combine functions thought to be involved in the Information and Arithmetic subtests. However, it is not clear how a low score on Information or Arithmetic (or on both) suggests a "weakness in the ability to assimilate given material and then provide a solution for the designated problem." Suggestion: "Her range of factual information and her ability in mental arithmetic are below average."

7. "By comparing some specific subtests within and between Performance and Verbal test categories, Joan achieved high Similarities standard scores and low Comprehension scores." The examinee's subtest scores are independent of any comparisons made with other subtest scores. For example, a score of 13 on Similarities is a strength in and of itself, whether it is higher or lower than another subtest score. The statement is also ungrammatical (for example, the examiner, not Joan, compared the subtests). Suggestion: "Joan has well-developed abstract

thinking ability but poorly developed ability to apply conceptualizing skills to solve problems in the social world."

8. "Her low score on the Arithmetic subtest may be due to her dislike of and disinterest in school mathematics classes." Cause-and-effect relationships are difficult to tease out without more information. It may be that she dislikes mathematics because she is not good at it.

9. The following statements were based on Profile 3.9 in Table K-1 (page 1113) for a girl who was 9 years, 6 months old: "At most activities requiring visual perception, Kirsten would excel, but when the motor aspect is introduced, she is in the average range. Physical activities may improve her motor coordination, bringing it to the same level as her other nonverbal skills." These statements are tenuous at best and provide the reader with potentially misleading information. First, five of the six Performance subtest scores are above average, and one subtest (Block Design) is at the upper end of the average range. Most of the Performance subtests involve motor coordination to some extent. Therefore, the statement "when the motor aspect is introduced, she is in the average range" is incorrect. The next statement, "Physical activities may improve her motor coordination . . . ," is conjectural. Second, all nonverbal skills are at the 75th percentile rank or higher. Thus, it is difficult to foresee how continuation of sports would improve her motor coordination in cognitive tasks. It would be better to emphasize the child's excellent nonverbal skills.

10. The following statement was based on an Information scaled score of 13 and a Comprehension scaled score of 16 for a 13-year-old girl: "Virginia achieved a lower score in her range of knowledge than in her ability to use social judgment, which suggests limited factual knowledge." This statement is misleading. A standard score of 13 indicates above-average ability. The fact that one subtest score is lower than another score does not mean that the lower score reflects limited ability. In this case, Information is not significantly lower than Comprehension (see Table L-3 in Appendix L). Suggestion: "Virginia's range of knowledge and ability to use social judgment are above average."

---

**Guideline 4. Describe the profile in a clear and unambiguous manner. State that two or more abilities reflect different levels of skill only when the scores are significantly different.**

---

## Discussion of Guideline 4

Consider all of the information you have in describing the test profile. Choose carefully the words you use to describe the child's performance. Subtests and scales overlap in their measurement properties; consequently, be careful not to make statements that are contradictory. Guideline 2 suggested terms that you can use to describe subtest scores.

Before you say that two abilities are different (or higher/lower or better/more poorly developed), be sure that the scores representing these abilities are *significantly* different. For example, you don't want to say "She may favor verbal expressive tasks that allow her to work at her own pace over more structured time-dependent tasks" when the examinee has a Verbal IQ of 106, a Performance IQ of 104, and a Full Scale IQ of 107. Because the Verbal and Performance IQs are about the same, there is little justification for making this inference. Similarly, you don't want to say "His verbal skills are slightly more well developed than his nonverbal skills" for a Verbal IQ of 83 and a Performance IQ of 82. When two (or more) scores are not significantly different, no inference should be made that one score is slightly better (or poorer) than the other one.

When the Verbal IQ is significantly higher than the Performance IQ, however, you can describe the difference with confidence. For example, for a Verbal IQ of 116 and a Performance IQ of 94, you can say "Her verbal comprehension skills (84th percentile) are better developed than her perceptual organizational skills (34th percentile)" rather than "Her verbal comprehension skills *may be* better developed. . . ."

Your report should clearly indicate when you are describing the examinee's own unique profile.

When you describe the examinee's scores, compare subtest scores, or compare the Verbal and Performance IQs, always give the level at which the scores fall and the direction of the differences between the scores. Thus, for example, the statement "She demonstrated a significant difference between Block Design and Object Assembly" is not informative *because it gives neither the level of the scores (average, above average, or below average) nor the direction of the difference (which score was higher or lower than the other).*

## Examples of Statements That Do Not Meet Guideline 4

1. The following statements were based on Profile 4.1 in Table K-1 (page 1113) for a 15-year-old male: "Jim's verbal and nonverbal skills are similarly developed and range from average to well below average. His vocabulary

ability is better developed than his social comprehension." Because the Vocabulary scaled score is not significantly higher than the Comprehension scaled score (9 vs. 8), this statement is misleading.

2. "Her average nonverbal and verbal skills varied in a range from average to above-average ability, with particular strengths and weaknesses in certain tasks." This is a confusing sentence. If all scores are average or above average, how can there be any weaknesses, since we define weaknesses to be skills that are below average (for example, scaled scores of 7 or lower)? Suggestion: Eliminate the last part of the sentence, beginning with "with particular strengths," or use other ways to describe the pattern of scores.

3. "Within Ginny's Verbal IQ, scores ranged from average to very superior." The phrase "within Ginny's Verbal IQ" is awkward and perhaps misleading. The Verbal IQ is one score, although we derive it from several subtest scores. Better: "Ginny's verbal skills range from average to superior."

4. "By comparing the standard scores based on her age group, she demonstrated a significant difference on arithmetic and digit span. High scores on these sub-tests may indicate a strength within the realm of visual-perceptual motor skills." The two sentences fail to give either the direction of the differences or the level at which the scores fall. In addition, subtest names are usually capitalized, and the word *subtests* is usually written without a hyphen. You do not have to put in the report how you proceeded to arrive at your statements. It is preferable to leave out the entire phrase "by comparing the standard scores based on her age group." Finally, the sentence is ungrammatical because the examinee didn't compare the standard scores.

5. The following statement was based on a Picture Completion score of 7 and a Block Design score of 12: "There is a marked difference between her visual perception and her visual-motor-spatial coordination." This statement is misleading because Block Design also involves visual perception. Suggestion: "Her attention to visual details is below average, whereas her spatial visualization ability is average."

6. "Within Becky's scores, a marked difference in ability was found between her Very Superior ability in abstract and concrete reasoning and her Low Average ability in spatial visualization." This is a confusing sentence. Part of the problem is that the opening phrase, "within Becky's scores," is immediately followed by a statement about ability levels. A better way might be to say "Her abstract reasoning ability is excellent, whereas her spatial visualization skills are less well developed but still within the lower limits of the average range." The qualita-

tive descriptions "Very Superior" and "Low Average," if used, should begin with lowercase letters. Capitalize qualitative descriptions only when you refer to the classifications associated with the Full Scale, Verbal Scale, and Performance Scale IQs.

7. The following statements were based on Profile 4.7 in Table K-1 (page 1113): "Jamie has one relative weakness in short-term memory. Within her other verbal scores, short-term memory is significantly less developed than her other scores. Her attention is less developed than her concentration. If, in class, Jamie's teacher asked her for some information just presented in class, Jamie probably would have been concentrating, but her average development in attention and short-term memory might cause her to forget the material."

This is a confusing paragraph. A scaled score of 9 is average and should not be considered weak. In addition, this child has excellent attention skills as noted by her performance on the other subtests. She shows somewhat less developed ability in nonmeaningful immediate auditory memory. I believe that it is inappropriate to speculate that the examinee would forget material presented in a class. In fact, with her outstanding ability, I would think that her recall ability was excellent. Do not stress any score in isolation from the total picture. The writing is also poor. It is incorrect to say that "Within her other verbal scores, short-term memory is. . . ." Finally, stating that "her average development in attention and short-term memory might cause her to forget the material" implies a cause-and-effect relationship that may be difficult to establish.

8. The following statement was based on a Block Design score of 7 and a Picture Completion score of 12: "Her performance on a spatial visual task was inconsistent with her performance on a task measuring alertness to details." This statement may lead the reader to believe that the two tasks should have yielded similar scores. It is preferable to refer to an examinee's scores in terms of strengths and weaknesses and the possible implications of the differences. Suggestion: "Her performance suggests that she has average nonspatial visual perceptual ability but below-average spatial visualization ability."

9. The following statement was written for Performance subtest scores ranging from 6 to 13: "In nonverbal areas Harry displayed uniformly developed skills." This statement is incorrect because this range of 7 scaled-score points (from below average to above average) indicates strengths as well as weaknesses.

10. "There is a 9-point difference between his Verbal and Performance IQs, which suggests that his nonverbal abilities are better developed than his verbal abilities." A 9-point difference is not significant, and thus the interpreta-

tion is incorrect. (See Table L-3 in Appendix L for required differences between the Verbal and Performance IQs at the .05 and .01 levels for the WISC-III.)

---

> **Guideline 5. Make recommendations carefully, using all available sources of information.**

### Discussion of Guideline 5

Recommendations are a valuable part of the report. However, if your assessment is for a class exercise and without a referral question, it may be difficult to arrive at meaningful recommendations. Try to develop one or more ideas that you believe may be appropriate. You want to be on relatively firm ground when you make predictions or recommendations. And you don't want to make statements that are potentially misleading.

Here is an example of recommendations made on the basis of Profile 5.0 in Table K-1 (page 1113):

It appears that Frida will have difficulty processing information, in either an auditory or a visual format, in the classroom. She will need to have material presented to her in a simplified manner in order for her to process, retain, and understand concepts. She would also benefit from lessons designed to help her understand logical and sequential cause-and-effect relationships. Frida's overall performance suggests that she can learn; however, the learning environment should be concrete and repetitive, with many examples provided.

### Examples of Statements That Do Not Meet Guideline 5

1. "Information regarding his academic performance is needed to determine the need for intervention in his areas of average ability." This is a confusing recommendation. Why would intervention be needed in areas of average ability?

2. This statement was made on the basis of a Verbal IQ of 108, Performance IQ of 102, and Full Scale IQ of 104: "Jim shows sufficient aptitude to attain advanced degrees, and I recommend that he be considered for a gifted program." This statement is misleading. First, an IQ of 104 may not be sufficient to allow a child to go on to graduate school. I would hesitate to go out on a limb to make such a prediction. Second, it is doubtful that a child with an IQ of 104 would be allowed into a gifted program unless the child

had special strengths in academic performance or other areas that would qualify him or her for the program.

3. The following statement was based on a Verbal IQ of 102, Performance IQ of 96, Full Scale IQ of 101, and Picture Completion score of 7: "Her visual perception skills may affect her duties as a camp counselor." With overall scores average, it is doubtful that a relatively low Picture Completion score would affect the examinee's work as a camp counselor. Predictions about success in occupations based solely on a single subtest score must be made with extreme caution, if at all.

4. "I believe that Jill's nervous behavior exhibited during the Verbal scale test administration was too profound to discount. It is recommended that this correlation between nervousness and verbal performance be considered before any definitive assessment is made." The examiner is concerned about the examinee's level of anxiety, but the recommendation is vague. What does the examiner mean by "before any definitive assessment is made"? Why use the term *correlation*? Why is her "nervous behavior . . . too profound to discount"? The recommendation should emphasize that the severity of the examinee's anxiety level needs to be further investigated. Did her level of anxiety affect the reliability of the test results? In addition, there are some minor stylistic problems. "Scale" should be capitalized and "test" is superfluous after "scale."

5. "Rachel wants to major in international business. It is recommended that she go into this area. Her strength in social judgment should be useful in international business because of the different cultures and protocols a person must use." This hypothesis is on shaky ground. A high score on the Comprehension subtest suggests good social reasoning, but it is highly culture bound. The social reasoning skills measured by the subtest therefore may not generalize to different cultures. Also, the term *protocols* is vague. Finally, what does it mean to say that she "must use" different cultures?

---

> **Guideline 6. Describe and use statistical concepts in an appropriate manner, check all calculations carefully, and report the reliability and validity of the test results as accurately as possible.**

### Discussion of Guideline 6

There are preferred ways to describe and use statistical concepts such as percentile rank, probability level, range, and so forth. Here are suggested ways of describing several statistical concepts:

• Percentile rank: "Her Full Scale IQ is at the 55th percentile." (This is preferable to "She is 55% better than other children.")

• Probability level: "The chances that the range of scores from 106 to 120 includes his true IQ are about 95 out of 100." (This is preferable to "There is a 95–100% probability that his true IQ falls between 106 and 120." The use of "100%" is questionable in the latter statement, and it depicts an improper conceptualization of probability levels.)

• Range or classification: "Her overall performance is in the High Average range." (Use the range or classification primarily for the Full Scale IQ and on occasion for the Verbal and Performance IQ. This is preferable to "Her Vocabulary ability is in the Superior classification.")

• Reliability and validity: "The present measure of her level of intellectual functioning appears to be reliable and valid. She was cooperative, motivated, and appeared to do her best." (This is preferable to "On the basis of her consistency, the current results appear to be reliable and valid." An examinee may be consistent, but the scores may still be invalid.)

## Examples of Statements That Do Not Meet Guideline 6

1. "Her fatigue and boredom during the latter portions of the test need to be considered in relation to her overall score. Although I don't believe that the test was invalid as a result of Patricia's behavior, I do think it may have influenced her abstract reasoning score somewhat. I would like to see her retested on this one task." The examiner is expressing some doubt about the validity of the test results. If you include an invalid subtest score in calculating the Full Scale IQ, then the Full Scale IQ is invalid as well. I would either eliminate the invalid subtest score when calculating the Full Scale IQ and Verbal Scale IQ (in this case) or point out that these scores also are not valid.

2. "The verbal scores may be an underestimation of his verbal ability because English is his second language. . . . The test results appear to be reliable and valid." These two sentences are contradictory. If part of the test appears to underestimate an examinee's ability, the test results cannot be valid.

3. "She enjoyed the performance subtests; hence, the results should be reliable." I do not think that "enjoyment" is a sufficient reason to conclude that the entire test results are reliable. Additional observations about her performance would be helpful.

4. "Jill was randomly referred for testing by her teacher." It is possible, but highly unlikely, that the teacher randomly referred the child for testing. The statement would be correct if all of the pupils' names were put in a hat and the teacher drew one name randomly or if the teacher used a table of random numbers to select a child for testing.

5. "Her range of knowledge is poor. This was demonstrated in her inability to identify Columbus or name three oceans." Poor knowledge is reflected in an examinee's low scores, not in missing one or two items on any particular subtest. A better example of her poor range of knowledge would be helpful.

---

**Guideline 7. Use words that have a low probability of being misinterpreted, that are nontechnical, and that convey as clearly as possible the examinee's performance.**

---

## Discussion of Guideline 7

This guideline and the one that follows address writing style. Guideline 7 focuses on the use of individual words (or word combinations), and Guideline 8 focuses more on the mechanics of writing. Your writing should be as accurate as possible. You want the reader to comprehend the report with a minimal amount of effort. However, you also want to make sure that your statements are clear and that readers will not misinterpret them. Whenever you detect some potential problem in your writing, revise your work so that the problem is solved.

## Examples of Statements That Do Not Meet Guideline 7

1. "His performance is a submaximal representation of his intellectual ability." The word *submaximal* is a poor choice. "His scores may underestimate his ability" would be better.

2. "Further support for the inference that Karl is detail oriented may be seen in his mazes." Instead of "in his mazes," it is preferable to say "in his performance on the Mazes subtest." This sentence should be followed by one that explains the "detail orientation."

3. "Helen was unable to let go of a task and referred back to it during the next task, either to correct her previous answer or to contaminate her current answer with the

previous one." This is an interesting and important observation, but the term *contaminate* may be somewhat difficult for the reader to understand; *spoil* or *confuse* might be a good substitute. A statement describing the possible implications of this performance would also be helpful, especially if the behavior occurred frequently during the examination.

4. "There is no reason to question the cultural validity of the WISC-III." *Cultural validity* is not a commonly accepted term. In addition, some psychologists do question the validity of intelligence tests for use with ethnic minority children (see Chapter 19).

5. "He had a tendency to elicit heavy sighs and become visibly frustrated when he was having difficulty with an item." The writer likely means "emit heavy sighs" and not "elicit heavy sighs."

6. "No evidence of abnormality on her verbal or perceptual skills was found in this testing." The term *abnormality* is likely to be confusing to most readers and potentially misleading. If you do use it, indicate what you mean by *abnormality*.

7. "Jane's IQ is an average of diverse abilities which make direct interpretation difficult." This statement is likely to be confusing to most readers. Although the statement is accurate, the profile of scores for a particular examinee can be interpreted. Despite the fact that the Full Scale IQ represents several different subscores, it is still used as a basis for classifying examinees in such areas as mental retardation, giftedness, and learning disability.

8. "The experimenter observed a significant difference between Jane's Perceptual Organizational factor score and Processing Speed factor score. A significant difference was also found between her Verbal Comprehension and Processing Speed factor scores." The first problem with these statements is that the preferred term is *examiner*, not *experimenter*. A second problem is that it may not be very informative for the average reader to read about factor scores by name. Suggestion: "Her verbal skills and perceptual organizational skills are better developed than her attention and concentration skills involving scanning and rapid eye-hand coordination." You can then point out the percentile ranks associated with each of these factor scores or use a qualitative description representing the level of her scores—such as average, above average, or below average.

9. "She also exhibited weaknesses in the Information and Arithmetic standard scores." The emphasis should be on abilities, not on scores per se. The scores are neither weak nor strong; rather, they are high or low. Abilities are weak or strong, or average or normal. You usually do not need to discuss in the report the type of scores (standard scores, raw scores, or age scores) that you are using as the basis for your statements.

10. "Within the subtests of information, arithmetic, and comprehension versus vocabulary, similarities, and digit span, Joan demonstrated a significantly decreased ability in analyzing long verbal questions versus short verbal questions." This is an awkward sentence. The reader is likely to be confused about the use of the terms *within* and *versus*. You don't need to mention the subtest names, but if you do, capitalize them. Also, what meaning may be attached to the difference between the examinee's performance on long and short verbal questions?

DRABBLE reprinted by permission of UFS, Inc.

**Guideline 8. Write clearly, cut words where possible, follow all rules of grammar and punctuation, use a consistent style, make clear transitions between different ideas or topics, and give examples of the examinee's abilities and behavior. Do not include, however, information that seems to have little or no value.**

## Discussion of Guideline 8

Technical and professional writing should leave little room for misinterpretation. Check carefully that the entire report is clearly written. Transition statements are valuable in a report. The reader expects a smooth flow between topics. When you plan to change topics, prepare the reader for the change. Lastly, judicious examples of the examinee's behavior will help the reader understand the assessment findings better.

## Examples of Statements That Do Not Meet Guideline 8

1. "His general performance would be described as being within the Average range." The words "would be described" are unnecessary. Suggestion: "His general performance is within the Average range."

2. "Jim was administered the WISC-III and Bender-Gestalt to provide training experience for students in the graduate assessment course at Blank University." It is not clear from the sentence whether the training experience was for Jim, who also could be a student in the assessment class, or for the examiner.

3. "Phil constantly kept finding things in a drawer of the desk he was being tested at to play with throughout the testing period, ie. paperclips, rubberbands, pens, etc." This is an awkward sentence. There are also punctuation mistakes, such as a period missing after the "i" in *i.e.* and a comma missing after the *i.e.* Suggestion: "Throughout the testing period, Phil played with paperclips, rubberbands, and pens that he found in the desk drawer."

4. "Virginia's behavior during the nonverbal subtests seemed to be more confident and less anxious." The sentence needs a reference point—a person has to be more confident and less anxious than she was in some other situation. In addition, grammatically speaking, "behavior" cannot be more confident or less anxious; only Virginia can. Behavior is a manifestation of the person. Suggestion: "Virginia was more confident and less anxious during the

nonverbal portion than during the verbal portion of the test."

5. "He often seemed bored during nonverbal items and often rested his head on his hand, slumped back in his chair, or laid his face down on the table. He displayed more interest in nonverbal items than in verbal items." These two sentences seem to be contradictory. If he was bored with nonverbal items, how could he display more interest in them than in verbal items? The examiner may have meant to write "bored during verbal items" but wrote "nonverbal items" instead. Careful proofreading will help to eliminate such errors.

6. The following statement was written in a report about an 8-year-old with a Verbal IQ of 92, a Performance IQ of 112, and a Full Scale IQ of 101: "Within a single subtest, his behavior and even speech seemed to deteriorate as the problems got successively more difficult." This statement has several problems. First, does the writer mean every subtest on the test, just one subtest, or a few subtests? Second, in what way did the examinee's behavior deteriorate? The word *deteriorate* carries connotations of severe impairment and must be used with caution. Third, in order to obtain average IQs, the examinee must have been able to perform adequately on several of the subtests. Consequently, whatever "deterioration" occurred must have been shortlived because he was able to perform on succeeding subtests.

7. "Gina's behavior during this assessment demonstrated her social intelligence." Without more information, there is no way to know what the word *behavior* refers to. In what way would an examinee's behavior demonstrate social intelligence? The writer may be referring to the examinee's performance on the Comprehension subtest, but this is not clear from the sentence.

8. The following statement was based on Profile 8.8 in Table K-1 (page 1113): "Her lack of reflection may prove to be problematic." This sentence contains two problems. First, does the writer really mean *lack of* reflection? If the examinee *lacked* reflection, how could she perform in the Average range, especially considering that tasks such as Similarities may require reflection, as may other WISC-III subtests? Second, the term *problematic* is not very meaningful. The writer likely means that the examinee's impulsiveness may lead to difficulties when she is faced with problem-solving situations.

9. "The most striking observation was the contrast between his level of interest and motivation during a visual-motor nonverbal task and during a task involving verbal conceptual reasoning. Before answering questions involving arithmetical reasoning, he looked at the examiner in disbelief." The second sentence doesn't follow from the

first sentence. The second sentence should explain the contrast in level of interest and motivation between the two tasks. Instead, a new task is described, and the description does not seem to be related to the prior sentence.

10. "At times, she would lose concentration and perform with less care than usual." This description would benefit from examples of the child's performance. Suggestion: "During the arithmetic items and during the items involving block designs, her concentration seemed to diminish and she became careless."

## SUGGESTIONS FOR DESCRIBING WISC-III SCALES AND SUBTESTS TO PARENTS AND THE REFERRAL SOURCE AND IN THE REPORT

Following are summaries of some of the essential features of the three WISC-III scales and 13 subtests. The information can be used to discuss the results with parents and the referral source, as well as in the writing of your report. (Appendix J provides more information about each subtest.)

### Full Scale

The Full Scale IQ is usually considered to be the best measure of cognitive ability in the test. It is considered to measure such abilities as general intelligence, scholastic aptitude, and readiness to master a school curriculum. The child's Full Scale IQ may be affected by his or her motivation, interests, cultural opportunities, natural endowment, neurological integrity, attention span, ability to process verbal information (particularly on the verbal subtests), and ability to process visual information (particularly on the performance subtests).

### Verbal Scale

The Verbal Scale IQ is a measure of verbal comprehension. This includes the application of verbal skills and information to the solution of new problems, ability to process verbal information, and ability to think with words. The Verbal Scale thus provides information about language processing, reasoning, attention, and verbal learning and memory. The child's Verbal Scale IQ may be affected by his or her motivation, interests, cultural opportunities, natural endowment, neurological integrity, attention span, and ability to process verbal information.

### Performance Scale

The Performance Scale IQ is a measure of perceptual organization. This includes the ability to think in visual images and to manipulate these images with fluency and relative speed, to reason without the use of words (in some cases), and to interpret visual material quickly. The Performance Scale thus provides information about visual processing, planning and organizational ability, attention, and nonverbal learning and memory. The child's Performance Scale IQ may be affected by his or her motivation, interests, cultural opportunities, natural endowment, neurological integrity, attention span, and ability to process visual information.

### Information

The Information subtest provides a measure of how much general factual knowledge the child has absorbed from his or her environment. The child is asked to answer a series of questions that cover a range of material on several subjects. The subtest provides valuable information about the child's range of factual knowledge and long-term memory. Performance may be influenced by cultural opportunities, outside

PEANUTS reprinted by permission of UFS, Inc.

interests, richness of early environment, reading, and school learning.

## Similarities

The Similarities subtest provides a measure of the child's ability to select and verbalize appropriate relationships between two objects or concepts. The child is asked to say in what way two things are alike. A response indicating an abstract classification receives more credit than a response indicating a concrete classification. The subtest provides valuable information about the child's verbal concept formation and long-term memory. Performance may be influenced by cultural opportunities, interests, reading habits, and school learning.

## Arithmetic

The Arithmetic subtest provides a measure of the child's facility in mental arithmetic. The child is asked to solve several different types of arithmetic problems involving addition, subtraction, multiplication, division, and problem solving. The subtest provides valuable information about the child's numerical reasoning ability, concentration, attention, short-term memory, and long-term memory. Performance may be influenced by the child's attitude toward school and by level of anxiety.

## Vocabulary

The Vocabulary subtest provides a measure of the child's word knowledge. The child is asked to define individual words of increasing difficulty. The subtest provides valuable information about the child's verbal skills, language development, and long-term memory. Performance may be influenced by cultural opportunities, education, reading habits, and familiarity with English.

## Comprehension

The Comprehension subtest provides a measure of the child's social judgment and common sense. The child is asked to answer questions dealing with various problem situations that, in part, involve interpersonal relations and social mores. The subtest provides valuable information about the child's knowledge of conventional standards of behavior. Performance may be influenced by cultural opportunities, ability to evaluate and draw from past experiences, and moral sense.

## Digit Span

The Digit Span subtest provides a measure of the child's short-term memory. The child is asked to repeat a series of digits given orally by the examiner. The child must repeat the series as given by the examiner on one part and say the series in the reverse order on the other part. The subtest provides valuable information about the child's rote memory, attention, and concentration. Performance may be influenced by level of anxiety.

## Picture Completion

The Picture Completion subtest provides a measure of the child's ability to differentiate essential from nonessential details. The child is shown pictures of objects from everyday life. The child is asked to indicate what important single part is missing from each picture. The subtest provides valuable information about the child's ability to concentrate on visually perceived material and alertness to details. Performance may be influenced by cultural experiences and alertness to the environment.

## Coding

The Coding subtest provides a measure of the child's ability to learn a code rapidly. The child is asked to look at a key that shows several symbols paired with other symbols. Then the child is shown one part of the pair and is asked to fill in the matching symbol in the blank space. The subtest provides valuable information about the child's speed and accuracy of eye-hand coordination, short-term memory, and attentional skills. Performance may be influenced by rate of motor activity and by motivation.

## Picture Arrangement

The Picture Arrangement subtest provides a measure of the child's ability to comprehend and evaluate social situations. The child is given pictures in a mixed-up order and is asked to rearrange them in a logical sequence. The pictures are similar to those used in short comic strips. The subtest provides valuable information about the child's ability to attend to details, alertness, planning ability, and visual sequencing. Performance may be influenced by cultural opportunities.

## Block Design

The Block Design subtest provides a measure of the child's spatial visualization and nonverbal reasoning ability. The child is required to use blocks to assemble a design that is identical to one made by the examiner or one pictured on a card. The subtest provides valuable information about the child's ability to analyze and synthesize visuospatial material and about the child's visual-motor coordination. Performance may be influenced by rate of motor activity and by degree of color vision.

### Object Assembly

The Object Assembly subtest provides a measure of the child's ability to synthesize concrete parts into meaningful wholes and of the child's visual-motor coordination. The child is asked to assemble jigsaw pieces correctly to form common objects. The subtest provides valuable information about the child's ability to visualize a whole from its parts, organizational ability, sense of spatial relations, and visual-motor coordination. Performance is influenced by rate of motor activity, persistence, and experience with part-whole relationships.

### Symbol Search

The Symbol Search subtest provides a measure of the child's visual discrimination and visual-perceptual scanning ability. The child looks first at the target symbol(s) and then at another group of symbols that may or may not contain the target symbol(s). The child is asked to indicate whether or not a target symbol is in the group of symbols. The subtest provides valuable information about the child's perceptual discrimination, speed and accuracy, attention and concentration, and short-term memory. Performance may be influenced by rate of motor activity and motivation and perhaps by cognitive flexibility (that is, the ability to shift between the target symbol and the other group of symbols as the target symbol and group of symbols change for each item).

### Mazes

The Mazes subtest provides a measure of the child's planning ability and the perceptual organizational ability involved in following a visual pattern. The child is shown a series of mazes of increasing difficulty and is requested to draw a continuous line that shows the way out of a maze without running into a blocked passage. The subtest provides valuable information about planning ability, foresight, visual-motor control, and attention and concentration. Performance may be influenced by visual-motor organization ability and ability to delay actions.

## PSYCHOLOGICAL EVALUATION

The psychological evaluation in Exhibit 8-2 (pages 183–187), which illustrates the application of the WISC-R

to a 7-year-, 4-month-old child, should help you understand the WISC-III as well. The report cites both qualitative and quantitative information obtained during the evaluation. Profile analysis is used to develop some assessment information, and recommendations are based on the test results and background information.

Exhibit K-1 presents an illustrative report based on the WISC-III. It gives a good description of the child's behavior during the evaluation. It discusses the difference between the child's Verbal and Performance IQs and briefly describes each subtest. It also provides recommendations for further testing.

After you complete the first draft of your report, use the checklist shown in Exhibit K-2 to help you evaluate whether you have included all the pertinent details. The checklist also may be used by your course instructor.

## TEST YOUR SKILL

The WISC-R Test-Your-Skill Exercises on pages 187–189 also pertain to the WISC-III, and you are encouraged to do those exercises. Here is another exercise, designed to help you develop the skills needed to write a psychological evaluation based on the WISC-III. There are three parts to the exercise. First, read the WISC-III report in Exhibit K-3, disregarding the superscript numbers. Then read the report in Exhibit K-3 again, focusing on the superscript numbers and the words, phrases, or information associated with each superscript number. Your task is to find the problem, such as an error in punctuation, style, spelling, quantitative information, or interpretation. Record your comments on a sheet of paper, using the numbers 1 to 81. Second, check your comments with those in the Comment section following the report in Exhibit K-3. Third, after reviewing the comments, read and study the suggested report in Exhibit K-4.

## THINKING THROUGH THE ISSUES

How does profile analysis help you to evaluate a child's WISC-III performance? How do the various forms of profile analysis complement each other? What are the problems associated with profile analysis?

How can an understanding of base rates help you in interpreting the WISC-III?

How might an evaluation of qualitative factors associated with the child's performance help you better understand the child's quantitative performance?

How will you decide whether or not to include certain kinds of information in the report?

"You're saved! I found a split infinitive in the burglary statutes!"

From the Wall Street Journal—Permission, Cartoon Features Syndicate.

What kinds of data would you like to have before making generalizations about a child's performance?

What steps could you take to improve your report writing skills?

The Verbal and Performance Scale IQs are important features of the WISC-III. How might a child function with a Verbal IQ of 120 and a Performance IQ of 80? How might another child function with a Verbal IQ of 80 and a Performance IQ of 120?

How might the WISC-III be improved?

What problems do you foresee in explaining the results of a psychological evaluation to a parent and to the referral source?

Based on the WISC-III, what would you say to a parent who asked, "What is my child's potential?"

Sign on Faculty Office Door:
COMMITTEE TO STAMP OUT AND ELIMINATE
REDUNDANCY COMMITTEE

## SUMMARY

1. Profile analysis on the WISC-III is similar to that on the WISC-R.

2. The primary approaches to profile analysis include comparing Verbal and Performance Scale IQs, comparing Verbal and Performance subtest scaled scores with the mean scores on the respective scales, comparing pairs of individual subtest scaled scores, comparing factor scores, and comparing subtest scaled scores with the average factor score on each factor.

3. Other approaches to profile analysis, based on frequency of occurrence in the population, include an evaluation of subtest scaled-score ranges, deviations of subtest scores from the child's own average, and Verbal-Performance Scale differences.

4. In interpreting the child's performance, look at the child's level of performance, the child's quality of performance, the relationship between level and quality of performance, and the problem-solving strategies used by the child to reach a solution.

5. You may still obtain valuable leads about how the child processes information even when the child has difficulty completing a task.

6. Describe carefully the behaviors you observe. Make inferences about underlying traits or processes with extreme caution, if at all.

7. Provide clear descriptions of abilities thought to be measured by the subtests, and use factor loadings to guide your interpretations of the subtests.

8. Relate inferences based on subtest scores or IQs to the cognitive processes measured (or thought to be measured) by the subtests and scales.

9. Describe the profile in a clear and unambiguous manner. State that two or more abilities reflect different levels of skill only when the scores are significantly different. Indicate clearly whether you are comparing the child's performance to the normative group or whether you are using the scores to describe the child's own profile.

10. Make recommendations carefully, using all available sources of information.

11. Describe and use statistical concepts in an appropriate manner, check all calculations carefully, and report the reliability and validity of the test results as accurately as possible.

12. Use words that have a low probability of being misinterpreted, that are nontechnical, and that convey as clearly as possible the examinee's performance.

13. Write clearly, cut words where possible, follow all rules of grammar and punctuation, use a consistent style, make clear transitions between different ideas or topics, and give examples of the examinee's abilities and behavior. Do not include, however, information that seems to have little or no value.

14. Knowledge of the essential features of the Wechsler scales and subtests presented in this chapter (and in other chapters of the text) will help in your work with parents and the referral source, and when you write reports.

## KEY TERMS, CONCEPTS, AND NAMES

■ **Exhibit K-I** ━━━━━━━━━━━━━━━━━━━━━━━━━━━━━━━━━━━━━━━

**Psychological Evaluation of a Boy with a Reading Problem**

*Name of examinee:* Bill
*Date of birth:* April 21, 1984
*Chronological age:* 7-8
*Grade*: First

*Date of examination:* Jan. 15, 1992
*Date of report:* Jan. 20, 1992
*Name of examiner:* Phyllis Brown

**Test Administered**

*Wechsler Intelligence Scale for Children — III (WISC-III):*

| VERBAL SCALE | | PERFORMANCE SCALE | |
|---|---|---|---|
| Information | 10 | Picture Completion | 14 |
| Similarities | 11 | Coding | 14 |
| Arithmetic | 9 | Picture Arrangement | 10 |
| Vocabulary | 7 | Block Design | 10 |
| Comprehension | 9 | Object Assembly | 10 |
| Digit Span | 7 | Mazes | 15 |

Verbal Scale IQ = 95
Performance Scale IQ = 111
Full Scale IQ = 103 ± 7 at the 95% confidence level

**Reason for Referral**

Bill volunteered to take the WISC-III in order for the examiner to obtain experience in administering the test.

**Background Information**

Bill, a 7-year-, 8-month-old boy, is currently in the first grade. His mother told me that he is experiencing reading difficulties. He states that his favorite subjects in school are spelling and math and that he likes to "work hard." Outside of school he enjoys building things with Legos.

**Behavioral Observations**

Bill was pleasant, cooperative, and motivated throughout the testing session. He conversed comfortably with me at the beginning of the session and between subtests. He told me that he was having problems learning to read. During both verbal and nonverbal tasks, he occasionally became fidgety and restless, moving back and forth in the chair, sitting on his knees, and laying his head down on the table. This restless behavior occurred more frequently toward the end of subtests (as the items became more difficult) and as the session progressed. However, despite his restlessness, Bill generally remained attentive and on task throughout the session. Bill was cooperative, put away the puzzle pieces in their boxes, and turned the pages of a subtest booklet when I asked him to do so. When frustrated, Bill occasionally asked me for help and exclaimed, "That's hard!" or "Can't do this!"

Bill's articulation was often poor, and he was occasionally difficult to understand. He often answered in the form of a question, as if unsure of his responses. During the verbal subtests that assessed social comprehension and language development, Bill frequently gave long answers, or several answers to the same question, some correct and some incorrect.

During two nonverbal subtests, one requiring visual sequencing and another requiring visual-spatial analytic and synthetic abilities, Bill proceeded quickly and systematically when the items were simple. However, as they became more difficult, he proceeded more slowly, often hesitating, and changing his mind about where to place the cards or blocks. Bill appeared particularly to enjoy puzzles and tasks involving making designs with blocks, and he was disappointed when these tasks were over. In fact, when the puzzle completion task was over, he was eager to go back and try to complete a puzzle that he could not do earlier.

**Assessment Results and Clinical Impressions**

With a chronological age of 7-8, Bill achieved a Verbal Scale IQ of 95 (37th percentile), a Performance Scale IQ of 111 (79th percentile), and a Full Scale IQ of 103 ± 7 on the WISC-III. His overall performance is classified in the Average range and is ranked at the 55th percentile. The chances that the range of scores from 96 to 110 includes his true IQ are about 95 out of 100. The present measure of his intellectual functioning appears to be reliable and valid because of his cooperativeness, willingness to try, and background characteristics.

There is a 16-point difference between Bill's Verbal and Performance IQs, which indicates that his nonverbal skills are better developed than his verbal skills. This difference may reflect a predominantly nonverbal cognitive style or greater interest and motivation during nonverbal than verbal tasks. As previously mentioned, he liked nonverbal tasks involving puzzles and creating designs with blocks. He also mentioned that he enjoyed building with Legos, a nonverbal spatially oriented activity.

In the verbal domain, his skills range from below average to average. His range of factual knowledge, logical and abstract reasoning, numerical reasoning, and social comprehension are all average for his age. However, his word knowledge and immediate auditory memory are below average for his age. His word knowledge is less well developed than his overall verbal skills. Within the nonverbal domain, his ability to analyze and synthesize visual-spatial material, his visual sequencing ability, and his ability to synthesize concrete parts

*(Exhibit continues next page)*

**Exhibit K-I (cont.)**

into meaningful wholes are average for his age. His ability to differentiate essential from nonessential details, speed and accuracy of eye-hand coordination, and visual-motor control are excellent for his age.

Bill's weakness in word knowledge may be related to his reading difficulties. Because of his reading problems, he may be acquiring verbal skills and word knowledge at a slower rate than is typical for children of his age. On the other hand, his weak word knowledge may be contributing in some way to his reading difficulties, though this is unclear. Further testing would be needed to determine the relationship between his poor word knowledge and his reading difficulties. Furthermore, the poor articulation he exhibited throughout the testing session could be related to his poor word knowledge.

His below-average word knowledge and his excellent psychomotor speed and visual-motor control indicate that Bill performs better on tasks having visual-motor components rather than language components. He performs especially well on tasks requiring visual-motor speed and precision. His excellent ability to differentiate essential from nonessential details, coupled with his poor language development, indicates that his ability to recognize and perceive details of objects visually is better developed than his ability to describe objects verbally.

His overall average verbal skills indicate that he has the ability to perform adequately in school subjects requiring verbal skills, but the reason for his reading difficulties remains unclear. Additional testing is needed to assess the nature of his reading problems. Furthermore, Bill's nonverbal skills are well developed for his age, and thus he has the ability to perform well in subjects with nonverbal components.

**Recommendations**

It is recommended that further testing be conducted to assess the nature of his reading difficulties. Bill may also benefit from exercises in articulation and verbalization of words and from exercises aimed at enhancing his word knowledge. It would be good to capitalize on his affinity for visual-spatial activities by providing him with picture books, objects, puzzles, and other construction activities. During these activities he should be encouraged to describe and explain his actions.

**Summary**

Although Bill, who is 7 years, 8 months old, was occasionally fidgety and restless during the test, he remained attentive, on task, friendly, and cooperative throughout the session. His articulation was somewhat poor, and he occasionally was difficult to understand. He appeared to enjoy particularly tasks involving puzzles and creating designs with blocks. Bill achieved an IQ of $103 \pm 7$ on the WISC-III. This IQ is at the 55th percentile and in the Average range. The chances that the range of scores from 96 to 110 includes his true IQ are about 95 out of 100. The test results appear to give a reliable and valid estimate of his present level of intellectual functioning. His nonverbal skills are better developed than his verbal skills. Within the verbal domain, most skills are average, except for word knowledge and immediate auditory memory, which are below average for his age. Within the nonverbal domain, he shows strengths in differentiating essential from nonessential details, speed and accuracy of eye-hand coordination, and visual-motor control, and he shows average ability in analyzing and synthesizing visual-spatial material, visual sequencing, and synthesizing concrete parts into meaningful wholes. It is unclear how his reading difficulties are related to his poor language development and vice versa. Further testing is needed to assess his reading difficulties. Remedial activities should capitalize on his affinity for visual-spatial materials.

Phyllis Brown, B.A., Examiner

# STUDY QUESTIONS

1. Discuss profile analysis on the WISC-III.

2. What are some important guidelines for interpreting and communicating WISC-III findings in the psychological report?

3. How would you go about describing each of the following parts of the WISC-III to a parent: Full Scale, Verbal Scale, Performance Scale, Information, Similarities, Arithmetic, Vocabulary, Comprehension, Digit Span, Picture Completion, Coding, Picture Arrangement, Block Design, Object Assembly, Symbol Search, and Mazes?

# REFERENCE

Holmes, J. M. (1988). Testing. In R. G. Rudel, *Assessment of developmental learning disorders* (pp. 166–201). New York: Basic Books.

■ **Exhibit K-2** ━━━━━━━━━━━━━━━━━━━━━━━━━━━━━━━━━━━━━━━━━━━━━━━━━━━━━━━━━

**Checklist for Accuracy and Completeness of an Intelligence Test Report**

*Student's name* _____   *Report number:* _____

*Examinee's name:* _____   *Date of report:* _____

*Directions:* Use this checklist to evaluate the accuracy and completeness of an intelligence test report. Place a checkmark in the box after you check the item in the report. Write "NA" next to items that are not applicable.

☐ 1. *Report Title*

   2. *Identifying Data*

☐   a. Examinee's name

☐   b. Date of birth

☐   c. Age

☐   d. Grade

☐   e. Date of examination

☐   f. Date of report

☐   g. Examiner's name

☐ 3. *Name of Test Administered*

☐ 4. *Reason for Referral*

☐ 5. *Background Information*

   6. *Behavioral Observations*

☐   a. Attitude toward examiner

☐   b. Attitude toward test situation

☐   c. Attitude toward self

☐   d. Work habits

☐   e. Reaction to successes

☐   f. Reaction to failures

☐   g. Speech

☐   h. Vocabulary

☐   i. Visual-motor abilities

☐   j. Motor abilities

   7. *Test Results and Impressions*

☐   a. Verbal IQ (based on 5 standard subtests when 6 subtests given)

☐   b. Performance IQ (based on 5 standard subtests when 6 or 7 subtests given)

☐   c. Full Scale IQ

☐   d. Percentile rank for Verbal IQ

☐   e. Percentile rank for Performance IQ

☐   f. Percentile rank for Full Scale IQ

☐   g. Range designation of Full Scale IQ

☐   h. Confidence interval for Full Scale IQ

☐   i. Statement describing confidence interval

☐   j. Statement about reliability of test results

☐   k. Statement about validity of test results

☐   l. Statements about a skill described by a percentile rank or qualitative statement (such as strength, weakness, average, above average, or below average)

☐   m. Statements comparing one skill with another skill based on significant differences between scores on which skills were based

☐   n. Interpretations based on substantial data

☐   o. Clear recommendations

   8. *Summary and End Matter*

☐   a. Summary short (about one paragraph)

☐   b. At least one statement included from each section of the report in the Summary

☐   c. Examiner's name typewritten at end of report

☐   d. Examiner's signature included at end of report

   9. *Technical Qualities*

☐   a. Report free of spelling errors

☐   b. Report free of grammatical errors

## Exhibit K-3

## Psychological Evaluation Illustrating Several Problems That May Occur in Writing a WISC-III Report

*Name of examinee:* Jane Doe
*Date of birth:* November 12, 1975
*Chronological age:* 16-8
*Grade:* High school junior

*Date of examination:* August, 1992[1]
*Date of report:* August, 1992[1]
*Name of examiner:* Alan K. Smith

### Test Administered

*Wechler Intelligence Scale for Children — III (WISC-III)*[2]

| VERBAL SCALE | | PERFORMANCE SCALE | |
|---|---|---|---|
| Information | 7 | Picture Completion | 9 |
| Similarities | 13 | Coding | 10 |
| Arithmetic | 7 | Picture Arrangement | 10 |
| Vocabulary | 11 | Block Design | 14 |
| Comprehension | 11 | Object Assembly | 13 |
| Digit Span | 10 | | |

Verbal Scale IQ = 99
Performance Scale IQ = 108
Full Scale IQ = 104 $\pm$ 6 (range of 97 to 110 at the 95% confidence level[3])

### Reason for Referral

Jane agreed to act as a subject for a course in psychological assessment at CSU.[4]

### Background Information

Jane is a sixteen[5]-year-, 9-month[6]-old white female in her junior year at Blank High School. She is enrolled in a pre-college curriculum and plans to go to college. She would like to become an Elementary School Teacher.[7] One practice of Janes that was mentioned during the interview was her involvement in a flag corp group.[8] The examiner had previously explained to Jane that she could not be shown her test results.[9] No further background information was obtained.

### Behavioral Observations

Jane was[10] a sixteen[5]-year-, 9-month[6]-old high school student[11] whose language and behavior appear appropriate to her age and the situation. The most prominent features about Jane were that[12] she was cheerful and cooperative while under observation and insecure during the testing situation.[13] She giggled frequently, especially before answering questions and when she was frustrated.[14] Her answers were often preceded by the word "Um", followed by disclaimers such as "I don't know", "I think", and "I'm no good".[15] These responses suggested some anxiety and nervousness.[16] She seemed more comfortable with the demands of material[17] that required visual attention, physical manipulation, and knowledge organization.[18] Consequently, some variability was apparent during subtests.[19]

Her answers were succinct on the initial portions of some subtests and wordy on the latter portion.[20] Her answers were extensive throughout other subtests.[21] She was not consistently methodical in her approach to problem solving[22] and occasionally acted in a haphazard fashion.[23] Her hands are[10] involved in a washing-like motion.[24] Related to the examiner in an approval-seeking manner.[25] She mimicked the examiner exactly during Digits Forward,[26] including timed delay.[27]On a vocabulary test,[28] she unsurely gave[29] multiple responses when a single answer would have sufficed.

### Assessment Results and Clinical Impressions

On the WISC-III Jane achieved a Verbal IQ of 99 (47th percentile, which places her in the average range),[30] a Performance IQ of 108 (70th percentile, which places her in the above average range),[30] and a combined full scale[31] IQ of 104 + 6[32] (61st percentile, which places her in the average range[33] of intellectual functioning). The Verbal IQ is near the mean, whereas the Performance IQ is 2/3 standard deviation above the mean.[34] The chances that the range of scores from 98 to 100[35] includes her true IQ are about 95 out of 100. Jane's voluntary participation suggests that the results represent a reliable[36] and valid estimate of her current level of intellectual functioning.

Janes[37] overall functioning is in the average range,[33] although with notable disparity between her verbal[38] and performance[38] IQs.[39] Her nonverbal skills are uniformly well developed,[40] but her verbal skills show considerably more variability.[41] Her verbal skills range from a low average to a superior classification,[42] whereas her nonverbal skills range from an average to superior classification.[42] Her Verbal Scale scores demonstrate accumulated experience[43] and indicate average performance in verbal skills and language development.[44]

On the six verbal subtests, Jane performed at or above the mean of the standardization sample one-half of the time (Similarities, Comprehension[45] and Digit Span).[46] Her performance on Information and Arithmetic subtests indicated the most notable skill deficits, with performance for each found to be one standard deviation below the mean of the norming sample.[47] Her scaled scores ($M = 10$, $SD = 3$)[48] on Arithmetic and Information were significantly lower than her own Verbal Scale mean score ($p < .05$ and $p < .01$, respectively).[49] Information is the second best measure of *g* among

*(Exhibit continues next page)*

**Exhibit K-3 (cont.)**

the Verbal Scale subtests.[50] Her performance on Information was anemic[51] and erratic[52] and at the Low Average range;[53] she sometimes answered more difficult items correctly and missed easier ones. On Arithmetic, she responded quickly to items involving simple calculations, but did not take time in responding to more difficult items.[54] Her verbal abilities are extremely diverse and do not fall within the Average range of performance; to characterize her verbal abilities as such would be in error.[55]

Within the non-verbal[56] performance[57] area, her perceptual organizational ability, attention to detail, and visual-motor coordination ability and speed are all well developed.[58] She assembled puzzles quickly in an object assembly task, scoring in the 75th percentile.[59] Her analytic and synthetic abilities, nonverbal reasoning ability, and sequencing are superior[60] as assessed by her performance on the Block Design subtest.[61] Block Design is the best measure of general intelligence (*g*) among the Performance Scale subtests.[62]

Her low fund of general information suggests that Jane has not been exposed to the kinds of information that average adolescents acquire through normal home and school experiences.[63] Her low arithmetical reasoning scores suggest that Jane was having difficulty sustaining attention, since this subtest is about halfway to the end of the test.[64] Her good social comprehension score suggests that her social skills are better developed than her other intellectual skills.[65] Overall, her intellectual level of functioning suggests that she will do well in her last two years of high school.[66] She appears to be a happy and goal oriented[67] girl,[68] and increased focus can be expected to add definition to her goals with time and increased high school experience.[69]

**Summary**

Jane, a healthy[70] 16-year-, 8-month-old high school student, volunteered to be examined for a demonstration of the WISC-III at a training clinic[71] at CSU.[72] Her test results seem to be reliable and valid.[73] She obtained a WISC-III Full Scale IQ of 104 ± 6, which is in the 51st percentile[74] and in the Average range. She was better overall in performance tasks (70th percentile) than in verbal tasks (47th percentile).[75] She has an uneven pattern of scores, as noted above.[76] She has strengths in three tasks and weaknesses in two others.[77] She should do well in her last two years of high school, but may not have been exposed to the kinds of information that other adolescents have been exposed to.[78] She appears to know where many of her improficiencies[79] lie and may often simply be fulfilling a "self-fulfilling prophecy."[80]

A.K.S.[81]

COMMENTS ON THE
PSYCHOLOGICAL EVALUATION

Note: The numbers below refer to the superscripts in the Psychological Evaluation.

1. The day should be included.
2. *Wechler* is a misspelling; it should be *Wechsler*.
3. The confidence interval is incorrect. It should be 98 to 110.
4. The name of the school should be spelled out completely. It is preferable not to use abbreviations, except for the name of the test. Under "Test Administered," the first use of the abbreviation follows the full name of the test.
5. Age is usually written in Arabic numerals.
6. The correct age is 16-8, not 16-9.
7. The first letter of each word in the phrase "elementary school teacher" should not be capitalized.
8. This sentence is awkward and contains a punctuation and a spelling error. *Janes* should have an apostrophe (Jane's), and *corp* should have an "s" (corps). The words "during the interview" are not appropriate. A formal interview was not conducted, and a test session should not be characterized as an interview. The sentence could be rewritten as follows: "Jane mentioned that she is a member of the flag corps at Blank High School."
9. Is this sentence needed in the report? It does provide some information about the testing session but doesn't contribute much to our understanding of the examinee. It would be better to delete it.
10. Use the *present tense* to describe the examinee's more enduring characteristics ("Jane is a 16-year-, 8-month-old") and the *past tense* to describe the examinee's behavior, dress, mood, and so forth during the examination ("She *was* cheerful"; "Her hands *were*...").
11. This information is in the Background Information section and therefore need not be repeated.
12. The first eight words ("The...that") are superfluous and should be deleted.
13. The phrases "while under observation" and "during the testing situation" imply two different periods of the examination. Isn't the examinee under observation throughout the examination? It is not clear when the examinee was cheerful and when she was insecure. Additionally, the words *the* and *situation* can be deleted in the phrase "insecure during the testing situation."
14. It would help if the writer indicated when the examinee giggled—on easy or difficult items, on verbal or nonverbal items.
15. The quotation mark *follows* the comma or period.
16. The words "and nervousness" are redundant.
17. The words "the demands of" are not needed.

*(Exhibit continues next page)*

**Exhibit K-3 (cont.)**

18. A comparative clause that begins with *than* is needed. "She was more comfortable with X *than* with Y." Additionally, the term *knowledge organization* is vague.

19. This sentence is vague because we don't know to what *variability* refers. For example, does it refer to behavior, test scores, affect, or something else? The variability should be clearly described.

20. The specific subtests should be mentioned.

21. Again, this sentence is vague because we don't know on what subtests (or subtest portions) she gave extensive answers.

22. It would be more helpful if her approach to problem solving were described.

23. *Haphazard* is a strong term and has negative clinical connotations. The examinee's specific behaviors should be mentioned, and an appropriate term used to describe these behaviors.

24. This sentence does not provide enough information to the reader, and it almost implies a Lady Macbeth syndrome. When were her hands making a washing-like motion—throughout the test or only on specific items? On what type of items were the hand movements observed?

25. This is not a complete sentence. Complete sentences should always be used in the body of the report. The statement also would benefit from a description of the behaviors associated with her "approval-seeking manner."

26. Most lay readers will not know what *Digits Forward* refers to; instead describe the task.

27. *Timed delay* is vague.

28. The 13 subtests are usually referred to as *subtests*, not tests. The word *test* should be used to describe a complete test, such as the WISC-III or the Detroit Test of Learning Aptitude.

29. "Unsurely gave" is an awkward expression; it should be revised.

30. It is best to use a classification category only for the Full Scale IQ. A report with more than one classification may confuse readers. The classification is also wrong.

31. The first letter of *full* and of *scale* should be capitalized (Full Scale).

32. The minus sign ($-$) is missing in the confidence interval; it should be $\pm 6$.

33. The first letter in *average* should be capitalized when the term designates a range.

34. This is technical information and is not needed in the report.

35. The confidence interval is incorrect. It should be 98 to 110.

36. Is voluntary participation a sufficient reason for concluding that the examinee's performance was reliable? Examinees can volunteer and still not try. The focus should be on the examinee's behavior and not on the reason for the examination, although that may play a role in certain cases.

37. *Janes* should be written with an apostrophe after the *e* (Jane's).

38. The initial letter in *verbal* and in *performance* should be capitalized when these terms refer to IQs or scales.

39. If the difference between the Verbal and Performance Scale IQs is not significant, report that both areas are developed at a similar level. The wording in this sentence is misleading.

40. Her scaled scores of 9 and 10 indicate average ability; thus the term *well developed* may be misleading. Additionally, the term *uniformly* is misleading because the scaled scores ranged from 9 to 15 on the Performance Scale.

41. The verbal scores range from 7 to 13 (6 points), and the performance scores range from 9 to 14 (5 points). Therefore, it is incorrect to say that the verbal scores show considerably more variability.

42. Subtest scaled scores should not be referred to as representing ranges or classifications such as *high average*. Terms such as *strength* (*above average*, *well developed*) or *weakness* (*below average*, *poorly developed*) are preferred (see Guideline 2 in this chapter). Additionally, using percentile ranks will help you to discuss subtest scores and the Verbal, Performance, and Full Scale IQs.

43. Both the Verbal Scale and the Performance Scale reflect accumulated experience; consequently, this phrase should be either eliminated or revised.

44. It is not clear how language development differs from verbal skills. Isn't language development a part of verbal development?

45. A comma would be helpful after the word *Comprehension*.

46. This statement is not accurate. Her Vocabulary score is also at or above the mean of the standardization group. Additionally, the statement is too technical and should be rewritten.

47. The sentence should be rewritten. This statement, although literally correct, is awkwardly written and too technical. Many readers may not know what the phrase "one standard deviation below the mean of the norming sample" refers to; it should be deleted.

48. It is not necessary to give the mean and standard deviation of the scaled scores.

49. The probability levels should not be included in a report.

50. This information is too technical and should be deleted.

51. *Anemic* is not the correct word in this context.

52. Use *variable* instead of *erratic*.

53. Individual subtest scores should not be classified into formal ranges or classifications (see number 42).

54. Instead of saying "but did not take time in responding to more difficult items," the examiner should describe how Jane responded to the more difficult items.

55. The logic of this sentence is unclear. The examinee's Verbal IQ is 99, which is clearly an average score. Consequently, it would be more appropriate to characterize her overall verbal skills as being average.

*(Exhibit continues next page)*

**Exhibit K-3 (cont.)**

56. A hyphen is not needed in *non-verbal* (nonverbal).

57. The word *performance* is redundant.

58. The phrases "attention to detail" and "visual-motor coordination ability and speed" likely pertain to the Picture Completion and Coding subtests, respectively. On these two subtests her scores were average: 9 and 10, respectively. Therefore, the sentence gives misleading information (that is, "are all well developed").

59. First, this sentence contains one error: the percentile rank should be 84th, not 75th, because the scaled score on Object Assembly is 13. Table C-41 on page 855 shows the percentile ranks for scaled scores. Second, the sentence can be rephrased to provide more meaningful information. The implications of her performance should be discussed rather than the specific tasks required by the subtest. For example, to describe her performance on Object Assembly, you could say "Her ability to arrange material under time pressure was excellent."

60. Block Design does not measure sequencing ability.

61. The remainder of the sentence ("as assessed by her performance on the Block Design subtest") is not needed.

62. This information is too technical and should be deleted.

63. There usually is no way of corroborating this hypothesis with the limited information obtained during an evaluation. Consequently, in this case this sentence should be deleted.

64. This is a puzzling inference, especially when you consider that some of her best scores were on Object Assembly and Block Design, which were administered during the second half of the test.

65. Comprehension, like all of the WISC-III subtests, is a measure of cognition. This subtest, therefore, likely measures social judgment and not social skills.

66. A Full Scale IQ of 104 probably indicates that the examinee has the ability to do at least average work in high school. However, because many other factors besides intelli-gence affect school grades, this statement should be rewritten (for example, "...she has the ability to complete high school").

67. Use a hyphen in *goal oriented* when it modifies a noun (goal-oriented student).

68. *Student* is preferable to *girl*.

69. The last half of this sentence is poorly written; it should be rewritten.

70. Because the term *healthy* was not mentioned in the body of the report, it should not be introduced in the summary. Additionally, unless you have information about the examinee's health, do not make statements about it.

71. The words *training clinic* were not mentioned previously and therefore should not be introduced for the first time in the summary. Additionally, the examinee was tested as part of a course requirement and not at a training clinic.

72. The summary should stand alone. Consequently, it is preferable not to use abbreviations, except for acronyms that are widely known and accepted (for example, *WISC-III*).

73. "Seem to be" is a vague phrase. Be more definite when discussing reliability and validity, if at all possible.

74. The correct percentile rank is 61st.

75. Because the Verbal and Performance IQs are not significantly different, this statement is misleading.

76. The summary should repeat the major findings and not refer readers to the body of the report.

77. This sentence is vague.

78. This is a speculative inference and should be deleted.

79. *Improficiencies* is not a word.

80. The concept of a "self-fulfilling prophecy" was not developed in the report proper and is likely to confuse the reader, especially as it comes at the end of the summary.

81. The examiner's full name should be typewritten in this space, followed by his or her degree (e.g., B.A., M.A., Ph.D.) and the word *Examiner*.

## Exhibit K-4

### Suggested Psychological Evaluation for Report in Exhibit K-3

*Name of examinee:* Jane Doe
*Date of birth:* November 12, 1975
*Chronological age:* 16-8
*Grade:* High school junior

*Date of examination:* August 2, 1992
*Date of report:* August 15, 1992
*Name of examiner:* Alan K. Smith

### Test Administered

*Wechsler Intelligence Scale for Children — III (WISC-III)*

### Reason for Referral

Jane agreed to be tested in order for the examiner to gain experience in administering the test.

### Background Information

Jane is a 16-year-, 8-month-old white female in her junior year at Blank High School. She is enrolled in a precollege curriculum and plans to attend college when she graduates. She lives at home with her parents and is a member of a flag corps at high school. No other information was obtained at the time of evaluation.

### Behavioral Observations

Jane is of average height for her age, slightly overweight, and right handed. She was comfortably dressed in jeans and an oversized tee shirt. Her blond hair was pulled back in a ponytail.

Jane was friendly and cooperative throughout the evaluation. However, she initially seemed anxious about being tested and frequently giggled, particularly when she was unsure of an answer. She was often tentative in her responses to verbal items, frequently saying "I think" or "I'm no good at that" when she had difficulty with an item. She often raised her voice at the end of her answers in a questioning way, as though seeking direction or reassurance from the examiner. Her behavior suggested that she has limited self-confidence in her verbal abilities. On nonverbal tasks, Jane worked quickly and calmly. Her attempts to solve problems were initially somewhat unsystematic. As the difficulty of a task increased, however, she became more methodical in her approach, organizing materials, such as blocks, one by one to complete the task. Jane stated that she was more confident about her performance on nonverbal tasks than on verbal tasks.

### Assessment Results and Clinical Impressions

Jane, at a chronological age of 16-8 years, achieved a Verbal Scale IQ of 99 (47th percentile), a Performance Scale IQ of 108 (70th percentile), and a Full Scale IQ of 104 ± 6 on the WISC-III. Her overall performance is classified in the Average range and is ranked in the 61st percentile. The chances that the range of scores from 98 to 110 includes her true IQ are about 95 out of 100. The present measure of her level of intellectual functioning appears to be reliable and valid because of her cooperativeness, willingness to try, and background characteristics.

Jane's overall verbal and nonverbal skills are at an average level of development. Within the verbal area, however, both weaknesses and strengths were exhibited in relation to her peer group. Her range of factual information and her numerical reasoning ability are weaknesses; both of them are at the 16th percentile. In contrast, her verbal concept formation is a strength (at the 84th percentile). Her average verbal abilities are in immediate auditory memory (50th percentile), word knowledge (63rd percentile), and social comprehension (63rd percentile).

Within the nonverbal area, she had two strengths and no weaknesses in relation to her peer group. Visual-motor spatial integration and coordination are strengths. She can analyze and synthesize effectively with spatial-visual material (91st percentile) and is well able to synthesize concrete parts into a meaningful whole (84th percentile). Her average nonverbal abilities are in differentiating essential from nonessential details (37th percentile), visual sequencing (50th percentile), and psychomotor speed (50th percentile).

Jane's overall average intellectual skills suggest that she possesses the ability to complete high school. However, she will likely have to work hard at some of her subjects. Her strengths lie in conceptual reasoning, both in verbal and in nonverbal areas. However, weaknesses in factual knowledge and in processing arithmetical concepts are likely to hamper her ability to master some course work.

Jane appears to be aware of her strengths in nonverbal skills but may be less aware of her strong verbal reasoning ability. Furthermore, her anxiety and low self-confidence on verbal tasks may interfere with her concentration, particularly on school-like tasks.

### Recommendations

Jane may benefit from feedback regarding both her strengths and her weaknesses, with particular emphasis on her strong reasoning skills. Information regarding her academic performance would be helpful in determining whether any intervention is needed.

*(Exhibit continues next page)*

### Exhibit K-4 (cont.)

**Summary**

Jane, a 16-year-, 8-month-old junior in high school, agreed to be tested in order for the examiner to gain testing experience. She obtained a Verbal IQ of 99, a Performance IQ of 108, and a Full Scale IQ of 104 $\pm$ 6 on the WISC-III. Her Full Scale IQ is in the Average range and at the 61st percentile. The chances that the range of scores from 98 to 110 includes her true IQ are about 95 out of 100. The present results appear to give a reliable and valid estimate of her present level of intellectual functioning. Overall, Jane's verbal and nonverbal skills are developed at an average level. She has, however, strengths in both verbal and nonverbal conceptual reasoning and in visualizing a whole from its parts. Her weaknesses are associated with her range of information and facility in mental arithmetic. Although she likely has the ability to complete high school, she may have difficulties in some course work.

Alan K. Smith, B.A., Examiner

# — APPENDIX L

# TABLES FOR THE WISC-III
# (AND OTHER WECHSLER SCALES)

See also Table C-12, "WISC-R Structure of Intellect Classifications" (page 821); Table C-13, "Interpretive Rationales, Implications of High and Low Scores, and Instructional Implications for WISC-R Subtests" (page 824); Table C-41, "Percentile Ranks and Suggested Qualitative Descriptions for the Wechsler Scales" (page 855); Table C-42, "Interpretive Rationales, Implications of High and Low Scores, and Instructional Implications for Wechsler Scales and Factor Scores" (page 856); and Table C-43, "Suggested Remediation Activities for Combinations of Wechsler Subtests."

**Table L-I**
**Confidence Intervals for WISC-III Scales Based on Obtained Score Only**

| Age level | Scale | Confidence level | | | | |
|---|---|---|---|---|---|---|
| | | 68% | 85% | 90% | 95% | 99% |
| **6** | Verbal Scale IQ | ± 4 | ± 6 | ± 7 | ± 8 | ± 10 |
| (6-0-0 through | Performance Scale IQ | ± 5 | ± 6 | ± 7 | ± 9 | ± 12 |
| 6-11-30) | Full Scale IQ | ± 3 | ± 5 | ± 6 | ± 7 | ± 9 |
| **7** | Verbal Scale IQ | ± 4 | ± 6 | ± 7 | ± 8 | ± 11 |
| (7-0-0 through | Performance Scale IQ | ± 5 | ± 7 | ± 8 | ± 9 | ± 12 |
| 7-11-30) | Full Scale IQ | ± 4 | ± 5 | ± 6 | ± 7 | ± 9 |
| **8** | Verbal Scale IQ | ± 3 | ± 4 | ± 5 | ± 6 | ± 8 |
| (8-0-0 through | Performance Scale IQ | ± 5 | ± 7 | ± 8 | ± 9 | ± 12 |
| 8-11-30) | Full Scale IQ | ± 3 | ± 4 | ± 5 | ± 6 | ± 8 |
| **9** | Verbal Scale IQ | ± 4 | ± 6 | ± 7 | ± 8 | ± 10 |
| (9-0-0 through | Performance Scale IQ | ± 5 | ± 6 | ± 7 | ± 9 | ± 12 |
| 9-11-30) | Full Scale IQ | ± 3 | ± 5 | ± 6 | ± 7 | ± 9 |
| **10** | Verbal Scale IQ | ± 3 | ± 5 | ± 6 | ± 7 | ± 9 |
| (10-0-0 through | Performance Scale IQ | ± 5 | ± 6 | ± 7 | ± 9 | ± 12 |
| 10-11-30) | Full Scale IQ | ± 3 | ± 4 | ± 5 | ± 6 | ± 8 |
| **11** | Verbal Scale IQ | ± 3 | ± 5 | ± 6 | ± 7 | ± 9 |
| (11-0-0 through | Performance Scale IQ | ± 5 | ± 7 | ± 8 | ± 9 | ± 12 |
| 11-11-30) | Full Scale IQ | ± 3 | ± 5 | ± 6 | ± 7 | ± 9 |
| **12** | Verbal Scale IQ | ± 3 | ± 5 | ± 6 | ± 7 | ± 9 |
| (12-0-0 through | Performance Scale IQ | ± 5 | ± 6 | ± 7 | ± 9 | ± 12 |
| 12-11-30) | Full Scale IQ | ± 3 | ± 4 | ± 5 | ± 6 | ± 8 |
| **13** | Verbal Scale IQ | ± 4 | ± 5 | ± 6 | ± 7 | ± 9 |
| (13-0-0 through | Performance Scale IQ | ± 5 | ± 7 | ± 8 | ± 9 | ± 12 |
| 13-11-30) | Full Scale IQ | ± 3 | ± 5 | ± 6 | ± 7 | ± 9 |
| **14** | Verbal Scale IQ | ± 3 | ± 5 | ± 6 | ± 7 | ± 9 |
| (14-0-0 through | Performance Scale IQ | ± 5 | ± 7 | ± 8 | ± 10 | ± 13 |
| 14-11-30) | Full Scale IQ | ± 3 | ± 5 | ± 6 | ± 7 | ± 9 |
| **15** | Verbal Scale IQ | ± 3 | ± 4 | ± 5 | ± 6 | ± 8 |
| (15-0-0 through | Performance Scale IQ | ± 4 | ± 5 | ± 6 | ± 7 | ± 9 |
| 15-11-30) | Full Scale IQ | ± 3 | ± 4 | ± 4 | ± 5 | ± 7 |
| **16** | Verbal Scale IQ | ± 3 | ± 5 | ± 6 | ± 7 | ± 9 |
| (16-0-0 through | Performance Scale IQ | ± 4 | ± 6 | ± 7 | ± 8 | ± 11 |
| 16-11-30) | Full Scale IQ | ± 3 | ± 4 | ± 5 | ± 6 | ± 8 |
| | Verbal Scale IQ | ± 4 | ± 5 | ± 6 | ± 7 | ± 9 |
| **Average** | Performance Scale IQ | ± 5 | ± 7 | ± 7 | ± 9 | ± 12 |
| | Full Scale IQ | ± 3 | ± 5 | ± 5 | ± 6 | ± 8 |

*Note.* See Table C-1 (page 813) for an explanation of the method used to obtain confidence intervals. Confidence intervals in Table L-1 were obtained by using the appropriate $SE_m$ located in Table 5.2 (page 168) in the WISC-III manual.

**Table L-2**
**Confidence Intervals for Wechsler Scales (and Other Tests) Based on Estimated True Score**

Use the following chart to locate the section of Table L-2 that shows confidence intervals based on estimated true scores for Wechsler scales.

### WISC-III

| Examinee's age | Verbal Scale | Performance Scale | Full Scale |
|---|:---:|:---:|:---:|
| 6  (6-0-0 to 6-11-30) | I | G | K |
| 7  (7-0-0 to 7-11-30) | H | F | J |
| 8  (8-0-0 to 8-11-30) | L | F | L |
| 9  (9-0-0 to 9-11-30) | I | G | K |
| 10 (10-0-0 to 10-11-30) | K | G | L |
| 11 (11-0-0 to 11-11-30) | K | F | K |
| 12 (12-0-0 to 12-11-30) | K | G | L |
| 13 (13-0-0 to 13-11-30) | J | F | K |
| 14 (14-0-0 to 14-11-30) | K | E | K |
| 15 (15-0-0 to 15-11-30) | L | J | M |
| 16 (16-0-0 to 16-11-30) | K | H | L |
| Average | K | G | L |

### WPPSI-R

| Examinee's age | Verbal Scale | Performance Scale | Full Scale |
|---|:---:|:---:|:---:|
| 3     (3-0-0 to 3-5-15) | I | L | M |
| 3½ (3-5-16 to 3-11-15) | I | L | M |
| 4   (3-11-16 to 4-5-15) | I | L | M |
| 4½ (4-5-16 to 4-11-15) | I | L | M |
| 5   (4-11-16 to 5-5-15) | H | K | L |
| 5½ (5-5-16 to 5-11-15) | F | J | K |
| 6   (5-11-16 to 6-5-15) | H | J | K |
| 6½ (6-5-16 to 6-11-15) | F | I | K |
| 7   (6-11-16 to 7-3-15) | A | B | F |
| Average | K | H | L |

### WAIS-R

| Examinee's age | Verbal Scale | Performance Scale | Full Scale |
|---|:---:|:---:|:---:|
| 16–17 | K | D | L |
| 18–19 | L | F | L |
| 20–24 | L | H | M |
| 25–34 | M | J | N |
| 35–44 | M | J | N |
| 45–54 | M | J | M |
| 55–64 | M | I | M |
| 65–69 | M | J | N |
| 70–74 | M | H | M |
| Average | M | I | M |

*(Table continues next page)*

**Table L-2 (cont.)**

## A. WPPSI-R – Verbal Scale – Age 7 ($r_{xx} = .85$)

| 68% | | | 85% | | | 90% | | | 95% | | | 99% | | |
|---|---|---|---|---|---|---|---|---|---|---|---|---|---|---|
| IQ | L | U | IQ | L | U | IQ | L | U | IQ | L | U | IQ | L | U |
| 40–42 | 4 | 14 | 40–42 | 2 | 16 | 40–42 | 1 | 17 | 40–41 | −1 | 19 | 40–41 | −4 | 22 |
| 43 | 4 | 13 | 43–44 | 1 | 16 | 43–44 | 0 | 17 | 42–45 | −1 | 18 | 42–45 | −4 | 21 |
| 44–49 | 3 | 13 | 45–49 | 1 | 15 | 45–49 | 0 | 16 | 46–47 | −2 | 18 | 46–48 | −5 | 21 |
| 50 | 3 | 12 | 50 | 0 | 15 | 50 | −1 | 16 | 48–52 | −2 | 17 | 49–51 | −5 | 20 |
| 51–56 | 2 | 12 | 51–55 | 0 | 14 | 51–55 | −1 | 15 | 53–54 | −3 | 17 | 52–54 | −6 | 20 |
| 57 | 2 | 11 | 56–57 | −1 | 14 | 56–57 | −2 | 15 | 55–58 | −3 | 16 | 55–58 | −6 | 19 |
| 58–62 | 1 | 11 | 58–62 | −1 | 13 | 58–62 | −2 | 14 | 59–61 | −4 | 16 | 59–61 | −7 | 19 |
| 63 | 1 | 10 | 63–64 | −2 | 13 | 63–64 | −3 | 14 | 62–65 | −4 | 15 | 62–65 | −7 | 18 |
| 64–69 | 0 | 10 | 65–69 | −2 | 12 | 65–69 | −3 | 13 | 66–67 | −5 | 15 | 66–68 | −8 | 18 |
| 70 | 0 | 9 | 70 | −3 | 12 | 70 | −4 | 13 | 68–72 | −5 | 14 | 69–71 | −8 | 17 |
| 71–76 | −1 | 9 | 71–75 | −3 | 11 | 71–75 | −4 | 12 | 73–74 | −6 | 14 | 72–74 | −9 | 17 |
| 77 | −1 | 8 | 76–77 | −4 | 11 | 76–77 | −5 | 12 | 75–78 | −6 | 13 | 75–78 | −9 | 16 |
| 78–82 | −2 | 8 | 78–82 | −4 | 10 | 78–82 | −5 | 11 | 79–81 | −7 | 13 | 79–81 | −10 | 16 |
| 83 | −2 | 7 | 83–84 | −5 | 10 | 83–84 | −6 | 11 | 82–85 | −7 | 12 | 82–85 | −10 | 15 |
| 84–89 | −3 | 7 | 85–89 | −5 | 9 | 85–89 | −6 | 10 | 86–87 | −8 | 12 | 86–88 | −11 | 15 |
| 90 | −3 | 6 | 90 | −6 | 9 | 90 | −7 | 10 | 88–92 | −8 | 11 | 89–91 | −11 | 14 |
| 91–96 | −4 | 6 | 91–95 | −6 | 8 | 91–95 | −7 | 9 | 93–94 | −9 | 11 | 92–94 | −12 | 14 |
| 97 | −4 | 5 | 96–97 | −7 | 8 | 96–97 | −8 | 9 | 95–98 | −9 | 10 | 95–98 | −12 | 13 |
| 98–102 | −5 | 5 | 98–102 | −7 | 7 | 98–102 | −8 | 8 | 99–101 | −10 | 10 | 99–101 | −13 | 13 |
| 103 | −5 | 4 | 103–104 | −8 | 7 | 103–104 | −9 | 8 | 102–105 | −10 | 9 | 102–105 | −13 | 12 |
| 104–109 | −6 | 4 | 105–109 | −8 | 6 | 105–109 | −9 | 7 | 106–107 | −11 | 9 | 106–108 | −14 | 12 |
| 110 | −6 | 3 | 110 | −9 | 6 | 110 | −10 | 7 | 108–112 | −11 | 8 | 109–111 | −14 | 11 |
| 111–116 | −7 | 3 | 111–115 | −9 | 5 | 111–115 | −10 | 6 | 113–114 | −12 | 8 | 112–114 | −15 | 11 |
| 117 | −7 | 2 | 116–117 | −10 | 5 | 116–117 | −11 | 6 | 115–118 | −12 | 7 | 115–118 | −15 | 10 |
| 118–122 | −8 | 2 | 118–122 | −10 | 4 | 118–122 | −11 | 5 | 119–121 | −13 | 7 | 119–121 | −16 | 10 |
| 123 | −8 | 1 | 123–124 | −11 | 4 | 123–124 | −12 | 5 | 122–125 | −13 | 6 | 122–125 | −16 | 9 |
| 124–129 | −9 | 1 | 125–129 | −11 | 3 | 125–129 | −12 | 4 | 126–127 | −14 | 6 | 126–128 | −17 | 9 |
| 130 | −9 | 0 | 130 | −12 | 3 | 130 | −13 | 4 | 128–132 | −14 | 5 | 129–131 | −17 | 8 |
| 131–136 | −10 | 0 | 131–135 | −12 | 2 | 131–135 | −13 | 3 | 133–134 | −15 | 5 | 132–134 | −18 | 8 |
| 137 | −10 | −1 | 136–137 | −13 | 2 | 136–137 | −14 | 3 | 135–138 | −15 | 4 | 135–138 | −18 | 7 |
| 138–142 | −11 | −1 | 138–142 | −13 | 1 | 138–142 | −14 | 2 | 139–141 | −16 | 4 | 139–141 | −19 | 7 |
| 143 | −11 | −2 | 143–144 | −14 | 1 | 143–144 | −15 | 2 | 142–145 | −16 | 3 | 142–145 | −19 | 6 |
| 144–149 | −12 | −2 | 145–149 | −14 | 0 | 145–149 | −15 | 1 | 146–147 | −17 | 3 | 146–148 | −20 | 6 |
| 150 | −12 | −3 | 150 | −15 | 0 | 150 | −16 | 1 | 148–152 | −17 | 2 | 149–151 | −20 | 5 |
| 151–156 | −13 | −3 | 151–155 | −15 | −1 | 151–155 | −16 | 0 | 153–154 | −18 | 2 | 152–154 | −21 | 5 |
| 157 | −13 | −4 | 156–157 | −16 | −1 | 156–157 | −17 | 0 | 155–158 | −18 | 1 | 155–158 | −21 | 4 |
| 158–160 | −14 | −4 | 158–160 | −16 | −2 | 158–160 | −17 | −1 | 159–160 | −19 | 1 | 159–160 | −22 | 4 |

*(Table continues next page)*

**Table L-2 (cont.)**

## B. WPPSI-R—Performance Scale—Age 7 ($r_{xx} = .86$)

| 68% | | | 85% | | | 90% | | | 95% | | | 99% | | |
|---|---|---|---|---|---|---|---|---|---|---|---|---|---|---|
| IQ | L | U | IQ | L | U | IQ | L | U | IQ | L | U | IQ | L | U |
| 40 | 4 | 13 | 40–46 | 1 | 15 | 40–46 | 0 | 16 | 40–42 | − 1 | 18 | 40–42 | − 4 | 21 |
| 41–45 | 3 | 13 | 47–53 | 0 | 14 | 47–53 | − 1 | 15 | 43 | − 1 | 17 | 43 | − 4 | 20 |
| 46–47 | 3 | 12 | 54–60 | − 1 | 13 | 54–60 | − 2 | 14 | 44–49 | − 2 | 17 | 44–49 | − 5 | 20 |
| 48–52 | 2 | 12 | 61 | − 1 | 12 | 61–67 | − 3 | 13 | 50 | − 2 | 16 | 50 | − 5 | 19 |
| 53–54 | 2 | 11 | 62–67 | − 2 | 12 | 68 | − 3 | 12 | 51–56 | − 3 | 16 | 51–56 | − 6 | 19 |
| 55–59 | 1 | 11 | 68 | − 2 | 11 | 69–74 | − 4 | 12 | 57 | − 3 | 15 | 57 | − 6 | 18 |
| 60–61 | 1 | 10 | 69–74 | − 3 | 11 | 75 | − 4 | 11 | 58–64 | − 4 | 15 | 58–63 | − 7 | 18 |
| 62–66 | 0 | 10 | 75 | − 3 | 10 | 76–81 | − 5 | 11 | 65–71 | − 5 | 14 | 64 | − 7 | 17 |
| 67–69 | 0 | 9 | 76–81 | − 4 | 10 | 82 | − 5 | 10 | 72–78 | − 6 | 13 | 65–71 | − 8 | 17 |
| 70–73 | − 1 | 9 | 82 | − 4 | 9 | 83–89 | − 6 | 10 | 79–85 | − 7 | 12 | 72–78 | − 9 | 16 |
| 74–76 | − 1 | 8 | 83–88 | − 5 | 9 | 90–96 | − 7 | 9 | 86–92 | − 8 | 11 | 79–85 | −10 | 15 |
| 77–80 | − 2 | 8 | 89 | − 5 | 8 | 97–103 | − 8 | 8 | 93 | − 8 | 10 | 86 | −10 | 14 |
| 81–83 | − 2 | 7 | 90–96 | − 6 | 8 | 104–110 | − 9 | 7 | 94–99 | − 9 | 10 | 87–92 | −11 | 14 |
| 84–88 | − 3 | 7 | 97–103 | − 7 | 7 | 111–117 | −10 | 6 | 100 | − 9 | 9 | 93 | −11 | 13 |
| 89–90 | − 3 | 6 | 104–110 | − 8 | 6 | 118 | −10 | 5 | 101–106 | −10 | 9 | 94–99 | −12 | 13 |
| 91–95 | − 4 | 6 | 111 | − 8 | 5 | 119–124 | −11 | 5 | 107 | −10 | 8 | 100 | −12 | 12 |
| 96–97 | − 4 | 5 | 112–117 | − 9 | 5 | 125 | −11 | 4 | 108–114 | −11 | 8 | 101–106 | −13 | 12 |
| 98–102 | − 5 | 5 | 118 | − 9 | 4 | 126–131 | −12 | 4 | 115–121 | −12 | 7 | 107 | −13 | 11 |
| 103–104 | − 5 | 4 | 119–124 | −10 | 4 | 132 | −12 | 3 | 122–128 | −13 | 6 | 108–113 | −14 | 11 |
| 105–109 | − 6 | 4 | 125 | −10 | 3 | 133–139 | −13 | 3 | 129–135 | −14 | 5 | 114 | −14 | 10 |
| 110–111 | − 6 | 3 | 126–131 | −11 | 3 | 140–146 | −14 | 2 | 136–142 | −15 | 4 | 115–121 | −15 | 10 |
| 112–116 | − 7 | 3 | 132 | −11 | 2 | 147–153 | −15 | 1 | 143 | −15 | 3 | 122–128 | −16 | 9 |
| 117–119 | − 7 | 2 | 133–138 | −12 | 2 | 154–160 | −16 | 0 | 144–149 | −16 | 3 | 129–135 | −17 | 8 |
| 120–123 | − 8 | 2 | 139 | −12 | 1 | | | | 150 | −16 | 2 | 136 | −17 | 7 |
| 124–126 | − 8 | 1 | 140–146 | −13 | 1 | | | | 151–156 | −17 | 2 | 137–142 | −18 | 7 |
| 127–130 | − 9 | 1 | 147–153 | −14 | 0 | | | | 157 | −17 | 1 | 143 | −18 | 6 |
| 131–133 | − 9 | 0 | 154–160 | −15 | −1 | | | | 158–160 | −18 | 1 | 144–149 | −19 | 6 |
| 134–138 | −10 | 0 | | | | | | | | | | 150 | −19 | 5 |
| 139–140 | −10 | −1 | | | | | | | | | | 151–156 | −20 | 5 |
| 141–145 | −11 | −1 | | | | | | | | | | 157 | −20 | 4 |
| 146–147 | −11 | −2 | | | | | | | | | | 158–160 | −21 | 4 |
| 148–152 | −12 | −2 | | | | | | | | | | | | |
| 153–154 | −12 | −3 | | | | | | | | | | | | |
| 155–159 | −13 | −3 | | | | | | | | | | | | |
| 160 | −13 | −4 | | | | | | | | | | | | |

*(Table continues next page)*

**Table L-2 (cont.)**

## C. No Wechsler Scale ($r_{xx} = .87$)

| 68% | | | 85% | | | 90% | | | 95% | | | 99% | | |
|---|---|---|---|---|---|---|---|---|---|---|---|---|---|---|
| IQ | L | U | IQ | L | U | IQ | L | U | IQ | L | U | IQ | L | U |
| 40 | 3 | 13 | 40 | 1 | 15 | 40 | 0 | 16 | 40 | −1 | 17 | 40–41 | −4 | 20 |
| 41–44 | 3 | 12 | 41–44 | 1 | 14 | 41–44 | 0 | 15 | 41–44 | −2 | 17 | 42–43 | −5 | 20 |
| 45–47 | 2 | 12 | 45–48 | 0 | 14 | 45–48 | −1 | 15 | 45–48 | −2 | 16 | 44–48 | −5 | 19 |
| 48–52 | 2 | 11 | 49–51 | 0 | 13 | 49–51 | −1 | 14 | 49–51 | −3 | 16 | 49–51 | −6 | 19 |
| 53–55 | 1 | 11 | 52–55 | −1 | 13 | 52–55 | −2 | 14 | 52–55 | −3 | 15 | 52–56 | −6 | 18 |
| 56–59 | 1 | 10 | 56–59 | −1 | 12 | 56–59 | −2 | 13 | 56–59 | −4 | 15 | 57–58 | −7 | 18 |
| 60–63 | 0 | 10 | 60–63 | −2 | 12 | 60–63 | −3 | 13 | 60–63 | −4 | 14 | 59–64 | −7 | 17 |
| 64–67 | 0 | 9 | 64–67 | −2 | 11 | 64–67 | −3 | 12 | 64–67 | −5 | 14 | 65–66 | −8 | 17 |
| 68–70 | −1 | 9 | 68–71 | −3 | 11 | 68–71 | −4 | 12 | 68–71 | −5 | 13 | 67–72 | −8 | 16 |
| 71–75 | −1 | 8 | 72–74 | −3 | 10 | 72–74 | −4 | 11 | 72–74 | −6 | 13 | 73–74 | −9 | 16 |
| 76–78 | −2 | 8 | 75–79 | −4 | 10 | 75–78 | −5 | 11 | 75–79 | −6 | 12 | 75–79 | −9 | 15 |
| 79–83 | −2 | 7 | 80–82 | −4 | 9 | 79–82 | −5 | 10 | 80–82 | −7 | 12 | 80–81 | −10 | 15 |
| 84–86 | −3 | 7 | 83–86 | −5 | 9 | 83–86 | −6 | 10 | 83–86 | −7 | 11 | 82–87 | −10 | 14 |
| 87–90 | −3 | 6 | 87–90 | −5 | 8 | 87–90 | −6 | 9 | 87–90 | −8 | 11 | 88–89 | −11 | 14 |
| 91–93 | −4 | 6 | 91–94 | −6 | 8 | 91–94 | −7 | 9 | 91–94 | −8 | 10 | 90–95 | −11 | 13 |
| 94–98 | −4 | 5 | 95–97 | −6 | 7 | 95–97 | −7 | 8 | 95–97 | −9 | 10 | 96–97 | −12 | 13 |
| 99–101 | −5 | 5 | 98–102 | −7 | 7 | 98–102 | −8 | 8 | 98–102 | −9 | 9 | 98–102 | −12 | 12 |
| 102–106 | −5 | 4 | 103–105 | −7 | 6 | 103–105 | −8 | 7 | 103–105 | −10 | 9 | 103–104 | −13 | 12 |
| 107–109 | −6 | 4 | 106–109 | −8 | 6 | 106–109 | −9 | 7 | 106–109 | −10 | 8 | 105–110 | −13 | 11 |
| 110–113 | −6 | 3 | 110–113 | −8 | 5 | 110–113 | −9 | 6 | 110–113 | −11 | 8 | 111–112 | −14 | 11 |
| 114–116 | −7 | 3 | 114–117 | −9 | 5 | 114–117 | −10 | 6 | 114–117 | −11 | 7 | 113–118 | −14 | 10 |
| 117–121 | −7 | 2 | 118–120 | −9 | 4 | 118–121 | −10 | 5 | 118–120 | −12 | 7 | 119–120 | −15 | 10 |
| 122–124 | −8 | 2 | 121–125 | −10 | 4 | 122–125 | −11 | 5 | 121–125 | −12 | 6 | 121–125 | −15 | 9 |
| 125–129 | −8 | 1 | 126–128 | −10 | 3 | 126–128 | −11 | 4 | 126–128 | −13 | 6 | 126–127 | −16 | 9 |
| 130–132 | −9 | 1 | 129–132 | −11 | 3 | 129–132 | −12 | 4 | 129–132 | −13 | 5 | 128–133 | −16 | 8 |
| 133–136 | −9 | 0 | 133–136 | −11 | 2 | 133–136 | −12 | 3 | 133–136 | −14 | 5 | 134–135 | −17 | 8 |
| 137–140 | −10 | 0 | 137–140 | −12 | 2 | 137–140 | −13 | 3 | 137–140 | −14 | 4 | 136–141 | −17 | 7 |
| 141–144 | −10 | −1 | 141–144 | −12 | 1 | 141–144 | −13 | 2 | 141–144 | −15 | 4 | 142–143 | −18 | 7 |
| 145–147 | −11 | −1 | 145–148 | −13 | 1 | 145–148 | −14 | 2 | 145–148 | −15 | 3 | 144–148 | −18 | 6 |
| 148–152 | −11 | −2 | 149–151 | −13 | 0 | 149–151 | −14 | 1 | 149–151 | −16 | 3 | 149–151 | −19 | 6 |
| 153–155 | −12 | −2 | 152–155 | −14 | 0 | 152–155 | −15 | 1 | 152–155 | −16 | 2 | 152–156 | −19 | 5 |
| 156–159 | −12 | −3 | 156–159 | −14 | −1 | 156–159 | −15 | 0 | 156–159 | −17 | 2 | 157–158 | −20 | 5 |
| 160 | −13 | −3 | 160 | −15 | −1 | 160 | −16 | 0 | 160 | −17 | 1 | 159–160 | −20 | 4 |

*(Table continues next page)*

**Table L-2 (cont.)**

### D. WAIS-R – Performance Scale – Ages 16–17 ($r_{xx} = .88$)

| 68% | | | 85% | | | 90% | | | 95% | | | 99% | | |
|---|---|---|---|---|---|---|---|---|---|---|---|---|---|---|
| *IQ* | *L* | *U* | *IQ* | *L* | *U* | *IQ* | *L* | *U* | *IQ* | *L* | *U* | *IQ* | *L* | *U* |
| 40–41 | 3 | 12 | 40 | 1 | 14 | 40–41 | 0 | 15 | 40–45 | − 2 | 16 | 40–44 | − 5 | 19 |
| 42 | 2 | 12 | 41–42 | 0 | 14 | 42 | − 1 | 15 | 46 | − 2 | 15 | 45–47 | − 5 | 18 |
| 43–49 | 2 | 11 | 43–49 | 0 | 13 | 43–49 | − 1 | 14 | 47–53 | − 3 | 15 | 48–52 | − 6 | 18 |
| 50 | 1 | 11 | 50 | − 1 | 13 | 50 | − 2 | 14 | 54 | − 3 | 14 | 53–55 | − 6 | 17 |
| 51–57 | 1 | 10 | 51–57 | − 1 | 12 | 51–57 | − 2 | 13 | 55–62 | − 4 | 14 | 56–60 | − 7 | 17 |
| 58 | 0 | 10 | 58–59 | − 2 | 12 | 58 | − 3 | 13 | 63–70 | − 5 | 13 | 61–64 | − 7 | 16 |
| 59–66 | 0 | 9 | 60–65 | − 2 | 11 | 59–66 | − 3 | 12 | 71 | − 5 | 12 | 65–69 | − 8 | 16 |
| 67 | − 1 | 9 | 66–67 | − 3 | 11 | 67 | − 4 | 12 | 72–78 | − 6 | 12 | 70–72 | − 8 | 15 |
| 68–74 | − 1 | 8 | 68–74 | − 3 | 10 | 68–74 | − 4 | 11 | 79 | − 6 | 11 | 73–77 | − 9 | 15 |
| 75 | − 2 | 8 | 75 | − 4 | 10 | 75 | − 5 | 11 | 80–87 | − 7 | 11 | 78–80 | − 9 | 14 |
| 76–82 | − 2 | 7 | 76–82 | − 4 | 9 | 76–82 | − 5 | 10 | 88–95 | − 8 | 10 | 81–85 | −10 | 14 |
| 83 | − 3 | 7 | 83–84 | − 5 | 9 | 83 | − 6 | 10 | 96 | − 8 | 9 | 86–89 | −10 | 13 |
| 84–91 | − 3 | 6 | 85–90 | − 5 | 8 | 84–91 | − 6 | 9 | 97–103 | − 9 | 9 | 90–94 | −11 | 13 |
| 92 | − 4 | 6 | 91–92 | − 6 | 8 | 92 | − 7 | 9 | 104 | − 9 | 8 | 95–97 | −11 | 12 |
| 93–99 | − 4 | 5 | 93–99 | − 6 | 7 | 93–99 | − 7 | 8 | 105–112 | −10 | 8 | 98–102 | −12 | 12 |
| 100 | − 5 | 5 | 100 | − 7 | 7 | 100 | − 8 | 8 | 113–120 | −11 | 7 | 103–105 | −12 | 11 |
| 101–107 | − 5 | 4 | 101–107 | − 7 | 6 | 101–107 | − 8 | 7 | 121 | −11 | 6 | 106–110 | −13 | 11 |
| 108 | − 6 | 4 | 108–109 | − 8 | 6 | 108 | − 9 | 7 | 122–128 | −12 | 6 | 111–114 | −13 | 10 |
| 109–116 | − 6 | 3 | 110–115 | − 8 | 5 | 109–116 | − 9 | 6 | 129 | −12 | 5 | 115–119 | −14 | 10 |
| 117 | − 7 | 3 | 116–117 | − 9 | 5 | 117 | −10 | 6 | 130–137 | −13 | 5 | 120–122 | −14 | 9 |
| 118–124 | − 7 | 2 | 118–124 | − 9 | 4 | 118–124 | −10 | 5 | 138–145 | −14 | 4 | 123–127 | −15 | 9 |
| 125 | − 8 | 2 | 125 | −10 | 4 | 125 | −11 | 5 | 146 | −14 | 3 | 128–130 | −15 | 8 |
| 126–132 | − 8 | 1 | 126–132 | −10 | 3 | 126–132 | −11 | 4 | 147–153 | −15 | 3 | 131–135 | −16 | 8 |
| 133 | − 9 | 1 | 133–134 | −11 | 3 | 133 | −12 | 4 | 154 | −15 | 2 | 136–139 | −16 | 7 |
| 134–141 | − 9 | 0 | 135–140 | −11 | 2 | 134–141 | −12 | 3 | 155–160 | −16 | 2 | 140–144 | −17 | 7 |
| 142 | −10 | 0 | 141–142 | −12 | 2 | 142 | −13 | 3 | | | | 145–147 | −17 | 6 |
| 143–149 | −10 | −1 | 143–149 | −12 | 1 | 143–149 | −13 | 2 | | | | 148–152 | −18 | 6 |
| 150 | −11 | −1 | 150 | −13 | 1 | 150 | −14 | 2 | | | | 153–155 | −18 | 5 |
| 151–157 | −11 | −2 | 151–157 | −13 | 0 | 151–157 | −14 | 1 | | | | 156–160 | −19 | 5 |
| 158 | −12 | −2 | 158–159 | −14 | 0 | 158 | −15 | 1 | | | | | | |
| 159–160 | −12 | −3 | 160 | −14 | −1 | 159–160 | −15 | 0 | | | | | | |

*(Table continues next page)*

**Table L-2 (cont.)**

### E. WISC-III — Performance Scale — Age 14 ($r_{xx} = .89$)

| 68% | | | 85% | | | 90% | | | 95% | | | 99% | | |
|---|---|---|---|---|---|---|---|---|---|---|---|---|---|---|
| IQ | L | U | IQ | L | U | IQ | L | U | IQ | L | U | IQ | L | U |
| 40–44 | 2 | 11 | 40–44 | 0 | 13 | 40–43 | − 1 | 14 | 40–43 | − 2 | 15 | 40–44 | − 5 | 18 |
| 45–46 | 2 | 10 | 45–46 | 0 | 12 | 44–47 | − 1 | 13 | 44–47 | − 3 | 15 | 45–46 | − 5 | 17 |
| 47–53 | 1 | 10 | 47–53 | − 1 | 12 | 48–52 | − 2 | 13 | 48–52 | − 3 | 14 | 47–53 | − 6 | 17 |
| 54–55 | 1 | 9 | 54–55 | − 1 | 11 | 53–56 | − 2 | 12 | 53–56 | − 4 | 14 | 54–55 | − 6 | 16 |
| 56–62 | 0 | 9 | 56–62 | − 2 | 11 | 57–61 | − 3 | 12 | 57–62 | − 4 | 13 | 56–62 | − 7 | 16 |
| 63–64 | 0 | 8 | 63–64 | − 2 | 10 | 62–65 | − 3 | 11 | 63–65 | − 5 | 13 | 63–64 | − 7 | 15 |
| 65–72 | − 1 | 8 | 65–71 | − 3 | 10 | 66–70 | − 4 | 11 | 66–71 | − 5 | 12 | 65–72 | − 8 | 15 |
| 73 | − 1 | 7 | 72–73 | − 3 | 9 | 71–74 | − 4 | 10 | 72–74 | − 6 | 12 | 73 | − 8 | 14 |
| 74–81 | − 2 | 7 | 74–80 | − 4 | 9 | 75–80 | − 5 | 10 | 75–80 | − 6 | 11 | 74–81 | − 9 | 14 |
| 82 | − 2 | 6 | 81–82 | − 4 | 8 | 81–83 | − 5 | 9 | 81–83 | − 7 | 11 | 82 | − 9 | 13 |
| 83–90 | − 3 | 6 | 83–89 | − 5 | 8 | 84–89 | − 6 | 9 | 84–89 | − 7 | 10 | 83–90 | −10 | 13 |
| 91 | − 3 | 5 | 90–92 | − 5 | 7 | 90–92 | − 6 | 8 | 90–92 | − 8 | 10 | 91 | −10 | 12 |
| 92–99 | − 4 | 5 | 93–98 | − 6 | 7 | 93–98 | − 7 | 8 | 93–98 | − 8 | 9 | 92–99 | −11 | 12 |
| 100 | − 4 | 4 | 99–101 | − 6 | 6 | 99–101 | − 7 | 7 | 99–101 | − 9 | 9 | 100 | −11 | 11 |
| 101–108 | − 5 | 4 | 102–107 | − 7 | 6 | 102–107 | − 8 | 7 | 102–107 | − 9 | 8 | 101–108 | −12 | 11 |
| 109 | − 5 | 3 | 108–110 | − 7 | 5 | 108–110 | − 8 | 6 | 108–110 | −10 | 8 | 109 | −12 | 10 |
| 110–117 | − 6 | 3 | 111–117 | − 8 | 5 | 111–116 | − 9 | 6 | 111–116 | −10 | 7 | 110–117 | −13 | 10 |
| 118 | − 6 | 2 | 118–119 | − 8 | 4 | 117–119 | − 9 | 5 | 117–119 | −11 | 7 | 118 | −13 | 9 |
| 119–126 | − 7 | 2 | 120–126 | − 9 | 4 | 120–125 | −10 | 5 | 120–125 | −11 | 6 | 119–126 | −14 | 9 |
| 127 | − 7 | 1 | 127–128 | − 9 | 3 | 126–129 | −10 | 4 | 126–128 | −12 | 6 | 127 | −14 | 8 |
| 128–135 | − 8 | 1 | 129–135 | −10 | 3 | 130–134 | −11 | 4 | 129–134 | −12 | 5 | 128–135 | −15 | 8 |
| 136–137 | − 8 | 0 | 136–137 | −10 | 2 | 135–138 | −11 | 3 | 135–137 | −13 | 5 | 136–137 | −15 | 7 |
| 138–144 | − 9 | 0 | 138–144 | −11 | 2 | 139–143 | −12 | 3 | 138–143 | −13 | 4 | 138–144 | −16 | 7 |
| 145–146 | − 9 | −1 | 145–146 | −11 | 1 | 144–147 | −12 | 2 | 144–147 | −14 | 4 | 145–146 | −16 | 6 |
| 147–153 | −10 | −1 | 147–153 | −12 | 1 | 148–152 | −13 | 2 | 148–152 | −14 | 3 | 147–153 | −17 | 6 |
| 154–155 | −10 | −2 | 154–155 | −12 | 0 | 153–156 | −13 | 1 | 153–156 | −15 | 3 | 154–155 | −17 | 5 |
| 156–160 | −11 | −2 | 156–160 | −13 | 0 | 157–160 | −14 | 1 | 157–160 | −15 | 2 | 156–160 | −18 | 5 |

*(Table continues next page)*

**Table L-2 (cont.)**

**F. WISC-III – Performance Scale – Ages 7, 8, 11, and 13; WPPSI-R – Verbal Scale – Ages 5½ and 6½; WPPSI-R – Full Scale – Age 7; WAIS-R – Performance Scale – Ages 18–19 ($r_{xx}$ = .90)**

| 68% | | | 85% | | | 90% | | | 95% | | | 99% | | |
|---|---|---|---|---|---|---|---|---|---|---|---|---|---|---|
| *IQ* | *L* | *U* | *IQ* | *L* | *U* | *IQ* | *L* | *U* | *IQ* | *L* | *U* | *IQ* | *L* | *U* |
| 40–42 | 2 | 10 | 40–43 | 0 | 12 | 40–44 | − 1 | 13 | 40–41 | − 2 | 14 | 40–44 | − 5 | 17 |
| 43–47 | 1 | 10 | 44–46 | − 1 | 12 | 45 | − 2 | 13 | 42–48 | − 3 | 14 | 45 | − 6 | 17 |
| 48–52 | 1 | 9 | 47–53 | − 1 | 11 | 46–54 | − 2 | 12 | 49–51 | − 3 | 13 | 46–54 | − 6 | 16 |
| 53–57 | 0 | 9 | 54–56 | − 2 | 11 | 55 | − 3 | 12 | 52–58 | − 4 | 13 | 55 | − 7 | 16 |
| 58–62 | 0 | 8 | 57–63 | − 2 | 10 | 56–64 | − 3 | 11 | 59–61 | − 4 | 12 | 56–64 | − 7 | 15 |
| 63–67 | − 1 | 8 | 64–66 | − 3 | 10 | 65 | − 4 | 11 | 62–68 | − 5 | 12 | 65 | − 8 | 15 |
| 68–72 | − 1 | 7 | 67–73 | − 3 | 9 | 66–74 | − 4 | 10 | 69–71 | − 5 | 11 | 66–74 | − 8 | 14 |
| 73–77 | − 2 | 7 | 74–76 | − 4 | 9 | 75 | − 5 | 10 | 72–78 | − 6 | 11 | 75 | − 9 | 14 |
| 78–82 | − 2 | 6 | 77–83 | − 4 | 8 | 76–84 | − 5 | 9 | 79–81 | − 6 | 10 | 76–84 | − 9 | 13 |
| 83–87 | − 3 | 6 | 84–86 | − 5 | 8 | 85 | − 6 | 9 | 82–88 | − 7 | 10 | 85 | −10 | 13 |
| 88–92 | − 3 | 5 | 87–93 | − 5 | 7 | 86–94 | − 6 | 8 | 89–91 | − 7 | 9 | 86–94 | −10 | 12 |
| 93–97 | − 4 | 5 | 94–96 | − 6 | 7 | 95 | − 7 | 8 | 92–98 | − 8 | 9 | 95 | −11 | 12 |
| 98–102 | − 4 | 4 | 97–103 | − 6 | 6 | 96–104 | − 7 | 7 | 99–101 | − 8 | 8 | 96–104 | −11 | 11 |
| 103–107 | − 5 | 4 | 104–106 | − 7 | 6 | 105 | − 8 | 7 | 102–108 | − 9 | 8 | 105 | −12 | 11 |
| 108–112 | − 5 | 3 | 107–113 | − 7 | 5 | 106–114 | − 8 | 6 | 109–111 | − 9 | 7 | 106–114 | −12 | 10 |
| 113–117 | − 6 | 3 | 114–116 | − 8 | 5 | 115 | − 9 | 6 | 112–118 | −10 | 7 | 115 | −13 | 10 |
| 118–122 | − 6 | 2 | 117–123 | − 8 | 4 | 116–124 | − 9 | 5 | 119–121 | −10 | 6 | 116–124 | −13 | 9 |
| 123–127 | − 7 | 2 | 124–126 | − 9 | 4 | 125 | −10 | 5 | 122–128 | −11 | 6 | 125 | −14 | 9 |
| 128–132 | − 7 | 1 | 127–133 | − 9 | 3 | 126–134 | −10 | 4 | 129–131 | −11 | 5 | 126–134 | −14 | 8 |
| 133–137 | − 8 | 1 | 134–136 | −10 | 3 | 135 | −11 | 4 | 132–138 | −12 | 5 | 135 | −15 | 8 |
| 138–142 | − 8 | 0 | 137–143 | −10 | 2 | 136–144 | −11 | 3 | 139–141 | −12 | 4 | 136–144 | −15 | 7 |
| 143–147 | − 9 | 0 | 144–146 | −11 | 2 | 145 | −12 | 3 | 142–148 | −13 | 4 | 145 | −16 | 7 |
| 148–152 | − 9 | −1 | 147–153 | −11 | 1 | 146–154 | −12 | 2 | 149–151 | −13 | 3 | 146–154 | −16 | 6 |
| 153–157 | −10 | −1 | 154–156 | −12 | 1 | 155 | −13 | 2 | 152–158 | −14 | 3 | 155 | −17 | 6 |
| 158–160 | −10 | −2 | 157–160 | −12 | 0 | 156–160 | −13 | 1 | 159–160 | −14 | 2 | 156–160 | −17 | 5 |

*(Table continues next page)*

**Table L-2 (cont.)**

### G. WISC-III – Performance Scale – Ages 6, 9, 10, 12, and Average ($r_{xx} = .91$)

| 68% | | | 85% | | | 90% | | | 95% | | | 99% | | |
|---|---|---|---|---|---|---|---|---|---|---|---|---|---|---|
| IQ | L | U | IQ | L | U | IQ | L | U | IQ | L | U | IQ | L | U |
| 40–48 | 1 | 9 | 40 | 0 | 11 | 40–41 | −1 | 12 | 40–49 | −3 | 13 | 40–43 | −5 | 16 |
| 49–51 | 0 | 9 | 41–48 | −1 | 11 | 42–47 | −2 | 12 | 50 | −4 | 13 | 44–45 | −6 | 16 |
| 52–60 | 0 | 8 | 49–51 | −1 | 10 | 48–52 | −2 | 11 | 51–60 | −4 | 12 | 46–54 | −6 | 15 |
| 61–62 | −1 | 8 | 52–59 | −2 | 10 | 53–58 | −3 | 11 | 61 | −5 | 12 | 55–56 | −7 | 15 |
| 63–71 | −1 | 7 | 60–62 | −2 | 9 | 59–63 | −3 | 10 | 62–71 | −5 | 11 | 57–65 | −7 | 14 |
| 72–73 | −2 | 7 | 63–71 | −3 | 9 | 64–69 | −4 | 10 | 72 | −6 | 11 | 66–67 | −8 | 14 |
| 74–82 | −2 | 6 | 72–73 | −3 | 8 | 70–74 | −4 | 9 | 73–83 | −6 | 10 | 68–77 | −8 | 13 |
| 83–84 | −3 | 6 | 74–82 | −4 | 8 | 75–80 | −5 | 9 | 84–94 | −7 | 9 | 78 | −9 | 13 |
| 85–93 | −3 | 5 | 83–84 | −4 | 7 | 81–86 | −5 | 8 | 95–105 | −8 | 8 | 79–88 | −9 | 12 |
| 94–95 | −4 | 5 | 85–93 | −5 | 7 | 87–91 | −6 | 8 | 106–116 | −9 | 7 | 89 | −10 | 12 |
| 96–104 | −4 | 4 | 94–95 | −5 | 6 | 92–97 | −6 | 7 | 117–127 | −10 | 6 | 90–99 | −10 | 11 |
| 105–106 | −5 | 4 | 96–104 | −6 | 6 | 98–102 | −7 | 7 | 128 | −11 | 6 | 100 | −11 | 11 |
| 107–115 | −5 | 3 | 105–106 | −6 | 5 | 103–108 | −7 | 6 | 129–138 | −11 | 5 | 101–110 | −11 | 10 |
| 116–117 | −6 | 3 | 107–115 | −7 | 5 | 109–113 | −8 | 6 | 139 | −12 | 5 | 111 | −12 | 10 |
| 118–126 | −6 | 2 | 116–117 | −7 | 4 | 114–119 | −8 | 5 | 140–149 | −12 | 4 | 112–121 | −12 | 9 |
| 127–128 | −7 | 2 | 118–126 | −8 | 4 | 120–125 | −9 | 5 | 150 | −13 | 4 | 122 | −13 | 9 |
| 129–137 | −7 | 1 | 127–128 | −8 | 3 | 126–130 | −9 | 4 | 151–160 | −13 | 3 | 123–132 | −13 | 8 |
| 138–139 | −8 | 1 | 129–137 | −9 | 3 | 131–136 | −10 | 4 | | | | 133–134 | −14 | 8 |
| 140–148 | −8 | 0 | 138–140 | −9 | 2 | 137–141 | −10 | 3 | | | | 135–143 | −14 | 7 |
| 149–151 | −9 | 0 | 141–148 | −10 | 2 | 142–147 | −11 | 3 | | | | 144–145 | −15 | 7 |
| 152–160 | −9 | −1 | 149–151 | −10 | 1 | 148–152 | −11 | 2 | | | | 146–154 | −15 | 6 |
| | | | 152–159 | −11 | 1 | 153–158 | −12 | 2 | | | | 155–156 | −16 | 6 |
| | | | 160 | −11 | 0 | 159–160 | −12 | 1 | | | | 157–160 | −16 | 5 |

*(Table continues next page)*

**Table L-2 (cont.)**

H. WISC-III – Verbal Scale – Age 7; WISC-III – Performance Scale – Age 16; WPPSI-R – Verbal Scale – Ages 5 and 6; WPPSI-R – Performance Scale – Average; WAIS-R – Performance Scale – Ages 20–24 and 70–74 ($r_{xx} = .92$)

| 68% | | | 85% | | | 90% | | | 95% | | | 99% | | |
|---|---|---|---|---|---|---|---|---|---|---|---|---|---|---|
| IQ | L | U | IQ | L | U | IQ | L | U | IQ | L | U | IQ | L | U |
| 40–42 | 1 | 9 | 40–48 | − 1 | 10 | 40–49 | − 2 | 11 | 40–48 | − 3 | 12 | 40–42 | − 5 | 15 |
| 43–44 | 1 | 8 | 49–51 | − 2 | 10 | 50 | − 2 | 10 | 49–51 | − 4 | 12 | 43–44 | − 6 | 15 |
| 45–55 | 0 | 8 | 52–60 | − 2 | 9 | 51–61 | − 3 | 10 | 52–60 | − 4 | 11 | 45–55 | − 6 | 14 |
| 56–57 | 0 | 7 | 61–64 | − 3 | 9 | 62–63 | − 3 | 9 | 61–64 | − 5 | 11 | 56–57 | − 7 | 14 |
| 58–67 | − 1 | 7 | 65–73 | − 3 | 8 | 64–74 | − 4 | 9 | 65–73 | − 5 | 10 | 58–67 | − 7 | 13 |
| 68–69 | − 1 | 6 | 74–76 | − 4 | 8 | 75 | − 4 | 8 | 74–76 | − 6 | 10 | 68–69 | − 8 | 13 |
| 70–80 | − 2 | 6 | 77–85 | − 4 | 7 | 76–86 | − 5 | 8 | 77–85 | − 6 | 9 | 70–80 | − 8 | 12 |
| 81–82 | − 2 | 5 | 86–89 | − 5 | 7 | 87–88 | − 5 | 7 | 86–89 | − 7 | 9 | 81–82 | − 9 | 12 |
| 83–92 | − 3 | 5 | 90–98 | − 5 | 6 | 89–99 | − 6 | 7 | 90–98 | − 7 | 8 | 83–92 | − 9 | 11 |
| 93–94 | − 3 | 4 | 99–101 | − 6 | 6 | 100 | − 6 | 6 | 99–101 | − 8 | 8 | 93–94 | −10 | 11 |
| 95–105 | − 4 | 4 | 102–110 | − 6 | 5 | 101–111 | − 7 | 6 | 102–110 | − 8 | 7 | 95–105 | −10 | 10 |
| 106–107 | − 4 | 3 | 111–114 | − 7 | 5 | 112–113 | − 7 | 5 | 111–114 | − 9 | 7 | 106–107 | −11 | 10 |
| 108–117 | − 5 | 3 | 115–123 | − 7 | 4 | 114–124 | − 8 | 5 | 115–123 | − 9 | 6 | 108–117 | −11 | 9 |
| 118–119 | − 5 | 2 | 124–126 | − 8 | 4 | 125 | − 8 | 4 | 124–126 | −10 | 6 | 118–119 | −12 | 9 |
| 120–130 | − 6 | 2 | 127–135 | − 8 | 3 | 126–136 | − 9 | 4 | 127–135 | −10 | 5 | 120–130 | −12 | 8 |
| 131–132 | − 6 | 1 | 136–139 | − 9 | 3 | 137–138 | − 9 | 3 | 136–139 | −11 | 5 | 131–132 | −13 | 8 |
| 133–142 | − 7 | 1 | 140–148 | − 9 | 2 | 139–149 | −10 | 3 | 140–148 | −11 | 4 | 133–142 | −13 | 7 |
| 143–144 | − 7 | 0 | 149–151 | −10 | 2 | 150 | −10 | 2 | 149–151 | −12 | 4 | 143–144 | −14 | 7 |
| 145–155 | − 8 | 0 | 152–160 | −10 | 1 | 151–160 | −11 | 2 | 152–160 | −12 | 3 | 145–155 | −14 | 6 |
| 156–157 | − 8 | −1 | | | | | | | | | | 156–157 | −15 | 6 |
| 158–160 | − 9 | −1 | | | | | | | | | | 158–160 | −15 | 5 |

*(Table continues next page)*

**Table L-2 (cont.)**

**I. WISC-III – Verbal Scale – Ages 6 and 9; WPPSI-R – Verbal Scale – Ages 3, 3½, 4, and 4½; WPPSI-R – Performance Scale – Age 6½; WAIS-R – Performance Scale – Ages 55–64 and Average ($r_{xx} = .93$)**

| 68% | | | 85% | | | 90% | | | 95% | | | 99% | | |
|---|---|---|---|---|---|---|---|---|---|---|---|---|---|---|
| IQ | L | U | IQ | L | U | IQ | L | U | IQ | L | U | IQ | L | U |
| 40 | 1 | 8 | 40 | − 1 | 10 | 40–48 | − 2 | 10 | 40–46 | − 3 | 11 | 40–42 | − 5 | 14 |
| 41–45 | 0 | 8 | 41–45 | − 1 | 9 | 49–51 | − 3 | 10 | 47–53 | − 4 | 11 | 43 | − 6 | 14 |
| 46–54 | 0 | 7 | 46–54 | − 2 | 9 | 52–63 | − 3 | 9 | 54–60 | − 4 | 10 | 44–56 | − 6 | 13 |
| 55–59 | − 1 | 7 | 55–59 | − 2 | 8 | 64–65 | − 4 | 9 | 61–67 | − 5 | 10 | 57 | − 7 | 13 |
| 60–68 | − 1 | 6 | 60–68 | − 3 | 8 | 66–77 | − 4 | 8 | 68–75 | − 5 | 9 | 58–71 | − 7 | 12 |
| 69–74 | − 2 | 6 | 69–74 | − 3 | 7 | 78–79 | − 5 | 8 | 76–81 | − 6 | 9 | 72–85 | − 8 | 11 |
| 75–82 | − 2 | 5 | 75–83 | − 4 | 7 | 80–91 | − 5 | 7 | 82–89 | − 6 | 8 | 86 | − 9 | 11 |
| 83–88 | − 3 | 5 | 84–88 | − 4 | 6 | 92–94 | − 6 | 7 | 90–96 | − 7 | 8 | 87–99 | − 9 | 10 |
| 89–97 | − 3 | 4 | 89–97 | − 5 | 6 | 95–105 | − 6 | 6 | 97–103 | − 7 | 7 | 100 | − 10 | 10 |
| 98–102 | − 4 | 4 | 98–102 | − 5 | 5 | 106–108 | − 7 | 6 | 104–110 | − 8 | 7 | 101–113 | − 10 | 9 |
| 103–111 | − 4 | 3 | 103–111 | − 6 | 5 | 109–120 | − 7 | 5 | 111–118 | − 8 | 6 | 114 | − 11 | 9 |
| 112–117 | − 5 | 3 | 112–116 | − 6 | 4 | 121–122 | − 8 | 5 | 119–124 | − 9 | 6 | 115–128 | − 11 | 8 |
| 118–125 | − 5 | 2 | 117–125 | − 7 | 4 | 123–134 | − 8 | 4 | 125–132 | − 9 | 5 | 129–142 | − 12 | 7 |
| 126–131 | − 6 | 2 | 126–131 | − 7 | 3 | 135–136 | − 9 | 4 | 133–139 | − 10 | 5 | 143 | − 13 | 7 |
| 132–140 | − 6 | 1 | 132–140 | − 8 | 3 | 137–148 | − 9 | 3 | 140–146 | − 10 | 4 | 144–156 | − 13 | 6 |
| 141–145 | − 7 | 1 | 141–145 | − 8 | 2 | 149–151 | − 10 | 3 | 147–153 | − 11 | 4 | 157 | − 14 | 6 |
| 146–154 | − 7 | 0 | 146–154 | − 9 | 2 | 152–160 | − 10 | 2 | 154–160 | − 11 | 3 | 158–160 | − 14 | 5 |
| 155–159 | − 8 | 0 | 155–159 | − 9 | 1 | | | | | | | | | |
| 160 | − 8 | −1 | 160 | − 10 | 1 | | | | | | | | | |

**J. WISC-III – Verbal Scale – Age 13; WISC-III – Performance Scale – Age 15; WISC-III – Full Scale – Age 7; WPPSI-R – Performance Scale – Ages 5½ and 6; WAIS-R – Performance Scale – Ages 25–34, 35–44, 45–54, and 65–69 ($r_{xx} = .94$)**

| 68% | | | 85% | | | 90% | | | 95% | | | 99% | | |
|---|---|---|---|---|---|---|---|---|---|---|---|---|---|---|
| IQ | L | U | IQ | L | U | IQ | L | U | IQ | L | U | IQ | L | U |
| 40–49 | 0 | 7 | 40–41 | − 1 | 9 | 40–46 | − 2 | 9 | 40–45 | − 3 | 10 | 40 | − 5 | 13 |
| 50 | 0 | 6 | 42 | − 1 | 8 | 47–53 | − 3 | 9 | 46–54 | − 4 | 10 | 41–43 | − 5 | 12 |
| 51–65 | − 1 | 6 | 43–57 | − 2 | 8 | 54–63 | − 3 | 8 | 55–62 | − 4 | 9 | 44–56 | − 6 | 12 |
| 66–67 | − 1 | 5 | 58 | − 2 | 7 | 64–69 | − 4 | 8 | 63–71 | − 5 | 9 | 57–59 | − 6 | 11 |
| 68–82 | − 2 | 5 | 59–74 | − 3 | 7 | 70–80 | − 4 | 7 | 72–78 | − 5 | 8 | 60–73 | − 7 | 11 |
| 83–84 | − 2 | 4 | 75 | − 3 | 6 | 81–86 | − 5 | 7 | 79–87 | − 6 | 8 | 74–76 | − 7 | 10 |
| 85–99 | − 3 | 4 | 76–91 | − 4 | 6 | 87–96 | − 5 | 6 | 88–95 | − 6 | 7 | 77–90 | − 8 | 10 |
| 100 | − 3 | 3 | 92 | − 4 | 5 | 97–103 | − 6 | 6 | 96–104 | − 7 | 7 | 91–93 | − 8 | 9 |
| 101–115 | − 4 | 3 | 93–107 | − 5 | 5 | 104–113 | − 6 | 5 | 105–112 | − 7 | 6 | 94–106 | − 9 | 9 |
| 116–117 | − 4 | 2 | 108 | − 5 | 4 | 114–119 | − 7 | 5 | 113–121 | − 8 | 6 | 107–109 | − 9 | 8 |
| 118–132 | − 5 | 2 | 109–124 | − 6 | 4 | 120–130 | − 7 | 4 | 122–128 | − 8 | 5 | 110–123 | − 10 | 8 |
| 133–134 | − 5 | 1 | 125 | − 6 | 3 | 131–136 | − 8 | 4 | 129–137 | − 9 | 5 | 124–126 | − 10 | 7 |
| 135–149 | − 6 | 1 | 126–141 | − 7 | 3 | 137–146 | − 8 | 3 | 138–145 | − 9 | 4 | 127–140 | − 11 | 7 |
| 150 | − 6 | 0 | 142 | − 7 | 2 | 147–153 | − 9 | 3 | 146–154 | − 10 | 4 | 141–143 | − 11 | 6 |
| 151–160 | − 7 | 0 | 143–157 | − 8 | 2 | 154–160 | -- 9 | 2 | 155–160 | − 10 | 3 | 144–156 | − 12 | 6 |
| | | | 158 | − 8 | 1 | | | | | | | 157–159 | − 12 | 5 |
| | | | 159–160 | − 9 | 1 | | | | | | | 160 | − 13 | 5 |

*(Table continues next page)*

**Table L-2 (cont.)**

**K. WISC-III – Verbal Scale – Ages 10, 11, 12, 14, 16, and Average; WISC-III – Full Scale – Ages 6, 9, 11, 13, and 14; WPPSI-R – Performance Scale – Age 5; WPPSI-R – Verbal Scale – Average; WPPSI-R – Full Scale – Ages 5½, 6, and 6½; WAIS-R – Verbal Scale – Ages 16–17 ($r_{xx} = .95$)**

| 68% | | | 85% | | | 90% | | | 95% | | | 99% | | |
|---|---|---|---|---|---|---|---|---|---|---|---|---|---|---|
| IQ | L | U | IQ | L | U | IQ | L | U | IQ | L | U | IQ | L | U |
| 40–46 | 0 | 6 | 40–41 | −2 | 8 | 40–44 | −2 | 8 | 40–45 | −3 | 9 | 40–45 | −5 | 11 |
| 47–53 | −1 | 6 | 42–58 | −2 | 7 | 45–55 | −3 | 8 | 46–54 | −4 | 9 | 46–54 | −6 | 11 |
| 54–66 | −1 | 5 | 59–61 | −3 | 7 | 56–64 | −3 | 7 | 55–65 | −4 | 8 | 55–65 | −6 | 10 |
| 67–73 | −2 | 5 | 62–78 | −3 | 6 | 65–75 | −4 | 7 | 66–74 | −5 | 8 | 66–74 | −7 | 10 |
| 74–86 | −2 | 4 | 79–81 | −4 | 6 | 76–84 | −4 | 6 | 75–85 | −5 | 7 | 75–85 | −7 | 9 |
| 87–93 | −3 | 4 | 82–98 | −4 | 5 | 85–95 | −5 | 6 | 86–94 | −6 | 7 | 86–94 | −8 | 9 |
| 94–106 | −3 | 3 | 99–101 | −5 | 5 | 96–104 | −5 | 5 | 95–105 | −6 | 6 | 95–105 | −8 | 8 |
| 107–113 | −4 | 3 | 102–118 | −5 | 4 | 105–115 | −6 | 5 | 106–114 | −7 | 6 | 106–114 | −9 | 8 |
| 114–126 | −4 | 2 | 119–121 | −6 | 4 | 116–124 | −6 | 4 | 115–125 | −7 | 5 | 115–125 | −9 | 7 |
| 127–133 | −5 | 2 | 122–138 | −6 | 3 | 125–135 | −7 | 4 | 126–134 | −8 | 5 | 126–134 | −10 | 7 |
| 134–146 | −5 | 1 | 139–141 | −7 | 3 | 136–144 | −7 | 3 | 135–145 | −8 | 4 | 135–145 | −10 | 6 |
| 147–153 | −6 | 1 | 142–158 | −7 | 2 | 145–155 | −8 | 3 | 146–154 | −9 | 4 | 146–154 | −11 | 6 |
| 154–160 | −6 | 0 | 159–160 | −8 | 2 | 156–160 | −8 | 2 | 155–160 | −9 | 3 | 155–160 | −11 | 5 |

**L. WISC-III – Verbal Scale – Ages 8 and 15; WISC-III – Full Scale – Ages 8, 10, 12, 16, and Average; WPPSI-R – Performance Scale – Ages 3, 3½, 4, and 4½; WPPSI-R – Full Scale – Age 5 and Average; WAIS-R – Verbal Scale – Ages 18–19 and 20–24; WAIS-R – Full Scale – Ages 16–17 and 18–19 ($r_{xx} = .96$)**

| 68% | | | 85% | | | 90% | | | 95% | | | 99% | | |
|---|---|---|---|---|---|---|---|---|---|---|---|---|---|---|
| IQ | L | U | IQ | L | U | IQ | L | U | IQ | L | U | IQ | L | U |
| 40 | 0 | 5 | 40–41 | −2 | 7 | 40–43 | −2 | 7 | 40–46 | −3 | 8 | 40–48 | −5 | 10 |
| 41–59 | −1 | 5 | 42–58 | −2 | 6 | 44–56 | −3 | 7 | 47–53 | −4 | 8 | 49–51 | −5 | 9 |
| 60–65 | −1 | 4 | 59–66 | −3 | 6 | 57–68 | −3 | 6 | 54–71 | −4 | 7 | 52–73 | −6 | 9 |
| 66–84 | −2 | 4 | 67–83 | −3 | 5 | 69–81 | −4 | 6 | 72–78 | −5 | 7 | 74–76 | −6 | 8 |
| 85–90 | −2 | 3 | 84–91 | −4 | 5 | 82–93 | −4 | 5 | 79–96 | −5 | 6 | 77–98 | −7 | 8 |
| 91–109 | −3 | 3 | 92–108 | −4 | 4 | 94–106 | −5 | 5 | 97–103 | −6 | 6 | 99–101 | −7 | 7 |
| 110–115 | −3 | 2 | 109–116 | −5 | 4 | 107–118 | −5 | 4 | 104–121 | −6 | 5 | 102–123 | −8 | 7 |
| 116–134 | −4 | 2 | 117–133 | −5 | 3 | 119–131 | −6 | 4 | 122–128 | −7 | 5 | 124–126 | −8 | 6 |
| 135–140 | −4 | 1 | 134–141 | −6 | 3 | 132–143 | −6 | 3 | 129–146 | −7 | 4 | 127–148 | −9 | 6 |
| 141–159 | −5 | 1 | 142–158 | −6 | 2 | 144–156 | −7 | 3 | 147–153 | −8 | 4 | 149–151 | −9 | 5 |
| 160 | −5 | 0 | 159–160 | −7 | 2 | 157–160 | −7 | 2 | 154–160 | −8 | 3 | 152–160 | −10 | 5 |

*(Table continues next page)*

**Table L-2 (cont.)**

**M.  WISC-III – Full Scale – Age 15; WPPSI-R – Full Scale – Ages 3, 3½, 4, and 4½; WAIS-R – Verbal Scale – Ages 25–34, 35–44, 45–54, 55–64, 65–69, 70–74, and Average; WAIS-R – Full Scale – Ages 20–24, 45–54, 55–64, 70–74, and Average ($r_{xx} = .97$)**

| 68% | | | 85% | | | 90% | | | 95% | | | 99% | | |
|---|---|---|---|---|---|---|---|---|---|---|---|---|---|---|
| *IQ* | *L* | *U* | *IQ* | *L* | *U* | *IQ* | *L* | *U* | *IQ* | *L* | *U* | *IQ* | *L* | *U* |
| 40–65 | − 1 | 4 | 40–62 | − 2 | 5 | 40–44 | − 2 | 6 | 40–47 | − 3 | 7 | 40–66 | − 5 | 8 |
| 66–67 | − 2 | 4 | 63–70 | − 3 | 5 | 45–55 | − 3 | 6 | 48–52 | − 3 | 6 | 67–99 | − 6 | 7 |
| 68–99 | − 2 | 3 | 71–95 | − 3 | 4 | 56–78 | − 3 | 5 | 53–81 | − 4 | 6 | 100 | − 7 | 7 |
| 100 | − 3 | 3 | 96–104 | − 4 | 4 | 79–88 | − 4 | 5 | 82–85 | − 4 | 5 | 101–133 | − 7 | 6 |
| 101–132 | − 3 | 2 | 105–129 | − 4 | 3 | 89–111 | − 4 | 4 | 86–114 | − 5 | 5 | 134–160 | − 8 | 5 |
| 133–134 | − 4 | 2 | 130–137 | − 5 | 3 | 112–121 | − 5 | 4 | 115–118 | − 5 | 4 | | | |
| 135–160 | − 4 | 1 | 138–160 | − 5 | 2 | 122–144 | − 5 | 3 | 119–147 | − 6 | 4 | | | |
| | | | | | | 145–155 | − 6 | 3 | 148–152 | − 6 | 3 | | | |
| | | | | | | 156–160 | − 6 | 2 | 153–160 | − 7 | 3 | | | |

**N.  WAIS-R – Full Scale – Ages 25–34, and 35–44 ($r_{xx} = .98$)**

| 68% | | | 85% | | | 90% | | | 95% | | | 99% | | |
|---|---|---|---|---|---|---|---|---|---|---|---|---|---|---|
| *IQ* | *L* | *U* | *IQ* | *L* | *U* | *IQ* | *L* | *U* | *IQ* | *L* | *U* | *IQ* | *L* | *U* |
| 40–71 | − 1 | 3 | 40–74 | − 2 | 4 | 40–46 | − 2 | 5 | 40–71 | − 3 | 5 | 40–43 | − 4 | 7 |
| 72–78 | − 2 | 3 | 75 | − 2 | 3 | 47–53 | − 2 | 4 | 72–78 | − 4 | 5 | 44–56 | − 4 | 6 |
| 79–121 | − 2 | 2 | 76–124 | − 3 | 3 | 54–96 | − 3 | 4 | 79–121 | − 4 | 4 | 57–93 | − 5 | 6 |
| 122–128 | − 3 | 2 | 125 | − 3 | 2 | 97–103 | − 3 | 3 | 122–128 | − 5 | 4 | 94–106 | − 5 | 5 |
| 129–160 | − 3 | 1 | 126–160 | − 4 | 2 | 104–146 | − 4 | 3 | 129–160 | − 5 | 3 | 107–143 | − 6 | 5 |
| | | | | | | 147–153 | − 4 | 2 | | | | 144–156 | − 6 | 4 |
| | | | | | | 154–160 | − 5 | 2 | | | | 157–160 | − 7 | 4 |

*Note.* Abbreviations: L = Lower limit of confidence interval, U = Upper limit of confidence interval. The values in the table, when added to the obtained IQ (in the first column), will form the confidence interval. For example, for a 7-year-old the confidence interval for an obtained IQ of 40 at the 99% confidence level for the WPPSI-R Verbal Scale (see Section A) is 36 to 62 (40 − 4 = 36; 40 + 22 = 62).

The confidence intervals in Table L-2 can be used for any test having the reliability coefficient shown in each section of the table ($r_{xx}$ range of .85 to .98) and a standard score distribution with $M = 100$ and $SD = 15$.

See page 1038 for an explanation of how confidence intervals were computed.

**Table L-3**
**Significant Differences Between Scaled Scores, Between IQs, and Between Factor Deviation Quotients (DQs) at Each of the 11 Age Levels of the WISC-III (.05/.01 significance levels)**

| Age level | | I | S | A | V | C | DS | PC | CD | PA | BD | OA | SS |
|---|---|---|---|---|---|---|---|---|---|---|---|---|---|
| **6** | S | 4/6 | — | | | | | | | | | | |
| (6-0-0 | A | 4/6 | 4/5 | — | | | | | | | | | |
| through | V | 4/6 | 4/5 | 4/5 | — | | | | | | | | |
| 6-11-30) | C | 5/6 | 4/6 | 4/6 | 4/5 | — | | | | | | | |
| | DS | 4/6 | 4/5 | 4/5 | 4/5 | 4/6 | — | | | | | | |
| | PC | 5/6 | 4/5 | 4/5 | 4/5 | 4/6 | 4/5 | — | | | | | |
| | CD | 5/6 | 4/6 | 4/6 | 4/5 | 5/6 | 4/6 | 4/6 | — | | | | |
| | PA | 4/6 | 4/5 | 4/5 | 4/5 | 4/5 | 4/5 | 4/5 | 4/5 | — | | | |
| | BD | 4/6 | 4/5 | 4/5 | 4/5 | 4/5 | 4/5 | 4/5 | 4/5 | 4/5 | — | | |
| | OA | 5/6 | 4/6 | 4/6 | 4/6 | 5/6 | 5/6 | 5/6 | 5/6 | 4/6 | 4/6 | — | |
| | SS | 5/6 | 5/6 | 5/6 | 5/6 | 5/6 | 5/6 | 5/6 | 5/6 | 5/6 | 5/6 | 5/6 | — |
| | MA | 4/6 | 4/5 | 4/5 | 4/5 | 4/6 | 4/5 | 4/5 | 4/6 | 4/5 | 4/5 | 5/6 | 5/6 |
| **7** | S | 4/6 | — | | | | | | | | | | |
| (7-0-0 | A | 5/6 | 5/6 | — | | | | | | | | | |
| through | V | 4/6 | 4/6 | 4/6 | — | | | | | | | | |
| 7-11-30) | C | 5/6 | 5/6 | 5/6 | 5/6 | — | | | | | | | |
| | DS | 4/5 | 4/5 | 4/6 | 4/5 | 4/6 | — | | | | | | |
| | PC | 4/5 | 4/5 | 4/5 | 4/5 | 4/6 | 4/5 | — | | | | | |
| | CD | 5/6 | 5/6 | 5/6 | 5/6 | 5/6 | 5/6 | 4/6 | — | | | | |
| | PA | 4/5 | 4/5 | 4/5 | 4/5 | 4/6 | 4/5 | 4/5 | 4/6 | — | | | |
| | BD | 4/6 | 4/6 | 5/6 | 4/6 | 5/6 | 4/5 | 4/5 | 5/6 | 4/5 | — | | |
| | OA | 5/6 | 5/6 | 5/6 | 5/6 | 5/7 | 5/6 | 5/6 | 5/7 | 5/6 | 5/6 | — | |
| | SS | 4/6 | 4/6 | 5/6 | 4/6 | 5/6 | 4/5 | 4/5 | 5/6 | 4/5 | 4/6 | 5/6 | — |
| | MA | 4/6 | 4/6 | 5/6 | 4/5 | 5/6 | 4/5 | 4/5 | 5/6 | 4/5 | 4/6 | 5/6 | 4/6 |
| **8** | S | 4/5 | — | | | | | | | | | | |
| (8-0-0 | A | 4/5 | 4/5 | — | | | | | | | | | |
| through | V | 3/4 | 4/4 | 4/5 | — | | | | | | | | |
| 8-11-30) | C | 4/5 | 4/5 | 4/5 | 3/4 | — | | | | | | | |
| | DS | 4/5 | 4/5 | 4/5 | 4/4 | 4/5 | — | | | | | | |
| | PC | 4/5 | 4/5 | 4/5 | 4/5 | 4/5 | 4/5 | — | | | | | |
| | CD | 4/5 | 4/5 | 4/6 | 4/5 | 4/5 | 4/5 | 4/5 | — | | | | |
| | PA | 4/5 | 4/6 | 5/6 | 4/5 | 4/5 | 4/6 | 4/6 | 5/6 | — | | | |
| | BD | 4/5 | 4/5 | 4/5 | 4/5 | 4/5 | 4/5 | 4/5 | 4/5 | 4/6 | — | | |
| | OA | 5/6 | 5/6 | 5/6 | 4/6 | 5/6 | 5/6 | 5/6 | 5/6 | 5/7 | 5/6 | — | |
| | SS | 4/5 | 4/6 | 5/6 | 4/5 | 4/5 | 4/6 | 4/6 | 5/6 | 5/6 | 4/6 | 5/7 | — |
| | MA | 4/5 | 4/5 | 4/6 | 4/5 | 4/5 | 4/5 | 4/5 | 4/6 | 5/6 | 4/5 | 5/6 | 5/6 |

Boxed Deviation Quotient values:

**Age 6:**
PSIQ  VSIQ 12/16
PODQ 14/18  VCDQ PSDQ 17/22
PSDQ 16/21

**Age 7:**
PSIQ  VSIQ 13/17
PODQ 14/18  VCDQ PSDQ 17/22
PSDQ 16/21

**Age 8:**
PSIQ  VSIQ 11/15
PODQ 12/16  VCDQ PSDQ 16/21
PSDQ 14/18

*(Table continues next page)*

**Table L-3 (cont.)**

| Age level | | I | S | A | V | C | DS | PC | CD | PA | BD | OA | SS |
|---|---|---|---|---|---|---|---|---|---|---|---|---|---|
| **9** | S | 4/5 | — | | | | | | VSIQ | | | VCDQ | PSDQ |
| (9-0-0 | A | 4/6 | 5/6 | — | | | PSIQ | 12/16 | | PODQ | 13/16 | | | 15/20 |
| through | V | 4/5 | 4/5 | 4/6 | — | | PSDQ | 14/19 | | | | | | |
| 9-11-30) | C | 4/6 | 4/6 | 5/6 | 4/6 | — | | | | | | | | |
| | DS | 4/5 | 4/5 | 4/6 | 4/5 | 4/6 | — | | | | | | | |
| | PC | 4/5 | 4/5 | 5/6 | 4/5 | 4/6 | 4/5 | — | | | | | | |
| | CD | 4/5 | 4/5 | 5/6 | 4/5 | 4/6 | 4/5 | 4/5 | — | | | | | |
| | PA | 4/6 | 4/6 | 5/6 | 4/6 | 5/6 | 4/6 | 4/6 | 5/6 | — | | | | |
| | BD | 4/5 | 4/5 | 4/6 | 4/5 | 4/5 | 4/5 | 4/5 | 4/5 | 4/5 | — | | | |
| | OA | 4/6 | 4/6 | 5/6 | 4/5 | 5/6 | 4/5 | 4/6 | 4/6 | 5/6 | 4/5 | — | | |
| | SS | 4/6 | 4/6 | 5/6 | 4/6 | 5/6 | 4/6 | 4/6 | 5/6 | 5/6 | 4/5 | 5/6 | — | |
| | MA | 5/6 | 5/6 | 5/7 | 5/6 | 5/6 | 5/6 | 5/6 | 5/6 | 5/7 | 5/6 | 5/6 | 5/7 | |
| **10** | S | 4/5 | — | | | | | | VSIQ | | | VCDQ | PSDQ |
| (10-0-0 | A | 4/5 | 4/5 | — | | | PSIQ | 11/15 | | PODQ | 13/16 | | | 16/21 |
| through | V | 4/5 | 4/5 | 4/5 | — | | PSDQ | 14/19 | | | | | | |
| 10-11-30) | C | 4/5 | 4/5 | 4/5 | 4/5 | — | | | | | | | | |
| | DS | 4/5 | 4/5 | 4/5 | 4/4 | 4/5 | — | | | | | | | |
| | PC | 4/6 | 4/6 | 4/6 | 4/5 | 4/6 | 4/5 | — | | | | | | |
| | CD | 4/5 | 4/5 | 4/5 | 4/5 | 4/5 | 4/5 | 4/6 | — | | | | | |
| | PA | 4/6 | 4/6 | 4/6 | 4/5 | 4/6 | 4/5 | 5/6 | 4/6 | — | | | | |
| | BD | 4/5 | 4/5 | 4/5 | 3/4 | 4/5 | 3/4 | 4/5 | 4/5 | 4/5 | — | | | |
| | OA | 5/6 | 5/6 | 5/6 | 4/5 | 5/6 | 4/6 | 5/6 | 5/6 | 5/6 | 4/5 | — | | |
| | SS | 4/6 | 4/6 | 5/6 | 4/5 | 5/6 | 4/6 | 5/6 | 5/6 | 5/6 | 4/5 | 5/6 | — | |
| | MA | 4/6 | 4/6 | 5/6 | 4/5 | 5/6 | 4/6 | 5/6 | 5/6 | 5/6 | 4/5 | 5/6 | 5/6 | |
| **11** | S | 4/5 | — | | | | | | VSIQ | | | VCDQ | PSDQ |
| (11-0-0 | A | 4/5 | 4/5 | — | | | PSIQ | 12/15 | | PODQ | 13/17 | | | 15/20 |
| through | V | 3/4 | 4/5 | 4/5 | — | | PSDQ | 13/17 | | | | | | |
| 11-11-30) | C | 4/5 | 4/5 | 4/6 | 4/5 | — | | | | | | | | |
| | DS | 4/5 | 4/5 | 4/5 | 4/4 | 4/5 | — | | | | | | | |
| | PC | 4/5 | 4/5 | 4/6 | 4/5 | 4/6 | 4/5 | — | | | | | | |
| | CD | 4/5 | 4/5 | 4/5 | 4/5 | 4/5 | 4/5 | 4/5 | — | | | | | |
| | PA | 4/6 | 4/6 | 5/6 | 4/5 | 5/6 | 4/6 | 5/6 | 4/6 | — | | | | |
| | BD | 4/5 | 4/5 | 4/5 | 4/4 | 4/5 | 4/5 | 4/5 | 4/5 | 4/6 | — | | | |
| | OA | 5/6 | 5/6 | 5/6 | 4/6 | 5/6 | 5/6 | 5/6 | 5/6 | 5/7 | 5/6 | — | | |
| | SS | 4/5 | 4/5 | 4/5 | 4/5 | 4/6 | 4/5 | 4/6 | 4/5 | 5/6 | 4/5 | 5/6 | — | |
| | MA | 4/6 | 5/6 | 5/6 | 4/6 | 5/6 | 4/6 | 5/6 | 5/6 | 5/6 | 4/6 | 5/7 | 5/6 | |
| **12** | S | 4/5 | — | | | | | | VSIQ | | | VCDQ | PSDQ |
| (12-0-0 | A | 4/5 | 4/5 | — | | | PSIQ | 11/15 | | PODQ | 12/16 | | | 15/19 |
| through | V | 3/4 | 3/4 | 4/5 | — | | PSDQ | 13/17 | | | | | | |
| 12-11-30) | C | 4/5 | 4/5 | 4/6 | 4/5 | — | | | | | | | | |
| | DS | 4/5 | 4/5 | 4/5 | 3/4 | 4/5 | — | | | | | | | |
| | PC | 4/5 | 4/6 | 5/6 | 4/5 | 4/6 | 4/5 | — | | | | | | |
| | CD | 4/5 | 4/5 | 4/6 | 4/5 | 4/5 | 4/5 | 4/6 | — | | | | | |
| | PA | 4/5 | 4/5 | 4/6 | 4/5 | 4/5 | 4/5 | 5/6 | 4/5 | — | | | | |
| | BD | 4/4 | 4/5 | 4/5 | 3/4 | 4/5 | 3/4 | 4/5 | 4/5 | 4/5 | — | | | |
| | OA | 4/6 | 4/6 | 5/6 | 4/5 | 5/6 | 4/6 | 5/6 | 5/6 | 5/6 | 4/6 | — | | |
| | SS | 4/5 | 4/5 | 4/6 | 4/5 | 4/5 | 4/5 | 5/6 | 4/5 | 4/5 | 4/5 | 5/6 | — | |
| | MA | 5/6 | 5/6 | 5/6 | 4/6 | 5/6 | 4/6 | 5/7 | 5/6 | 5/6 | 4/6 | 5/7 | 5/6 | |

*(Table continues next page)*

**Table L-3 (cont.)**

| Age level | | I | S | A | V | C | DS | PC | CD | PA | BD | OA | SS |
|---|---|---|---|---|---|---|---|---|---|---|---|---|---|
| **13** | S | 4/5 | — | | | | | | | | | | |
| (13-0-0 | A | 4/5 | 4/6 | — | | | | | | | | | |
| through | V | 3/4 | 4/5 | 4/5 | — | | | | | | | | |
| 13-11-30) | C | 4/5 | 5/6 | 4/6 | 4/5 | — | | | | | | | |
| | DS | 4/4 | 4/5 | 4/5 | 3/4 | 4/5 | — | | | | | | |
| | PC | 4/5 | 5/6 | 4/6 | 4/5 | 5/6 | 4/5 | — | | | | | |
| | CD | 4/6 | 5/6 | 5/6 | 4/5 | 5/6 | 4/5 | 5/6 | — | | | | |
| | PA | 4/5 | 5/6 | 4/5 | 4/5 | 5/6 | 4/5 | 5/6 | 5/6 | — | | | |
| | BD | 3/4 | 4/5 | 4/5 | 3/4 | 4/5 | 3/4 | 4/5 | 4/5 | 4/5 | — | | |
| | OA | 4/5 | 5/6 | 4/6 | 4/5 | 5/6 | 4/5 | 5/6 | 5/6 | 5/6 | 4/5 | — | |
| | SS | 4/5 | 5/6 | 4/6 | 4/5 | 5/6 | 4/5 | 5/6 | 5/6 | 5/6 | 4/5 | 5/6 | — |
| | MA | 4/6 | 5/6 | 5/6 | 4/5 | 5/6 | 4/5 | 5/6 | 5/6 | 5/6 | 4/5 | 5/6 | 5/6 |

Age 13 — PSIQ: VSIQ 12/16; PODQ: VCDQ 13/16, PSDQ 16/21; PSDQ: 15/20

| Age level | | I | S | A | V | C | DS | PC | CD | PA | BD | OA | SS |
|---|---|---|---|---|---|---|---|---|---|---|---|---|---|
| **14** | S | 4/5 | — | | | | | | | | | | |
| (14-0-0 | A | 4/5 | 4/5 | — | | | | | | | | | |
| through | V | 3/4 | 3/4 | 4/5 | — | | | | | | | | |
| 14-11-30) | C | 4/5 | 4/5 | 4/6 | 4/5 | — | | | | | | | |
| | DS | 4/5 | 4/5 | 4/5 | 3/4 | 4/5 | — | | | | | | |
| | PC | 4/5 | 4/6 | 5/6 | 4/5 | 5/6 | 4/6 | — | | | | | |
| | CD | 4/5 | 4/6 | 5/6 | 4/5 | 5/6 | 4/6 | 5/6 | — | | | | |
| | PA | 4/5 | 4/5 | 4/6 | 4/5 | 4/6 | 4/5 | 5/6 | 5/6 | — | | | |
| | BD | 3/4 | 3/4 | 4/5 | 3/4 | 4/5 | 3/4 | 4/5 | 4/5 | 4/5 | — | | |
| | OA | 5/6 | 5/6 | 5/7 | 5/6 | 5/7 | 5/6 | 5/7 | 5/7 | 5/7 | 5/6 | — | |
| | SS | 4/5 | 4/5 | 4/6 | 4/5 | 5/6 | 4/5 | 5/6 | 5/6 | 4/6 | 4/5 | 5/7 | — |
| | MA | 4/5 | 4/6 | 5/6 | 4/5 | 5/6 | 4/6 | 5/6 | 5/6 | 5/6 | 4/5 | 5/7 | 5/6 |

Age 14 — PSIQ: VSIQ 12/16; PODQ: VCDQ 13/17, PSDQ 17/22; PSDQ: 15/19

| Age level | | I | S | A | V | C | DS | PC | CD | PA | BD | OA | SS |
|---|---|---|---|---|---|---|---|---|---|---|---|---|---|
| **15** | S | 4/5 | — | | | | | | | | | | |
| (15-0-0 | A | 4/5 | 4/5 | — | | | | | | | | | |
| through | V | 3/4 | 4/5 | 4/5 | — | | | | | | | | |
| 15-11-30) | C | 4/5 | 4/5 | 4/5 | 4/5 | — | | | | | | | |
| | DS | 3/4 | 4/5 | 4/5 | 3/4 | 4/5 | — | | | | | | |
| | PC | 4/5 | 4/5 | 4/5 | 3/4 | 4/5 | 3/4 | — | | | | | |
| | CD | 3/4 | 4/5 | 4/5 | 3/4 | 4/5 | 3/4 | 4/4 | — | | | | |
| | PA | 4/5 | 4/6 | 4/6 | 4/5 | 4/6 | 4/5 | 4/6 | 4/5 | — | | | |
| | BD | 3/4 | 3/4 | 3/4 | 3/4 | 4/4 | 3/4 | 3/4 | 3/4 | 4/5 | — | | |
| | OA | 4/5 | 4/5 | 4/5 | 4/5 | 4/6 | 4/5 | 4/5 | 4/5 | 5/6 | 4/5 | — | |
| | SS | 4/5 | 4/5 | 4/5 | 3/4 | 4/5 | 3/4 | 4/5 | 4/4 | 4/6 | 3/4 | 4/5 | — |
| | MA | 5/6 | 5/6 | 5/6 | 4/6 | 5/6 | 4/6 | 5/6 | 5/6 | 5/7 | 4/6 | 5/7 | 5/6 |

Age 15 — PSIQ: VSIQ 10/13; PODQ: VCDQ 11/14, PSDQ 13/16; PSDQ: 11/15

| Age level | | I | S | A | V | C | DS | PC | CD | PA | BD | OA | SS |
|---|---|---|---|---|---|---|---|---|---|---|---|---|---|
| **16** | S | 4/4 | — | | | | | | | | | | |
| (16-0-0 | A | 4/5 | 4/5 | — | | | | | | | | | |
| through | V | 3/4 | 3/4 | 4/5 | — | | | | | | | | |
| 16-11-30) | C | 4/5 | 4/5 | 4/6 | 4/5 | — | | | | | | | |
| | DS | 3/4 | 3/4 | 4/5 | 3/4 | 4/5 | — | | | | | | |
| | PC | 4/5 | 4/5 | 4/5 | 4/5 | 5/6 | 4/5 | — | | | | | |
| | CD | 3/4 | 3/4 | 4/4 | 3/4 | 4/5 | 3/4 | 4/5 | — | | | | |
| | PA | 4/5 | 4/5 | 4/6 | 4/5 | 5/6 | 4/5 | 5/6 | 4/5 | — | | | |
| | BD | 3/4 | 3/4 | 4/4 | 3/4 | 4/5 | 3/4 | 4/5 | 3/4 | 4/5 | — | | |
| | OA | 4/5 | 4/6 | 4/6 | 4/5 | 5/6 | 4/5 | 5/6 | 4/5 | 5/6 | 4/5 | — | |
| | SS | 4/5 | 4/5 | 4/5 | 4/5 | 4/6 | 4/5 | 4/5 | 4/4 | 4/6 | 4/4 | 4/6 | — |
| | MA | 4/6 | 5/6 | 5/6 | 4/6 | 5/6 | 4/6 | 5/6 | 4/5 | 5/6 | 4/5 | 5/6 | 5/6 |

Age 16 — PSIQ: VSIQ 11/14; PODQ: VCDQ 12/16, PSDQ 13/17; PSDQ: 12/15

*(Table continues next page)*

**Table L-3 (cont.)**

| Age level | | I | S | A | V | C | DS | PC | CD | PA | BD | OA | SS |
|---|---|---|---|---|---|---|---|---|---|---|---|---|---|
| **Average** | S | 4/5 | – | | | | | | | | | | |
| | A | 4/5 | 4/5 | – | | | | | | | | | |
| | V | 4/5 | 4/5 | 4/5 | – | | | | | | | | |
| | C | 4/5 | 4/5 | 4/6 | 4/5 | – | | | | | | | |
| | DS | 4/5 | 4/5 | 4/5 | 4/5 | 4/5 | – | | | | | | |
| | PC | 4/5 | 4/5 | 4/6 | 4/5 | 4/6 | 4/5 | – | | | | | |
| | CD | 4/5 | 4/5 | 4/6 | 4/5 | 4/6 | 4/5 | 4/6 | – | | | | |
| | PA | 4/5 | 4/5 | 4/6 | 4/5 | 4/6 | 4/5 | 4/6 | 4/6 | – | | | |
| | BD | 4/5 | 4/5 | 4/5 | 3/4 | 4/5 | 4/5 | 4/5 | 4/5 | 4/5 | – | | |
| | OA | 4/6 | 5/6 | 5/6 | 4/6 | 5/6 | 4/6 | 5/6 | 5/6 | 5/6 | 4/6 | – | |
| | SS | 4/5 | 4/5 | 4/6 | 4/5 | 4/6 | 4/5 | 4/6 | 4/6 | 5/6 | 4/5 | 5/6 | – |
| | MA | 4/6 | 5/6 | 5/6 | 4/5 | 5/6 | 4/6 | 5/6 | 5/6 | 5/6 | 4/6 | 5/6 | 5/6 |

Box 1:
|  |  |
|---|---|
|  | VSIQ |
| PSIQ | 12/15 |

Box 2:
|  | VCDQ | PSDQ |
|---|---|---|
| PODQ | 13/17 | 16/21 |
| PSDQ | 15/20 | |

*Note.* Abbreviations: I = Information; S = Similarities; A = Arithmetic; V = Vocabulary; C = Comprehension; DS = Digit Span; PC = Picture Completion; CD = Coding; PA = Picture Arrangement; BD = Block Design; OA = Object Assembly; SS = Symbol Search; MA = Mazes; VSIQ = Verbal Scale IQ; PSIQ = Performance Scale IQ; VCDQ = Verbal Comprehension Deviation Quotient; PODQ = Perceptual Organization Deviation Quotient; PSDQ = Processing Speed Deviation Quotient.

The factor scores are composed of the following subtests: Verbal Comprehension: Information, Similarities, Vocabulary, and Comprehension; Perceptual Organization: Picture Completion, Block Design, and Object Assembly; Processing Speed: Coding and Symbol Search.

Sample reading: At the 6-0-0 year level, a difference of 4 points between scaled scores on the Information and Similarities subtests is significant at the 5 percent level; a difference of 6 points is significant at the 1 percent level. The first small box shows that a 12-point difference between the Verbal Scale IQ and the Performance Scale IQ is needed for the 5 percent level, and a 16-point difference is needed for the 1 percent level. The second small box shows that a difference of 14 points is needed between the Verbal Comprehension Deviation Quotient and the Perceptual Organization Deviation Quotient at the 5 percent level, and a difference of 18 points is needed at the 1 percent level.

The values in this table for the subtest comparisons are overly liberal when more than one comparison is made for a subtest. They are more accurate when a priori planned comparisons are made, such as Information vs. Comprehension or Digit Span vs. Arithmetic.

All values in this table have been rounded up to the next higher number.

See Chapter 8, Exhibit 8-1 (page 168) for an explanation of the method used to arrive at magnitude of differences.

See Exhibit I-4 in Appendix I for the procedure used to obtain the reliability coefficients for the factor scores.

**Table L-4**
**Differences Required for Significance When Each Subtest Scaled Score Is Compared to the Mean Subtest Scaled Score for Any Individual Child at Each of the 11 Age Levels of the WISC-III**

| | Age 6-0-0 through 6-11-30 | | | | | | | | | | | |
|---|---|---|---|---|---|---|---|---|---|---|---|---|
| | Mean of 4 subtests[a] | | Mean of 5 subtests[b] | | Mean of 6 subtests[c] | | Mean of 6 subtests | | Mean of 7 subtests | | Mean of 10 subtests | |
| Subtest | .05 | .01 | .05 | .01 | .05 | .01 | .05 | .01 | .05 | .01 | .05 | .01 |
| Information | 3.27 | 3.96 | 3.51 | 4.20 | 3.64 | 4.38 | — | — | — | — | 4.11 | 4.82 |
| Similarities | 2.91 | 3.52 | 3.07 | 3.68 | 3.16 | 3.80 | — | — | — | — | 3.52 | 4.12 |
| Arithmetic | — | — | 3.07 | 3.68 | 3.16 | 3.80 | — | — | — | — | 3.52 | 4.12 |
| Vocabulary | 2.86 | 3.46 | 3.01 | 3.60 | 3.09 | 3.72 | — | — | — | — | 3.43 | 4.02 |
| Comprehension | 3.19 | 3.85 | 3.40 | 4.07 | 3.52 | 4.24 | — | — | — | — | 3.97 | 4.65 |
| Digit Span | — | — | — | — | 3.28 | 3.95 | — | — | — | — | — | — |
| Picture Completion | 3.04 | 3.67 | 3.25 | 3.90 | 3.38 | 4.07 | 3.35 | 4.03 | 3.52 | 4.18 | 3.75 | 4.39 |
| Coding | — | — | 3.42 | 4.09 | 3.56 | 4.28 | 3.53 | 4.25 | 3.71 | 4.40 | 3.97 | 4.65 |
| Picture Arrangement | 2.85 | 3.44 | 3.03 | 3.62 | 3.13 | 3.76 | 3.10 | 3.73 | 3.25 | 3.85 | 3.43 | 4.02 |
| Block Design | 2.85 | 3.44 | 3.03 | 3.62 | 3.13 | 3.76 | 3.10 | 3.73 | 3.25 | 3.85 | 3.43 | 4.02 |
| Object Assembly | 3.35 | 4.05 | 3.62 | 4.34 | 3.78 | 4.55 | 3.76 | 4.52 | 3.96 | 4.69 | 4.25 | 4.97 |
| Symbol Search | — | — | — | — | 3.89 | 4.68 | — | — | 4.07 | 4.83 | — | — |
| Mazes | — | — | — | — | — | — | 3.23 | 3.88 | 3.39 | 4.02 | — | — |
| | Mean of 11 subtests | | Mean of 11 subtests | | Mean of 11 subtests | | Mean of 12 subtests | | Mean of 12 subtests | | Mean of 13 subtests | |
| Subtest | .05 | .01 | .05 | .01 | .05 | .01 | .05 | .01 | .05 | .01 | .05 | .01 |
| Information | 4.18 | 4.89 | 4.19 | 4.90 | 4.18 | 4.89 | 4.25 | 5.11 | 4.25 | 5.10 | 4.43 | 5.00 |
| Similarities | 3.57 | 4.17 | 3.58 | 4.18 | 3.57 | 4.17 | 3.62 | 4.36 | 3.62 | 4.35 | 3.77 | 4.25 |
| Arithmetic | 3.57 | 4.17 | 3.58 | 4.18 | 3.57 | 4.17 | 3.62 | 4.36 | 3.62 | 4.35 | 3.77 | 4.25 |
| Vocabulary | 3.48 | 4.07 | 3.49 | 4.08 | 3.48 | 4.07 | 3.54 | 4.25 | 3.53 | 4.24 | 3.68 | 4.15 |
| Comprehension | 4.04 | 4.72 | 4.04 | 4.73 | 4.04 | 4.72 | 4.10 | 4.93 | 4.10 | 4.93 | 4.28 | 4.82 |
| Digit Span | 3.73 | 4.36 | — | — | — | — | 3.79 | 4.56 | 3.78 | 4.55 | 3.95 | 4.45 |
| Picture Completion | 3.81 | 4.45 | 3.82 | 4.46 | 3.81 | 4.45 | 3.87 | 4.65 | 3.86 | 4.65 | 4.03 | 4.55 |
| Coding | 4.04 | 4.72 | 4.04 | 4.73 | 4.04 | 4.72 | 4.10 | 4.93 | 4.10 | 4.93 | 4.28 | 4.82 |
| Picture Arrangement | 3.48 | 4.07 | 3.49 | 4.08 | 3.48 | 4.07 | 3.54 | 4.25 | 3.53 | 4.24 | 3.68 | 4.15 |
| Block Design | 3.48 | 4.07 | 3.49 | 4.08 | 3.48 | 4.07 | 3.54 | 4.25 | 3.53 | 4.24 | 3.68 | 4.15 |
| Object Assembly | 4.32 | 5.05 | 4.33 | 5.06 | 4.32 | 5.05 | 4.39 | 5.28 | 4.39 | 5.28 | 4.58 | 5.17 |
| Symbol Search | — | — | 4.46 | 5.22 | — | — | 4.53 | 5.45 | — | — | 4.73 | 5.33 |
| Mazes | — | — | — | — | 3.65 | 4.27 | — | — | 3.70 | 4.45 | 3.86 | 4.35 |

*(Table continues next page)*

**Table L-4 (cont.)**

| | Mean of 4 subtests[a] | | Mean of 5 subtests[b] | | Mean of 6 subtests[c] | | Mean of 6 subtests | | Mean of 7 subtests | | Mean of 10 subtests | |
|---|---|---|---|---|---|---|---|---|---|---|---|---|
| Subtest | .05 | .01 | .05 | .01 | .05 | .01 | .05 | .01 | .05 | .01 | .05 | .01 |
| Information | 3.18 | 3.84 | 3.40 | 4.07 | 3.50 | 4.21 | — | — | — | — | 3.92 | 4.59 |
| Similarities | 3.14 | 3.79 | 3.35 | 4.01 | 3.44 | 4.14 | — | — | — | — | 3.85 | 4.50 |
| Arithmetic | — | — | 3.56 | 4.26 | 3.67 | 4.41 | — | — | — | — | 4.13 | 4.84 |
| Vocabulary | 3.05 | 3.68 | 3.24 | 3.88 | 3.32 | 3.99 | — | — | — | — | 3.70 | 4.33 |
| Comprehension | 3.35 | 4.05 | 3.61 | 4.32 | 3.72 | 4.48 | — | — | — | — | 4.20 | 4.92 |
| Digit Span | — | — | — | — | 3.19 | 3.84 | — | — | — | — | — | — |
| Picture Completion | 2.77 | 3.34 | 2.94 | 3.52 | 3.00 | 3.61 | 2.99 | 3.60 | 3.11 | 3.68 | 3.29 | 3.85 |
| Coding | — | — | 3.70 | 4.43 | 3.84 | 4.61 | 3.83 | 4.61 | 4.02 | 4.77 | 4.33 | 5.07 |
| Picture Arrangement | 2.77 | 3.34 | 2.94 | 3.52 | 3.00 | 3.61 | 2.99 | 3.60 | 3.11 | 3.68 | 3.29 | 3.85 |
| Block Design | 3.10 | 3.75 | 3.34 | 4.00 | 3.44 | 4.14 | 3.44 | 4.14 | 3.59 | 4.26 | 3.85 | 4.50 |
| Object Assembly | 3.61 | 4.36 | 3.93 | 4.71 | 4.09 | 4.92 | 4.09 | 4.92 | 4.30 | 5.10 | 4.65 | 5.44 |
| Symbol Search | — | — | — | — | 3.50 | 4.21 | — | — | 3.66 | 4.34 | — | — |
| Mazes | — | — | — | — | — | — | 3.38 | 4.06 | 3.53 | 4.18 | — | — |

| | Mean of 11 subtests | | Mean of 11 subtests | | Mean of 11 subtests | | Mean of 12 subtests | | Mean of 12 subtests | | Mean of 13 subtests | |
|---|---|---|---|---|---|---|---|---|---|---|---|---|
| Subtest | .05 | .01 | .05 | .01 | .05 | .01 | .05 | .01 | .05 | .01 | .05 | .01 |
| Information | 3.98 | 4.65 | 3.98 | 4.65 | 3.98 | 4.65 | 4.04 | 4.85 | 4.04 | 4.85 | 4.21 | 4.74 |
| Similarities | 3.90 | 4.56 | 3.91 | 4.57 | 3.91 | 4.57 | 3.96 | 4.76 | 3.96 | 4.76 | 4.12 | 4.65 |
| Arithmetic | 4.20 | 4.91 | 4.20 | 4.91 | 4.20 | 4.91 | 4.26 | 5.12 | 4.26 | 5.12 | 4.44 | 5.01 |
| Vocabulary | 3.75 | 4.38 | 3.75 | 4.39 | 3.75 | 4.38 | 3.80 | 4.57 | 3.80 | 4.57 | 3.96 | 4.46 |
| Comprehension | 4.27 | 4.99 | 4.27 | 4.99 | 4.27 | 4.99 | 4.33 | 5.21 | 4.33 | 5.21 | 4.52 | 5.09 |
| Digit Span | 3.59 | 4.19 | — | — | — | — | 3.63 | 4.37 | 3.63 | 4.37 | 3.78 | 4.26 |
| Picture Completion | 3.33 | 3.89 | 3.33 | 3.90 | 3.33 | 3.89 | 3.37 | 4.05 | 3.37 | 4.05 | 3.50 | 3.95 |
| Coding | 4.40 | 5.15 | 4.41 | 5.15 | 4.41 | 5.15 | 4.47 | 5.38 | 4.47 | 5.38 | 4.66 | 5.26 |
| Picture Arrangement | 3.33 | 3.89 | 3.33 | 3.90 | 3.33 | 3.89 | 3.37 | 4.05 | 3.37 | 4.05 | 3.50 | 3.95 |
| Block Design | 3.90 | 4.56 | 3.91 | 4.57 | 3.91 | 4.57 | 3.96 | 4.76 | 3.96 | 4.76 | 4.12 | 4.65 |
| Object Assembly | 4.73 | 5.53 | 4.73 | 5.53 | 4.73 | 5.53 | 4.81 | 5.78 | 4.80 | 5.78 | 5.01 | 5.65 |
| Symbol Search | — | — | 3.98 | 4.65 | — | — | 4.04 | 4.85 | — | — | 4.21 | 4.74 |
| Mazes | — | — | — | — | 3.83 | 4.48 | — | — | 3.88 | 4.66 | 4.04 | 4.56 |

*Age 7-0-0 through 7-11-30*

*(Table continues next page)*

**Table L-4 (cont.)**

| | Mean of 4 subtests[a] | | Mean of 5 subtests[b] | | Mean of 6 subtests[c] | | Mean of 6 subtests | | Mean of 7 subtests | | Mean of 10 subtests | |
|---|---|---|---|---|---|---|---|---|---|---|---|---|
| Subtest | .05 | .01 | .05 | .01 | .05 | .01 | .05 | .01 | .05 | .01 | .05 | .01 |
| Information | 2.44 | 2.94 | 2.63 | 3.15 | 2.71 | 3.26 | — | — | — | — | 3.06 | 3.59 |
| Similarities | 2.55 | 3.08 | 2.76 | 3.31 | 2.86 | 3.44 | — | — | — | — | 3.24 | 3.80 |
| Arithmetic | — | — | 3.13 | 3.75 | 3.26 | 3.92 | — | — | — | — | 3.73 | 4.37 |
| Vocabulary | 2.32 | 2.80 | 2.49 | 2.98 | 2.55 | 3.07 | — | — | — | — | 2.87 | 3.36 |
| Comprehension | 2.49 | 3.01 | 2.70 | 3.23 | 2.78 | 3.35 | — | — | — | — | 3.15 | 3.69 |
| Digit Span | — | — | — | — | 2.86 | 3.44 | — | — | — | — | — | — |
| Picture Completion | 2.97 | 3.59 | 3.12 | 3.74 | 3.21 | 3.86 | 3.20 | 3.85 | 3.34 | 3.96 | 3.50 | 4.09 |
| Coding | — | — | 3.29 | 3.94 | 3.40 | 4.09 | 3.39 | 4.07 | 3.54 | 4.20 | 3.73 | 4.37 |
| Picture Arrangement | 3.37 | 4.07 | 3.60 | 4.31 | 3.74 | 4.50 | 3.73 | 4.49 | 3.91 | 4.64 | 4.16 | 4.88 |
| Block Design | 2.87 | 3.47 | 3.00 | 3.60 | 3.08 | 3.71 | 3.07 | 3.69 | 3.19 | 3.79 | 3.33 | 3.90 |
| Object Assembly | 3.65 | 4.41 | 3.93 | 4.71 | 4.10 | 4.94 | 4.10 | 4.93 | 4.31 | 5.11 | 4.62 | 5.41 |
| Symbol Search | — | — | — | — | 3.74 | 4.50 | — | — | 3.91 | 4.64 | — | — |
| Mazes | — | — | — | — | — | — | 3.50 | 4.22 | 3.67 | 4.35 | — | — |

| | Mean of 11 subtests | | Mean of 11 subtests | | Mean of 11 subtests | | Mean of 12 subtests | | Mean of 12 subtests | | Mean of 13 subtests | |
|---|---|---|---|---|---|---|---|---|---|---|---|---|
| Subtest | .05 | .01 | .05 | .01 | .05 | .01 | .05 | .01 | .05 | .01 | .05 | .01 |
| Information | 3.10 | 3.62 | 3.11 | 3.64 | 3.11 | 3.63 | 3.15 | 3.78 | 3.14 | 3.78 | 3.28 | 3.69 |
| Similarities | 3.29 | 3.84 | 3.30 | 3.85 | 3.29 | 3.85 | 3.34 | 4.01 | 3.33 | 4.01 | 3.48 | 3.92 |
| Arithmetic | 3.79 | 4.43 | 3.80 | 4.44 | 3.80 | 4.44 | 3.85 | 4.63 | 3.85 | 4.63 | 4.02 | 4.53 |
| Vocabulary | 2.90 | 3.39 | 2.91 | 3.41 | 2.91 | 3.40 | 2.94 | 3.54 | 2.94 | 3.54 | 3.06 | 3.45 |
| Comprehension | 3.19 | 3.73 | 3.21 | 3.75 | 3.20 | 3.74 | 3.24 | 3.90 | 3.24 | 3.90 | 3.38 | 3.81 |
| Digit Span | 3.29 | 3.84 | — | — | — | — | 3.34 | 4.01 | 3.33 | 4.01 | 3.48 | 3.92 |
| Picture Completion | 3.55 | 4.15 | 3.56 | 4.16 | 3.55 | 4.15 | 3.60 | 4.33 | 3.60 | 4.33 | 3.76 | 4.24 |
| Coding | 3.79 | 4.43 | 3.80 | 4.44 | 3.80 | 4.44 | 3.85 | 4.63 | 3.85 | 4.63 | 4.02 | 4.53 |
| Picture Arrangement | 4.23 | 4.95 | 4.24 | 4.96 | 4.24 | 4.96 | 4.31 | 5.18 | 4.31 | 5.18 | 4.49 | 5.07 |
| Block Design | 3.38 | 3.95 | 3.39 | 3.96 | 3.38 | 3.95 | 3.43 | 4.12 | 3.43 | 4.12 | 3.57 | 4.03 |
| Object Assembly | 4.70 | 5.49 | 4.71 | 5.50 | 4.70 | 5.50 | 4.78 | 5.75 | 4.78 | 5.75 | 4.99 | 5.63 |
| Symbol Search | — | — | 4.24 | 4.96 | — | — | 4.31 | 5.18 | — | — | 4.49 | 5.07 |
| Mazes | — | — | — | — | 3.95 | 4.62 | — | — | 4.01 | 4.82 | 4.18 | 4.72 |

Age 8-0-0 through 8-11-30

*(Table continues next page)*

**Table L-4 (cont.)**

## Age 9-0-0 through 9-11-30

| Subtest | Mean of 4 subtests[a] | | Mean of 5 subtests[b] | | Mean of 6 subtests[c] | | Mean of 6 subtests | | Mean of 7 subtests | | Mean of 10 subtests | |
|---|---|---|---|---|---|---|---|---|---|---|---|---|
| | .05 | .01 | .05 | .01 | .05 | .01 | .05 | .01 | .05 | .01 | .05 | .01 |
| Information | 2.87 | 3.47 | 3.08 | 3.69 | 3.16 | 3.80 | – | – | – | – | 3.52 | 4.12 |
| Similarities | 2.92 | 3.53 | 3.14 | 3.76 | 3.22 | 3.88 | – | – | – | – | 3.60 | 4.21 |
| Arithmetic | – | – | 3.62 | 4.34 | 3.75 | 4.51 | – | – | – | – | 4.25 | 4.98 |
| Vocabulary | 2.82 | 3.41 | 3.03 | 3.62 | 3.09 | 3.72 | – | – | – | – | 3.44 | 4.02 |
| Comprehension | 3.20 | 3.86 | 3.47 | 4.15 | 3.58 | 4.31 | – | – | – | – | 4.04 | 4.74 |
| Digit Span | – | – | – | – | 3.09 | 3.72 | – | – | – | – | – | – |
| Picture Completion | 2.95 | 3.57 | 3.13 | 3.75 | 3.24 | 3.90 | 3.26 | 3.92 | 3.40 | 4.04 | 3.60 | 4.21 |
| Coding | – | – | 3.25 | 3.89 | 3.37 | 4.05 | 3.38 | 4.07 | 3.54 | 4.20 | 3.75 | 4.39 |
| Picture Arrangement | 3.31 | 4.00 | 3.56 | 4.27 | 3.71 | 4.47 | 3.73 | 4.48 | 3.91 | 4.64 | 4.18 | 4.90 |
| Block Design | 2.70 | 3.27 | 2.83 | 3.39 | 2.91 | 3.50 | 2.93 | 3.52 | 3.04 | 3.61 | 3.18 | 3.72 |
| Object Assembly | 3.18 | 3.84 | 3.41 | 4.08 | 3.55 | 4.27 | 3.56 | 4.28 | 3.73 | 4.42 | 3.97 | 4.65 |
| Symbol Search | – | – | – | – | 3.71 | 4.47 | – | – | 3.91 | 4.64 | – | – |
| Mazes | – | – | – | – | – | – | 4.04 | 4.86 | 4.25 | 5.05 | – | – |

| Subtest | Mean of 11 subtests | | Mean of 11 subtests | | Mean of 11 subtests | | Mean of 12 subtests | | Mean of 12 subtests | | Mean of 13 subtests | |
|---|---|---|---|---|---|---|---|---|---|---|---|---|
| | .05 | .01 | .05 | .01 | .05 | .01 | .05 | .01 | .05 | .01 | .05 | .01 |
| Information | 3.57 | 4.17 | 3.58 | 4.18 | 3.58 | 4.19 | 3.62 | 4.35 | 3.63 | 4.36 | 3.78 | 4.26 |
| Similarities | 3.65 | 4.27 | 3.66 | 4.28 | 3.66 | 4.28 | 3.71 | 4.46 | 3.71 | 4.46 | 3.87 | 4.36 |
| Arithmetic | 4.32 | 5.05 | 4.33 | 5.06 | 4.33 | 5.06 | 4.39 | 5.28 | 4.40 | 5.28 | 4.59 | 5.17 |
| Vocabulary | 3.48 | 4.07 | 3.49 | 4.08 | 3.50 | 4.09 | 3.54 | 4.25 | 3.54 | 4.26 | 3.69 | 4.16 |
| Comprehension | 4.11 | 4.80 | 4.12 | 4.81 | 4.12 | 4.82 | 4.18 | 5.02 | 4.18 | 5.02 | 4.36 | 4.92 |
| Digit Span | 3.48 | 4.07 | – | – | – | – | 3.54 | 4.25 | 3.54 | 4.26 | 3.69 | 4.16 |
| Picture Completion | 3.65 | 4.27 | 3.66 | 4.28 | 3.66 | 4.28 | 3.71 | 4.46 | 3.71 | 4.46 | 3.87 | 4.36 |
| Coding | 3.81 | 4.45 | 3.82 | 4.46 | 3.82 | 4.47 | 3.87 | 4.65 | 3.87 | 4.66 | 4.04 | 4.55 |
| Picture Arrangement | 4.25 | 4.97 | 4.26 | 4.98 | 4.26 | 4.98 | 4.32 | 5.20 | 4.33 | 5.20 | 4.51 | 5.09 |
| Block Design | 3.22 | 3.76 | 3.23 | 3.77 | 3.23 | 3.78 | 3.26 | 3.92 | 3.27 | 3.93 | 3.40 | 3.84 |
| Object Assembly | 4.04 | 4.72 | 4.04 | 4.73 | 4.05 | 4.73 | 4.10 | 4.93 | 4.11 | 4.94 | 4.28 | 4.83 |
| Symbol Search | – | – | 4.26 | 4.98 | – | – | 4.32 | 5.20 | – | – | 4.51 | 5.09 |
| Mazes | – | – | – | – | 4.66 | 5.45 | – | – | 4.73 | 5.69 | 4.94 | 5.57 |

*(Table continues next page)*

**Table L-4 (cont.)**

| | Age 10-0-0 through 10-11-30 | | | | | | | | | | | |
|---|---|---|---|---|---|---|---|---|---|---|---|---|
| | Mean of 4 subtests[a] | | Mean of 5 subtests[b] | | Mean of 6 subtests[c] | | Mean of 6 subtests | | Mean of 7 subtests | | Mean of 10 subtests | |
| Subtest | .05 | .01 | .05 | .01 | .05 | .01 | .05 | .01 | .05 | .01 | .05 | .01 |
| Information | 2.74 | 3.31 | 2.94 | 3.52 | 3.03 | 3.64 | — | — | — | — | 3.42 | 4.00 |
| Similarities | 2.74 | 3.31 | 2.94 | 3.52 | 3.03 | 3.64 | — | — | — | — | 3.42 | 4.00 |
| Arithmetic | — | — | 3.12 | 3.73 | 3.22 | 3.88 | — | — | — | — | 3.66 | 4.29 |
| Vocabulary | 2.41 | 2.91 | 2.54 | 3.05 | 2.59 | 3.12 | — | — | — | — | 2.88 | 3.37 |
| Comprehension | 2.89 | 3.49 | 3.12 | 3.73 | 3.22 | 3.88 | — | — | — | — | 3.66 | 4.29 |
| Digit Span | — | — | — | — | 2.89 | 3.48 | — | — | — | — | — | — |
| Picture Completion | 3.26 | 3.94 | 3.48 | 4.17 | 3.62 | 4.35 | 3.62 | 4.36 | 3.80 | 4.50 | 4.03 | 4.72 |
| Coding | — | — | 3.27 | 3.92 | 3.38 | 4.07 | 3.39 | 4.08 | 3.54 | 4.20 | 3.74 | 4.38 |
| Picture Arrangement | 3.26 | 3.94 | 3.48 | 4.17 | 3.62 | 4.35 | 3.62 | 4.36 | 3.80 | 4.50 | 4.03 | 4.72 |
| Block Design | 2.53 | 3.06 | 2.59 | 3.11 | 2.64 | 3.17 | 2.64 | 3.18 | 2.73 | 3.23 | 2.78 | 3.25 |
| Object Assembly | 3.47 | 4.19 | 3.73 | 4.47 | 3.89 | 4.68 | 3.89 | 4.68 | 4.09 | 4.85 | 4.37 | 5.12 |
| Symbol Search | — | — | — | — | 3.73 | 4.48 | — | — | 3.92 | 4.64 | — | — |
| Mazes | — | — | — | — | — | — | 3.84 | 4.62 | 4.03 | 4.78 | — | — |
| | Mean of 11 subtests | | Mean of 11 subtests | | Mean of 11 subtests | | Mean of 12 subtests | | Mean of 12 subtests | | Mean of 13 subtests | |
| Subtest | .05 | .01 | .05 | .01 | .05 | .01 | .05 | .01 | .05 | .01 | .05 | .01 |
| Information | 3.47 | 4.05 | 3.48 | 4.07 | 3.48 | 4.07 | 3.52 | 4.23 | 3.52 | 4.24 | 3.67 | 4.14 |
| Similarities | 3.47 | 4.05 | 3.48 | 4.07 | 3.48 | 4.07 | 3.52 | 4.23 | 3.52 | 4.24 | 3.67 | 4.14 |
| Arithmetic | 3.72 | 4.34 | 3.73 | 4.35 | 3.73 | 4.36 | 3.78 | 4.54 | 3.78 | 4.54 | 3.94 | 4.44 |
| Vocabulary | 2.91 | 3.40 | 2.92 | 3.41 | 2.92 | 3.42 | 2.95 | 3.55 | 2.95 | 3.55 | 3.07 | 3.46 |
| Comprehension | 3.72 | 4.34 | 3.73 | 4.35 | 3.73 | 4.36 | 3.78 | 4.54 | 3.78 | 4.54 | 3.94 | 4.44 |
| Digit Span | 3.29 | 3.85 | — | — | — | — | 3.34 | 4.02 | 3.34 | 4.02 | 3.48 | 3.93 |
| Picture Completion | 4.10 | 4.79 | 4.10 | 4.80 | 4.11 | 4.80 | 4.17 | 5.01 | 4.17 | 5.01 | 4.35 | 4.90 |
| Coding | 3.79 | 4.44 | 3.80 | 4.45 | 3.81 | 4.45 | 3.86 | 4.64 | 3.86 | 4.64 | 4.03 | 4.54 |
| Picture Arrangement | 4.10 | 4.79 | 4.10 | 4.80 | 4.11 | 4.80 | 4.17 | 5.01 | 4.17 | 5.01 | 4.35 | 4.90 |
| Block Design | 2.80 | 3.28 | 2.82 | 3.29 | 2.82 | 3.30 | 2.84 | 3.42 | 2.84 | 3.42 | 2.96 | 3.34 |
| Object Assembly | 4.44 | 5.19 | 4.45 | 5.20 | 4.45 | 5.21 | 4.52 | 5.43 | 4.52 | 5.44 | 4.72 | 5.32 |
| Symbol Search | — | — | 4.25 | 4.96 | — | — | 4.31 | 5.18 | — | — | 4.50 | 5.08 |
| Mazes | — | — | — | — | 4.39 | 5.13 | — | — | 4.45 | 5.35 | 4.65 | 5.24 |

(Table continues next page)

**Table L-4 (cont.)**

### Age 11-0-0 through 11-11-30

| Subtest | Mean of 4 subtests[a] | | Mean of 5 subtests[b] | | Mean of 6 subtests[c] | | Mean of 6 subtests | | Mean of 7 subtests | | Mean of 10 subtests | |
|---|---|---|---|---|---|---|---|---|---|---|---|---|
| | .05 | .01 | .05 | .01 | .05 | .01 | .05 | .01 | .05 | .01 | .05 | .01 |
| Information | 2.58 | 3.11 | 2.75 | 3.29 | 2.82 | 3.39 | – | – | – | – | 3.17 | 3.71 |
| Similarities | 2.74 | 3.31 | 2.94 | 3.52 | 3.03 | 3.64 | – | – | – | – | 3.43 | 4.01 |
| Arithmetic | – | – | 3.12 | 3.73 | 3.22 | 3.88 | – | – | – | – | 3.67 | 4.29 |
| Vocabulary | 2.41 | 2.91 | 2.54 | 3.05 | 2.59 | 3.12 | – | – | – | – | 2.89 | 3.38 |
| Comprehension | 3.03 | 3.66 | 3.28 | 3.93 | 3.41 | 4.10 | – | – | – | – | 3.89 | 4.56 |
| Digit Span | – | – | – | – | 2.89 | 3.48 | – | – | – | – | – | – |
| Picture Completion | 3.23 | 3.90 | 3.40 | 4.07 | 3.50 | 4.21 | 3.53 | 4.24 | 3.67 | 4.36 | 3.89 | 4.56 |
| Coding | – | – | 3.07 | 3.68 | 3.13 | 3.77 | 3.16 | 3.80 | 3.27 | 3.88 | 3.43 | 4.01 |
| Picture Arrangement | 3.48 | 4.21 | 3.71 | 4.44 | 3.84 | 4.61 | 3.86 | 4.64 | 4.04 | 4.79 | 4.31 | 5.05 |
| Block Design | 2.86 | 3.46 | 2.95 | 3.53 | 3.00 | 3.61 | 3.03 | 3.64 | 3.13 | 3.71 | 3.26 | 3.81 |
| Object Assembly | 3.68 | 4.44 | 3.94 | 4.72 | 4.09 | 4.92 | 4.12 | 4.95 | 4.32 | 5.12 | 4.63 | 5.42 |
| Symbol Search | – | – | – | – | 3.32 | 4.00 | – | – | 3.48 | 4.13 | – | – |
| Mazes | – | – | – | – | – | – | 3.96 | 4.77 | 4.15 | 4.92 | – | – |

| Subtest | Mean of 11 subtests | | Mean of 11 subtests | | Mean of 11 subtests | | Mean of 12 subtests | | Mean of 12 subtests | | Mean of 13 subtests | |
|---|---|---|---|---|---|---|---|---|---|---|---|---|
| | .05 | .01 | .05 | .01 | .05 | .01 | .05 | .01 | .05 | .01 | .05 | .01 |
| Information | 3.21 | 3.75 | 3.21 | 3.75 | 3.22 | 3.77 | 3.25 | 3.91 | 3.26 | 3.92 | 3.39 | 3.82 |
| Similarities | 3.47 | 4.06 | 3.48 | 4.07 | 3.49 | 4.08 | 3.52 | 4.23 | 3.53 | 4.24 | 3.68 | 4.14 |
| Arithmetic | 3.72 | 4.35 | 3.73 | 4.35 | 3.73 | 4.37 | 3.78 | 4.54 | 3.78 | 4.55 | 3.94 | 4.44 |
| Vocabulary | 2.92 | 3.41 | 2.92 | 3.41 | 2.93 | 3.43 | 2.95 | 3.55 | 2.96 | 3.56 | 3.07 | 3.47 |
| Comprehension | 3.95 | 4.62 | 3.96 | 4.63 | 3.97 | 4.64 | 4.01 | 4.83 | 4.02 | 4.83 | 4.19 | 4.73 |
| Digit Span | 3.30 | 3.86 | – | – | – | – | 3.34 | 4.02 | 3.35 | 4.03 | 3.49 | 3.93 |
| Picture Completion | 3.95 | 4.62 | 3.96 | 4.63 | 3.97 | 4.64 | 4.01 | 4.83 | 4.02 | 4.83 | 4.19 | 4.73 |
| Coding | 3.47 | 4.06 | 3.48 | 4.07 | 3.49 | 4.08 | 3.52 | 4.23 | 3.53 | 4.24 | 3.68 | 4.14 |
| Picture Arrangement | 4.38 | 5.12 | 4.38 | 5.13 | 4.39 | 5.13 | 4.45 | 5.35 | 4.46 | 5.36 | 4.65 | 5.24 |
| Block Design | 3.30 | 3.86 | 3.30 | 3.86 | 3.31 | 3.87 | 3.34 | 4.02 | 3.35 | 4.03 | 3.49 | 3.93 |
| Object Assembly | 4.71 | 5.50 | 4.71 | 5.51 | 4.72 | 5.52 | 4.79 | 5.75 | 4.79 | 5.76 | 5.00 | 5.64 |
| Symbol Search | – | – | 3.73 | 4.35 | – | – | 3.78 | 4.54 | – | – | 3.94 | 4.44 |
| Mazes | – | – | – | – | 4.52 | 5.29 | – | – | 4.59 | 5.52 | 4.79 | 5.40 |

*(Table continues next page)*

**Table L-4 (cont.)**

| | Mean of 4 subtests[a] | | Mean of 5 subtests[b] | | Mean of 6 subtests[c] | | Mean of 6 subtests | | Mean of 7 subtests | | Mean of 10 subtests | |
|---|---|---|---|---|---|---|---|---|---|---|---|---|
| Subtest | .05 | .01 | .05 | .01 | .05 | .01 | .05 | .01 | .05 | .01 | .05 | .01 |
| Information | 2.52 | 3.05 | 2.73 | 3.27 | 2.80 | 3.37 | — | — | — | — | 3.15 | 3.69 |
| Similarities | 2.58 | 3.11 | 2.80 | 3.35 | 2.87 | 3.45 | — | — | — | — | 3.24 | 3.80 |
| Arithmetic | — | — | 3.38 | 4.05 | 3.51 | 4.22 | — | — | — | — | 4.02 | 4.71 |
| Vocabulary | 2.29 | 2.76 | 2.46 | 2.94 | 2.49 | 3.00 | — | — | — | — | 2.77 | 3.24 |
| Comprehension | 2.74 | 3.31 | 2.99 | 3.58 | 3.08 | 3.70 | — | — | — | — | 3.50 | 4.09 |
| Digit Span | — | — | — | — | 2.65 | 3.19 | — | — | — | — | — | — |
| Picture Completion | 3.34 | 4.04 | 3.57 | 4.28 | 3.70 | 4.45 | 3.73 | 4.49 | 3.90 | 4.63 | 4.16 | 4.87 |
| Coding | — | — | 3.03 | 3.62 | 3.10 | 3.73 | 3.14 | 3.77 | 3.25 | 3.86 | 3.41 | 4.00 |
| Picture Arrangement | 3.03 | 3.67 | 3.20 | 3.83 | 3.29 | 3.96 | 3.33 | 4.00 | 3.46 | 4.11 | 3.65 | 4.28 |
| Block Design | 2.64 | 3.19 | 2.71 | 3.25 | 2.75 | 3.31 | 2.79 | 3.36 | 2.88 | 3.41 | 2.97 | 3.47 |
| Object Assembly | 3.51 | 4.24 | 3.77 | 4.51 | 3.92 | 4.71 | 3.95 | 4.75 | 4.14 | 4.90 | 4.43 | 5.18 |
| Symbol Search | — | — | — | — | 3.29 | 3.96 | — | — | 3.46 | 4.11 | — | — |
| Mazes | — | — | — | — | — | — | 4.05 | 4.87 | 4.25 | 5.04 | — | — |

| | Mean of 11 subtests | | Mean of 11 subtests | | Mean of 11 subtests | | Mean of 12 subtests | | Mean of 12 subtests | | Mean of 13 subtests | |
|---|---|---|---|---|---|---|---|---|---|---|---|---|
| Subtest | .05 | .01 | .05 | .01 | .05 | .01 | .05 | .01 | .05 | .01 | .05 | .01 |
| Information | 3.19 | 3.73 | 3.20 | 3.74 | 3.21 | 3.75 | 3.24 | 3.89 | 3.25 | 3.90 | 3.38 | 3.81 |
| Similarities | 3.28 | 3.84 | 3.29 | 3.85 | 3.30 | 3.86 | 3.33 | 4.00 | 3.34 | 4.01 | 3.48 | 3.92 |
| Arithmetic | 4.09 | 4.78 | 4.09 | 4.79 | 4.10 | 4.80 | 4.15 | 4.99 | 4.16 | 5.00 | 4.34 | 4.89 |
| Vocabulary | 2.79 | 3.27 | 2.80 | 3.28 | 2.82 | 3.29 | 2.83 | 3.40 | 2.84 | 3.41 | 2.95 | 3.33 |
| Comprehension | 3.54 | 4.14 | 3.55 | 4.15 | 3.56 | 4.16 | 3.60 | 4.32 | 3.61 | 4.33 | 3.76 | 4.24 |
| Digit Span | 3.00 | 3.51 | — | — | — | — | 3.04 | 3.65 | 3.05 | 3.67 | 3.17 | 3.58 |
| Picture Completion | 4.23 | 4.95 | 4.24 | 4.95 | 4.25 | 4.96 | 4.30 | 5.17 | 4.31 | 5.18 | 4.49 | 5.07 |
| Coding | 3.46 | 4.04 | 3.47 | 4.05 | 3.48 | 4.06 | 3.51 | 4.22 | 3.52 | 4.23 | 3.67 | 4.13 |
| Picture Arrangement | 3.71 | 4.33 | 3.71 | 4.34 | 3.72 | 4.35 | 3.76 | 4.53 | 3.77 | 4.54 | 3.93 | 4.43 |
| Block Design | 3.00 | 3.51 | 3.01 | 3.51 | 3.02 | 3.53 | 3.04 | 3.65 | 3.05 | 3.67 | 3.17 | 3.58 |
| Object Assembly | 4.50 | 5.26 | 4.51 | 5.27 | 4.52 | 5.28 | 4.58 | 5.50 | 4.59 | 5.51 | 4.79 | 5.40 |
| Symbol Search | — | — | 3.71 | 4.34 | — | — | 3.76 | 4.53 | — | — | 3.93 | 4.43 |
| Mazes | — | — | — | — | 4.65 | 5.43 | — | — | 4.72 | 5.67 | 4.93 | 5.55 |

*(Table continues next page)*

**Table L-4 (cont.)**

| | Mean of 4 subtests[a] | | Mean of 5 subtests[b] | | Mean of 6 subtests[c] | | Mean of 6 subtests | | Mean of 7 subtests | | Mean of 10 subtests | |
|---|---|---|---|---|---|---|---|---|---|---|---|---|
| **Subtest** | *.05* | *.01* | *.05* | *.01* | *.05* | *.01* | *.05* | *.01* | *.05* | *.01* | *.05* | *.01* |
| Information | 2.65 | 3.20 | 2.78 | 3.33 | 2.83 | 3.41 | — | — | — | — | 3.17 | 3.71 |
| Similarities | 3.18 | 3.84 | 3.42 | 4.10 | 3.54 | 4.26 | — | — | — | — | 4.04 | 4.73 |
| Arithmetic | — | — | 3.03 | 3.63 | 3.11 | 3.74 | — | — | — | — | 3.51 | 4.11 |
| Vocabulary | 2.42 | 2.93 | 2.51 | 3.01 | 2.53 | 3.04 | — | — | — | — | 2.79 | 3.27 |
| Comprehension | 3.22 | 3.89 | 3.47 | 4.16 | 3.60 | 4.33 | — | — | — | — | 4.11 | 4.81 |
| Digit Span | — | — | — | — | 2.68 | 3.23 | — | — | — | — | — | — |
| Picture Completion | 3.31 | 3.99 | 3.59 | 4.30 | 3.72 | 4.48 | 3.73 | 4.49 | 3.91 | 4.64 | 4.18 | 4.89 |
| Coding | — | — | 3.69 | 4.41 | 3.83 | 4.61 | 3.84 | 4.62 | 4.03 | 4.78 | 4.31 | 5.05 |
| Picture Arrangement | 3.13 | 3.78 | 3.38 | 4.05 | 3.50 | 4.21 | 3.51 | 4.22 | 3.67 | 4.35 | 3.90 | 4.56 |
| Block Design | 2.42 | 2.93 | 2.53 | 3.03 | 2.55 | 3.07 | 2.57 | 3.09 | 2.63 | 3.12 | 2.69 | 3.14 |
| Object Assembly | 3.18 | 3.84 | 3.43 | 4.11 | 3.55 | 4.28 | 3.57 | 4.29 | 3.73 | 4.42 | 3.97 | 4.65 |
| Symbol Search | — | — | — | — | 3.55 | 4.28 | — | — | 3.73 | 4.42 | — | — |
| Mazes | — | — | — | — | — | — | 3.84 | 4.62 | 4.03 | 4.78 | — | — |

| | Mean of 11 subtests | | Mean of 11 subtests | | Mean of 11 subtests | | Mean of 12 subtests | | Mean of 12 subtests | | Mean of 13 subtests | |
|---|---|---|---|---|---|---|---|---|---|---|---|---|
| **Subtest** | *.05* | *.01* | *.05* | *.01* | *.05* | *.01* | *.05* | *.01* | *.05* | *.01* | *.05* | *.01* |
| Information | 3.21 | 3.75 | 3.22 | 3.76 | 3.22 | 3.77 | 3.25 | 3.91 | 3.25 | 3.91 | 3.39 | 3.82 |
| Similarities | 4.10 | 4.79 | 4.11 | 4.80 | 4.11 | 4.81 | 4.17 | 5.01 | 4.17 | 5.01 | 4.35 | 4.90 |
| Arithmetic | 3.56 | 4.16 | 3.57 | 4.17 | 3.57 | 4.17 | 3.61 | 4.34 | 3.61 | 4.35 | 3.77 | 4.25 |
| Vocabulary | 2.81 | 3.29 | 2.82 | 3.30 | 2.83 | 3.31 | 2.85 | 3.42 | 2.85 | 3.43 | 2.96 | 3.34 |
| Comprehension | 4.17 | 4.88 | 4.18 | 4.89 | 4.18 | 4.89 | 4.24 | 5.10 | 4.24 | 5.10 | 4.43 | 4.99 |
| Digit Span | 3.01 | 3.52 | — | — | — | — | 3.06 | 3.67 | 3.06 | 3.68 | 3.18 | 3.59 |
| Picture Completion | 4.24 | 4.96 | 4.25 | 4.97 | 4.25 | 4.97 | 4.31 | 5.18 | 4.32 | 5.19 | 4.50 | 5.08 |
| Coding | 4.38 | 5.12 | 4.39 | 5.13 | 4.39 | 5.13 | 4.45 | 5.35 | 4.46 | 5.36 | 4.65 | 5.24 |
| Picture Arrangement | 3.95 | 4.62 | 3.96 | 4.63 | 3.97 | 4.64 | 4.02 | 4.83 | 4.02 | 4.83 | 4.19 | 4.73 |
| Block Design | 2.70 | 3.16 | 2.72 | 3.18 | 2.72 | 3.18 | 2.73 | 3.29 | 2.74 | 3.29 | 2.85 | 3.21 |
| Object Assembly | 4.03 | 4.71 | 4.04 | 4.72 | 4.04 | 4.72 | 4.09 | 4.92 | 4.10 | 4.92 | 4.27 | 4.82 |
| Symbol Search | — | — | 4.04 | 4.72 | — | — | 4.09 | 4.92 | — | — | 4.27 | 4.82 |
| Mazes | — | — | — | — | 4.39 | 5.13 | — | — | 4.46 | 5.36 | 4.65 | 5.24 |

*(Table continues next page)*

**Table L-4 (cont.)**

| | Age 14-0-0 through 14-11-30 | | | | | | | | | | | |
| --- | --- | --- | --- | --- | --- | --- | --- | --- | --- | --- | --- | --- |
| | Mean of 4 subtests[a] | | Mean of 5 subtests[b] | | Mean of 6 subtests[c] | | Mean of 6 subtests | | Mean of 7 subtests | | Mean of 10 subtests | |
| Subtest | .05 | .01 | .05 | .01 | .05 | .01 | .05 | .01 | .05 | .01 | .05 | .01 |
| Information | 2.42 | 2.92 | 2.59 | 3.10 | 2.65 | 3.19 | — | — | — | — | 2.99 | 3.50 |
| Similarities | 2.58 | 3.12 | 2.79 | 3.34 | 2.87 | 3.46 | — | — | — | — | 3.26 | 3.82 |
| Arithmetic | — | — | 3.21 | 3.84 | 3.33 | 4.01 | — | — | — | — | 3.82 | 4.47 |
| Vocabulary | 2.17 | 2.62 | 2.30 | 2.75 | 2.32 | 2.80 | — | — | — | — | 2.58 | 3.02 |
| Comprehension | 2.99 | 3.61 | 3.27 | 3.91 | 3.40 | 4.09 | — | — | — | — | 3.90 | 4.56 |
| Digit Span | — | — | — | — | 2.87 | 3.46 | — | — | — | — | — | — |
| Picture Completion | 3.38 | 4.08 | 3.63 | 4.35 | 3.75 | 4.51 | 3.76 | 4.53 | 3.93 | 4.67 | 4.18 | 4.89 |
| Coding | — | — | 3.73 | 4.47 | 3.86 | 4.64 | 3.87 | 4.66 | 4.05 | 4.80 | 4.31 | 5.05 |
| Picture Arrangement | 3.11 | 3.76 | 3.32 | 3.98 | 3.41 | 4.10 | 3.42 | 4.12 | 3.56 | 4.22 | 3.75 | 4.39 |
| Block Design | 2.52 | 3.04 | 2.59 | 3.10 | 2.59 | 3.12 | 2.61 | 3.14 | 2.67 | 3.16 | 2.69 | 3.14 |
| Object Assembly | 3.84 | 4.64 | 4.18 | 5.01 | 4.36 | 5.24 | 4.37 | 5.25 | 4.59 | 5.44 | 4.93 | 5.77 |
| Symbol Search | — | — | — | — | 3.59 | 4.31 | — | — | 3.75 | 4.45 | — | — |
| Mazes | — | — | — | — | — | — | 3.87 | 4.66 | 4.05 | 4.80 | — | — |
| | Mean of 11 subtests | | Mean of 11 subtests | | Mean of 11 subtests | | Mean of 12 subtests | | Mean of 12 subtests | | Mean of 13 subtests | |
| Subtest | .05 | .01 | .05 | .01 | .05 | .01 | .05 | .01 | .05 | .01 | .05 | .01 |
| Information | 3.02 | 3.53 | 3.03 | 3.54 | 3.03 | 3.54 | 3.06 | 3.68 | 3.06 | 3.68 | 3.18 | 3.59 |
| Similarities | 3.30 | 3.86 | 3.31 | 3.87 | 3.31 | 3.87 | 3.35 | 4.02 | 3.35 | 4.03 | 3.49 | 3.93 |
| Arithmetic | 3.88 | 4.53 | 3.89 | 4.54 | 3.89 | 4.55 | 3.94 | 4.74 | 3.94 | 4.74 | 4.11 | 4.64 |
| Vocabulary | 2.59 | 3.03 | 2.60 | 3.05 | 2.61 | 3.05 | 2.62 | 3.15 | 2.63 | 3.16 | 2.73 | 3.08 |
| Comprehension | 3.95 | 4.62 | 3.96 | 4.63 | 3.97 | 4.64 | 4.02 | 4.83 | 4.02 | 4.83 | 4.19 | 4.73 |
| Digit Span | 3.30 | 3.86 | — | — | — | — | 3.35 | 4.02 | 3.35 | 4.03 | 3.49 | 3.93 |
| Picture Completion | 4.24 | 4.96 | 4.25 | 4.97 | 4.25 | 4.97 | 4.31 | 5.19 | 4.32 | 5.19 | 4.50 | 5.08 |
| Coding | 4.38 | 5.12 | 4.39 | 5.13 | 4.39 | 5.13 | 4.46 | 5.36 | 4.46 | 5.36 | 4.65 | 5.25 |
| Picture Arrangement | 3.80 | 4.44 | 3.81 | 4.45 | 3.81 | 4.46 | 3.86 | 4.64 | 3.86 | 4.65 | 4.03 | 4.54 |
| Block Design | 2.71 | 3.16 | 2.72 | 3.18 | 2.72 | 3.18 | 2.74 | 3.29 | 2.74 | 3.30 | 2.85 | 3.21 |
| Object Assembly | 5.01 | 5.86 | 5.02 | 5.87 | 5.02 | 5.87 | 5.10 | 6.13 | 5.10 | 6.14 | 5.33 | 6.01 |
| Symbol Search | — | — | 4.04 | 4.72 | — | — | 4.09 | 4.92 | — | — | 4.27 | 4.82 |
| Mazes | — | — | — | — | 4.39 | 5.13 | — | — | 4.46 | 5.36 | 4.65 | 5.25 |

*(Table continues next page)*

**Table L-4 (cont.)**

| | Age 15-0-0 through 15-11-30 | | | | | | | | | | | |
|---|---|---|---|---|---|---|---|---|---|---|---|---|
| | Mean of 4 subtests[a] | | Mean of 5 subtests[b] | | Mean of 6 subtests[c] | | Mean of 6 subtests | | Mean of 7 subtests | | Mean of 10 subtests | |
| Subtest | .05 | .01 | .05 | .01 | .05 | .01 | .05 | .01 | .05 | .01 | .05 | .01 |
| Information | 2.34 | 2.83 | 2.49 | 2.98 | 2.53 | 3.04 | — | — | — | — | 2.83 | 3.31 |
| Similarities | 2.73 | 3.30 | 2.95 | 3.54 | 3.04 | 3.66 | — | — | — | — | 3.46 | 4.05 |
| Arithmetic | — | — | 2.95 | 3.54 | 3.04 | 3.66 | — | — | — | — | 3.46 | 4.05 |
| Vocabulary | 2.15 | 2.60 | 2.26 | 2.71 | 2.28 | 2.74 | — | — | — | — | 2.51 | 2.94 |
| Comprehension | 2.78 | 3.36 | 3.01 | 3.61 | 3.11 | 3.74 | — | — | — | — | 3.54 | 4.15 |
| Digit Span | — | — | — | — | 2.28 | 2.74 | — | — | — | — | — | — |
| Picture Completion | 2.79 | 3.37 | 2.92 | 3.50 | 3.02 | 3.64 | 3.08 | 3.71 | 3.21 | 3.80 | 3.38 | 3.96 |
| Coding | — | — | 2.38 | 2.85 | 2.42 | 2.92 | 2.50 | 3.00 | 2.56 | 3.04 | 2.62 | 3.07 |
| Picture Arrangement | 3.21 | 3.88 | 3.43 | 4.11 | 3.58 | 4.31 | 3.63 | 4.37 | 3.80 | 4.51 | 4.07 | 4.76 |
| Block Design | 2.23 | 2.69 | 2.23 | 2.67 | 2.25 | 2.71 | 2.33 | 2.80 | 2.37 | 2.82 | 2.39 | 2.80 |
| Object Assembly | 3.08 | 3.71 | 3.27 | 3.92 | 3.41 | 4.10 | 3.46 | 4.16 | 3.62 | 4.29 | 3.85 | 4.51 |
| Symbol Search | — | — | — | — | 3.02 | 3.64 | — | — | 3.21 | 3.80 | — | — |
| Mazes | — | — | — | — | — | — | 4.25 | 5.12 | 4.48 | 5.31 | — | — |
| | Mean of 11 subtests | | Mean of 11 subtests | | Mean of 11 subtests | | Mean of 12 subtests | | Mean of 12 subtests | | Mean of 13 subtests | |
| Subtest | .05 | .01 | .05 | .01 | .05 | .01 | .05 | .01 | .05 | .01 | .05 | .01 |
| Information | 2.86 | 3.34 | 2.87 | 3.35 | 2.89 | 3.38 | 2.90 | 3.49 | 2.92 | 3.51 | 3.04 | 3.42 |
| Similarities | 3.51 | 4.11 | 3.52 | 4.11 | 3.54 | 4.14 | 3.57 | 4.29 | 3.58 | 4.31 | 3.73 | 4.21 |
| Arithmetic | 3.51 | 4.11 | 3.52 | 4.11 | 3.54 | 4.14 | 3.57 | 4.29 | 3.58 | 4.31 | 3.73 | 4.21 |
| Vocabulary | 2.53 | 2.96 | 2.54 | 2.97 | 2.56 | 3.00 | 2.56 | 3.08 | 2.58 | 3.10 | 2.68 | 3.02 |
| Comprehension | 3.60 | 4.20 | 3.60 | 4.21 | 3.62 | 4.23 | 3.65 | 4.39 | 3.67 | 4.41 | 3.82 | 4.31 |
| Digit Span | 2.53 | 2.96 | — | — | — | — | 2.56 | 3.08 | 2.58 | 3.10 | 2.68 | 3.02 |
| Picture Completion | 3.43 | 4.01 | 3.43 | 4.01 | 3.45 | 4.04 | 3.48 | 4.18 | 3.50 | 4.20 | 3.64 | 4.11 |
| Coding | 2.64 | 3.09 | 2.65 | 3.10 | 2.68 | 3.13 | 2.68 | 3.22 | 2.70 | 3.24 | 2.80 | 3.16 |
| Picture Arrangement | 4.13 | 4.83 | 4.14 | 4.84 | 4.16 | 4.86 | 4.20 | 5.05 | 4.22 | 5.07 | 4.40 | 4.96 |
| Block Design | 2.41 | 2.82 | 2.42 | 2.83 | 2.45 | 2.86 | 2.44 | 2.93 | 2.46 | 2.96 | 2.55 | 2.88 |
| Object Assembly | 3.91 | 4.57 | 3.92 | 4.58 | 3.93 | 4.60 | 3.98 | 4.78 | 3.99 | 4.80 | 4.16 | 4.69 |
| Symbol Search | — | — | 3.43 | 4.01 | — | — | 3.48 | 4.18 | — | — | 3.64 | 4.11 |
| Mazes | — | — | — | — | 4.94 | 5.77 | — | — | 5.02 | 6.03 | 5.24 | 5.91 |

*(Table continues next page)*

**Table L-4 (cont.)**

| Subtest | Mean of 4 subtests[a] | | Mean of 5 subtests[b] | | Mean of 6 subtests[c] | | Mean of 6 subtests | | Mean of 7 subtests | | Mean of 10 subtests | |
|---|---|---|---|---|---|---|---|---|---|---|---|---|
| | .05 | .01 | .05 | .01 | .05 | .01 | .05 | .01 | .05 | .01 | .05 | .01 |
| Information | 2.39 | 2.88 | 2.52 | 3.01 | 2.55 | 3.07 | — | — | — | — | 2.85 | 3.34 |
| Similarities | 2.61 | 3.15 | 2.79 | 3.34 | 2.86 | 3.44 | — | — | — | — | 3.23 | 3.78 |
| Arithmetic | — | — | 2.91 | 3.49 | 3.00 | 3.60 | — | — | — | — | 3.40 | 3.98 |
| Vocabulary | 2.33 | 2.81 | 2.44 | 2.93 | 2.47 | 2.97 | — | — | — | — | 2.75 | 3.22 |
| Comprehension | 3.15 | 3.80 | 3.42 | 4.10 | 3.56 | 4.28 | — | — | — | — | 4.08 | 4.78 |
| Digit Span | — | — | — | — | 2.47 | 2.97 | — | — | — | — | — | — |
| Picture Completion | 3.20 | 3.86 | 3.38 | 4.04 | 3.50 | 4.21 | 3.54 | 4.25 | 3.69 | 4.38 | 3.94 | 4.61 |
| Coding | — | — | 2.45 | 2.94 | 2.47 | 2.97 | 2.52 | 3.04 | 2.58 | 3.06 | 2.65 | 3.10 |
| Picture Arrangement | 3.29 | 3.97 | 3.48 | 4.17 | 3.61 | 4.35 | 3.65 | 4.39 | 3.82 | 4.53 | 4.08 | 4.78 |
| Block Design | 2.45 | 2.96 | 2.45 | 2.94 | 2.47 | 2.97 | 2.52 | 3.04 | 2.58 | 3.06 | 2.65 | 3.10 |
| Object Assembly | 3.37 | 4.07 | 3.58 | 4.29 | 3.73 | 4.48 | 3.76 | 4.52 | 3.94 | 4.67 | 4.22 | 4.94 |
| Symbol Search | — | — | — | — | 3.06 | 3.69 | — | — | 3.22 | 3.82 | — | — |
| Mazes | — | — | — | — | — | — | 3.97 | 4.78 | 4.17 | 4.94 | — | — |

| Subtest | Mean of 11 subtests | | Mean of 11 subtests | | Mean of 11 subtests | | Mean of 12 subtests | | Mean of 12 subtests | | Mean of 13 subtests | |
|---|---|---|---|---|---|---|---|---|---|---|---|---|
| | .05 | .01 | .05 | .01 | .05 | .01 | .05 | .01 | .05 | .01 | .05 | .01 |
| Information | 2.88 | 3.37 | 2.89 | 3.38 | 2.90 | 3.40 | 2.92 | 3.51 | 2.93 | 3.52 | 3.05 | 3.44 |
| Similarities | 3.27 | 3.82 | 3.27 | 3.83 | 3.29 | 3.84 | 3.31 | 3.98 | 3.33 | 4.00 | 3.46 | 3.90 |
| Arithmetic | 3.44 | 4.03 | 3.45 | 4.03 | 3.46 | 4.05 | 3.50 | 4.20 | 3.51 | 4.22 | 3.65 | 4.12 |
| Vocabulary | 2.78 | 3.25 | 2.78 | 3.25 | 2.80 | 3.27 | 2.81 | 3.38 | 2.82 | 3.39 | 2.93 | 3.31 |
| Comprehension | 4.15 | 4.85 | 4.15 | 4.86 | 4.16 | 4.87 | 4.22 | 5.07 | 4.23 | 5.08 | 4.41 | 4.97 |
| Digit Span | 2.78 | 3.25 | — | — | — | — | 2.81 | 3.38 | 2.82 | 3.39 | 2.93 | 3.31 |
| Picture Completion | 4.00 | 4.68 | 4.01 | 4.69 | 4.02 | 4.70 | 4.07 | 4.89 | 4.08 | 4.90 | 4.25 | 4.79 |
| Coding | 2.67 | 3.12 | 2.68 | 3.13 | 2.69 | 3.15 | 2.70 | 3.24 | 2.71 | 3.26 | 2.82 | 3.18 |
| Picture Arrangement | 4.15 | 4.85 | 4.15 | 4.86 | 4.16 | 4.87 | 4.22 | 5.07 | 4.23 | 5.08 | 4.41 | 4.97 |
| Block Design | 2.67 | 3.12 | 2.68 | 3.13 | 2.69 | 3.15 | 2.70 | 3.24 | 2.71 | 3.26 | 2.82 | 3.18 |
| Object Assembly | 4.29 | 5.01 | 4.29 | 5.02 | 4.30 | 5.03 | 4.36 | 5.24 | 4.37 | 5.25 | 4.56 | 5.14 |
| Symbol Search | — | — | 3.45 | 4.03 | — | — | 3.50 | 4.20 | — | — | 3.65 | 4.12 |
| Mazes | — | — | — | — | 4.57 | 5.35 | — | — | 4.64 | 5.58 | 4.85 | 5.46 |

*(Table continues next page)*

**Table L-4 (cont.)**

**Average**

| Subtest | Mean of 4 subtests[a] | | Mean of 5 subtests[b] | | Mean of 6 subtests[c] | | Mean of 6 subtests | | Mean of 7 subtests | | Mean of 10 subtests | |
|---|---|---|---|---|---|---|---|---|---|---|---|---|
| | .05 | .01 | .05 | .01 | .05 | .01 | .05 | .01 | .05 | .01 | .05 | .01 |
| Information | 2.65 | 3.20 | 2.82 | 3.38 | 2.89 | 3.48 | — | — | — | — | 3.25 | 3.80 |
| Similarities | 2.80 | 3.38 | 3.01 | 3.60 | 3.10 | 3.73 | — | — | — | — | 3.50 | 4.10 |
| Arithmetic | — | — | 3.18 | 3.81 | 3.29 | 3.96 | — | — | — | — | 3.74 | 4.38 |
| Vocabulary | 2.48 | 3.00 | 2.63 | 3.15 | 2.67 | 3.22 | — | — | — | — | 2.97 | 3.48 |
| Comprehension | 2.99 | 3.62 | 3.24 | 3.88 | 3.35 | 4.03 | — | — | — | — | 3.81 | 4.46 |
| Digit Span | — | — | — | — | 2.82 | 3.40 | — | — | — | — | — | — |
| Picture Completion | 3.11 | 3.76 | 3.31 | 3.96 | 3.42 | 4.12 | 3.44 | 4.14 | 3.59 | 4.26 | 3.81 | 4.46 |
| Coding | — | — | 3.20 | 3.83 | 3.30 | 3.97 | 3.32 | 3.99 | 3.46 | 4.10 | 3.66 | 4.29 |
| Picture Arrangement | 3.15 | 3.81 | 3.36 | 4.03 | 3.48 | 4.19 | 3.50 | 4.21 | 3.66 | 4.34 | 3.89 | 4.55 |
| Block Design | 2.62 | 3.16 | 2.71 | 3.25 | 2.76 | 3.32 | 2.78 | 3.35 | 2.87 | 3.41 | 2.97 | 3.48 |
| Object Assembly | 3.45 | 4.17 | 3.72 | 4.45 | 3.87 | 4.66 | 3.88 | 4.67 | 4.08 | 4.84 | 4.37 | 5.11 |
| Symbol Search | — | — | — | — | 3.48 | 4.19 | — | — | 3.66 | 4.34 | — | — |
| Mazes | — | — | — | — | — | — | 3.83 | 4.61 | 4.02 | 4.77 | — | — |

| Subtest | Mean of 11 subtests | | Mean of 11 subtests | | Mean of 11 subtests | | Mean of 12 subtests | | Mean of 12 subtests | | Mean of 13 subtests | |
|---|---|---|---|---|---|---|---|---|---|---|---|---|
| | .05 | .01 | .05 | .01 | .05 | .01 | .05 | .01 | .05 | .01 | .05 | .01 |
| Information | 3.29 | 3.85 | 3.30 | 3.86 | 3.30 | 3.86 | 3.34 | 4.01 | 3.34 | 4.02 | 3.48 | 3.92 |
| Similarities | 3.55 | 4.15 | 3.56 | 4.16 | 3.56 | 4.17 | 3.60 | 4.33 | 3.61 | 4.34 | 3.76 | 4.24 |
| Arithmetic | 3.79 | 4.43 | 3.80 | 4.44 | 3.80 | 4.45 | 3.85 | 4.63 | 3.86 | 4.64 | 4.02 | 4.53 |
| Vocabulary | 3.01 | 3.51 | 3.02 | 3.53 | 3.02 | 3.53 | 3.05 | 3.66 | 3.05 | 3.67 | 3.18 | 3.58 |
| Comprehension | 3.87 | 4.52 | 3.88 | 4.53 | 3.88 | 4.54 | 3.93 | 4.73 | 3.94 | 4.73 | 4.10 | 4.63 |
| Digit Span | 3.20 | 3.74 | — | — | — | — | 3.24 | 3.90 | 3.25 | 3.91 | 3.38 | 3.81 |
| Picture Completion | 3.87 | 4.52 | 3.88 | 4.53 | 3.88 | 4.54 | 3.93 | 4.73 | 3.94 | 4.73 | 4.10 | 4.63 |
| Coding | 3.71 | 4.34 | 3.72 | 4.35 | 3.73 | 4.36 | 3.77 | 4.53 | 3.78 | 4.54 | 3.94 | 4.44 |
| Picture Arrangement | 3.95 | 4.61 | 3.95 | 4.62 | 3.96 | 4.63 | 4.01 | 4.82 | 4.01 | 4.83 | 4.19 | 4.72 |
| Block Design | 3.01 | 3.51 | 3.02 | 3.53 | 3.02 | 3.53 | 3.05 | 3.66 | 3.05 | 3.67 | 3.18 | 3.58 |
| Object Assembly | 4.44 | 5.19 | 4.45 | 5.20 | 4.45 | 5.20 | 4.52 | 5.43 | 4.52 | 5.43 | 4.72 | 5.32 |
| Symbol Search | — | — | 3.95 | 4.62 | — | — | 4.01 | 4.82 | — | — | 4.19 | 4.72 |
| Mazes | — | — | — | — | 4.38 | 5.13 | — | — | 4.45 | 5.35 | 4.65 | 5.24 |

*Note.* Table L-4 shows the minimum deviations from an individual's average subtest scaled score that are significant at the .05 and .01 levels. See the note in Table C-3 (page 815) for an explanation of the method used to obtain the deviations.

[a] In this column, the entries for Information, Similarities, Vocabulary, and Comprehension are compared to the mean of these four subtests. Similarly, the entries for Picture Completion, Picture Arrangement, Block Design, and Object Assembly are compared to the mean of these four subtests.

[b] In this column, the entries for Information, Similarities, Arithmetic, Vocabulary, and Comprehension are compared to the mean of these five subtests. Similarly, the entries for Picture Completion, Coding, Picture Arrangement, Block Design, and Object Assembly are compared to the mean of these five subtests.

[c] In this column, the entries for Information, Similarities, Arithmetic, Vocabulary, Comprehension, and Digit Span are compared to the mean of these six subtests. Similarly, the entries for Picture Completion, Coding, Picture Arrangement, Block Design, Object Assembly, and Symbol Search are compared to the mean of these six subtests.

**Table L-5**
**Differences Required for Significance When Each WISC-III Subtest Scaled Score Is Compared to the Respective Mean Factor Scaled Score for Any Individual Child**

| Subtest | Mean of Verbal Comprehension subtests | | Mean of Perceptual Organization subtests | | Mean of Processing Speed subtests | |
|---|---|---|---|---|---|---|
| | .05 | .01 | .05 | .01 | .05 | .01 |
| Information | 2.69 | 3.26 | — | — | — | — |
| Similarities | 2.79 | 3.38 | — | — | — | — |
| Arithmetic | — | — | — | — | — | — |
| Vocabulary | 2.48 | 3.01 | — | — | — | — |
| Comprehension | 3.02 | 3.65 | — | — | — | — |
| Digit Span | — | — | — | — | — | — |
| Picture Completion | — | — | 2.80 | 3.43 | — | — |
| Coding | — | — | — | — | 2.30 | 2.88 |
| Picture Arrangement | — | — | — | — | — | — |
| Block Design | — | — | 2.49 | 3.05 | — | — |
| Object Assembly | — | — | 3.03 | 3.71 | — | — |
| Symbol Search | — | — | — | — | 2.30 | 2.88 |
| Mazes | — | — | — | — | — | — |

*Note*. Table L-5 shows the minimum deviations from an individual's mean factor scaled score that are significant at the .05 and .01 levels. See Note in Table C-3 (page 815) in Appendix C for an explanation of how differences were obtained. The following Bonferroni corrections were used: .05 = 2.500, .01 = 3.025 for Verbal Comprehension; .05 = 2.39, .01 = 2.93 for Perceptual Organization; .05 = 2.24, .01 = 2.81 for Processing Speed. The values in this table are based on the total sample.

**Table L-6**
**Estimates of the Differences Obtained by Various Percentages of the WISC-III Standardization Sample When Each WISC-III Subtest Scaled Score is Compared to the Mean Scaled Score for Any Individual Child**

| Subtest | Verbal average (5 subtests) | | | | Verbal average (6 subtests) | | | | | | | |
|---|---|---|---|---|---|---|---|---|---|---|---|---|
| | 10% | 5% | 2% | 1% | 10% | 5% | 2% | 1% | | | | |
| Information | 2.62 | 3.12 | 3.70 | 4.10 | 2.80 | 3.33 | 3.96 | 4.39 | | | | |
| Similarities | 2.62 | 3.12 | 3.70 | 4.10 | 2.80 | 3.33 | 3.96 | 4.39 | | | | |
| Arithmetic | 3.23 | 3.84 | 4.57 | 5.06 | 3.17 | 3.76 | 4.47 | 4.95 | | | | |
| Vocabulary | 2.48 | 2.94 | 3.50 | 3.87 | 2.66 | 3.16 | 3.75 | 4.15 | | | | |
| Comprehension | 3.02 | 3.59 | 4.26 | 4.72 | 3.17 | 3.76 | 4.47 | 4.95 | | | | |
| Digit Span | – | – | – | – | 4.08 | 4.84 | 5.76 | 6.37 | | | | |

| Subtest | Performance average (5 subtests) | | | | Performance average (6 subtests) | | | | Performance average (6 subtests) | | | |
|---|---|---|---|---|---|---|---|---|---|---|---|---|
| | 10% | 5% | 2% | 1% | 10% | 5% | 2% | 1% | 10% | 5% | 2% | 1% |
| Picture Completion | 3.42 | 4.06 | 4.82 | 5.34 | 3.58 | 4.25 | 5.06 | 5.60 | 3.53 | 4.19 | 4.99 | 5.52 |
| Coding | 4.17 | 4.96 | 5.89 | 6.53 | 4.01 | 4.76 | 5.66 | 6.27 | 4.24 | 5.04 | 5.99 | 6.63 |
| Picture Arrangement | 3.60 | 4.27 | 5.08 | 5.62 | 3.70 | 4.39 | 5.22 | 5.78 | 3.70 | 4.39 | 5.22 | 5.78 |
| Block Design | 3.04 | 3.61 | 4.29 | 4.75 | 3.14 | 3.72 | 4.43 | 4.90 | 3.14 | 3.72 | 4.43 | 4.90 |
| Object Assembly | 3.18 | 3.78 | 4.50 | 4.98 | 3.35 | 3.98 | 4.73 | 5.24 | 3.28 | 3.90 | 4.64 | 5.13 |
| Symbol Search | – | – | – | – | 3.40 | 4.04 | 4.80 | 5.31 | – | – | – | – |
| Mazes | – | – | – | – | – | – | – | – | 4.14 | 4.92 | 5.85 | 6.48 |

| Subtest | Full Scale average (10 subtests) | | | | Full Scale average (11 subtests) | | | | Full Scale average (11 subtests) | | | |
|---|---|---|---|---|---|---|---|---|---|---|---|---|
| | 10% | 5% | 2% | 1% | 10% | 5% | 2% | 1% | 10% | 5% | 2% | 1% |
| Information | 3.10 | 3.68 | 4.38 | 4.85 | 3.15 | 3.74 | 4.45 | 4.93 | 3.20 | 3.80 | 4.52 | 5.01 |
| Similarities | 3.12 | 3.70 | 4.40 | 4.88 | 3.17 | 3.76 | 4.47 | 4.95 | 3.22 | 3.82 | 4.52 | 5.03 |
| Arithmetic | 3.42 | 4.06 | 4.82 | 5.34 | 3.37 | 4.00 | 4.75 | 5.26 | 3.43 | 4.08 | 4.85 | 5.37 |
| Vocabulary | 3.04 | 3.61 | 4.29 | 4.75 | 3.09 | 3.67 | 4.36 | 4.82 | 3.14 | 3.72 | 4.43 | 4.90 |
| Comprehension | 3.47 | 4.12 | 4.89 | 5.42 | 3.50 | 4.16 | 4.94 | 5.47 | 3.51 | 4.17 | 4.96 | 5.50 |
| Digit Span | – | – | – | – | 4.22 | 5.02 | 5.96 | 6.60 | – | – | – | – |
| Picture Completion | 3.65 | 4.33 | 5.15 | 5.70 | 3.70 | 4.39 | 5.22 | 5.78 | 3.70 | 4.39 | 5.22 | 5.78 |
| Coding | 4.57 | 5.43 | 6.45 | 7.15 | 4.54 | 5.39 | 6.41 | 7.10 | 4.44 | 5.27 | 6.27 | 6.94 |
| Picture Arrangement | 3.89 | 4.63 | 5.50 | 6.09 | 3.94 | 4.68 | 5.57 | 6.17 | 3.91 | 4.65 | 5.52 | 6.11 |
| Block Design | 3.33 | 3.96 | 4.71 | 5.21 | 3.37 | 4.00 | 4.75 | 5.26 | 3.33 | 3.96 | 4.71 | 5.21 |
| Object Assembly | 3.66 | 4.35 | 5.17 | 5.73 | 3.71 | 4.41 | 5.24 | 5.81 | 3.68 | 4.37 | 5.20 | 5.75 |
| Symbol Search | – | – | – | – | – | – | – | – | 3.81 | 4.53 | 5.38 | 5.96 |
| Mazes | – | – | – | – | – | – | – | – | – | – | – | – |

(Table continues next page)

**Table L-6 (cont.)**

| Subtest | Full Scale average (11 subtests) | | | | Full Scale average (12 subtests) | | | | Full Scale average (12 subtests) | | | |
|---|---|---|---|---|---|---|---|---|---|---|---|---|
| | 10% | 5% | 2% | 1% | 10% | 5% | 2% | 1% | 10% | 5% | 2% | 1% |
| Information | 3.20 | 3.80 | 4.52 | 5.01 | 3.23 | 3.84 | 4.57 | 5.06 | 3.23 | 3.84 | 4.57 | 5.06 |
| Similarities | 3.22 | 3.82 | 4.54 | 5.03 | 3.23 | 3.84 | 4.57 | 5.06 | 3.25 | 3.86 | 4.59 | 5.08 |
| Arithmetic | 3.45 | 4.10 | 4.87 | 5.39 | 3.38 | 4.02 | 4.78 | 5.29 | 3.42 | 4.06 | 4.82 | 5.34 |
| Vocabulary | 3.15 | 3.74 | 4.45 | 4.93 | 3.17 | 3.76 | 4.47 | 4.95 | 3.18 | 3.78 | 4.50 | 4.98 |
| Comprehension | 3.53 | 4.19 | 4.99 | 5.52 | 3.55 | 4.21 | 5.01 | 5.55 | 3.56 | 4.23 | 5.03 | 5.57 |
| Digit Span | — | — | — | — | 4.24 | 5.04 | 5.99 | 6.63 | 4.24 | 5.04 | 5.99 | 6.63 |
| Picture Completion | 3.66 | 4.35 | 5.17 | 5.73 | 3.73 | 4.43 | 5.27 | 5.83 | 3.71 | 4.41 | 5.24 | 5.80 |
| Coding | 4.54 | 5.39 | 6.41 | 7.10 | 4.42 | 5.25 | 6.24 | 6.91 | 4.52 | 5.37 | 6.38 | 7.07 |
| Picture Arrangement | 3.89 | 4.63 | 5.50 | 6.09 | 3.94 | 4.68 | 5.57 | 6.17 | 3.94 | 4.68 | 5.57 | 6.17 |
| Block Design | 3.32 | 3.94 | 4.68 | 5.19 | 3.37 | 4.00 | 4.57 | 5.26 | 3.37 | 4.00 | 4.75 | 5.26 |
| Object Assembly | 3.65 | 4.33 | 5.15 | 5.70 | 3.71 | 4.41 | 5.24 | 5.80 | 3.68 | 4.37 | 5.20 | 5.75 |
| Symbol Search | — | — | — | — | 3.81 | 4.53 | 5.38 | 5.96 | — | — | — | — |
| Mazes | 4.64 | 5.51 | 6.55 | 7.25 | — | — | — | — | 4.64 | 5.51 | 6.55 | 7.25 |

| Subtest | Full Scale average (13 subtests) | | | |
|---|---|---|---|---|
| | 10% | 5% | 2% | 1% |
| Information | 3.30 | 3.92 | 4.66 | 5.16 |
| Similarities | 3.32 | 3.94 | 4.68 | 5.19 |
| Arithmetic | 3.43 | 4.08 | 4.85 | 5.37 |
| Vocabulary | 3.25 | 3.86 | 4.59 | 5.08 |
| Comprehension | 3.56 | 4.23 | 5.03 | 5.57 |
| Digit Span | 4.26 | 5.06 | 6.01 | 6.66 |
| Picture Completion | 3.73 | 4.43 | 5.27 | 5.83 |
| Coding | 4.41 | 5.23 | 6.22 | 6.89 |
| Picture Arrangement | 3.94 | 4.68 | 5.57 | 6.17 |
| Block Design | 3.35 | 3.98 | 4.73 | 5.24 |
| Object Assembly | 3.70 | 4.39 | 5.22 | 5.78 |
| Symbol Search | 3.81 | 4.53 | 5.38 | 5.96 |
| Mazes | 4.64 | 5.51 | 6.55 | 7.25 |

*Note.* The formula used to obtain the values in this table was obtained from Silverstein (1984):

$$SD_{Da} = 3\sqrt{1 + \overline{G} - 2\,\overline{T}_a}$$

where $SD_{Da}$ is the standard deviation of the difference for subtest a, 3 is the standard deviation of the scaled scores on each of the subtests, $\overline{G}$ is the mean of all the elements in the matrix (including the diagonal), and $\overline{T}_a$ is the mean of the elements in row or column a of the matrix (again including the diagonal).

**Table L-7**
**Estimates of the Probability of Obtaining Designated Differences Between Individual WISC-III Verbal and Performance IQs by Chance**

| Probability of obtaining given or greater discrepancy by chance | Age level 6 | 7 | 8 | 9 | 10 | 11 | 12 | 13 | 14 | 15 | 16 | Av.[a] |
|---|---|---|---|---|---|---|---|---|---|---|---|---|
| .50 | 4.02 | 4.26 | 3.76 | 4.02 | 3.76 | 3.89 | 3.76 | 4.02 | 4.02 | 3.18 | 3.62 | 3.76 |
| .25 | 6.90 | 7.32 | 6.45 | 6.90 | 6.45 | 6.68 | 6.45 | 6.90 | 6.90 | 5.45 | 6.22 | 6.45 |
| .20 | 7.68 | 8.15 | 7.18 | 7.68 | 7.18 | 7.44 | 7.18 | 7.68 | 7.68 | 6.07 | 6.92 | 7.18 |
| .10 | 9.90 | 10.50 | 9.26 | 9.90 | 9.26 | 9.59 | 9.26 | 9.90 | 9.90 | 7.83 | 8.92 | 9.26 |
| .05 | 11.76 | 12.47 | 11.00 | 11.76 | 11.00 | 11.39 | 11.00 | 11.76 | 11.76 | 9.30 | 10.60 | 11.00 |
| .02 | 13.98 | 14.83 | 13.08 | 13.98 | 13.08 | 13.54 | 13.08 | 13.98 | 13.98 | 11.05 | 12.60 | 13.08 |
| .01 | 15.48 | 16.42 | 14.48 | 15.48 | 14.48 | 14.99 | 14.48 | 15.48 | 15.48 | 12.24 | 13.95 | 14.48 |
| .001 | 19.74 | 20.94 | 18.47 | 19.74 | 18.47 | 19.11 | 18.47 | 19.74 | 19.74 | 15.61 | 17.79 | 18.47 |

*Note.* Table L-7 is entered in the column appropriate to the examinee's age. The discrepancy that is just less than the discrepancy obtained by the examinee is located. The entry in the first column in the same row gives the probability of obtaining a given or greater discrepancy by chance. For example, the hypothesis that a 6-year-old examinee obtained a Verbal-Performance discrepancy of 17 by chance can be rejected at the .01 level of significance. Table L-7 is two-tailed. See Chapter 8, Exhibit 8-1 (page 168) for an explanation of the method used to arrive at magnitude of differences.
[a] Av. = Average of 11 age groups.

**Table L-8**
**Estimates of the Percentage of the Population Obtaining Discrepancies Between WISC-III Verbal and Performance IQs**

| Percentage obtaining given or greater discrepancy in either direction | Age level 6 | 7 | 8 | 9 | 10 | 11 | 12 | 13 | 14 | 15 | 16 | Av.[a] | Percentage obtaining given or greater discrepancy in a specific direction |
|---|---|---|---|---|---|---|---|---|---|---|---|---|---|
| 50 | 8.41 | 9.32 | 7.78 | 8.16 | 8.65 | 8.76 | 8.29 | 8.53 | 8.76 | 6.96 | 8.29 | 8.29 | 25 |
| 25 | 14.43 | 16.00 | 13.36 | 14.01 | 14.84 | 15.04 | 14.22 | 14.64 | 15.04 | 11.95 | 14.22 | 14.22 | 12.5 |
| 20 | 16.06 | 17.81 | 14.87 | 15.60 | 16.52 | 16.74 | 15.83 | 16.29 | 16.74 | 13.30 | 15.83 | 15.83 | 10 |
| 10 | 20.71 | 22.95 | 19.17 | 20.11 | 21.29 | 21.58 | 20.41 | 21.00 | 21.58 | 17.15 | 20.41 | 20.41 | 5 |
| 5 | 24.60 | 27.26 | 22.77 | 23.88 | 25.29 | 25.63 | 24.24 | 24.95 | 25.63 | 20.37 | 24.24 | 24.24 | 2.5 |
| 2 | 29.24 | 32.41 | 27.07 | 28.39 | 30.07 | 30.47 | 28.82 | 29.66 | 30.47 | 24.21 | 28.82 | 28.82 | 1 |
| 1 | 32.38 | 35.89 | 29.98 | 31.44 | 33.29 | 33.74 | 31.91 | 32.84 | 33.74 | 26.81 | 31.91 | 31.91 | .5 |
| .1 | 41.29 | 45.77 | 38.23 | 40.09 | 42.45 | 43.02 | 40.70 | 41.87 | 43.02 | 34.19 | 40.70 | 40.70 | .05 |

*Note.* Table L-8 is entered in the column appropriate to the examinee's age. The discrepancy that is just less than the discrepancy obtained by the examinee is located. The entry in the first column in the same row gives the percentage of the standardization population obtaining discrepancies as large as or larger than the located discrepancy. For example, a 6-year-old examinee with a Verbal-Performance discrepancy of 14 on the WISC-III will be found in between 25 and 50 percent of the standardization population. However, a Verbal-Performance discrepancy of 14 in one direction only (that is, Verbal > Performance *or* Performance > Verbal) will be found in between 12.5 and 25 percent of the standardization population.

The method used to compute the discrepancy between the Verbal and Performance Scale IQs that reflects the percentage of the population obtaining the discrepancy is as follows: Discrepancy $= \sigma_1 z \sqrt{2 - 2r_{xy}}$. The first term is the standard deviation of the test, the second is the selected $z$ value, and the last is the correlation between the two scales. For example, for a 6-year-old child, the discrepancy between the WISC-III Verbal and Performance Scale IQs that represents 5 percent of the population is $15(1.96)\sqrt{2 - 2(.65)} = 24.60$.
[a] Av. = Average of 11 age groups.

**Table L-9**
**Estimates of the Probability of Obtaining Designated Differences Between Individual WISC-III Factor Score Deviation Quotients (DQs) by Chance**

| Probability of obtaining given or greater discrepancy by chance | Verbal Comprehension DQ vs. Perceptual Organization DQ | Verbal Comprehension DQ vs. Processing Speed DQ | Perceptual Organization DQ vs. Processing Speed DQ |
|---|---|---|---|
| .50 | 4.12 | 4.88 | 5.34 |
| .25 | 7.07 | 8.38 | 9.16 |
| .20 | 7.87 | 9.33 | 10.20 |
| .10 | 10.14 | 12.02 | 13.14 |
| .05 | 12.05 | 14.28 | 15.61 |
| .02 | 14.32 | 16.98 | 18.56 |
| .01 | 15.86 | 18.80 | 20.55 |
| .001 | 20.23 | 23.97 | 26.21 |

*Note.* The values in Table L-9 are based on the total group. The discrepancy that is just less than the discrepancy obtained by the examinee is located. The entry in the first column in the same row gives the probability of obtaining a given or greater discrepancy by chance. For example, the hypothesis that an examinee obtained a Verbal Comprehension–Perceptual Organization discrepancy of 12 by chance can be rejected at the .10 level of significance. Table L-9 is two-tailed. See Chapter 8, Exhibit 8-1 (page 168) for an explanation of the method used to arrive at the magnitude of differences.

**Table L-10**
**Estimates of the Percentage of the Population Obtaining Discrepancies Between WISC-III Factor Deviation Quotients (DQs)**

| Percentage obtaining given or greater discrepancy in either direction | Verbal Comprehension DQ vs. Perceptual Organization DQ | Verbal Comprehension DQ vs. Processing Speed DQ | Perceptual Organization DQ vs. Processing Speed DQ | Percentage obtaining given or greater discrepancy in a specific direction |
|---|---|---|---|---|
| 50 | 8.94 | 11.13 | 10.79 | 25 |
| 25 | 15.34 | 19.11 | 18.52 | 12.5 |
| 20 | 17.08 | 21.27 | 20.62 | 10 |
| 10 | 22.01 | 27.42 | 26.58 | 5 |
| 5 | 26.15 | 32.57 | 31.57 | 2.5 |
| 2 | 31.09 | 38.72 | 37.53 | 1 |
| 1 | 34.42 | 42.87 | 41.56 | .5 |
| .1 | 43.90 | 54.67 | 53.00 | .05 |

*Note.* The procedure used to calculate the values in this table is similar to that used by Clampitt, Adair, & Strenio (1983). The $z$ values used were as follows: $z = .67$ for 50%, $z = 1.15$ for 25%, $z = 1.28$ for 20%, $z = 1.65$ for 10%, $z = 1.96$ for 5%, $z = 2.33$ for 2%, $z = 2.58$ for 1%, $z = 3.29$ for .1%. Values in this table are based on the total group.

Verbal Comprehension subtests are Information, Similarities, Vocabulary, and Comprehension. Perceptual Organization subtests are Picture Completion, Block Design, and Object Assembly. Processing Speed subtests are Coding and Symbol Search.

**Table L-11**
**Reliability and Validity Coefficients of Proposed WISC-III Short Forms**

| Dyad | | | | Triad | | | | | Tetrad | | | | | Pentad | | | | | | |
|---|---|---|---|---|---|---|---|---|---|---|---|---|---|---|---|---|---|---|---|---|
| Short form | | $r_{tt}$ | $r$ | Short form | | | $r_{tt}$ | $r$ | Short form | | | | $r_{tt}$ | $r$ | Short form | | | | | $r_{tt}$ | $r$ |
| I | V | .915 | .803 | I | V | BD | .933 | .881 | I | S | V | BD | .944 | .886 | I | S | A | V | BD | .949 | .899 |
| V | BD | .911 | .862 | I | S | V | .932 | .829 | I | A | V | BD | .939 | .895 | I | S | V | C | BD | .949 | .889 |
| S | V | .905 | .802 | S | V | BD | .928 | .878 | I | S | V | C | .939 | .839 | I | S | V | DS | BD | .948 | .899 |
| I | BD | .902 | .848 | I | V | DS | .924 | .827 | I | V | DS | BD | .939 | .890 | I | S | V | PC | BD | .947 | .898 |
| V | DS | .896 | .764 | I | V | C | .924 | .821 | I | S | A | V | .939 | .860 | I | A | V | DS | BD | .945 | .899 |
| I | S | .895 | .802 | I | S | BD | .923 | .874 | I | S | V | DS | .938 | .852 | I | S | A | V | C | .945 | .867 |
| DS | BD | .894 | .760 | I | A | V | .923 | .847 | I | V | C | BD | .938 | .885 | I | S | A | V | DS | .945 | .872 |
| S | BD | .893 | .842 | V | DS | BD | .922 | .864 | S | A | V | BD | .936 | .895 | I | A | V | C | BD | .945 | .901 |
| V | C | .890 | .777 | A | V | BD | .921 | .884 | I | V | PC | BD | .936 | .889 | I | S | V | PA | BD | .944 | .902 |
| A | V | .886 | .825 | S | V | C | .920 | .816 | S | V | C | BD | .935 | .881 | I | S | V | C | DS | .944 | .863 |

*Note.* Abbreviations: I = Information, V = Vocabulary, BD = Block Design, S = Similarities, DS = Digit Span, A = Arithmetic, PC = Picture Completion, PA = Picture Arrangement, SS = Symbol Search, C = Comprehension.

It is recommended that short-form combinations involving Digit Span or Symbol Search not be used because these two subtests were not used in the construction of the IQ tables.

For screening children who have severe hearing problems, the best two-subtest short-form combinations are Picture Completion and Block Design ($r_{tt}$ = .882, $r$ = .777), followed by Block Design and Symbol Search ($r_{tt}$ = .872, $r$ = .784) and Picture Arrangement and Block Design ($r_{tt}$ = .869, $r$ = .777); the best three-subtest short-form combinations are Coding, Block Design, and Symbol Search ($r_{tt}$ = .895, $r$ = .765); Picture Completion, Block Design, and Symbol Search ($r_{tt}$ = .893, $r$ = .830); Picture Completion, Picture Arrangement, and Block Design ($r_{tt}$ = .893, $r$ = .817); and Picture Completion, Block Design, and Object Assembly ($r_{tt}$ = .893, $r$ = .794).

For screening children with severe visual deficits, any of the short-form combinations shown in the table involving subtests in the Verbal Scale can be used, such as Information and Vocabulary or Similarities and Vocabulary.

Tables L-12, L-13, L-14, and L-15 provide estimated Deviation Quotients associated with the ten best dyads, triads, tetrads, and pentads, respectively.

This table was constructed using a computer program developed by L. Atkinson and G. Yoshida (1989), "A BASIC Program for Determining Reliability and Validity of Subtest Combination Short Forms," *Educational and Psychological Measurement, 49*, 141–143. The program is based on formulas provided by Tellegen and Briggs (1967).

**Table L-12**
**Estimated WISC-III Full Scale Deviation Quotients for Sum of Scaled Scores for Ten Best Short-Form Dyads**

| | Combination | | | | Combination | | |
|---|---|---|---|---|---|---|---|
| Sum of scaled scores | Col. 1[a] V + DS DS + BD | Col. 2[b] V + BD I + BD S + BD | Col. 3 I + V S + V I + S V + C A + V | Sum of scaled scores | Col. 1[a] V + DS DS + BD | Col. 2[b] V + BD I + BD S + BD | Col. 3 I + V S + V I + S V + C A + V |
| | | | | 20 | 100 | 100 | 100 |
| | | | | 21 | 103 | 103 | 103 |
| 2 | 45 | 48 | 51 | 22 | 106 | 106 | 105 |
| 3 | 48 | 51 | 54 | 23 | 109 | 109 | 108 |
| 4 | 51 | 54 | 57 | 24 | 112 | 112 | 111 |
| 5 | 54 | 56 | 59 | 25 | 115 | 115 | 114 |
| 6 | 57 | 59 | 62 | 26 | 118 | 117 | 116 |
| 7 | 60 | 62 | 65 | 27 | 121 | 120 | 119 |
| 8 | 63 | 65 | 67 | 28 | 124 | 123 | 122 |
| 9 | 67 | 68 | 70 | 29 | 127 | 126 | 124 |
| 10 | 70 | 71 | 73 | 30 | 130 | 129 | 127 |
| 11 | 73 | 74 | 76 | 31 | 133 | 132 | 130 |
| 12 | 76 | 77 | 78 | 32 | 137 | 135 | 133 |
| 13 | 79 | 80 | 81 | 33 | 140 | 138 | 135 |
| 14 | 82 | 83 | 84 | 34 | 143 | 141 | 138 |
| 15 | 85 | 85 | 86 | 35 | 146 | 144 | 141 |
| 16 | 88 | 88 | 89 | 36 | 149 | 146 | 143 |
| 17 | 91 | 91 | 92 | 37 | 152 | 149 | 146 |
| 18 | 94 | 94 | 95 | 38 | 155 | 152 | 149 |
| 19 | 97 | 97 | 97 | | | | |

*Note.* Abbreviations: V = Vocabulary, DS = Digit Span, BD = Block Design, I = Information, S = Similarities, CD = Coding, SS = Symbol Search, C = Comprehension, A = Arithmetic, PC = Picture Completion, PA = Picture Arrangement.

Reliability and validity coefficients associated with each short-form combination for the ten best dyads are shown in Table L-11. See Exhibit I-4 in Appendix I for an explanation of the procedure used to obtain the estimated Deviation Quotients.

[a] This column can also be used for the PC + BD combination and for the PA + BD combination useful for screening hard-of-hearing children.

[b] This column can also be used for the BD + SS combination useful for screening hard-of-hearing children and for the I + PC combination useful for a rapid screening.

**Table L-I3**
**Estimated WISC-III Full Scale Deviation Quotients for Sum of Scaled Scores for Ten Best Short-Form Triads and Perceptual Organization Factor Score**

| | Combination | | | | | Combination | | | |
|---|---|---|---|---|---|---|---|---|---|
| | Col. 1[a] | Col. 2[b] | Col. 3 | Col. 4 | | Col. 1[a] | Col. 2[b] | Col. 3 | Col. 4 |
| Sum of scaled scores | V+DS+BD | I+V+DS | I + V +BD<br>S + V +BD<br>I + S +BD<br>A + V +BD<br>PC+BD+OA[c] | I+S+V<br>I+V+C<br>I+A+C<br>S+V+C | Sum of scaled scores | V+DS+BD | I+V+DS | I + V +BD<br>S + V +BD<br>I + S +BD<br>A + V +BD<br>PC+BD+OA[c] | I+S+V<br>I+V+C<br>I+A+C<br>S+V+C |
| | | | | | 30 | 100 | 100 | 100 | 100 |
| | | | | | 31 | 102 | 102 | 102 | 102 |
| | | | | | 32 | 104 | 104 | 104 | 104 |
| 3 | 41 | 44 | 46 | 48 | 33 | 107 | 106 | 106 | 106 |
| 4 | 43 | 46 | 48 | 49 | 34 | 109 | 108 | 108 | 108 |
| 5 | 45 | 48 | 50 | 51 | 35 | 111 | 110 | 110 | 110 |
| 6 | 48 | 50 | 52 | 53 | 36 | 113 | 112 | 112 | 112 |
| 7 | 50 | 52 | 54 | 55 | 37 | 115 | 115 | 114 | 114 |
| 8 | 52 | 54 | 56 | 57 | 38 | 117 | 117 | 116 | 116 |
| 9 | 54 | 56 | 58 | 59 | 39 | 120 | 119 | 118 | 117 |
| 10 | 56 | 58 | 60 | 61 | 40 | 122 | 121 | 120 | 119 |
| 11 | 59 | 60 | 62 | 63 | 41 | 124 | 123 | 122 | 121 |
| 12 | 61 | 63 | 64 | 65 | 42 | 126 | 125 | 124 | 123 |
| 13 | 63 | 65 | 66 | 67 | 43 | 128 | 127 | 126 | 125 |
| 14 | 65 | 67 | 68 | 69 | 44 | 131 | 129 | 128 | 127 |
| 15 | 67 | 69 | 70 | 71 | 45 | 133 | 131 | 130 | 129 |
| 16 | 69 | 71 | 72 | 73 | 46 | 135 | 133 | 132 | 131 |
| 17 | 72 | 73 | 74 | 75 | 47 | 137 | 135 | 134 | 133 |
| 18 | 74 | 75 | 76 | 77 | 48 | 139 | 137 | 136 | 135 |
| 19 | 76 | 77 | 78 | 79 | 49 | 141 | 140 | 138 | 137 |
| 20 | 78 | 79 | 80 | 81 | 50 | 144 | 142 | 140 | 139 |
| 21 | 80 | 81 | 82 | 83 | 51 | 146 | 144 | 142 | 141 |
| 22 | 83 | 83 | 84 | 84 | 52 | 148 | 146 | 144 | 143 |
| 23 | 85 | 85 | 86 | 86 | 53 | 150 | 148 | 146 | 145 |
| 24 | 87 | 88 | 88 | 88 | 54 | 152 | 150 | 148 | 147 |
| 25 | 89 | 90 | 90 | 90 | 55 | 155 | 152 | 150 | 149 |
| 26 | 91 | 92 | 92 | 92 | 56 | 157 | 154 | 152 | 151 |
| 27 | 93 | 94 | 94 | 94 | 57 | 159 | 156 | 154 | 152 |
| 28 | 96 | 96 | 96 | 96 | 58 | 161 | 158 | 156 | 154 |
| 29 | 98 | 98 | 98 | 98 | | | | | |

*Note.* Abbreviations: V = Vocabulary, DS = Digit Span, BD = Block Design, I = Information, S = Similarities, A = Arithmetic, PC = Picture Completion, OA = Object Assembly, C = Comprehension, CD = Coding, SS = Symbol Search, PA = Picture Arrangement.

Reliability and validity coefficients associated with each short-form combination for the ten best triads are shown in Table L-11. See Exhibit I-4 in Appendix I for an explanation of the procedure used to obtain the estimated Deviation Quotients.

[a] This column can also be used for the CD + BD + SS combination useful for screening hard-of-hearing children.

[b] This column can also be used for the PC + BD + SS combination and for the PC + PA + BD combination useful for screening hard-of-hearing children.

[c] The Perceptual Organization factor score is formed by PC + BD + OA. This combination is also useful for screening hard-of-hearing children.

**Table L-14**
**Estimated WISC-III Full Scale Deviation Quotients for Sum of Scaled Scores for Ten Best Short-Form Tetrads**

| | Combination | | | Combination | |
|---|---|---|---|---|---|
| | Col. 1[a] | Col. 2 | | Col. 1[a] | Col. 2 |
| Sum of scaled scores | $I+V+DS+BD$<br>$I+S+V+DS$<br>$I+V+PC+BD$ | $I+S+V+BD$<br>$I+A+V+BD$<br>$I+S+V+C$<br>$I+S+A+V$<br>$I+V+C+BD$<br>$S+A+V+BD$<br>$S+V+C+BD$ | Sum of scaled scores | $I+V+DS+BD$<br>$I+S+V+DS$<br>$I+V+PC+BD$ | $I+S+V+BD$<br>$I+A+V+BD$<br>$I+S+V+C^b$<br>$I+S+A+V$<br>$I+V+C+BD$<br>$S+A+V+BD$<br>$S+V+C+BD$ |
| | | | 40 | 100 | 100 |
| | | | 41 | 102 | 102 |
| | | | 42 | 103 | 103 |
| | | | 43 | 105 | 105 |
| 4 | 44 | 45 | 44 | 106 | 106 |
| 5 | 45 | 46 | 45 | 108 | 108 |
| 6 | 47 | 48 | 46 | 109 | 109 |
| 7 | 48 | 49 | 47 | 111 | 111 |
| 8 | 50 | 51 | 48 | 113 | 112 |
| 9 | 51 | 52 | 49 | 114 | 114 |
| 10 | 53 | 54 | 50 | 116 | 115 |
| 11 | 55 | 55 | 51 | 117 | 117 |
| 12 | 56 | 57 | 52 | 119 | 118 |
| 13 | 58 | 58 | 53 | 120 | 120 |
| 14 | 59 | 60 | 54 | 122 | 122 |
| 15 | 61 | 61 | 55 | 124 | 123 |
| 16 | 62 | 63 | 56 | 125 | 125 |
| 17 | 64 | 65 | 57 | 127 | 126 |
| 18 | 65 | 66 | 58 | 128 | 128 |
| 19 | 67 | 68 | 59 | 130 | 129 |
| 20 | 69 | 69 | 60 | 131 | 131 |
| 21 | 70 | 71 | 61 | 133 | 132 |
| 22 | 72 | 72 | 62 | 135 | 134 |
| 23 | 73 | 74 | 63 | 136 | 135 |
| 24 | 75 | 75 | 64 | 138 | 137 |
| 25 | 76 | 77 | 65 | 139 | 139 |
| 26 | 78 | 78 | 66 | 141 | 140 |
| 27 | 80 | 80 | 67 | 142 | 142 |
| 28 | 81 | 82 | 68 | 144 | 143 |
| 29 | 83 | 83 | 69 | 145 | 145 |

(Table continues next page)

**Table L-14 (cont.)**

| Sum of scaled scores | Combination | | Sum of scaled scores | Combination | |
|---|---|---|---|---|---|
| | Col. 1[a] | Col. 2 | | Col. 1[a] | Col. 2 |
| | $I+V+DS+BD$ $I+S+V+DS$ $I+V+PC+BD$ | $I+S+V+BD$ $I+A+V+BD$ $I+S+V+C$ $I+S+A+V$ $I+V+C+BD$ $S+A+V+BD$ $S+V+C+BD$ | | $I+V+DS+BD$ $I+S+V+DS$ $I+V+PC+BD$ | $I+S+V+BD$ $I+A+V+BD$ $I+S+V+C^{b}$ $I+S+A+V$ $I+V+C+BD$ $S+A+V+BD$ $S+V+C+BD$ |
| 30 | 84 | 85 | 70 | 147 | 146 |
| 31 | 86 | 86 | 71 | 149 | 148 |
| 32 | 87 | 88 | 72 | 150 | 149 |
| 33 | 89 | 89 | 73 | 152 | 151 |
| 34 | 91 | 91 | 74 | 153 | 152 |
| 35 | 92 | 92 | 75 | 155 | 154 |
| 36 | 94 | 94 | 76 | 156 | 155 |
| 37 | 95 | 95 | | | |
| 38 | 97 | 97 | | | |
| 39 | 98 | 98 | | | |

*Note.* Abbreviations: I = Information, V = Vocabulary, DS = Digit Span, BD = Block Design, S = Similarities, PC = Picture Completion, A = Arithmetic, C = Comprehension, PA = Picture Arrangement, OA = Object Assembly.

Reliability and validity coefficients associated with each short-form combination for the ten best tetrads are shown in Table L-11. See Exhibit I-4 in Appendix I for an explanation of the procedure used to obtain the estimated Deviation Quotients.

[a] This column can be used to estimate the Deviation Quotients for the PC + PA + BD + OA combination.

[b] This short-form combination represents the Verbal Comprehension factor score. See Table A.5 (page 255) in the WISC-III manual for Deviation Quotients for this short-form combination. The method used by The Psychological Corporation (discussed on pages 30 and 31 of the WISC-III manual) differs from that used in constructing this table. Their weighting and smoothing procedures may account for the difference in their values and the values in this table.

**Table L-I5**
**Estimated WISC-III Full Scale Deviation Quotients for Sum of Scaled Scores for Ten Best Short-Form Pentads**

| Sum of scaled scores | Combination | | Sum of scaled scores | Combination | |
|---|---|---|---|---|---|
| | Col. 1 | Col. 2 | | Col. 1 | Col. 2 |
| | $I+S+A+V+BD$ $I+S+A+V+C$ | $I+S+V+C+BD$ $I+S+V+DS+BD$ $I+S+V+PC+BD$ $I+A+V+DS+BD$ $I+S+A+V+DS$ $I+A+V+C+BD$ $I+S+V+PA+BD$ $I+S+V+C+DS$ | | $I+S+A+V+BD$ $I+S+A+V+C$ | $I+S+V+C+BD$ $I+S+V+DS+BD$ $I+S+V+PC+BD$ $I+A+V+DS+BD$ $I+S+A+V+DS$ $I+A+V+C+BD$ $I+S+V+PA+BD$ $I+S+V+C+DS$ |
| | | | 30 | 75 | 74 |
| | | | 31 | 76 | 76 |
| | | | 32 | 78 | 77 |
| | | | 33 | 79 | 78 |
| | | | 34 | 80 | 80 |
| 5 | 44 | 43 | 35 | 81 | 81 |
| 6 | 46 | 44 | 36 | 83 | 82 |
| 7 | 47 | 45 | 37 | 84 | 83 |
| 8 | 48 | 46 | 38 | 85 | 85 |
| 9 | 49 | 48 | 39 | 86 | 86 |
| 10 | 50 | 49 | 40 | 88 | 87 |
| 11 | 52 | 50 | 41 | 89 | 89 |
| 12 | 53 | 51 | 42 | 90 | 90 |
| 13 | 54 | 53 | 43 | 91 | 91 |
| 14 | 55 | 54 | 44 | 93 | 92 |
| 15 | 57 | 55 | 45 | 94 | 94 |
| 16 | 58 | 57 | 46 | 95 | 95 |
| 17 | 59 | 58 | 47 | 96 | 96 |
| 18 | 60 | 59 | 48 | 98 | 97 |
| 19 | 62 | 60 | 49 | 99 | 99 |
| 20 | 63 | 62 | 50 | 100 | 100 |
| 21 | 64 | 63 | 51 | 101 | 101 |
| 22 | 65 | 64 | 52 | 102 | 103 |
| 23 | 67 | 66 | 53 | 104 | 104 |
| 24 | 68 | 67 | 54 | 105 | 105 |
| 25 | 69 | 68 | 55 | 106 | 106 |
| 26 | 70 | 69 | 56 | 107 | 108 |
| 27 | 72 | 71 | 57 | 109 | 109 |
| 28 | 73 | 72 | 58 | 110 | 110 |
| 29 | 74 | 73 | 59 | 111 | 111 |

*(Table continues next page)*

**Table L-l5 (cont.)**

| Sum of scaled scores | Combination Col. 1 $I+S+A+V+BD$ $I+S+A+V+C$ | Combination Col. 2 $I+S+V+C+BD$ $I+S+V+DS+BD$ $I+S+V+PC+BD$ $I+A+V+DS+BD$ $I+S+A+V+DS$ $I+A+V+C+BD$ $I+S+V+PA+BD$ $I+S+V+C+DS$ | Sum of scaled scores | Combination Col. 1 $I+S+A+V+BD$ $I+S+A+V+C$ | Combination Col. 2 $I+S+V+C+BD$ $I+S+V+DS+BD$ $I+S+V+PC+BD$ $I+A+V+DS+BD$ $I+S+A+V+DS$ $I+A+V+C+BD$ $I+S+V+PA+BD$ $I+S+V+C+DS$ |
|---|---|---|---|---|---|
| 60 | 112 | 113 | 80 | 137 | 138 |
| 61 | 114 | 114 | 81 | 138 | 140 |
| 62 | 115 | 115 | 82 | 140 | 141 |
| 63 | 116 | 117 | 83 | 141 | 142 |
| 64 | 117 | 118 | 84 | 142 | 143 |
| 65 | 119 | 119 | 85 | 143 | 145 |
| 66 | 120 | 120 | 86 | 145 | 146 |
| 67 | 121 | 122 | 87 | 146 | 147 |
| 68 | 122 | 123 | 88 | 147 | 149 |
| 69 | 124 | 124 | 89 | 148 | 150 |
| 70 | 125 | 126 | 90 | 150 | 151 |
| 71 | 126 | 127 | 91 | 151 | 152 |
| 72 | 127 | 128 | 92 | 152 | 154 |
| 73 | 128 | 129 | 93 | 153 | 155 |
| 74 | 130 | 131 | 94 | 154 | 156 |
| 75 | 131 | 132 | | | |
| 76 | 132 | 133 | | | |
| 77 | 133 | 134 | | | |
| 78 | 135 | 136 | | | |
| 79 | 136 | 137 | | | |

*Note.* Abbreviations: I = Information, S = Similarities, A = Arithmetic, V = Vocabulary, BD = Block Design, C = Comprehension, DS = Digit Span, PC = Picture Completion, PA = Picture Arrangement.

Reliability and validity coefficients associated with each short-form combination for the ten best pentads are shown in Table L-11. See Exhibit I-4 in Appendix I for an explanation of the procedure used to obtain the estimated Deviation Quotients.

**Table L-16**
**Interpretive Rationale, Implications of High and Low Scores, and Instructional Implications for the WISC-III Symbol Search Subtest**

| Ability | Background factors | Possible implications of high scores | Possible implications of low scores | Instructional implications |
|---|---|---|---|---|
| | | **Symbol Search** | | |
| Processing speed | Rate of motor activity | Good processing speed | Poor processing speed | Use visual-motor scanning exercises, such as having child look at two or more objects and decide if they are the same or different |
| Perceptual discrimination | Motivation | Good perceptual discrimination ability | Poor perceptual discrimination ability | |
| Speed of mental operation | | | Distractibility | |
| Psychomotor speed | | Good attention and concentration | Visual defects | |
| Attention and concentration skills | | Sustained energy or persistence | Lethargy | |
| Short-term memory | | Good motivation or desire for achievement | Poor motivation | |
| Visual-motor coordination | | | | |
| Cognitive flexibility | | | | |

# _ APPENDIX M _____

# MODIFIED INSTRUCTIONS FOR ADMINISTERING THE WISC-III SYMBOL SEARCH SUBTEST TO DEAF CHILDREN

The WISC-III materials plus an instruction sheet prepared by the examiner are needed.

## PROCEDURE FOR SYMBOL SEARCH A (FOR CHILDREN AGES 6–7)

The instructions cover the sample items, practice items, and subtest items.

### Sample Items

With the Symbol Search Response Booklet before the child, move your finger in a sweeping motion, from the child's left to right, across the entire row of the first sample item in Part A. Then point to the single target symbol in the first column. Next point to the first symbol in the search group. Then catch the child's eye and shake your head "no" to indicate that the first search symbol does not match the target symbol. You must make sure the child is looking at you each time you shake your head "yes" or "no" or when you nod your head for any other purpose.

Repeat this procedure two more times. Point to the single target symbol and then to the second search symbol. Shake your head "no." Again point to the single target symbol and then to the third search symbol. This time shake your head "yes" to indicate that the search symbol matches the target symbol. With a no. 2 pencil, mark a slash in the "YES" box.

For the second sample item in Part A, generally follow the same procedure. However, for this item shake your head "no" for each search symbol. After demonstrating the third search symbol, mark a slash in the "NO" box.

### Practice Items

Give the child a no. 2 pencil. Point to the first row of the practice items and move your finger in a sweeping motion, from the child's left to right, along the entire first row. Nod your head to indicate to the child to begin. If the child places a slash mark in the "YES" box, nod your head to indicate "good" and go to the second practice item.

If the child marks "NO" on the first practice item, point to the target symbol and then to the second search symbol. Shake your head to indicate "yes." Then immediately place a slash through the "YES" box. Do not demonstrate the third symbol.

Point to the second practice item and, by nodding your head, encourage the child to do it. If the child marks "NO," nod your head to indicate "good" and proceed to the regular subtest items (see below). If the child marks "YES," correct the child. Point to the target symbol and each of the three search symbols in turn, shaking your head to indicate "no" each time. Then place a slash through the "NO" box.

Do not go on to the regular subtest items until the child understands the task. You may have to erase your marks and the child's marks and ask the child to do the sample and/or practice items again.

## Subtest Items

When the child understands the task, open the Symbol Search Booklet to the second page and fold the page over. If the child can read, hand him or her the instruction sheet. This sheet should contain the information beginning in the last paragraph on page 146 and ending with the fifth line on page 147 of the WISC-III manual ("When . . . questions?"). Only copy the material in color. After the child has read the directions, point to the first row to indicate that the child should begin the task.

If the child cannot read, run your finger down the entire second page. Next turn the booklet to the third page, and again run your finger down the entire page. Then turn to the fourth page, and again run your finger down the entire page. After showing the child the three pages of items, turn back to the second page of the booklet. Point to the pencil and then to the first row of the second page, then run your finger down the page, and then nod your head to indicate to the child to begin.

If a child ceases to work after completing the first row, redirect the child's attention to the second row by pointing to the entire second row in a sweeping motion and encourage the child to continue. If a child stops at the end of the second page, turn the booklet to the third page and encourage the child to continue. If the child stops at the end of the third page, turn the booklet to the fourth page and encourage the child to continue. Allow 120 seconds.

## PROCEDURE FOR SYMBOL SEARCH B (FOR CHILDREN AGES 8–16)

The instructions cover the sample items, practice items, and subtest items.

## Sample Items

With the Symbol Search Response Booklet before the child, move your finger in a sweeping motion, from the child's left to right, across the entire row of the first sample item in Part B. Then point to the two target symbols in the first column. Next point to the first symbol in the search group. Then catch the child's eye and shake your head "yes" to indicate that the first search symbol matches the target symbol. With a no. 2 pencil, immediately mark a slash in the "YES" box. You must make sure the child is looking at you each time you shake your head "yes" or "no" or when you nod your head for any other purpose. Go to the second sample item, without demonstrating the remaining symbols in the first sample item.

For the second sample item in Part B, point to the two target symbols and then to the first search symbol. Shake your head "no" to indicate that the search symbol does not match either of the target symbols. Repeat this procedure four more times. In each case point to the two target symbols and then to the search symbol. Shake your head "no" each time. After the last search symbol, make a slash in the "NO" box.

## Practice Items

Give the child a no. 2 pencil. Point to the first row of the practice items and move your finger in a sweeping motion, from the child's left to right, along the entire first row. Nod your head to indicate to the child to begin. If the child places a slash mark in the "YES" box, nod your head to indicate "good" and go to the second practice item.

If the child marks "NO" on the first practice item, correct the child. Point to the two target symbols and then to the *second* search symbol. Shake your head to indicate "yes." Then immediately place a slash through the "YES" box. Do not demonstrate the remaining three symbols. Go to the second practice item.

Point to the second practice item and, by nodding your head, encourage the child to do it. If the child marks "NO," nod your head to indicate "good" and proceed to the regular subtest items (see below). If the child marks "YES," correct the child. Point to the two target symbols and each of the five search symbols in turn, shaking your head to indicate "no" each time. Then place a slash through the "NO" box.

Do not go on to the regular subtest items until the child understands the task. You may have to erase your marks and the child's marks and ask the child to do the sample and/ or practice items again.

## Subtest Items

When the child understands the task, open the Symbol Search Booklet to the sixth page and fold it over. If the child can read, hand him or her the instruction sheet. This sheet should contain the information beginning in the last paragraph on page 146 and ending with the fifth line on page 147 of the WISC-III manual ("When . . . questions?"). Only copy the material in color. After the child has read the directions, point to the first row to indicate that the child should begin the task.

If the child cannot read, run your finger down the entire sixth page. Next turn the booklet to the seventh page, and again run your finger down the entire page. Then turn to the eighth page, and again run your finger down the entire page. After showing the child the three pages of items, turn back to the sixth page of the booklet. Point to the pencil and then to the first row of the sixth page, then run your finger down the page, and then nod your head to indicate to the child to begin.

If a child ceases to work after completing the first row, redirect the child's attention to the second row by pointing to the entire second row in a sweeping motion and encourage the child to continue. If a child stops at the end of the sixth page, turn the booklet to the seventh page. If the child stops at the end of the seventh page, turn the booklet to the eighth page. Allow 120 seconds.

# NAME INDEX

# _ SUBJECT INDEX _____